MAY 3 0 1975 NOV 1 8 1975 MAY 2 9 1976 FEB 4 1982	Date Due		
MAR 1 4 1985			
MAR 2 4 1987 JUN 2 2 1987			
JUL 7 1989			
JUL 1 7 1990 R AUG 1 3 1990			
NOV 2 4 1990			
MAY 1 6 1994			

Education: Ontario's preoccupation

W.G. FLEMING

Education: Ontario's preoccupation

UNIVERSITY OF TORONTO PRESS

© University of Toronto Press 1972
Toronto and Buffalo

Printed in Canada

ISBN 0-8020-3274-5
LC 78-186280

Ontario's Educative Society volumes I-VII and
Education: Ontario's Preoccupation (set of 8 volumes)
ISBN 0-8020-3284-2
Microfiche ISBN 0-8020-0079-7
LC 77-166928

Preface

Education: Ontario's Preoccupation was written as a companion volume to the much more lengthy and detailed work entitled ONTARIO'S EDUCATIVE SOCIETY. The two share the objective of exploring the recent development of education in the province of Ontario, particularly since the end of the Second World War. The treatment of certain themes involves a brief review of the earlier historical background, with information derived largely from secondary sources. This material is presented on the familiar grounds that recent developments are comprehensible only in terms of their historical antecedents, and that to omit reference to these antecedents is to deprive readers who are not steeped in history of the means of appreciating the significance of much of what has happened in the recent past. In some major fields of education, the period after the Second World War saw the first serious effort to modify structures and practices that were basically established in the nineteenth century. The organization of local school systems and teacher education are examples that come readily to mind.

An attempt was made to bring the account presented in the two works up to date as far as the rather lengthy process of publication would permit. These works might thus be appropriately described as contemporary history. There are, of course, many authorities who regard such a term as self-contradictory, feeling that the perspective provided by the passage of a considerable amount of time is essential before any true history can be written. If those who hold such a point of view prefer some other designation for my work, I have no objection. I certainly make no claim to have discovered a way of shortening the process by which the real significance of certain events emerges from the ephemeral and the trivial.

Whether or not a particular reader will agree with the expressions of opinion interspersed among the facts will depend to a considerable extent on his philosophical position. My point of view is basically progressive, as opposed to that of the traditionalist or essentialist. It is a position that I reached only after many years of experience at various levels of the educational system, and in fact represents a reversal of my earlier views. Although it is the position toward which I feel the available evidence points, I acknowledge freely that it could be in error, and am thus not prepared to expound it as a fanatical believer. Yet, while making no apology for espousing a particular philosophical position with respect to education, or for basing my interpretation of various developments on a particular set of beliefs, I recognize a major responsibility to select the facts and present them with maximum objectivity. I have attempted to distinguish clearly between fact and opinion, and can only hope the reader will agree that I have been successful in this endeavour.

Both *Education: Ontario's Preoccupation* and ONTARIO'S EDUCATIVE SOCIETY adopt a broad definition of education, concerning themselves with organizations and activities beyond the formal system. Attention is given, for example, to government departments not usually considered to exist for educational purposes, to agencies with primarily cultural objectives, and to associations of many kinds. Since some limits must obviously be drawn, there has been no attempt to deal more than casually with completely informal activities in the family and in other social spheres. An effort to cover every ramification of education in the very widest sense would have been unmanageable.

In my treatment of the subject, I have drawn no sharp distinction between those activities that are commonly termed training and those reserved for a somewhat circumscribed category designated as education. This treatment does not deny the value of such a distinction as an aid to thought and action. There is a danger, however, that too much attention to the difference between the two concepts may obscure their essential relationship. To the administrator, the problems involved in providing education and training are often very similar.

Education: Ontario's Preoccupation contains little material that is not to be found in ONTARIO'S EDUCATIVE SOCIETY, except that certain topics have been updated at the editorial stage. The two works differ chiefly in organization and length. The briefer work is intended primarily for those who do not have the time or interest to read seven rather substantial volumes and for those who may find value in an overview of developments in the period under consideration. In some cases, the book may be read profitably with the seven volume series at hand for reference.

A brief indication of the contents of ONTARIO'S EDUCATIVE SOCIETY is offered here for the benefit of those to whom it is not immediately available. Volume I, *The expansion of the educational system*, provides an introduction to the whole series, offering a discussion of some of the major contemporary issues and problems in education. It is, however, primarily a quantitative history of the recent period, presenting most of the statistical material relevant to the series. This treatment is designed both for the maximum convenience of the reader interested in such data and as a means of keeping other volumes clear of material that might interrupt the smooth flow of verbal exposition or narrative. Volume II, *The administrative structure,* deals with the development and functions of the Department of Education and of local school systems, the financing of education, and educational activities of the provincial and federal governments. Volume III, *Schools, pupils, and teachers*, covers the evolution of schools as institutions and of curriculum, and shows how the process of education has operated up to the end of secondary school. It outlines the role of media and indicates basic principles of measurement to show how these aspects of education have affected the operation of Ontario schools. Separate chapters deal with special education and the education of minority groups. The role of the teacher and the development of measures to improve teacher welfare are examined. Volume IV, *Post-secondary and adult education*, deals with many facets of the development of universities, including government-university relationships, the establishment and growth of individual universities, university government, teaching, research, student activities, and the status and welfare of faculty. Further chapters are concerned with institutes of technology, institutions for trades training, colleges of applied arts and technology, nursing education, manpower training, and training in industry. Volume V, *Supporting institutions and services*, deals with teacher education, educational research and development, external examination and testing services, the provision of facilities for educational television, libraries, and miscellaneous institutions combining cultural and educational functions. Volume VI, *Significant developments in local school systems*, indicates some of the educational contributions arising chiefly from local initiative. It presents examples of the way changes in curriculum, administrative and teaching procedures, styles in school architecture, and other innovations have affected educational practice. Volume VII, *Educational contributions of associations*, attempts to demonstrate the extent to which educative activities in Ontario have been initiated and conducted through voluntary effort as a supplement to formal and official services. The approach involves brief accounts of the early history, objectives, and activities of a representative group of associations.

Education: Ontario's Preoccupation contains what may be regarded as the highlights of the period presented in relatively brief form under a restricted list of chapter headings. Some topics dealt with at length in the longer work have been passed over rather lightly or even omitted altogether. A number of footnotes have been provided to assist the reader who may wish to refer to ONTARIO'S EDUCATIVE SOCIETY for a fuller treatment.

At this point there may be some value in attempting to summarize in a few words the main stages of educational development in Ontario during the post-war period, with all the inaccuracy that such brevity entails. Immediately after 1945 the elementary and secondary schools returned briefly to the relative stability of the years just preceding the war while the universities struggled valiantly and successfully to cope with large numbers of men and women released from the armed services. Despite a partial implementation of George Drew's promise to ease the burden of local taxation for the support of the school system, schools continued to be financed mainly in the traditional manner. Returned veterans were dealt with in such a way that no permanent change in government-university relations or in university finance resulted.

The 1950s, a period roughly corresponding to W.J. Dunlop's tenure of office as minister of education but one in which Premier Leslie Frost probably exerted much more real influence on the educational system, saw a desperate effort to accommodate rising enrolments in the elementary and secondary schools and to find sufficient teachers. While the physical expansion of the school system was impressive, there was relatively little progress in improving the quality of education. Where only ill-trained teachers were available there was undoubtedly substantial deterioration. Relative stability prevailed in the universities with respect to enrolment and status in the community. Post-secondary institutions for technological and trades training were struggling into existence.

The 1960s witnessed a continuation of accommodation problems, with the emphasis shifting from elementary to secondary schools and even more to institutions of post-secondary education. Also, beginning modestly under J.P. Robarts, minister of education from 1959 to 1962, and rapidly gathering momentum under William G. Davis, his successor in the portfolio of Education from 1962 to 1971 and holder of the portfolio of University Affairs for most of the same period, was a series of fundamental changes in the organization of the system and in the educational process itself. The universities adapted to a new role in society and staggered toward the status of components of a publicly financed system of post-secondary education, struggling to maintain the essence of their traditional autonomy. In the latter effort they were largely successful, although there were many dangers to be faced in the future. A whole new dimension was added to post-secondary education in the creation and expansion of the colleges of applied arts and technology.

Most of the decade of the 1960s may be characterized as one of relatively uncritical confidence in the efficacy of education as a means of improving the economy, of solving social problems, and particularly of ensuring the material welfare of the recipient by guaranteeing him a good job. There was also a large element of confidence that education would improve society and enhance the virtues of the individual, although this element cannot be considered the dominant one in the strong popular support for the expansion of education during the period. Whatever their mixture of motives, the people of Ontario bore the rapidly expanding costs of education with no more grumbling than may ordinarily be expected from taxpayers, although there were many complaints that the burden was not distributed fairly. Most of the new programs introduced by Davis in the mid-sixties were regarded as money well spent. The political opposition attempted for the most part to score points on the grounds that not enough was being done for various groups.

The period of disillusionment developed rather quickly toward the end of the decade. Davis suddenly found himself with a reputation as a spender to live down, and there was genuine pressure from the population and the press to cut costs. The fact that the new mood was not by any means confined to one province, or to Canada alone, did not make the problem easier to deal with in Ontario. There was particular concern because the rising curve of expenditure was not only steep, but showed no sign of levelling out in the foreseeable future. Alarmists warned that existing trends would have to be changed if education was to be prevented from ultimately consuming all public revenue.

Perhaps the atmosphere of disillusionment was less a result of concern over rising costs than of a growing impression that education had failed to live up to its promise. The recession that ended the old decade and ushered in the new one saw unemployment for the first time since the war affecting large groups of educated people. Education was no longer a guarantee of economic security. Furthermore, conspicuous groups of ostensibly educated young people seemed more adept than their predecessors at showing their contempt for the values held by their elders. Many a parent wondered in retrospect whether financial sacrifices to put his son or daughter through university had been worthwhile. Also, despite a perceptible rise in the educational level of the population as a whole, many social ills stubbornly persisted and new ones appeared.

A better perspective may well indicate that the disillusionment of the early 1970s was not as serious as it sometimes appeared. Public pressure was actually exerted in favour of a less rapid acceleration in costs rather than an absolute reduction. Most young people who had an opportunity for post-secondary education were willing to take the chance that it would improve their social status and earning power, even though the former confidence had weakened. Most people still assumed that an educated population would be best able to improve its material and cultural environment.

Ontario faced many problems that appeared, if not entirely soluble through education, quite certainly insoluble without a substantial contribution from that source. If an educated citizenry could not be sure of rewarding and remunerative employment, the prospects for an uneducated one were much less favourable. The threat posed to the Canadian economy by harsh measures adopted by the American government in the summer of 1971 to solve its foreign trade and balance of payments problems made it obvious as never before that Canada would have to make the most judicious use of its human resources if it was not to be left largely as an exporter of raw materials.

As the major centre of industrial activity in Canada, Ontario had perhaps the most to lose if the other nations of the world organized themselves into trading blocks and erected ever higher barriers against one another. While the fate of the country and of the province were in part at the mercy of external forces, and judicious foreign and domestic government policy could protect the interests of the people only in part, there was no question that a population with a high level of skill in the arts of production, transportation, communication, and public service could best survive and prosper in a world grown suddenly difficult or even hostile.

There were many domestic problems that the pessimists thought insoluble and the optimists could see yielding only to an educated population – educated not merely in terms of economic competence and occupational skill, but also possessing a keen awareness of the individual's social responsibilities. While there was no guarantee that education would not, by encouraging the development of extreme individualism, help to upset the delicate balance between freedom and restraint that makes civilization possible, there was a hope that it might provide a basis for the avoidance of some of the conditions that were rapidly making the central cores of American cities uninhabitable. Educated citizens and the kind of leaders they could be expected to elect might support long-term planning of city growth, even if it involved some immediate sacrifices. They might be able to solve problems of the automobile, of housing, of waste disposal, and others of an equally threatening nature.

At the beginning of the 1970s the inhabitants of Ontario cities could still congratulate themselves on the fact that they could walk the streets in daylight and darkness with relative safety. As in other parts of the western world, however, crime was rising, and there was no guarantee of the permanence of existing conditions. A continued increase in challenges to the law would evoke the danger of police repression, accompanied by a reversal of the traditional attitude toward the policeman as a friend and protector. The chief hope that such a change would not occur lay in the ordinary citizen's obtaining a better understanding of his legal rights and obligations and maintaining a healthy attitude toward law enforcement.

The very complexity of social and political organization posed an increasing threat to human freedom and dignity. Government boards and agencies were constantly occupied in devising new regulations and constraints and in finding ways of enforcing them. Private persuaders exercised their ingenuity in breaking down psychological barriers to their messages. It was ever more obvious that an ignorant population would inevitably fail to maintain true freedom. The citizen had not only to know his rights, but also to possess the will and the competence to defeat the forces that threatened them.

A particular challenge to the continued existence of healthy communities in both urban and rural areas was the survival of poverty. There was little evidence that, despite all the ostensible concern demonstrated over the issue, the self-satisfied middle and upper income groups in Ontario really understood what was involved. There were, after all, no little match girls freezing to death on the streets. Citizens who coped successfully with the intricate and complex structure of modern society showed little capacity to empathize with those whose lack of education or of basic physical and mental capacities condemned them to hover on the fringes of affluence, their appetites constantly whetted and the means of gratification always out of reach. Exhortations to work, to save, and to compete were more and more unrealistic and irrelevant. The problem of poverty made two demands on education which it might or might not be able to meet, but certainly no other force could: first, to improve the potentiality of the poor, or at least of their children, to solve their own problems and second, to arouse the social conscience of the affluent so that they would devise long-term solutions rather than palliatives and make whatever sacrifices were necessary to implement them.

What could hardly have been imagined a decade or so earlier was the tremendous amount of attention being given in the early 1970s to the problems of environmental pollution. Governments were concluding that there was not only public pressure to take the steps to save the environment that could be carried out with little expense or effort, but also support for measures that would perceptibly lower standards of living. Yet it was obvious that the battle had hardly yet been effectively joined. The average citizen had still to be educated to identify the many ways in which he himself could contribute to the reduction of pollution. He also needed a better understanding of ultimate implications of the problem before he could be expected to call for and accept the sacrifices that would be needed.

Like other societies in the 1960s and 1970s, that of Ontario showed many signs of lack of confidence in where it was going. Feeling a need for guidance in dealing with the dilemmas of life that must be lived in surroundings and under conditions that no previous generation had faced, people groped for the elements that should be included in an adequate definition of morality. Traditional attitudes toward work, worship, leisure, recreation, the family, sex, and stimulants had to be carefully examined to see if they contributed to the unfolding of human personality in a socially constructive manner. The church, which often seemed more confused than its communicants, had lost much of its power to stabilize the social order. While there was no prospect that education could lay down definitive principles for life in a new age, it might attempt the less ambitious task of assisting people to devise intelligent and rational solutions to their problems.

Neglected educational opportunities were being held in part responsible for the precariousness of the country's existence as a single political entity. In his disturbing book *What Culture? What Heritage?*, A.B. Hodgetts had recently made important additions to the accumulating evidence that education had failed deplorably to help bridge the gap between the two main linguistic and cultural groups.* Generations of school children emerged from school without an adequate knowledge of or pride in their own history or a sympathetic understanding of that of their compatriots of the other culture. While an improved educational approach might work too slowly to contribute much to the solution of the immediate crisis, it would be an essential element in the maintenance of an ultimate accommodation.

With so much for education to do, and so much that it alone could do, for the preservation and improvement of a society in which the individual could live, grow, and fulfil himself, it would indeed be unfortunate if disillusionment with the process ran too deep. There was plenty of scope, of course, for a critical examination of the immediate objectives being pursued and the methods being followed in the province's schools, colleges, and universities. A better use of financial resources might well be essential for the survival of a productive educational system. To engage in criticism, and in many cases to oppose the proponents of some form of expansion of the educational system, were by no means necessarily a demonstration of lack of faith in education. It would be unfortunate if one led to the other.

*A.B. Hodgetts, *What Culture? What Heritage?: A Study of Civic Education in Canada,* Report of the National History Project, Curriculum Series No. 5 (Toronto: The Ontario Institute for Studies in Education, 1968).

Acknowledgments

I am deeply indebted to the Honourable William G. Davis who, as Minister of Education and of University Affairs, provided me with the full co-operation of his departments in the production of the series of volumes constituting *Ontario's Educative Society* as well as the present volume entitled *Education: Ontario's Preoccupation*. In this task I was given access to all pertinent material in the two departments under his direction. His officials at the time the work was undertaken, headed by Dr J.R. McCarthy, Deputy Minister of Education, and Dr E.E. Stewart, Deputy Minister of University Affairs, were also extraordinarily co-operative and helpful. I am particularly grateful to these officials for enabling me to pursue the work in a way that most appeals to a member of the university community: that is, I was completely free to choose, present, and interpret the facts according to my own best judgment. I did not feel the slightest pressure to adapt or modify the material in any way so as to present an "official" version of educational developments in Ontario. As a consequence, I am completely responsible for any opinions or interpretations of the facts that the work contains. The generous assistance for the project provided by the Ontario government, without which publication would have been impossible, does not involve any responsibility for the contents.

I would like to express my particular gratitude to those who assisted me so devotedly in the project: Miss L. McGuire, my loyal secretary, who served from the time the work began in the spring of 1968, Mrs E. West, who also served with extraordinary devotion and competence during most of the same period, and Mrs S. Constable, Miss D. McDowell, Mrs G.J. Moore, and Mr Alex French, each of whom participated during an extended period. Mr C.H. Westcott, formerly Executive Assistant to the Minister of Education and University Affairs, gave me continuous encouragement and helped to deal with practical problems relating to production and publication. Particularly helpful advice and information were given by Dr C.A. Brown, Professor E.B. Rideout, and Dr J.A. Keddy. Arrangements by Dr G.E. Flower to relieve me of the majority of my other professional obligations during most of a three-year period are also greatly appreciated. In addition, I would like to acknowledge my general indebtedness to the hundreds of people who supplied information so willingly in a variety of forms. That I am unable to name them all individually does not mean that I am any the less grateful for their contributions.

W.G. FLEMING
May 1972

Contents

Preface / v

Acknowledgments / xiii

1
The growing importance of formal education for
utilitarian purposes / 1

2
The expanding system / 32

3
The quest for organizational efficiency in the school system / 62

4
Province and university come to terms / 117

5
Educational agencies outside the formal system / 142

6
New practices and procedures in the educational process / 171

7
Early research efforts and the development of the
Ontario Institute for Studies in Education / 231

8
Religion and language / 252

9
The burden of support / 272

10
Future prospects for formal education / 303

Notes / 312

General index / 317

Index of persons / 329

Education: Ontario's preoccupation

ONE

The growing importance
of formal education
for utilitarian purposes

Education became an increasingly important phenomenon for the Ontario citizen and for the society in which he lived between the Second World War and the early 1970s. This development owed a great deal to economic considerations. While the economic aspects may not have been the only important ones, there is strong support for the view that, no matter how their feelings were verbalized, the people of Ontario actually looked to education primarily for economic results, and that they were willing to support a multiplication of investment in various educational endeavours principally for this reason. Such a judgment does not mean that non-economic outcomes were not of profound importance, or that they could not in actual fact have overshadowed those with direct economic implications. But education could never have risen to the top of the list of priorities for public expenditure if the ordinary taxpayer had thought his money was being used mainly to support cultural creation and appreciation, moral uplift, or the development of a more sensitive and intelligent social conscience. He really slackened his grip on his wallet, or permitted it to be pried open, at the prospect of a good job and the material rewards and social status that go with it, if not for himself, then certainly for his children. Other benefits were in fact treated as incidental, despite the verbal tribute so freely paid to them.

The war itself created a powerful impetus for the development of many kinds of practical training. The rapid growth of an industrial superstructure to support the war machine called for on-the-job training for large numbers of previously unskilled employees. The demand for female labour helped to create new employment expectations and aspirations for many women. Although for some, war work represented a temporary call to duty, the stage was set for the steady increase in the proportion of women in the work force that marked the entire post-war period. The armed forces themselves were in a sense a great training school, providing many men and some women with skills that served both for the prosecution of the war and for peace-time occupations. In many cases there was direct continuity between what was done in war and the further education obtained with the help of the Department of Veterans Affairs after the cessation of hostilities.

THE EFFECT OF POST-WAR INDUSTRIALIZATION
AND ADVANCING TECHNOLOGY ON OCCUPATIONAL
SKILL REQUIREMENTS

Ontario emerged into the post-war period with an economy largely operated by people with a low level of formal education. According to the
census of 1941 only 44.6 per cent of the population at or above eighteen
years of age had attended high school at all, and only 8.8 per cent had
more than twelve years of schooling.[1] The farmer, the proprietor of a small
business, the factory worker, and the employee in any of the multitude of
service industries could manage quite well if they read and calculated at
about the grade 6 level. For a very large proportion of jobs, it hardly mattered, in fact, whether or not the employee was even literate.

Three factors were mainly responsible for the shift in levels of education and training demanded of the labour force as a whole. First, some
occupations that retained their essential characteristics throughout the
post-war period required higher paper qualifications of those who sought
admission to them. Secondly, other occupations, possibly without undergoing any change in name, became increasingly complex and difficult as
advancing technology transformed them. Thirdly, still others were eliminated altogether as new ones with higher skill requirements appeared in
their place.

A good many service occupations fell in the first category. Sales people
in commercial establishments, for example, might need about the same
computational skills in 1972 as they did in 1946, along with certain qualities not directly related to formal education, such as patience, a pleasant
manner in meeting the public, a concern for accuracy, and a conscientious
desire to give a satisfactory performance. In filling positions of this kind,
an employer at the later date was not likely to be satisfied with an appli-
cant with the same level of education as his earlier counterpart simply because people with desirable personal qualities were likely to have moved
up at least one level in the educational system.

The same phenomenon was encountered at all levels of education. Immediately after the war a girl who had completed grade 11, possibly in
one of the secondary schools in the province that offered the commercial
program, and had then taken the special commercial course in the same
school or a course in a privately operated commercial school to acquire
typing speed and develop her competence in shorthand, might be hired for
an office position leading eventually to a substantial amount of responsibility. The corresponding position in 1972 might in some respects actually
require less rather than more intensive preparation, since the universal
availability of dictaphones had done much to eliminate the use of shorthand, while typing and other office procedures had remained substantially
the same. Yet an employer was likely to suspect that a girl who had not
completed grade 12 was among the minority who were incapable of doing
so or, if she lacked the drive to make the attempt, might demonstrate the

same attitude toward her job. Even a grade 12 graduate might be under suspicion, and a grade 13 diploma insisted upon, not because much in the academic grade 13 program could be identified as direct preparation for the work to be done, but because of what the diploma implied about the ability and character of the individual who had completed the year. Paradoxically, the less meaningful the grade 13 course became as an educational experience, and the grimmer the struggle to succeed in the all-important departmental examinations, the more useful it probably became as a screening device for many kinds of employment. Most employers were not really interested in finding highly cultured recruits for office work, let alone those who had a propensity to "think" in the sense of identifying absurdities, inconsistencies, or unethical practices in what they were doing. They wanted employees who would work hard and persistently to attain a goal, who had a high tolerance for boredom, and who were reasonably docile and obedient. It was hard to get through grade 13 without some measure of these qualities.

At a higher educational level, there was a very substantial change in the attitude of business and commercial establishments toward the employment of university graduates. Before returned veterans taking advantage of their DVA benefits flooded the universities immediately after the war and began to create a new image for the graduate, these establishments were inclined to be suspicious of him or ignorant of the contribution he might potentially make. They tended to regard him as a highbrow, probably full of impractical ideas, and possibly too contemptuous of practical routines to be very dependable. What he had studied seemed likely to have had even less direct application to the demands of the job than had the grade 13 program. His normal course of action seemed to be to enter one of the professions. The much more favourable attitude that developed among employers in the fifties and sixties was often attributed to the optimistic assumption that a university education enhanced such qualities as flexibility, ingenuity, and adaptability to change. While one would hope that this assumption had some validity, what was probably a more important factor was that employers were realizing that the young people who tended to be flexible, ingenious, and adaptable to change were moving up one level in the educational system, and had to be sought there. As those with higher levels of education came to be more in demand in the business and commercial worlds, the contribution of the educational process to the occupational competence of the holder of the certificate, diploma, or degree was frequently overestimated. Thus part of what was thought to be the economic return from investment in education was no doubt illusory.

Some occupations in the service field are unlikely, by their very nature, ever to require an increased degree of human skill. The educational system has, however, discovered a responsibility to those who are destined to enter them. During the 1960s junior vocational schools and occupational programs introduced as an aspect of the Robarts Plan increasingly attempted to prepare students with little ability or inclination in academic fields to work in service stations, laundries, hairdressing establishments, horticultural enterprises, and the like.* It was not so much that the school needed to give the boy a knowledge of how to operate a gasoline pump, or to teach the girl how to handle a cash register, although such practical exercises might be included, but that, in helping them define realistic goals that enhanced their feeling of personal security and usefulness, it might do something to make them more responsible citizens and better persons. Vocational school graduates sometimes had an edge in the job market over those who remained in an inappropriate academic or technical course until they reached the age when they were mercifully permitted to drop out. Of course the larger problem of job security remained for both groups, since employment at this skill level tended to decline or disappear with advancing technology. For such a problem the educators had no answer.

In the second group of occupations mentioned earlier, a large proportion were strongly affected during the post-war period, continuing an already well established trend, by the advancement of science and technology and by the accumulation of capital, which made it possible to apply new techniques. This development was pronounced in agriculture. The Ontario farmer found it increasingly difficult to prosper, or even to make ends meet, without acquiring a greater knowledge of soils, fertilizers, pesticides, varieties of crops, animal breeding, plant and animal diseases, mechanics, marketing, and legal matters. The changes were perhaps more of degree than of kind, but nevertheless profound. They were reflected to some extent in the purposes for which young men studied at the colleges of agricultural technology, formerly called agricultural schools, at Kemptville, Ridgetown, Centralia, and New Liskeard, and in certain courses at the University of Guelph, which continued after its establishment in 1964 to carry on the program of the Guelph Agricultural College. It seemed increasingly natural to attend these institutions in order to become a better farmer, rather than to prepare for some farm-related occupation in government or business, although the latter remained a legitimate objective. One of the major consequences of the higher training, skill, and capital required by the farmer was to increase the number of both rural and urban poor. More efficient production kept farm prices at a level where the unskilled could not compete, and they either clung to small plots of land in growing privation or left to join the ranks of the least employable in the cities. These developments, incidentally, had a great deal to do with some of the major organizational and administrative changes in post-war education,

*The Reorganized Program, or Robarts Plan, was introduced into grade 9 of Ontario high schools in the fall of 1962, to a large extent as a result of the new accessibility of federal funds for the support of technical and vocational education. It is dealt with more fully in chapter 6 of the prseent volume and in ONTARIO'S EDUCATIVE SOCIETY, volume III, chapters 4, 5, and 6.

such as school consolidation, with provision for bussing students, and the enlargement of school districts. Such changes are dealt with mainly in Chapter 3.

Typical of entirely new occupations, the third occupational category listed earlier, were those associated with electronic data processing. Some of these occupations, particularly in the earlier years, demanded routine skills and a capacity to withstand boredom under monotonous conditions. Information could be processed by machine only after laborious coding, card punching, and verifying, the operation of tabulators had to be supplemented by sorters and collators, the inefficiency of the earlier machines meant regular pauses to repair the damage caused by card jams, and routine card checking at many stages was the price of accurate work. Rapidly advancing technology in the field proved particularly effective in eliminating the relatively unskilled tasks in favour of those that offered the greatest challenge. While the transfer of data to tapes became automatic and the auxiliary machines came to require less tending or disappeared altogether, technicians were required to learn how to program the computer, a task that often put human ingenuity to a serious test. As the process of addressing the computer became further simplified, it seemed that computer technology would ulimately provide employment only for those who formulated the problems and interpreted and applied the results, and perhaps for those who repaired the machines and kept them in operation.

The formal school system did not begin to acknowledge any serious responsibility in the field of data processing until the mid-1960s. Perhaps earlier action was not to be expected in view of the expense of machine rental or purchase, the rapid obsolescence of equipment, and uncertainty about the number and nature of relevant employment opportunities. Those who felt that the role of technical education was not simply to teach skills or to prepare students directly for occupational competence, but rather to educate through a combination of liberal studies and technical subjects with a strong theoretical component, were not sure of the place that data processing should occupy. Training was initially offered almost entirely by the firms that supplied the equipment. As time went on, their contributions were supplemented by those of private commercial enterprises which provided training for those not already employed in the field. By the mid-1960s the Department of Education began to encourage curricular adaptations to enable students to learn the principles of computer operations, to solve problems by means of the computer, and in some cases to acquire skills that might be useful on the job market. At the same time that it was pioneering in the introduction of these innovations, the North York school system, at the urging of its noted director of education, Frederick W. Minkler, was making increasing use of computers to conduct its own business operations. Most systems that began to make use of the new techniques at an early stage ran into many frustrations and problems, and the officials involved often wondered aloud whether the old manual methods were not easier and more efficient; however, they usually found increasing reasons for satisfaction as time went on.

The universities recognized computer technology as a development worthy of some of their best brains working in applied mathematics. A Computation Centre at the University of Toronto developed into an Institute of Computer Science, and the vigorous and innovative University of Waterloo soon became a leader in this area. Universities had a major interest in advancing computer technology and in the utilization of computers for research, while training in their use tended to be an incidental function.

One of the most significant developments during the post-war period in the job training field was the appearance of occupational categories between the position of the skilled artisan or tradesman and that of the university trained professional. When the so-called 'Rehab School' was operated on the site of the old Toronto Normal School in downtown Toronto immediately after the war to help veterans readjust to the occupational demands of civilian life, there was no serious problem in determining what course to offer a prospective sheet metal worker, for example, or to foresee his role in the labour force. The trades training aspect of the program of the successor Ryerson Institute of Technology, which began operations under its new name in 1948, was reasonably clearcut. Three years later, when the Provincial Institute of Trades was split off and assigned the task of carrying on the trades training program, Ryerson was left to clarify a less definite role. Despite the fact that it was actually the fourth institution of its kind established in Ontario, having been preceded by the Hamilton Institute of Textiles, the Provincial Institute of Mining at Haileybury, and the Lakehead Technical Institute, Ryerson bore the main burden of defining the term "technologist" in relation to "technician" and "engineer" so that it would be meaningful in terms of the kind and length of preparation required and the kind of service its bearer could render to the economy. In actual fact Ryerson graduates found it reasonably easy to find rewarding employment. During the period of rapid industrial expansion in the 1950s, Ontario could have used many more of such graduates, and in fact was able to carry on only by utilizing the skills of European immigrants.

The appearance of the graduate of the technology course at Ryerson, which ordinarily called for three years of study beyond grade 12, was accompanied by and helped to cause a change in the role of the professional engineer. University courses in engineering around 1950 are said by members of the Ryerson faculty to have been comparable in their practical orientation to some Ryerson courses of the late sixties. The trend from that time on was to place more emphasis on theory and research. When he became employed, the professional engineer could make better use of what advanced training he had because there were others qualified to implement plans and designs. In the early part of the period, graduate work in engineering in Ontario universities was rare. By the 1960s, when there were enough schools of engineering, and probably too many for efficient operation, graduate enrolment was increasing very quickly while undergraduate enrolment rose more slowly. A study carried out for the Committee of Presidents of Universities of Ontario by a Committee of Ontario Deans of Engineering, and reported in November 1970 under the title *Ring of Iron*, indicated the expectation of substantial rises in enrolment in the future at both the undergraduate and graduate levels.[2] Such a development would gradually modify the criticism that some of the schools were too small to function effectively. If the purpose of the study was realized, the expansion of enrolment in the major engineering schools would continue on a more orderly basis than in the past while some of the smaller schools would be restricted. The committee did not appear to see a serious danger of a surplus of engineers in view of the widening range of roles opening up for engineers in Ontario society.

Many of the new occupations and changes in existing ones in the post-war period resulted from an extension of bureaucratic superstructure in private corporations and government. In the corporations this phenomenon was in part a result of more sophisticated and complex activities in such areas as industrial research, market analysis, and advance planning based on studies of economic and social trends, and in part of the elaboration of various theories of administration. Government agencies grew with the increased public assumption of certain functions in areas such as welfare, the stimulation and regulation of economic activity, and the preservation of the environment. There was a growing recognition of a need for formal preparation for administrators as a supplement to appropriate natural talents and inclinations. Training began to be provided in a variety of forms, including short courses and seminars offered by industrial firms for their own employees, government-sponsored programs of a similar type, and university courses. The universities tended to begin their activities in the extension field and in some cases moved on to the establishment of regular departments. From the earliest years of its existence, Carleton University in Ottawa showed a particularly keen awareness of the need for a contribution in this area. By 1970 it was possible to earn some type of degree in administration, or at least enrol in some course or program of this kind, in most Ontario universities.

CHANGES IN REQUIREMENTS FOR ADMISSION
TO THE PROFESSIONS

The majority of the professions, with a conspicuous exception discussed later, continuously upgraded their preparatory courses in the years after the Second World War. Most groups that called themselves professional had or acquired a responsibility for deciding who would be admitted to membership and who would be allowed to practise under a legally recognized designation. Accountancy offered a good example of the evolution of methods of ensuring adequate preparation for membership. Originally the Institute of Chartered Accountants of Ontario concerned itself with setting examinations for candidates who were largely responsible for their own preparation. Then, in co-operation with the Canadian Institute of Chartered Accountants, the Ontario institute assumed increasing responsibility for providing training courses through correspondence. A more recent development involved an increasing reliance on universities to provide suitable courses while the professional organization concentrated on its original function of certifying those regarded as qualified to practise. This type of development was in part a recognition of the superiority of the facilities and learning environment offered by the university and in part an acknowledgment of the growing demands on practitioners of the profession, which called for higher educational attainments.

The extent to which other professions were calling for higher levels of preparation depended to a considerable extent on how much they were influenced by technology. As a result of rapidly accumulating knowledge in the medical field, the basic medical degree was more and more regarded as only a preliminary to a period of specialization, typically lasting for several years. As a concomitant to welcome progress in the treatment of human ills, there were serious problems of selecting candidates for training, providing the expensive facilities required in the program, and finding enough private or public funds to remunerate those who eventually emerged ready for practice.

The medical profession demonstrated clearly some of the problems resulting from the specialization which was increasingly necessitated by the rapid accumulation of knowledge. The extension of the required period of training involved higher costs for initial and in-service training and a longer delay before the trainee entered his period of service. When he began to practise, more complex organization was required to ensure that his specialized knowledge and skills were co-ordinated with those of other specialists in the interest of the patient as an individual. The fact that at least someone should be capable of an overview of the patient's physical and mental state gave continued importance to the general practitioner. Yet the latter found increasing difficulty in maintaining his prestige in view of the specialist's lengthier training and higher remuneration.

The development of nursing education illustrated the tendency for a profession to upgrade itself and, in doing so, to leave room for a group with less advanced training to perform relatively unskilled tasks. Immediately after the Second World War, the organized nursing profession was uncertain about how to handle those who at that time began to be known as registered nursing assistants. The decision was made to recognize this group and to control admission and training standards so that the position of the registered nurse would be protected and the quality of nursing care maintained. As members of the nursing profession observed the growing complexity of their task and urged that university training facilities be expanded in relation to the more traditional hospital schools, they increasingly realized the value of utilizing a body of sub-professionals so that their own more advanced training could be employed to best advantage.

In the 1950s and 1960s the nursing profession demonstrated the apparent paradox of attempting to improve the quality of preparation by shortening the period devoted to it. The objective was to separate real training from the ill-paid and often menial service with which it had long been inextricably mingled. Experimental programs demonstrated that two years of concentrated training under independent administration constituted a more satisfactory kind of preparation than a three-year combination of study and service offered as an integral part of the hospital's activities. It was difficult to make a change, however, because many teaching hospitals had become completely dependent on the services of the trainees. A classic example of the vicious circle had developed. Unattractive training conditions contributed to such a serious shortage of nurses that it was extremely difficult to move to a system that offered a real chance of alleviating the shortage. During the 1960s the profession was reluctantly forced to accept a "two plus one" program that constituted a kind of compromise between the traditional approach and one considered more suitable for the modern age. This program involved two years of concentrated theoretical training followed by a year of practical experience in a service role. A complete transition to the desired program was not seen as a practical possibility until the mid-seventies. The effect of the elimination of the shortage of nurses in the early 1970s, a development that was occurring more rapidly than had been anticipated in the mid-1960s, was likely to be an increase in the level of training required, at least for some nursing roles.

For many years the legal profession was characterized by an unusual capacity to resist change. Those who controlled the Law Society of Upper Canada appeared to regard a university education as an entirely unnecessary diversion on the route to mastery of the technician's skills needed to practise law. They seemed unaware of the accumulation of knowledge in the humanities and social science disciplines that might enable their practitioners to exercise a responsible role in leading and shaping the evolving society in which they lived. The monopoly of training vested in Osgoode Hall was exercised in favour of an arrangement for a kind of peripheral, part-time instructional program supplementing a form of apprenticeship governed by articles. The immediate post-war years were notable for a battle between the traditionalists and the revived Faculty of Law at the University of Toronto. Arrangements made in 1957 opened the way for other universities to establish such faculties and to present their programs as a practicable way for candidates to prepare for entry into the profession. The change was in part an acknowledgment of the need for better educated lawyers and in part a result of the inability of Osgoode Hall to provide the facilities needed for the increasing number of applicants.

Most professional associations recognized a need for continuing education to enable their members to keep up to date with new developments in their field and to refurbish the skills they had acquired in their period of initial preparation. With variations according to the size and wealth of their membership, the rate of change in their recognized body of professional knowledge, and their degree of professional responsibility, they offered refresher courses, seminars, workshops, and conferences. Many of them produced and distributed professional journals and other publications. In some cases they employed closed-circuit television or films on specialized subjects. Money was raised for scholarships and fellowships for advanced study for a few fortunate recipients.

The increase in educational requirements for entrance to the professions caused disquiet in some circles. In a preliminary treatment of issues in the fall of 1970, the Commission on Post-Secondary Education in Ontario expressed some of its misgivings. It commented that the higher qualifications required for admission were at times justified on the grounds that increased professional quality brought about returns in better professional services. It observed, however, that professional quality was often equated with years spent in school, which might or might not provide relevant experience. The result was a vicious circle that provided for the initiation or maintenance of high fees for professional services on the grounds of the long period of training required, while the additional years of schooling were justified on the basis of the prospective high income.[3] The commission suggested that the rigidities and abuses of certification might be reduced by curtailing the powers of organizations representing individual practitioners, that is, by more government intervention.

Given the rapid assumption of public responsibility for maintaining the universities and other educational and training institutions, and in the light of the increasing assumption by governments of the burden of ensuring health, welfare, and legal services for the population as a whole, more government regulation of all fields of professional education seemed inevitable. The advantage of preventing selfish groups from putting their own interests first had to be weighed against the disadvantage of introducing the effects of political expediency into the regulatory process. Traditional government control over teacher training had aroused substantial criticism.

Under normal circumstances, teaching might have been expected to have followed the same trend as did many other occupations by requiring continuously higher levels of preparation for the real or ostensible purpose of handling a more sophisticated and demanding task. For most of the post-war period, no such upgrading occurred. Although philosophers and theorists in various countries were busy defining what should have been more productive educational approaches, the Ontario system continued to operate with recruits whose educational background almost ensured that most of them would lean heavily on the prescribed courses of study, textbooks, and routines supplied by a paternalistic bureaucracy. Curriculum makers in the Department of Education, turning to Great Britain for forward-looking models and ideas which actually originated in the United States, and in an unusual effort to take advantage of the experience of leading Ontario teachers, produced a curriculum for grades 1 to 6 in 1937 that even thirty years later was regarded by the Provincial Committee on Aims and Objectives of Education in the Schools of Ontario (the Hall-Dennis Committee) as difficult to improve upon. Its successful implementation would have required a teaching force of highly mature and self-confident individuals, knowledgeable about the natural world and human affairs, steeped in the culture of their own age and appreciative of the legacies of the past, creative, sympathetic, humane, and imbued with a desire to serve. These qualities are by no means all derived from high levels of education, but some of them are almost certain to be scarce when a large proportion of schools are staffed by young people in their late adolescence who are admitted to teaching even though they could not qualify academically for other professions, some of which could never be considered of the same importance for the welfare of society. The shell of the 1937 curriculum survived and no doubt, as critics alleged, provided the excuse for a great deal of shoddy work, but few classrooms really reflected its spirit. The system or, to be more accurate, the teachers were not ready for it, and it is doubtful whether many inspectors were either.

The facts of the story of teacher preparation are dismal enough.* A move to require elementary school teachers to return to normal school for a second year was reversed in the early thirties, to some extent because of lack of imagination on the part of those who were responsible for the program. Teachers were naturally resentful at having to return after a year of initial preparation followed by experience in the field only to encounter much of the same course content they had covered the first time around. The depression itself was a major factor in the return to the shorter program. The government was not averse to saving the funds required to operate a longer program of teacher education, and school boards often placed more value on being able to employ cheaply produced teachers than on ensuring a high quality of instruction. With the return to the one-year formal program, the Department of Education for a time tried to maintain academic standards by requiring for permanent certification the equivalent of a further year of study in credits that might be obtained by extramural university work. As the teacher surplus of the depression years gave way to a shortage during and after the war, requirements for admission to normal schools dropped. In 1940 the number of grade 13 credits

*The development of teacher education in Ontario is recounted in ONTARIO'S EDUCATIVE SOCIETY, vol. V, chapters 1–9.

required for admission to the course leading to the Interim First Class Certificate was reduced from nine to eight. In 1944 and 1945 the requirement was reduced in succession to seven and five credits, but until 1948 the candidate received only a Deferred Interim First Class Certificate until he obtained sufficient credits to make a total of eight. Between 1948 and 1953 there was no upgrading requirement; in the latter year, however, the entrance standard of 1940 was restored, and eight credits were again demanded.

In the early 1950s two new routes to teaching were opened, both of which could be entered by grade 12 graduates who were not necessarily capable of meeting the academic standards of grade 13. The more defensible of the programs involved two years at normal school, where a much more limited academic program than that ordinarily offered in grade 13 was combined with professional subjects and practice teaching. At the beginning, partly because normal school staffs had little warning of what was coming, and therefore had no time for adequate planning, the second-year students got treatment comparable to that experienced by those in the two-year program of the thirties: they covered much the same ground a second time. Although this defect was corrected, the two-year course continued to be regarded as inferior to the one-year course for grade 13 graduates. In theory it might have been as good or, with professional work and practice teaching stretched over a longer period, even better than the latter, but to insist on grade 13 standards of academic work would have defeated the major objective, which was to recruit from among those with a lower level of achievement and ability.

The second program for grade 12 graduates required attendance at a six-week initial summer course, followed by a year of teaching, a second summer course, another year of teaching, and a year of attendance at normal school. A considerable number, particularly of those whose work between training periods was adequately supervised, may have emerged with as high a level of teaching competence as the graduates of other programs, but the fact was that many did not continue beyond the first year or two. Thus pupils in areas of the province where good teachers were disinclined to go were often taught by a succession of individuals with only six or twelve weeks of formal preparation.

Of the two programs that could be entered from grade 12, that involving summer courses and one year of normal school attendance was abolished in 1961, and the two-year course in 1966, although teachers with lesser academic qualifications could still prepare for service in what were then called the bilingual schools. In 1966 the stage was finally set for an increase in the minimum level of preparation of elementary school teachers over that maintained in the 1930s. The report of the Minister's Committee on the Training of Elementary School Teachers (the MacLeod Committee) recommended that every teacher at this level eventually be required to have a degree obtained in some appropriate type of university program.

Mainly because of the difficulty in negotiating the necessary arrangements between the universities and the government, the implementation of the recommendation was slow.

Where agreements had been concluded, and these involved the Lakehead Teachers' College and Lakehead University, the University of Ottawa Teachers' College and the University of Ottawa, and the Windsor Teachers' College and the University of Windsor in 1970 and the St Catharines Teachers' College and Brock University and the Lakeshore Teachers' College and York University in 1971, a gradual evolution from a one-year to a four-year program was undertaken. The first real over-all advance since the Second World War was made in 1969, when normal school applicants were expected to meet the same minimum requirements as those seeking admission to universities. A further major forward step followed in 1971–2, when candidates for admission had to have one year of university credit or equivalent beyond the grade 13 level. A rapidly developing surplus of teachers made it possible to announce plans for a minimum entrance requirement of a university degree, beginning in 1973–4.

Ostensibly at least, the post-war shortage of secondary school teachers did not result in as serious a blow to standards as that suffered at the elementary level. In the opinion of a considerable number of people who believe that academic study is sufficient, and that professional preparation is a waste of time, there was no decline in minimum standards at all, since the degree requirement was maintained for all teachers of academic subjects. The chief concern of this group was that the proportion of honours graduates in college of education programs underwent a steady decline. Some indication of the trend may be gained from the fact that the percentage of college students in Type A courses (most, although not all, of whom were honours graduates) fell from 46.8 in 1950 to a low point of 22.2 in 1969. A major change in this respect occurred in 1970 when for the first time in many years there were far more applicants than could be accommodated, and preference could be given to those whose qualifications were higher than the minimum. The surplus of candidates, both for training and for teaching positions, grew rapidly after that time, and became a serious problem in itself.

Those who believed that a post-graduate year of preparation for secondary school teaching offered an opportunity for a significant improvement in teachers' competence were unhappy at the apparent necessity of substituting summer courses for the traditional program in 1955. Although summer courses of varying lengths were offered for other groups from time to time, this so-called special summer course was by far the most important in terms of the numbers involved. Since it offered a speedier route to a remunerative position, it naturally attracted many who would otherwise have attended the college for a winter session immediately after university graduation, as well as others who, had it not been available, would never have entered teaching at all. By the mid-sixties, a considerable majority of teachers in Ontario secondary schools had qualified by the summer course route. The course caused increasing dissatisfaction among college staff and other concerned educators, who felt that the contrived opportunities for practice teaching during the summer were hardly more than a farce, and that the other aspects of the program could not be given satisfactorily in summer sessions. After 1969 the special summer course in its original form was discontinued, and the only applicants allowed to qualify through summer courses were those who had had a specified amount of work experience or work experience plus further study after receiving an undergraduate degree. A temporary exception was made when Lakehead University was permitted in 1969 to offer a special summer program for teachers who promised to teach for a minimum period of time in northern Ontario, where the shortage of qualified people remained serious. This program was terminated in 1972. Thus requirements for preparation for secondary school teaching were largely restored to the level of the immediate post-war period.

Teaching is like many other professions in that demands on the knowledge and skill of the practitioner increase as the years pass. After the war, the swift growth of knowledge belatedly produced a situation in the schools where curricula could no longer be drawn up to last a generation, but underwent drastic revision every few years. A good teacher could no longer depend exclusively on intuition to handle human problems, but had an obligation to keep up with at least some of the major psychological findings about the learning process as well as with the results of research into other aspects of school education. The role of new aids and educational media needed to be studied, understood, and assessed. More important still, the more quickly social structures and modes of living changed, the more important it was for teachers to understand, and help to define, the changing role of the school. The success of the entire retinue of administrators, supervisors, researchers, and developers in introducing innovations and improvements depended directly on the ability of teachers to assimilate and apply their recommendations, and that ability was closely related to the level of education they attained and maintained.

During most of the post-war period, it seemed distressingly obvious that the uncritical copying of the teachers they had observed in their own school days played a predominant part in the behaviour of a large proportion of the teaching force. Attempts to introduce educational improvements produced meagre results in view of teachers' lack of capacity to comprehend or apply them. The situation provided what seemed to many sincere Department of Education officials to be sufficient justification for detailed regulation of the schools, a view that contributed to the prolongation of an unsatisfactory state of affairs. An attempt to compensate for inadequate pre-service courses, as well as to contribute to the continuing development of teacher competence, was made by the department, the universities, local school boards, and the teachers' federations. All these agencies found their efforts hampered by the fact that the teachers with the least education were also the least interested in upgrading their qualifications.

In industrial operations, the conditions of the market ultimately bring pressure to bear to ensure that those who hold certain positions are adequately prepared for them. If, for example, a substantial shortage of draftsmen were to develop because the occupation exercised a declining attraction for young people, the response would not be to lower the level of competence required of trainees, since the obvious consequences would be to endanger the success of the entire operation, but rather to make the work more rewarding in financial or other respects. If advancing technology made the occupation more challenging and difficult, training requirements would go up regardless of other factors. The same process does not operate in education. There is too much disagreement about the desired outcomes and too much uncertainty about the importance of various factors in achieving them. Since the consequences of lowering the standards for admission to teacher training institutions are not immediately evident, it is possible for many people to persuade themselves that undesirable results can be escaped. Thus political expediency can often operate to damage the educational system without those responsible suffering unfavourable consequences.

The superficial, and in a sense quite valid, explanation for lowering standards of teacher preparation in the 1950s, and in fact for failing to raise them continuously throughout the post-war period to correspond with occupational trends in general, was that the pool of potential teachers was too small to meet the need. The age group from which recruits had to be drawn came from the 1930s when the birth rate was at a low point, while school enrolment reflected the high birth rate of the immediate post-war years. It is of course always valid to ask whether the pool of potentially good teachers is large enough to provide the kind of education that the idealists want. Many utopian schemes would be workable only if there were a stable of archangels at hand eager to rush into service. Much of the disappointment with the products of the schools may well be traceable ultimately to a lack of enough people with the talent and temperament to realize even fairly modest objectives. Whatever the reality may have been, it is clear that Ontario society did not in general hold education in high enough esteem in the 1950s to take certain measures that might have eased the situation considerably. First of all, there might have been a much greater effort to retain in the profession those teachers who had already been trained. There were no publicly operated day nurseries where working mothers might have left their children during the day while they taught school. There was actually a good deal of residue of the antipathy to married women teachers which prevailed during the depression when a working wife provided the family with a second income while some other family was thereby deprived of any income at all. Also, many school boards objected to the inconvenience resulting from the propensity of married women to get pregnant. Secondly, more teachers might have been attracted and retained if salaries had been increased and working conditions improved much more rapidly than they actually were. It is unconvincing to claim that the economy could not have afforded it in view of the steady rise in incomes in general. A society that puts a really high value on education will face the prospect of using a major proportion, or even all, of its income gains for the improvement of education. Even some reduction in the standard of living may not be regarded as an unthinkable sacrifice. Thirdly, there was no serious effort to redefine the teaching task in order to make the most efficient use of resources of trained teachers. The employment of teachers' aides or assistants, with an accompanying increase in the number of pupils per teacher, was not seriously contemplated. Little effort was made to employ educational media to make the work of the individual teacher more effective.

MANPOWER DEVELOPMENT

A new dimension was added to the educational enterprise in the latter part of the post-war period through the provision of programs for manpower development. Major precedents were established during and after the Second World War when the Department of Veterans Affairs in the federal government made a major effort to prepare returned men and women for civilian life. The project went considerably beyond compensating them for the educational and employment opportunities they might have lost by serving in the armed forces; in many cases they were enabled to reach a much higher educational level than they had ever aspired to, particularly under the stringent economic conditions of the late depression years. It was not very difficult to deduce that the welfare of non-veterans might be enhanced and the state of the economy improved if government money continued to be used to stimulate various forms of training.

There were always sensitive issues involved in the use of federal money for educational purposes, even when every effort was made to draw a distinction between education and training. Although financed by the federal government, the DVA program did not arouse any particular protest from the provinces. Not only was it seen as a response to an emergency, but it also reflected the desire of a grateful citizenry to express tangible appreciation for the services of those who had defended their country. Further, the federal government worked as far as possible through provincial institutions rather than setting up a rival network of facilities. While federally sponsored programs in the 1950s continued to cover the full cost of such training for veterans as continued to be needed, most of the effort was made through shared-cost programs. There was some provincial grumbling that a federal offer to pay half the cost of a program removed the initiative from provincial hands, since it was politically difficult for a provincial government to refuse such an offer. Some federal incentives were ineffective, however, simply because even a half-contribution exceeded provincial capacity. A very serious disadvantage of the shared-cost type of program was that it provided the most help to those provinces that were best able to respond, that is, to those in the least need of help. Naturally Ontario was a conspicuous member of this group.

Efforts to assist the unemployed and the under-employed to adjust to the higher educational demands of the job market were on too small a scale to have much effect before 1960. The major innovations of the *Technical and Vocational Training Assistance Act* of that year and of the federal-provincial agreements that followed were to provide massive assistance for the construction and initial maintenance of secondary school facilities for vocational education and to increase the dimensions of the entire assistance program. A closely related outcome was that the Reorganized Program, or Robarts Plan, introduced in 1962, became a practical and politically desirable reality. Of particular significance for Ontario were the contributions to the building and equipping of post-secondary institutes of technology, trades institutes, and vocational centres, to the development of programs for upgrading those already employed in industry, and particularly to the training of the unemployed. A gratifying number of the latter were assisted under Program 5, although the improved employment situation was much more attributable to a booming economy. The cooperation of school boards was enlisted to help make the program a success.

During the mid-1960s the federal government became increasingly unhappy about certain developments resulting from the 1960 act and related agreements. Although efforts had been made to prevent the retraining program for the unemployed from becoming an alternative to formal educational facilities, the main beneficiaries were young people. Partly because of the inadequate levels of financial support, comparatively few older men with families, many of whom were in the greatest need of assistance, were able to participate. A further disadvantage was the one inherent in shared-cost programs already referred to. Federal officials felt that the greatest effort should be expended in those parts of the country where unemployment was most serious. The *Adult Occupational Training Act* of 1967 was an attempt to remedy the situation by requiring a longer waiting period between the end of formal education and eligibility for assistance, by providing more adequate support for men with families, and by ending the shared-cost feature of earlier programs. Taking responsibility more directly into its own hands, the federal government undertook to appraise the needs of applicants in its Canada Manpower Centres and to purchase appropriate training for them in existing educational institutions, or to create its own where these did not exist. In Ontario in 1968, the colleges of applied arts and technology took over from the larger school boards the function of providing facilities and courses.

Provisions for manpower retraining in the late sixties had one very serious defect: many of the unemployed lacked the academic background to participate successfully. Although provision was made for up to one year of work in basic school subjects, this period of time was inadequate to overcome the deficiencies of a person who functioned at the grade 4 level, or even lower. According to 1961 figures, about 6.1 per cent of the population aged fifteen or over had fewer than five years of schooling.[4] Thus the real "hard-core" unemployed were left untouched. Federal officials seemed to feel that it would be too costly to finance a program that would materially benefit this group. Although a considerable proportion no doubt lacked the capacity or the drive to advance from a level of near-illiteracy, it would appear that the least expensive approach in the long run would be to enable those with the ability and desire to overcome their deficiencies to do so.

There was increasing criticism of the manpower program during the recession that marked the end of the 1960s and the beginning of the 1970s on the grounds that many of the trainees were unsuccessful in finding work. It was an unfortunate fact that most of them remained at an educational level where jobs were disappearing most rapidly. Even a return to a booming economy offered little hope that the situation would be remedied.

OTHER ADULT EDUCATION ACTIVITIES

Adult education activities without direct vocational implications flourished throughout the post-war period. School boards offering evening courses found their enrolments surging upward year by year. University extension activities were so popular that traditionally oriented administrators feared that resources and effort thrown into them would seriously damage their capacity to maintain the strength of their full-time programs. The success of York University's Atkinson College, the first such institution devoted to part-time students, was so overwhelming that it left planners nonplussed. The evening courses offered by the colleges of applied arts and technology exerted an immediate and wide appeal. A multitude of associations, organized for a great variety of social, protective, and philanthropic purposes, found their educational programs eagerly received.

Substantial numbers of adults demonstrated the ability to plan and stick to an academic program long enough to attain impressive goals. Atkinson College officials claimed that they found no need to compromise the standards maintained in the full-time programs of the university. The English-language classes offered by many agencies showed that large numbers of immigrants were prepared to make a determined effort to overcome the handicaps of a strange society. There was more doubt about some of the courses with cultural or recreational purposes. Enrolment typically fell off drastically during the latter part of the winter as resolution faded and alternative activities exerted more attraction. It was often suspected that attendance at many of the classes was more of a social than a learning experience. Thus it was not surprising that evidence of real cultural uplift was not very obvious. However, since evening courses could be provided for comparatively small cost, there was reason for satisfaction, even if few housewives' oil paintings could be regarded as a major contribution to the artistic treasures of the ages, and few English-speaking aspirants to bilingualism could go much beyond "Bonjour Mme Thibeau."

EFFECT OF RISING DEMAND FOR EDUCATION
ON EDUCATIONAL INSTITUTIONS

The rising educational requirements for a large proportion of existing occupations caused a profound transformation in the nature and range of Ontario's educational institutions. Only at the elementary school level was the effect not strongly felt. It might almost be said that, the further up the educational ladder one proceeded, the greater were the changes. In the secondary school, there was a great broadening of programs and a change in the relative importance of those of different types. At the post-secondary level, the assumption of a substantially modified role by the universities (if not in terms of the nature of their offerings, then at least in terms of the proportion of young people they dealt with) was accompanied by the creation of a whole network of new institutions, the colleges of applied arts and technology.

An extension of vocational facilities occurred after the Second World War with the construction of composite schools, which offered technical and commercial courses along with the academic or General course. Unfortunately, Department of Education records do not provide any convenient means of determining the number or percentage of secondary school students who were enrolled in such schools. Vocational education was not at that time held in high esteem, a situation reflected in the Department of Education practice of paying vocational inspectors at a lower rate than their academic counterparts. For a time it appeared that a substantial effort might be made to improve the situation. The report of the Royal Commission on Education, which appeared in 1950 after five years of laborious investigation, showed a realistic awareness of the need for secondary and post-secondary programs with a strong vocational orientation. Little progress was made, however, during the eight years from 1951 to 1959 when W.J. Dunlop was Minister of Education. Dunlop saw secondary education as primarily a means of cultivating the intellect through the book-based treasures of the ages. The quality of technical and commercial programs actually deteriorated, at least in relative terms, largely as a result of the government's failure to provide the necessary financial resources. A thoroughgoing traditionalist had great difficulty swallowing the idea that substantially more money needed to be spent on each vocational student than on his counterpart in the General course to ensure a program of adequate quality.

To some extent the failure of vocational education to develop during this period as the changing nature of Ontario society seemed to demand can be attributed to the discrepancy between what it was supposed to be and what it all too often demonstrably was. According to the theorists, it was not designed to give the student the specific occupational competencies that he needed to fit smoothly into a skilled or even a semi-skilled job immediately after graduation. The school was recognized as a very inefficient agent for the performance of this task, which was better left to on-the-job training or specific, concentrated short courses provided by industries themselves. Particularly in areas where technical progress was rapid, it was impossible to keep either the equipment or the teachers strictly up to date. Therefore, instead of trying to compete in areas where it was unlikely to succeed, the school was supposed to concentrate on producing an educated individual and member of society through a combination of academic and practical studies. Work with his hands and the study of the practical arts would give him an insight into important aspects of his social environment, a knowledge of the basic principles of certain technologies, and an orientation that would pave the way for a quick adaptation to a chosen occupation. In actual fact, most vocational teachers completely failed to grasp this concept, and provided straightforward skill training, often of an obsolescent nature. Leading educators found it difficult to promote an expansion of this type of offering. Thus it was that Ontario, during a period of rapid industrial expansion, was supporting a relatively unresponsive secondary school system.

As already indicated, something of a turning point came with the passage of the federal *Technical and Vocational Training Assistance Act* of 1960, under the terms of which the Canadian and Ontario governments worked out the Federal-Provincial Technical and Vocational Training Agreement in 1961. These measures did not appear at first to break any radically new ground. It was the apparent intention of the federal government in 1960 to continue in the existing tradition, although with a more generous arrangement than before in view of the growing realization of the importance of training, particularly at a time of rising unemployment. What really introduced a new era in secondary education was the acceptance by the federal government of an obligation to provide a major share of the funds for the construction and extension of vocational school facilities throughout the province. The provincial government, which in the fall of 1961 became the Robarts government, had no difficulty in seeing the possibilities, and no hesitation in agreeing to pay the remainder of the costs of the new construction. It also gratefully accepted federal contributions toward the maintenance of the extended vocational programs. For the first two years after the agreement was signed, when conditions were most favourable, school boards could expand their vocational offerings at no pain to the local taxpayer and subject only to the provision that they submit satisfactory plans to the two higher levels of government. Expenditures for the construction of secondary schools rose from $39,169,000 in 1960 to $81,611,000 in 1963. Of course, so precipitous an expansion involved a good deal of waste. Suppliers of equipment, for example, were unprepared to fill the unanticipated volume of orders, and school boards often had to make do with substitutes. In many cases school officials did not know what they needed, or what they would need a few years later, and made ill-judged purchases. The whole development, with responsibilities split among three levels of government, was far from ideal from the point of view of the taxpayer, the ultimate source of the funds. In retrospect, however, the money was perhaps spent as productively as it would have been had it been used for certain other purposes that governments are adept at devising.

When the agreement of 1961 was signed, education officials are said to have begun to look around for an appropriate school program. The department was not actually caught unprepared to quite that extent. S.D. Rendall, Superintendent of Secondary Education, was one of those who had realized the deficiencies of the system and had urged that better provision be made for vocational education. He was therefore ready with some ideas that circumstances now gave him the opportunity to implement. By the fall of 1962, the Reorganized Program or Robarts Plan had been delineated and was introduced into grade 9. For the time being few real changes could be made in view of the haste involved, but new directions had been defined. The program was a scheme designed both to raise the quality and prestige of vocational courses and to give greater recognition to variations in individual capacities. The first of these objectives was to be achieved by substituting for the General, Commercial, and Technical courses three corresponding branches entitled Arts and Science, Business and Commerce, and Science, Technology, and Trades, all of which would provide for a five-year university preparatory program or stream. The second objective was to be realized by offering two other programs in each branch, a four-year and a two-year program.

The change was not as drastic as it was sometimes made to appear. The Business and Commerce Branch received most of the students who would have gone into the old Commercial course, and the Science, Technology, and Trades Branch most of those who would have gone into the Technical course. These two branches attracted an increasing proportion of secondary school students, perhaps less because of a shift in interest away from academic studies than because the federal-provincial agreement had made vocational facilities available in far more communities than before, and students were better able to follow their preferences. Retention in the two branches was better than in the courses which they replaced, and improved steadily, but perhaps as much because of the continuously rising levels of education being demanded by employers as of the attractiveness of the programs themselves. The overwhelming majority of those who intended to seek admission to university chose the five-year program of the Arts and Science Branch rather than that of one of the other two branches. The two-year program was seldom offered in the Arts and Science Branch, although it attracted a significant proportion of students in the other two branches. Most students who clearly lacked the capacity or inclination to complete four or five years of secondary school were accommodated, as indicated earlier, in the Occupational program, which gave them a year or two of work with a heavily practical orientation.

The system had made a fairly creditable response to the demands of society for higher levels of education at the secondary school level. The process was, however, still far from complete. It soon became quite clear that a two-year program was a dead end, and that those who were capable of going further should not be encouraged to enter it. By the time the Reorganized Program was properly launched, it was also becoming evident that four years of secondary school education was inadequate to provide access to a large proportion of the more interesting, challenging, and remunerative occupations. The next logical step was a great expansion of non-university post-secondary educational facilities.

What followed has been described by critics as the development of a kind of holding procedure to occupy young people who would otherwise be unemployed. While it would be unduly cynical to suggest that such an idea entered into the consciousness of those who planned the expansion of the system, it seems fair to say that their efforts had that result. Such an observation is not necessarily entirely derogatory, since a society that has not found means of employing the efforts of young people for economic gain could do worse than provide educational institutions where they can occupy their enforced leisure. It would of course be a much healthier situation if they had a genuine choice between employment and full-time education. Furthermore, the provision of the necessary educational institutions is not the least expensive solution that can be imagined.

There was already a base for the development of the new colleges. Ryerson Institute of Technology, which had become Ryerson Polytechnical Institute under the control of its own Board of Governors in 1963, had done much to show the way. Other institutions with more modest enrolment and more limited scope but similar purposes were functioning in Hamilton, Haileybury, Ottawa, Windsor, and Kirkland Lake. There were three trade institutes in Toronto and vocational centres in London, Ottawa, and Sault Ste Marie by 1965.

A simple expansion of the institutes of technology and the trades institutes and vocational centres might have appealed as a reasonable course of action. Despite the fact that these institutions were providing a valuable service, however, they had certain limitations. Many of their programs were narrowly vocational, preparing the students for very specific jobs. Although they were in a much better position than the secondary schools to keep up to date with market demands, rapid industrial progress led to the criticism that their graduates were not as well prepared as they should be to adjust to job obsolescence. What was called for was a much larger component of general education, which would presumably produce a more flexible and adaptable graduate. Further, in addition to jobs requiring technicians and technologists, there was a wide spectrum of occupations in business and applied arts fields in which candidates might perform more satisfactorily after a preparatory program lasting from one to three years. Examples of these were in journalism, photography, specialized secretarial work, and health services.

Ryerson Polytechnical Institute had been extending the range of its programs and leavening job-oriented training with increasing amounts of liberal education. Although the Minister of Education and his planners and advisers travelled across North America in search of ideas before introducing the system of colleges of applied arts and technology, the new institutions deviated in few essential respects from the Ryerson model.* By the end of the decade, Ryerson had been so successfully copied that it was plunged into a crisis of role definition. That it was still considerably larger than any of the colleges, that it offered a few four-year programs, and that it did not attempet to provide an umbrella for manpower retraining programs, apprenticeship programs, and a variety of short, specifically job-oriented courses did not provide it with a sufficiently distinctive identity to enable potential students to explain why they should attend it rather than one of the more readily accessible colleges. The alternatives appeared to be relative stagnation on the one hand and conversion to degree-granting status, with the possible addition of other accoutrements of a university, on the other. The Commission on Post-Secondary Education in Ontario pushed the institute in the second of these two directions, and in 1971 the provincial government accepted the proposed policy. The question was whether enough provincial money would be made available to ensure an effective transition. It would take a good deal of academic upgrading to make the staff acceptable as a university faculty.

The colleges of applied arts and technology expanded in an extraordinary fashion, despite the fact that only Centennial College in Scarborough succeeded in opening its doors in October 1966, and the system did not get effectively under way until the fall of 1967. Apart from apprenticeship programs and manpower programs, which were switched from school board auspices, and thus did not represent a net gain in numbers in the provincial system, enrolment grew from approximately 11,700 in 1967–8 to 36,936 in 1971–2. This increase was in large measure attributable to the forces already noted: more young people in the relevant age group, a larger proportion completing grades 12 and 13, and an awareness of the tendency of employers to ask for higher educational qualifications. There were also potent psychological influences. There was a great deal more appeal in attending a college than an institute, a factor which would have existed regardless of any difference in the programs. This influence was

*For a review of the ideas that were taken into account in the planning of the colleges of applied arts and technology, see ONTARIO'S EDUCATIVE SOCIETY, volume IV, chapter 15.

particularly noted by those responsible for recruiting staff in the institutes of technology and in their successor colleges. Where formerly they had to conduct an assiduous search for qualified and competent instructors, they rather suddenly found themselves confronted with lengthy lists of promising applicants. The promotional activities conducted by officials in the Department of Education, such as N.A. Sisco, Director of the Applied Arts and Technology Branch when the college system was introduced, and L.M. Johnston, his predecessor in that office who moved up to become an assistant deputy minister, were particularly effective in stressing the novel aspects of the colleges. There were also many effective spokesmen in the colleges themselves and on their boards of governors. Many students who had struggled through secondary school, constantly under the shadow of those who were destined for university, and feeling that no one really cared much whether they continued or dropped out, were now convinced that society was making substantial efforts on their behalf. The rather unpromising employment situation of 1970–2 exerted a somewhat dampening influence on early enthusiasm, although the college students in some branches of training had reason to feel that they had at least as good a chance of finding work as had their university counterparts.

The institutes of technology, the provincial institutes of trades, and the vocational centres had been under the direct control of the Department of Education. While this form of control was not necessarily inefficient, and did not necessarily prevent the institutions from responding to the needs of the surrounding community, the transfer of responsibility to boards of governors made up of local citizens was a move that fitted in with Davis's program of reducing the role of the Department of Education in favour of local agencies. It was hoped that the new arrangement would give these institutions something of the role of community colleges. Although the department limited the powers of the boards, and retained the kind of co-ordinating authority that no government agency had over the universities, the parallel between the CAATs and the universities helped give the CAATs a substantial degree of prestige.

The provincial government was determined that the CAATs would begin with and retain distinct qualities that marked them off from the universities. Unlike their closest counterparts in the United States and in some other parts of Canada, they were not to offer an identifiable university preparatory program. Students who felt that their proper destination was university were to be encouraged to proceed in that direction through grade 13. The colleges would do no more than assist students to transfer if they discovered that their original choice had been wrong or if they developed new interests that gave the university an attraction that it had not had originally. It was felt that to do more would be to distort the whole purpose in establishing the CAATs and to encourage them to deteriorate into second-rate liberal arts colleges. The hope for their success lay in building up the prestige of occupationally-oriented courses so that those whose needs they best met would not feel apologetic about taking them. Since the tendency to look down upon such programs was deep-rooted in Ontario society, this hope was not fully realized, but very commendable progress was made. The ultimate verdict, of course, would depend primarily on the acceptability of the graduates to employers.

Those who criticized the government for failing to provide university preparatory programs in the CAATs passed rather lightly over the fact that year after year the universities expanded rapidly enough to be able to accept every qualified grade 13 graduate. Some critics indeed reflected a view not uncommonly held by present-day radicals – that any scheme to prepare young people to fill jobs in the existing economy is an evil plot to destroy their souls by making them slaves of a ruthless capitalist system.

The creation of the CAAT system was accompanied by a change of direction in the secondary schools. Since fewer students were headed directly for the job market, there was less temptation to emphasize the teaching of specific vocational skills, a role that could be left to the colleges. Vocational teachers could not so easily escape the more complex and difficult task of educating through vocational courses, just as the theorists had always said they should be doing. Observers saw major changes beginning to take place around 1964 and 1965, although the strongest impetus for change did not come until two or three years later. Pressure rapidly built up against the rather rigid streaming of the Robarts Plan. To the curriculum innovators of the late 1960s there seemed no good reason why a student whose interests were primarily academic could not include a technical or commercial course in his program if he had a secondary interest in one of those areas, or why a student with technical or vocational interests could not take more than the minimum of academic work.

A reduction in emphasis on job-preparatory aspects of the curriculum raised questions about the validity of some of the programs and made it more difficult to deal with a certain type of student. Oriented toward immediate gratification, he had been prepared to apply himself to courses of an extremely practical nature that pointed to satisfactory employment in the immediate offing. To try to teach him the beauties of English literature or the significance of the past had been a distinctly unrewarding task. Now that the direct incentives were weakening and the importance of general education was receiving greater emphasis, he was more likely to become a discipline problem. To carry him to a higher level in the school system was a challenge to the dedication and ingenuity of the best of teachers. The school was under mounting pressure to deal successfully with him, because it was becoming less convincing to declare that, if he could not be persuaded to learn, it would be better for him to go to work.

The situation underlined certain vital questions about the role of the school in relation to society. What were the school's obligations toward the youth who continued to attend simply because there was no very desirable alternative? To what extent had it a responsibility to reorient him

toward more distant and intangible goals when the prospect of immediate employment disappeared? To the extent that it had such a responsibility, how was it to be discharged? If the school found that it had nothing to offer, on what other social agencies might the responsibility devolve?

The Hall-Dennis Committee demonstrated a clear understanding of the changing role that the secondary school would have to play with respect to vocational education. This committee propounded the view that the student would be best prepared for occupational success if he developed his individual capacities and talents in a challenging atmosphere of freedom. If he had the right attitudes and outlook, he would be well prepared to acquire the job skills he needed at the proper time. For the majority of students, this time was after, not during, their school career.

CHANGES IN UNIVERSITY EDUCATION

Changes in the role of the school were closely related to the opening of university doors to a continuously rising proportion of young people. The decision on the part of the Robarts government early in the 1960s to make a university education accessible to all those who met the traditional requirements, or the nearest counterpart to such requirements that could be identified, was indeed a bold one. There were indications in the early 1970s that it might, at least if continued, prove to be an impractical one in view of rapidly rising costs. Some of the expensive library, laboratory, and other facilities for independent study and research might prove beyond the capacity of even a wealthy society to provide for students in their freshman and sophomore years. If such turned out to be the case, serious consideration would have to be given to the possibility of reserving the universities for more advanced students and providing for a less expensive substitute in advanced programs in secondary schools, in an adaptation of the CAATs to assume the role of junior colleges offering a liberal arts program in accordance with the pattern in California and some other states, or in work-study programs. The Commission on Post-Secondary Education was arousing lively discussion of such possibilities. Whether the CAATs would be permitted to continue and expand according to the original plan was uncertain.

The rising demands of the job market for at least the appearance of educational achievement brought about noticeable changes in the quality of university life. It is virtually impossible to make any objective comparisons between the academic abilities of the groups separated by the twenty years between 1950 and 1970. Grade 13 examination results are of little help since, as is well known among those who are aware of how the grade 13 departmental examination system was operated, the level of marks and the proportion of successful candidates were adjusted to the quality of the candidates over a period of time. It is particularly difficult to interpret the sudden rise in mark levels when the schools assumed the responsibility for appraising success in grade 13 in 1968. It would be unduly cynical to attribute the phenomenon simply to a decline in standards, since the basic purpose of the change was to improve the quality of education, an improvement that should have been reflected in better marks. Over-simplified reasoning would suggest that every increase in the percentage of young people attending university should mean a closely related decline in the level of abilities being drawn upon, and thus in the standards of achievement. However, as the Atkinson Study of Utilization of Student Resources and other related research demonstrated, financial and other selective factors tended to let many individuals with a rather low level of competence in while excluding many others who were demonstrably more capable. It is thus possible to admit a rising proportion of individuals to university without lowering standards provided that it is done through an improvement in the processes of selection, both formal and informal.

However difficult it may be to assess the difference in learning capacity between the student of the early 1970s and his earlier counterpart, many university professors claimed to see a definite change in attitude and outlook. Apart from the veterans of the Second World War, who constituted an unusually serious, highly motivated, unique group, and thus must be left out of the comparison, these professors thought that the early post-war student body contained a higher proportion of students who were drawn there by the attractions of scholarship. According to the theory, they were naturally interested in future occupational opportunities, just as any other young people, but there was a wider variety of acceptable non-university routes toward occupational success. Economic influences exerted less pressure on them to produce that precious piece of paper that only the university could provide before they were given a chance to demonstrate their worth. Although no doubt humiliating, it was less economically damaging to fail. The university, less dependent on government financial contributions, and thus less subject to public pressure than it later became, could weed out the uncommitted students with more equanimity.

Throughout the post-war years, traditionalist professors complained that the university would be prevented from making the vital contributions to scholarship for which it was uniquely fitted if it had to deal with hordes of apathetic or resentful students seeking the appearance of education but contemptuous of the substance. Their protest was, however, futile in the face of powerful economic, social, and political forces. They were compelled to take what seemed to be the next best course of action and find the means within the university structure to preserve standards of serious scholarship. Where an honours undergraduate degree would once serve professional purposes, a master's degree was demanded, and where a master's degree formerly served, a PhD was barely adequate. Many of the specialized courses were preserved for the student with a real interest in learning, while arts and science constituted the receptacle for the uncommitted and the uncertain.

The effect was somewhat comparable to the imposition of compulsory education at lower levels. In a sense, many university students were there because they were compelled to be there – compelled, if not by law, then by their parents, their peers, their attachment to the material comforts and social amenities that they could more readily learn to disparage than to dispense with. They demanded to be interested, to be persuaded to learn. They were less willing to tolerate ineffective teaching. They wanted convincing reasons why they should concern themselves with particular areas of knowledge structured according to an ancient scheme that might or might not remain valid. An underlying anger at what society was doing to them was said to have eroded their reluctance to resort to the professional essay-writer.

There was even considerable doubt that the mass of students were any less interested in learning than they ever had been. In contrast to the view just referred to, some suggested that complaints of declining interest and application were based mainly on the illusory effects of fading memory. Records showed that the universities had always been burdened with individuals flitting in and out for social reasons having little to do with scholarship. It seemed possible that the hangers-on were simply more numerous in the absolute rather than in the relative sense, and perhaps more vociferous and unabashed in making their dissatisfaction known.

Learning to deal with a large number of such students was not without its salutary effects on many of the professors. They were forced to examine the role of teaching in relation to their other functions, and to improve their methods, to the advantage of the students with scholarly inclinations as well as the others. They also discovered how often the horse dragged unwillingly to the pool finds that the waters of learning quench a hitherto unapprehended thirst. Young people whose entire educational experience had tended to turn them away from further voluntary learning might at last, in the jargon of the age, be "turned on." There were always grounds for hope that something stimulating, thought-provoking, or inspiring would rub off even on the unwilling student. In actual fact, of course, if most students were not imbued with strong scholarly interests, neither were they truly antagonistic. Coming in various combinations of idealism, interest, assertiveness, uncertainty, respect for authority and learning, determination to establish their own personal independence, inclination to oversimplify, iconoclasm, and good will, they gave the true teacher as challenging an opportunity to exercise his calling as his predecessors ever faced.

One of the articles of faith during the fifties and much of the sixties was that education provided a reasonably firm guarantee against unemployment. Although there were some highly specialized occupations that could absorb only a restricted number of entrants, generally speaking it was felt that the higher the educational level one attained, the more one's services would be in demand. The nature of the economic growth during that period gave strong support for such a belief. The scarcities were in the skilled trades and technological fields and in the professions. It was assumed that the employment of the highly skilled in key occupations offered the best assurance that more jobs would be created to employ the relatively unskilled.

As early as the late fifties, a few prognosticators began to warn of fundamental changes to come. The revolution that automation was beginning to create would tend at first to eliminate the assembly-line type of job that had been or could be reduced to a mechanical routine. Ultimately, however, it would endanger employment among the most highly skilled. It was no longer to be expected that the technological advance that eliminated one job would create three new ones in its place. The superior efficiency and the cheapness of the machine would finally triumph, and the Luddite theory that industrial progress was the enemy of the worker would come into its own. Those who foresaw this development felt that work would ultimately have to be rationed and that socially approved and individually rewarding alternatives would have to be created. More important, they suggested that basic attitudes toward labour, leisure, and recreation would have to be changed. Work could no longer be regarded as the chief means by which success and prestige were won. The hope of greater occupational opportunity could no longer be the main force driving people to higher levels of educational attainment.

There were observers ready to see some of these prophecies being fulfilled in the economic slump that developed in 1960 and 1961. It seemed possible that employment would not return to the high levels reached in the fifties. During the prosperity of the next few years, however, such gloomy appraisals seemed to be discredited, and less was heard about the problems being created by automation. Demographers were noting, however, that much larger numbers of young people than hitherto would soon be released on the labour market, and that new patterns of economic activity would be needed if there was to be a reasonable prospect of absorbing them. Unlike educators, civil servants, and politicians, these demographers were thus not unprepared for the difficulties that appeared during the combination of inflation and recession that characterized 1969 and the following years. Just at this time the realization was dawning that the world's limited natural resources would not for long permit a continuation of the economic expansion that had hitherto made it possible to maintain a reasonably high level of employment.

Disturbing data were produced in November 1970 to suggest that education was losing its effectiveness as the ultimate guarantor of job security. The Graduate Students' Union of the University of Toronto, after a study of employment prospects for graduates with doctoral degrees, announced that, of 190 PhD graduates from the university that year, only 105 had found work. Fewer than half of the 158 seeking employment in universities had received appointments. A rapidly worsening situation was foreseen in later years when the mass enrolments of the 1960s produced floods of new graduates. The tendency was for those with master's degrees who could not find employment to seek the Ph D, and for unemployed Ph Ds to do post-doctoral work with the assistance of research fellowships.

On the face of the matter, a report issued by the Ontario Council on Graduate Studies in January 1971 made the situation appear somewhat less alarming.[5] This report indicated that, of 624 PhD graduates from Ontario universities in convocations between autumn 1969 and spring 1970, 257 had obtained employment in university teaching positions within or outside Ontario, 58 had obtained positions in industry, 169 had received research fellowships, 28 were employed in private research institutes, 61 had obtained government positions, 15 were unemployed, 18 were otherwise accounted for, and the employment status of the remaining 18 was unknown. These figures did not explain how many of those who accepted research fellowships for further study did so because they could not find the kind of jobs they wanted. Nor was there indication of how many of those who were employed had an opportunity to use the specialized skills which had cost the public so much to produce.

In any case, there was no question that Ontario confronted a problem that might be expected to grow in the future. A considerable amount of blame for the situation was placed on American domination of the economy, which ensured that research and other occupations requiring a high level of education were being reserved for corporation headquarters in the United States. Whatever the reason, it was evident that educational facilities had outrun the capacity of the economy to absorb the product. There appeared to be considerable risk in assuming that the pattern would adjust automatically so that the accretion of human resources in the new form could be fully utilized.

There was little sign in 1972 that Ontario society, or any other society for that matter, was attempting to make an innovative adjustment to a permanent scarcity of work. The distribution of income was such that the unemployed and underemployed had every reason to feel deprived, impotent, and condemned. There was always some municipal official ready to declare that handouts ruined the moral fibres of the recipients, and that the able-bodied at least ought to be forced to work for their subsidies even if make-work projects had to be contrived. No serious consideration was given to schemes whereby work might be treated as a diminishing commodity which ought to be rationed so that the benefits could be shared by all. People were admired for being work addicts, and gained respect from the admission that they had no hobby but work. Young people who showed leanings toward the hippy culture were scorned for a willingness to live off the fruits of other people's efforts while making no contribution of their own. Ontario society had missed a major point of continuing education, that of helping people adapt to a new balance between work and leisure.

The educatonal system had a great deal of adjusting yet to do if it was to lead the way to a new ethic. True, it had the Hall-Dennis Report, *Living and Learning*, which, if it did not exactly provide a specific blueprint by which children could be prepared for a diminished emphasis on material amenities in an age of leisure, at least amply expounded the spirit with which such a task might be approached. *Living and Learning*, however, remained largely an expression of ideals. In every type of educational institution beyond the elementary school, there was an underlying understanding that students were being prepared for careers, whether through highly academic or strictly practical courses, and that success and satisfaction awaited him who was prepared to carve off for himself a segment of that unlimited commodity, work. The tendency to place more emphasis on academic studies, as already noted, may have reflected a yearning on the part of educators for more cultural uplift and a better appreciation of the finer things in life, but it was at least as often defended as a means of producing the ability to generalize from experience, to respond flexibly to challenges, and to adapt to changing occupational demands. The colleges of applied arts and technology were particularly vulnerable to a shift in values. Although they represented an appropriate and impressive response to conditions in the 1960s, they would have to make a drastic change in the balance of their programs if they were to take a leading part in cultivating the art of living as contrasted with the art of earning a living. The seeds of such a shift could perhaps be found in some of the liberal arts courses they were offering, and particularly in their night-school programs.

While the new age held little promise of full-time, productive employment for everyone, it did not, of course, offer visions of a workless life for all. The most ingenious minds and the most creative imaginations would be required to keep the complex machinery of civilization running in increasingly effective ways for the general welfare. Assuming an escape from such perils as uncontrolled overpopulation, the exhaustion of usable natural resources, and nuclear holocaust, perhaps the greatest social problem would be to utilize those talents that could make a contribution to the continued advance of science and technology without an intolerable widening of the gulf between their possessors and those whose main role was consumption and self-fulfilling leisure.

The educational system would still have to provide intensive preparation for certain kinds of employment. There could be no question of a complete dismantling of its machinery for vocational preparation. It would have the delicate task of turning out a decreasing proportion of graduates with highly-honed technical skills while at the same time dealing humanely with others destined for a less productive role. Both objectives would have to be pursued in such a way as to avoid allowing one to impinge destructively on the other. There is an obvious parallel with the university's chronic problem of reconciling its desire to remain a comfortable home for the seekers of knowledge for its own sake while preparing large numbers of young people lacking strong scholarly inclinations for immediately practical pursuits.

TWO

The expanding system

The post-war period was one of extraordinary expansion in the educational systems of all provinces, and most particularly in Ontario. Although the problems were not comparable to those of some underdeveloped countries, which found themselves struggling to make two or three centuries' progress in as many decades, the challenge was perhaps greater than that in any of the other so-called developed countries. During the period of most rapid growth in the elementary schools in particular, there was a constant atmosphere of crisis. It is not surprising, perhaps, that qualitative improvement was neglected, and that in some respects the effectiveness of educational programs declined.

GENERAL TRENDS IN SCHOOL ENROLMENT
In 1945–6 there were 664,780 pupils in the publicly supported schools of Ontario, of whom 545,007 were in elementary schools and 119,773 in secondary schools.* This meant that approximately one in six of the population was attending school at either the elementary or the secondary level. Breaking the figure down further, we find that about 13.6 per cent of the population were in elementary schools and just under 3 per cent in secondary schools. Compulsory education was operating with sufficient effectiveness to ensure that the percentage of the eligible age group attending elementary schools was about as high as it could realistically be expected to go under existing legal provisions and given the kind of facilities provided. Small further increments awaited the elimination of the arrangement by which pupils could be excused from school attendance at the age of fourteen if their parents claimed they were needed to help at home. This change was made in 1968, thus producing a uniform school-leaving age of sixteen. The percentage of enrolment also improved somewhat over the post-war period as a result of the increased provision for children with certain types of handicaps who at one time were considered uneducable. At the pre-grade 1 level there was of course a large increase as kinder-

---

*Most of the statistics presented in this volume were obtained from one of four sources: 1 / the *Reports* of the Minister of Education, 2 / the *Reports* of the Minister of University Affairs, 3 / departments of the Ontario government other than Education and University Affairs, and 4 / the Dominion Bureau of Statistics. Specific sources for particular figures are given in ONTARIO'S EDUCATIVE SOCIETY.

garten facilities were extended. In the secondary school system there was a great deal of room for further improvement. Enrolment at that level constituted only about 37 per cent of the age group between fifteen and nineteen years of age.

During the post-war period the Ontario population grew at a most impressive rate. The four million figure of 1945 rose to over 7.8 million in 1971, an increase of about 95 per cent in twenty-six years. This rate of growth, which was somewhat greater than that for Canada as a whole, was attributable to a combination of a high birth rate and a large influx of immigrants. Other provinces shared, or even exceeded, the Ontario birth rate, but over half the immigrants consistently chose to settle in Ontario.

The birth rate in Ontario was low throughout the depression period of the 1930s, reaching the bottom of a trough in 1937 at 16.9 births per thousand of the population. There was an erratic rise during the war years, with a temporary peak at 20.7 in 1943, followed by a small decline. The sharp climb to 23.8 in 1946 and 26.1 in 1947 was expected as a result of the return of the servicemen. Also anticipated was the decline to 24.3 in 1948 and 1949, which was commonly regarded as the beginning of a trend toward what had seemed to be a more normal situation in earlier years. For reasons that are not thoroughly understood, however, large families became popular and, with considerable numbers of young immigrants arriving, the rate rose above 25 per thousand, where it remained until after 1961. The Ontario record of 26.8, reached in 1957, was somewhat below that of the whole of Canada. After 1961 there was a steady decline until the situation by 1970 was comparable to that in 1937. This reduction actually became evident before the widespread adoption of birth control pills, although these no doubt accelerated it. Other contributory factors were considered to be the increased tendency of married women to continue in employment, the rising costs of educating children, and various effects of urbanization.

Immigration into Ontario was approximately thirty thousand in 1946, and a little more than twice that figure in 1948. In subsequent years it fluctuated erratically, jumping from 39,000 in 1950 to 105,000 in 1951, and falling from a peak of 147,000 in 1957 to 64,000 in 1958 and to 37,000 in 1961. A second minor peak of 117,000 was reached in 1967. The variations were attributable partly to economic conditions in Canada and in the countries from which the immigrants came. The number arriving from certain parts of the world, such as the West Indies, was influenced by changes in immigration regulations, when skill level rather than more blatantly racial factors became the chief criterion for admission. During the twenty-year period between 1947 and 1966, Ontario gained a total of about 1.34 million people from immigration. Assuming that the province lost people from emigration at about the same rate as Canada as a whole, the exodus amounted to about 420,000 and the net gain to about 840,000.

This increase was about 20 per cent of the population at the beginning of the period. A comparison with the United States shows that, in relation to its population, Ontario received four times as many immigrants in 1961, six times as many in 1964, and nearly nine times as many in 1967. During the same twenty-year period, Ontario is estimated to have gained about 260,000 people who moved to the province from other parts of Canada.

Of great importance for the provision of educational facilities was the post-war change in the age distribution of the population. The effect of the low birth rate in the 1930s was to leave the younger age groups relatively depleted in numbers. In fact the number in every single-year age group between twelve and twenty-one actually declined between 1941 and 1951. The decrease in what is ordinarily considered to be the high school age group, that is, those between fifteen and nineteen, was from 338,000 to 316,000. Even the larger number of children in the younger age groups did not counteract this trend to any great extent during the 1940s. Between 1941 and 1951 the total number from five to nineteen increased only from 964,000 to 1,040,000, or by slightly less than 8 per cent. In 1941 they constituted 25.5 per cent of the population, and in 1951 only 22.7 per cent.

From that time on, the situation changed quickly. Between 1951 and 1961 what may be termed the school age population, that is, the number in the same age group increased from 1,040,000 to 1,704,000, or by nearly 64 per cent. Even by the latter date, the post-war baby boom had had its major effect only on the elementary schools, and was just beginning to affect the high schools. During the fifties, the number between fifteen and nineteen increased from 316,000 to 437,000, or by about 38 per cent. This increase was of course substantial, although much smaller, relatively speaking, than that at the elementary school level. Combined with the rapidly rising percentage of young people from that age group attending school, it was enough to cause serious problems of accommodation and staffing. In 1961 the total school age population as defined here reached 27.3 per cent of the entire population of all ages.

Five years later the school age population reached 2,059,000, a further increase of 21 per cent. During this interval, the elementary school age group between five and fourteen increased by about 15 per cent while the high school age group between fifteen and nineteen increased by nearly 38 per cent. This was clearly the period during which the most serious problems were shifting to the secondary level. In 1966 the school age population at both levels together constituted nearly 30 per cent of the total population.

Reports by the Department of Treasury and Economics for 1971 indicated a total population of 7,815,000.* In 1970–1 there were 1,588,800

*Actual figures from the Dominion Bureau of Statistics (Statistics Canada), produced after this account was written, gave the population of Ontario as 7,815,000 in July 1971.

between five and fourteen and 716,100 between fifteen and nineteen. The whole school age group would be almost the same percentage of the total population as in 1966, at slightly over 30 per cent. The increase in the elementary school age group for the decade between 1961 and 1971 was over 25 per cent and that for the high school age group about 64 per cent. The years between 1971 and 1981 were expected to see an absolute decline in the former group and a reduced rate of increase in the latter.

SCHOOL ENROLMENT
Enrolment in the elementary schools of the province constituted 87.8 per cent of the elementary school age group in 1945–6, and rose to 91.7 per cent in 1955–6. During most of the 1960s the figure was somewhat above 93 per cent, with the remaining percentage presumably unable to attend because of illness, severe handicap, or remoteness from a school, or absent because of failure to enforce the compulsory education laws. Thus the story of rising enrolments closely paralleled that of the population increase in the relevant age group. Totals for 1945–6, 1950–1, 1955–6, 1960–1, 1965–6, and 1970–1, rounded to the nearest thousand, were respectively 545,000, 612,000, 864,000, 1,126,000, 1,320,000, and 1,465,000, with a slight decrease to 1,457,000 in 1971–2. That is, the system had to accommodate almost three times as many pupils at the end of the period as at the beginning. Because of the large increase in the percentage of the relevant age group attending secondary school, the situation was more complicated at that level. The percentage for 1950–1 was 41.0, for 1955–6, 51.1, for 1960–1, 62.6, for 1965–6, 73.3, and for 1970–1 and 1971–2, over 80. The secondary school enrolments for five-year intervals beginning in 1945–6 were respectively 120,000, 131,000, 175,000, 263,000, 419,000, and 557,000, with a further increase to 575,000 in 1971–2. Enrolment at this level was thus between four and one-half and five times as great in 1970–1 as in 1945–6. Enrolment at the elementary and secondary levels combined was a little more than 26 per cent of the entire population of the province in 1970–1 and 1971–2.

There was a substantial change in the balance of enrolment between the public elementary and the Roman Catholic separate schools, the latter of which had students up to the end of grade 10. Between 1945–6 and 1970–1, enrolment in the former increased from 437,000 to 1,047,000 and in the latter from 108,000 to 418,000, or by less than two and one-half times in the former and nearly four times in the latter. To put it another way, the ratio of pupils attending Roman Catholic separate schools to the total in all elementary schools was about one to five in 1945–6 and about one to three and one-half in 1970–1. The change was attributable to an increase in the proportion of Roman Catholics in the population of the province and to the growing attractiveness of the separate schools, which were relatively better financed at the end of the period.

A particularly notable development in the elementary schools during

CHART 2-1

Enrolment trends in publicly supported elementary and secondary schools in Ontario, 1945–71

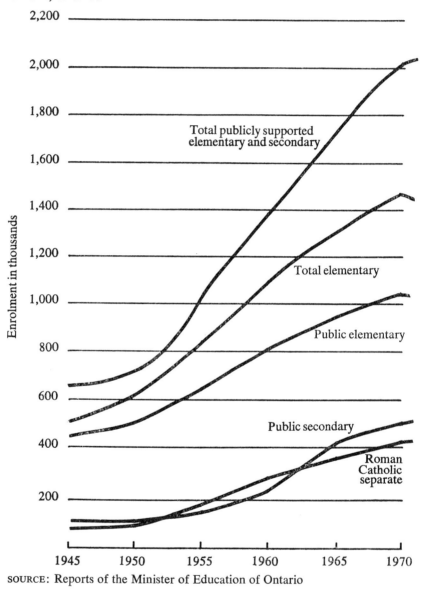

SOURCE: Reports of the Minister of Education of Ontario

the post-war period was the increase in kindergarten classes. In 1945–6, there were 24,000 children in these classes in the public elementary schools, as compared with 61,000 in grade 1. By 1970–1, the corresponding figures were 112,832 and 121,801, declining to 106,815 and 113,032 respectively in 1971–2. The change was considerably more impressive in the Roman Catholic separate schools, where the kindergarten enrolment increased from 272 to 41,633 from 1945–6 to 1970–1 and to 42,333 in 1971–2. Since the grade 1 enrolment in the latter year was 42,019, it was obvious that, in these schools too, kindergartens had become practically universal by the end of the 1960s.

The bilingual elementary schools, more recently called French schools, in which pupils received their early instruction in French and were gradually introduced to English as a second language, were, generally speaking, supposed to have existed in a more tolerant and congenial atmosphere in the early 1970s than in 1945. Their enrolment increased more slowly, however, than did that of the elementary school system as a whole during the twenty-five year period. The total of 90,225 in 1970–1 was only about twice that at the end of the war. In 1971–2, enrolment decreased to 87,496. Until the mid-fifties, about 8 per cent of the bilingual school enrolment was in public elementary schools, but by 1971–2 this percentage was less than 2.4. The declining percentage of children in bilingual schools reflected population trends in general. According to the census of 1941, the percentage of the population up to fourteen years of age acknowledging French as the mother tongue was over 10, while in 1971 it was below 7. This phenomenon was apparently partly attributable to assimilation of Franco-Ontarians into the English-language group and partly to the overwhelming tendency of immigrants from foreign countries to swell the same group. Even if many of the newcomers could not claim English as their mother tongue, their children commonly did.

ELEMENTARY SCHOOL BUILDING

The number of school buildings required to house the greatly increased number of elementary school children declined from 6,852 in 1945–6 to 4,207 in 1971–2. As far as the public schools were concerned, the trend was fairly continuous, although there was a small rise in the 1950s. By 1971–2, there were only about half as many schools as in the earlier year. The Roman Catholic separate schools, however, followed a different pattern. Reflecting both increases in enrolment and the extension of facilities to new areas, the number rose rapidly until 1960 and then slowly until a peak of 1,430 was reached in 1964–5, followed by a decline to 1,345 in 1971–2. The general trend was mainly a result of the abandonment of small rural schools, particularly those with only one room, in favour of larger central schools with three, four, or more classrooms. This change accompanied the gradual amalgamation of school sections into township school areas, a process that was completed by legislation which took effect at the beginning of 1965. The formation of larger units of administration in 1969 was likely to ensure a continuation of this trend. A second factor of major importance was the program of road construction and maintenance that made it possible to transport pupils efficiently in all kinds of weather.

CHART 2-2

Number of additional pupil places provided by new schools and additions
completed in Ontario each year between 1945 and 1971

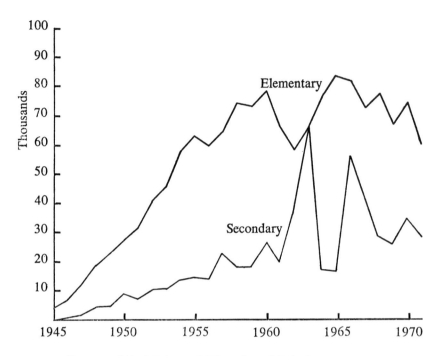

SOURCE: Reports of the Minister of Education of Ontario

The extent to which teaching resources were being wasted while emergency programs were being maintained to alleviate the teacher shortage is
indicated by the fact that in 1960–1 there were 113 public and separate
schools with fewer than ten pupils. The number of teachers in such schools
was not, of course, a very large proportion of the total force. Where the
teachers were reasonably competent, as happened in some of the communities that were able to secure the services of a resident married woman,
the pupils benefited from a large amount of individual assistance. In total
the 2,147 schools in the next size category, those with ten to twenty-nine
pupils, were a much greater problem. The smallest of these wasted teacher
power while the largest, especially when the pupils were scattered over
eight grades, gave the pupils too little attention. By 1971–2 the situation
had been much improved, with the number of schools in the smallest enrolment category reduced to five and the number in the second category to
forty-six. During the same eleven-year interval, the number of schools with
thirty to forty-nine pupils declined from 1,154 to 78, and the number with
fifty to ninety-nine, from 861 to 268. Most of the enlarged enrolment was

accommodated in schools with between two hundred and seven hundred pupils. There was no trend toward very large schools, which would have lacked any obvious administrative advantages at the elementary level. The situation was not comparable to that in secondary schools, where large size made possible a wide range of courses, a highly specialized teaching staff, and elaborate equipment. Both in 1960–1 and 1969–70 there were only twenty-nine schools with an enrolment of 1,000 and above. In 1971–2, however, the number of such schools rose to forty-six.

Building activity was extremely vigorous during most of the post-war period. Although only fifty-three and eighty-nine projects, including new buildings and modifications of existing buildings, were completed during 1945 and 1946 respectively, the pace began to quicken thereafter.* During the period between 1955 and 1966, more than four hundred new projects were completed in every year except two, and more than sixty thousand new pupil places were provided in every year except one. The number of projects declined after that, although the number of new pupil places remained fairly high, reflecting the trend toward larger schools. Between 1945 and 1971, 8,745 elementary school projects were completed, providing places for 1,467,451 pupils at an estimated cost of $1,407 million.

ELEMENTARY SCHOOL PUPIL-TEACHER RATIOS
The increase in the number of pupils in the elementary schools was accompanied by an even sharper rise in the number of teachers, since the pupil-teacher ratio was reduced, despite a slight rise in the 1950s, from 29.9 to 23.6 in the public schools and from 32.2 to 29.9 in the Roman Catholic separate schools between 1945–6 and 1971–2. These ratios are calculated by dividing the total number of pupils by the total number of staff, including administrators and consultants, with part-time staff treated as the appropriate fraction of full-time staff. Since the increase in the number of administrators and consultants was relatively much greater than that of teachers, the size of the average class decreased less than the figures seem to imply. Some of the reduction was also attributable to an inrceased provision of special classes with very small numbers. The total elementary school teaching force, again with part-time staff pro-rated according to teaching time, numbered 17,970 in 1945–6 and 62,166 in 1970–1; that is, it was multiplied by about 3.5 times. The five-year period of most rapid growth was between 1950–1 and 1955–6, but for much of the rest of the period the rate of increase was not much less. The rate of attrition rose from less than 9 per cent in 1945–6 to more than 14 per cent during the 1960s. Because of the substantial additions each year, the teaching force became an extremely youthful one. Although documentation of the point is unreliable, it is said that the median amount of experience for much of

*The available statistics do not distinguish between replacements for existing buildings and entirely new structures.

the period was less than three years. If the new teachers had gone through a long and thorough pre-service training course, it might have been a very propitious time to introduce educational innovations. When youth was combined with very slight preparation, however, the effect was the exact opposite. Many teachers coped with their problems by clinging to models remembered from their own elementary school days along with the formulas picked up later.

SECONDARY SCHOOL ENROLMENT

Secondary school enrolment was relatively stable during the first five years after the war. Although the numbers in the eligible age group continued to decline, a rise in enrolment as a proportion of this age group from about 37 per cent in 1945–6 to 41 per cent in 1950–1 more than counteracted this trend, and produced a small numerical increase from almost 120,000 to over 131,000. During the next five years there was an extraordinary jump in the attendance rate to 51 per cent of the eligible age group and a 33 per cent numerical increase to 175,000. Two factors stand out as reasons for the increased attendance rate: the increasing value being placed on education for utilitarian purposes, as dealt with in Chapter 1, and the availability of more and better secondary schools. After this time the continuously rising rate combined with the increasing number in the relevant age group to produce a considerably more spectacular growth in enrolment. Between 1955–6 and 1960–1, the figure rose by over 50 per cent to reach 263,000. This growth rate continued at a high level during the sixties, producing another doubling of the enrolment during the next ten years, at the end of which time enrolment constituted about 80 per cent of the group between fifteen and nineteen. Enrolment in 1971–2 was between four and five times as great as in 1945–6. It is hardly surprising that this period, particularly the latter part of it, was characterized by an atmosphere of crisis.

The increasing powers of retention of the secondary schools are demonstrated by calculations of the percentage of students reaching certain levels a given number of years after entering grade 9. For example, of every hundred students who entered grade 9 in 1951, forty-two reached grade 12 three years later, twenty-one reached grade 13 four years later, twelve received an Ontario Secondary School Honour Graduation Diploma five years later, and seven indicated their intention of entering university. After intervals of the same length, of every hundred who entered grade 9 in 1965, sixty-eight reached grade 12, thirty-six reached grade 13, twenty-seven received the diploma, and eighteen planned to enter university (in 1970).

Until the early 1960s nearly all secondary school students were enrolled in the academic General course, the Commercial course, or the Industrial (Technical) course. Very small numbers took the Home Economics or the Art course. There was a growing enrolment in non-diploma, ungraded courses, but the number was never more than a small proportion of the total. In 1945–6, 75 per cent of all secondary school students were in the General course. In 1955–6 this percentage was nearly 76, and in 1961–2, the year before the Reorganized Program was introduced, it was still almost unchanged. One reason why such a large proportion were taking this course was that many of them had no choice. A majority of the high schools and all the continuation schools offered nothing else. A wider range of opportunities would no doubt have been provided over a larger part of the province if it had not been for the strength of the snobbish belief, held in varying degrees by many Department of Education officials, teachers, students, parents, and members of the general public alike, that vocational courses were meant only for an inferior type of student.

For several years the Reorganized Program existed side by side with its predecessor as revised courses were added at the rate of a grade level each year. Between 1963–4 and 1968–9, the percentage in the Arts and Science Branch decreased from about 65 to about 56 per cent of the total. After the latter year, the lines between branches as well as those between five-year and four-year programs became blurred, and it was more difficult to try to trace the trend. Between 1963–4 and 1969–70, the number in the Occupational program, which was ungraded, increased from 9,922 to 15,569, and that in the Special Vocational course from 5,177 to 15,132. The changes in these programs, taken together, give some indication of the growing attempt to accommodate students who did not fit into the regular streams.

Secondary schools with very small enrolments tended, like the smallest elementary schools, to disappear rapidly during the 1960s. The continuation schools, which were reduced in number from fifty to twenty-two between 1955–6 and 1960–1, disappeared altogther in the 1960s. There were twenty-seven schools with an enrolment below one hundred in 1960–1 and only four in 1971–2. It was only among schools with an enrolment of more than five hundred that there was an absolute increase in numbers. In contrast to the elementary schools, there was a definite trend toward very large (at least by Ontario standards) secondary schools. There were twenty-one schools with 1,900 students and over in 1971–2 as compared with only three in 1960–1.

SECONDARY SCHOOL BUILDING

The secondary school building boom, like that in the elementary school field, got under way rather slowly during the late 1940s. Fewer than five thousand new places were provided by the twenty-seven projects completed in 1948 and the nineteen completed in 1949. During the fifties, the annual number of projects ranged from twenty-nine to seventy-one, and the number of new places from a little over 7,000 to nearly 23,000. The rush to take advantage of the financial terms of the Federal-Provincial

Technical and Vocational Training Agreement of 1961 produced a peak of 174 projects in 1963, providing nearly 67,000 new places. After a two-year slump, the number of projects reached 116, providing about 56,000 places. Between 1945 and 1971 the total number of projects was 1,573, the number of student places, 559,690, and the estimated cost, $1,360 million. From July 1961 until July 1970 the federal government contributed $349,506,400 to vocational school building at the secondary and post-secondary school levels in Ontario.*

SCHOOLS FOR THE BLIND AND DEAF
Throughout the post-war period, the provincial educational establishment included schools for the blind and deaf operating under the direct control of and financed by the Department of Education. The first School for the Deaf was opened at Belleville in 1869, and a second one at Milton in 1967. The School for the Blind at Brantford dates from 1872. Enrolment at Belleville in 1945–6 was 284, and at Belleville and Milton in 1970–1, 999. That at the Brantford school was 164 and 233 in the same years respectively. The trend by the early 1970s was strongly against segregation of those afflicted with these handicaps if there was any way of educating them in proximity with or in regular school classes. Thus there seemed to be little future for such isolated institutions.

PRIVATE SCHOOL ENROLMENT
Private schools did not, generally speaking, have an easy time financially during the post-war period. In 1945–6, approximately 2.4 per cent of students at all levels, mostly at the secondary school level, attended such schools. The secondary private schools were often grouped for convenience into two categories: Roman Catholic private schools and independent schools. The former were by no means the only ones, however, with a strong religious orientation. In 1960–1, private school enrolment was 25,-000, or 1.8 per cent of the total in all schools. By 1971–2 the number had reached 44,000, and the percentage had risen slightly to 2.1. Given existing trends, the prospects for private secondary school education were not very favourable, mainly because costs were rising so quickly that the traditional sources of revenue, including fees, could not keep up. The trend in private schools offering elementary grades only was opposite to that of the group as a whole. Enrolment in these schools rose from about 7,000 in 1963–4 to 13,035 in 1971–2. Although costs were increasing at the elemenary level, they were still much lower than those at the secondary level, and within the reach of a certain number of families. The schools proved attractive to some parents who feared the results of extremely progressive approaches in the schools, and to others whose neighbourhood school continued to operate according to the pattern of the 1920s, and who wanted something more up-to-date.

*Figure supplied by a Department of Education official.

Despite the increase in vocational school facilities in the publicly supported system, private trade schools flourished in the 1960s. The number
of these increased from thirty-five to eighty-two between 1960–1 and
1968–9, and their full-time enrolment rose from 1,331 to 3,182 during the
same period. The opposite trend was in evidence in the private business
colleges, where the number in operation, after rising slightly from seventy-
seven in 1960–1 to eighty-one in 1962–3, fell steadily to thirty-five in
1968–9. Full-time enrolment in these colleges was 5,645 in 1960–1 and
2,615 in 1968–9.[1]

TEACHERS' COLLEGE ENROLMENT
In 1945 there were eight teachers' colleges, which continued to be called
normal schools until 1953. Five more were added by the time the report
of the Minister's Committee on the Training of Elementary School Teachers (the MacLeod Committee) was released in 1966, resulting in an official
decision to arrange for the transfer of pre-service preparation of elementary school teachers to the universities. Enrolment grew substantially until
the end of the 1960s, but not in the regular fashion of most educational
institutions. The lowering and raising of requirements for admission tended
to be accompanied by irregular increases and decreases. Between 1951
and 1966, while the two-year program was in operation, enrolment was
inflated in relation to the number of graduates turned out each year, since
the same students, provided they returned for the second year, were
counted in two successive years. During this period an attempt was made
to accommodate all applicants who met the minimum requirements in view
of the continuing shortage of teachers, which the government felt obliged
to alleviate in some fashion or other.

The oldest and largest of the institutions, the Toronto Teachers' College, was founded in 1847. Its enrolment of 269 in 1945–6 rose to 484 in
1950–1, and more than doubled again during the next five years. The new
building provided in 1955 was obviously an urgent necessity. During the
peak year of 1968–9, enrolment was 2,036, but sank back to 1,771 in
1969–70. The Ottawa Teachers' College, the second in terms of seniority,
having been founded in 1875, had an enrolment of 118 in 1945–6. In
1968–9 the aged structure which it had occupied from the beginning had
to make a pretence at housing 1,097 students. Even the 910 who attended
in 1969–70 grossly overstrained facilities. The third oldest, the London
Teachers' College, founded in 1900, moved into a new building in 1958.
It had its highest enrolment in 1960, when it housed 1,009 students. There
was a small decline in 1961–2 and a much larger one in 1962–3 when the
Windsor Teachers' College was opened. Between that year and 1968–9,
enrolment climbed from 501 to 816. The year 1908 saw the establishment
of colleges at Hamilton, Peterborough, and Stratford, followed by the one
in North Bay in 1909. The first of these got a new building in 1957 while
the latter three were still making do with their original structures in the

early 1970s. Enrolment at the Hamilton Teachers' College ranged from 908 in 1960–1 to 804 in 1964–5, and then fell to 626 the following year when a new college was opened in St Catharines. The Peterborough and Stratford Teachers' Colleges, which had 91 and 113 students respectively in 1945–6, had serious accommodation problems in handling enrolments of 501 and 481 in 1968–9. The North Bay Teachers' College had similar problems with an enrolment growing from 66 in 1945–6 to 546 in 1968–9. The University of Ottawa Teachers' College was opened in 1927 to prepare teachers for the bilingual schools. Its enrolment rose from 147 in 1945–6 to 364 in 1960–1, fell to 218 in 1964–5, and rose again to 316 in 1967–8. This college, along with its counterpart in Sudbury, which opened in 1963–4, did not experience the crisis of abundance experienced by the other colleges in 1968–9. The Lakeshore Teachers' College, dating from 1960, was from the beginning one of the largest. Its initial enrolment of 989 fell to 612 in 1962–3 and then increased to 1,195 in 1968–9. The Lakehead Teachers' College opened with 207 students in 1960–1, and continued with a fairly stable enrolment until 1965–6, when the number fell to 141. It had 260 students in 1968–9, the year before it was taken over by Lakehead University. Total enrolment in all the colleges was 1,019 in 1945–6, hovered around the six thousand level during most of the 1960s, rose to 9,277 in 1968–9, and then fell back to 7,896 the next year and to 7,571 in 1970–1. The peak enrolment of 1968–9 was partly explained by a rush of candidates to obtain certificates before minimum standards for admission were made the same as those for university entrance. In 1971–2 the considerably reduced number of teachers' colleges had 4,250 students.

There were 75 instructors in the eight teachers' colleges operating in 1945–6, and the student/teacher ratio was slightly under 13.5 to 1. There were thus no grounds for complaint at that time that the colleges were inadequately staffed. In 1968–9, however, the situation was quite different. The overall ratio had risen to 28.5 to 1, and in the hardest hit of the colleges was not far below 40 to 1. As a consequence, the existing staff were seriously overworked and the students undoubtedly obtained a less satisfactory education than they had a right to expect. The reason for this unfortunate situation, as well as for the deplorable overcrowding in most of the colleges, particularly the older ones, was the long process of transition between the one-year program and the more adequate preparation that was to be provided by the universities when they eventually assumed responsibility for the process in accordance with the recommendations of the Minister's Committee on the Training of Elementary School Teachers. During the interim period, the government could not be expected to invest in expensive new buildings which might not meet the needs or desires of the universities. Moreover, since most of the universities were engaging in considerable soul-searching before agreeing to absorb the teachers' college staffs, the government could not exacerbate the problem by making

CHART 2.5

Enrolment in teacher training institutions in Ontario, 1945–72

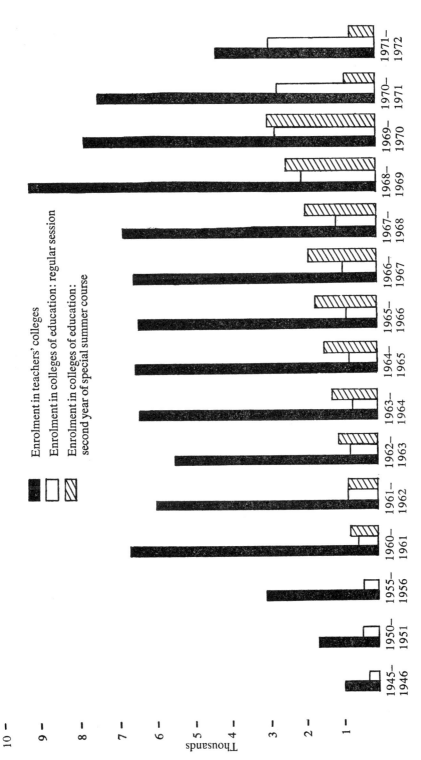

Enrolment in teachers' colleges

Enrolment in colleges of education: regular session

Enrolment in colleges of education:
second year of special summer course

Thousands

the large number of new appointments that would have been necessary to restore the student/teacher ratio to reasonable proportions, even if enough candidates of satisfactory calibre could have been found to serve under the conditions of uncertainty that prevailed. In the early stages, at least, the universities could not be held altogether to blame, since they had a responsibility to ensure that the function of teacher preparation was accepted and integrated in such a way as to strengthen rather than weaken their other programs. They were also determined to ensure that the programs were adequately financed. For various reasons months and years went by with only minor progress made. While there were matters of principle at stake before the Committee of Presidents and the minister announced an agreement in the spring of 1969, no comparable excuse for delay existed after that. Some of the negotiators, in acting as if they had all eternity to haggle over the specific terms of agreement, might well have given some thought to the damage that was resulting from the perpetuation of the uncertain state which only they could end.* In any case, by 1971 six universities were at some stage in the process of absorbing and integrating teachers' colleges: Brock, Lakehead, Laurentian, Ottawa, Windsor, and York.

ENROLMENT IN COLLEGES OF EDUCATION
For most of the post-war period, facilities for the professional preparation of secondary school teachers were concentrated in the Ontario College of Education of the University of Toronto. Immediately after the war, this arrangement seemed the only sensible one for, although there were dangers of complacency and even of stagnation in the absence of competition, enrolment was too small to justify splitting up the resources needed to maintain the program. Thus, bringing the prospective vocational teachers from the Ontario Vocational College in Hamilton into the college in 1946 appeared to be a logical step. In 1945–6 total enrolment was 289, consisting of 153 students taking the High School Assistant's course, Type B, 131 taking the High School Assistant's Course, Type A, along with the Type B course, and five students taking the Intermediate Home Economics course.† In 1950–1 the numbers in these courses had increased by similar proportions to a total of 442. There were, in addition, nineteen students in the Ordinary Vocational program and fifteen in the Industrial Arts and Crafts program.

A gradual rise in enrolment in the Types A and B programs proved inadequate to meet the increasing needs in the schools, and in 1955 the special summer course was introduced, with an enrolment of 418, ostensibly as an emergency measure. Although this course did have the virtue of re-

*For a more complete account of these events, see ONTARIO'S EDUCATIVE SOCIETY, volume v, chapter 4.
†The High School Assistant's course, Type B, led, after satisfactory experience, to the High School Assistant's Certificate, and the Type A course to the High School Specialist's Certificate.

cruiting many excellent graduates who wished to transfer from other occupations and could not have done so for financial or other reasons if they had had to spend a full year in attendance, it also provided a short and unsatisfactory route to the profession for those emerging from the universities who would have been able and willing to take a full academic year of pre-service preparation if there had been no alternative. During the winter following the introduction of the emergency course there were only 308 students in the Academic Department. This total rose rather slowly, and not altogether steadily, reaching a peak of 583 in 1962–3 and standing at 566 in 1964–5, the last year before alternative facilities were opened at Althouse College of the University of Western Ontario. After a brief period of relative stability, what became known as the College of Education, University of Toronto, faced a rapid rise in the number of regular session students. In 1968–9, the academic enrolment was 1,172 and the following year, the first one in which inexperienced university graduates were excluded from the special summer course, it increased to 1,741. In 1970–1, 1,240 students were enrolled. Enrolment in the Academic Department in Althouse College rose from 169 in 1965–6 to 706 in 1970–1. McArthur College of Queen's University began with 194 academic students in 1968–9, and had 334 two years later. Enrolment in the secondary program in the University of Ottawa was eighty in 1969–70 and 163 in 1970–1.

After the first special summer course was offered at the college in Toronto in 1955, accommodation had to be found for both a first and a second session. By 1960 enrolment in these sessions had reached 1,035 and 866 respectively, and facilities were used in London and Kingston under the supervision of the Ontario College of Education until responsibility was assumed for the London operation by Althouse College. Enrolment in the summer courses increased regularly and rapidly until 1968, when 3,225 students attended the first session and 2,519 the second. In 1969 the number in the first session was reduced by new conditions of admission to 812, while that in the second session was 3,041. Despite the general cut-back in summer courses, a new and temporary program was introduced at Lakehead University to prepare teachers for schools in northern Ontario. Summer session enrolment in all courses in all the colleges was 6,672 in the summer of 1970.* Special summer courses of all kinds were rather quickly abolished after that time.

The greatest challenge for the Vocational Department of the Ontario College of Education came as a result of the Federal-Provincial Technical and Vocational Training Agreement of 1961, which involved federal financial support for the preparation of vocational teachers to handle the Reorganized Program introduced in 1962. Enrolment in the Ordinary Vocational program jumped from 77 in 1960–1 to 281 in 1961–2 and remained approximately at that level for several years. The new facilities

*A discussion of certain aspects of the quality of these programs is found in
ONTARIO'S EDUCATIVE SOCIETY, volume V, chapters 5 to 8.

and programs ended the need for training teachers in industrial arts and crafts, and the course in 1961–2, attended by forty-seven students, was the last of its kind. Althouse College had a relatively small enrolment in its Vocational Department and, after it began to make a contribution in 1965–6, the two colleges together enrolled between two and three hundred trainees each year.

FOUNDING AND EXPANSION OF INSTITUTIONS FOR
TECHNOLOGICAL AND TRADES TRAINING

The system of provincially administered and supported institutions for technological and trades training covered the period from 1945, when the Provincial Institute of Mining was established at Haileybury, until 1968, when the Provincial Institute of Trades and the Provincial Institute of Trades and Occupations were absorbed into George Brown College of Applied Arts and Technology. Among the institutes of technology, Ryerson was overwhelmingly the largest. In 1963–4, the year before it began to operate under its own Board of Governors, it had 2,899 full-time students as compared with 1,600 in the four other institutes of technology and the Provincial Institute of Mining combined. In 1966–7, the year before the latter institutions were merged with the colleges of applied arts and technology, Ryerson had 4,494 students and they had 3,144. Much of the contribution of these institutes was through night school programs. In 1962–3 Ryerson had 4,671 night school students and the others had 967. In 1966–7 the corresponding figures were 9,000 and 2,784.

The Provincial Institute of Trades, established in 1951, was the only one of its kind during the first ten years of its existence. In 1962 the Provincial Institute of Automotive and Allied Trades and the Provincial Institute of Trades and Occupations were split off from it. Ontario vocational centres were set up in Ottawa and London in 1964 and in Sault Ste Marie in 1965. By 1966–7, the year before some of them were merged with the CAATs, these centres had a total full-time enrolment of 4,111 and a night school enrolment of 4,883. The senior one among them, the Provincial Institute of Trades, remained the largest, with a full-time enrolment of 1,319 and a night school enrolment of 2,463.

FOUNDING AND EXPANSION OF COLLEGES OF
APPLIED ARTS AND TECHNOLOGY

Between the opening of Centennial College in Scarborough in October 1966 and the same time the following year, seventeen additional colleges began operations. Two others joined them in 1968–9. The complete network at that time, in addition to Centennial, consisted of the following: Algonquin, with campuses in Ottawa and manpower retraining centres in various locations; St Lawrence, with campuses in Cornwall and Kingston; Loyalist in Belleville; Sir Sandford Fleming, with campuses in Peterborough and Lindsay; Durham in Oshawa; Humber in Etobicoke; Seneca in

North York; Sheridan in Brampton; Mohawk in Hamilton; Niagara in Welland; Fanshawe in London; St Clair in Windsor; Lambton in Sarnia; Conestoga in Kitchener; Georgian in Barrie; Cambrian, with campuses in Sudbury, Sault Ste Marie, and North Bay; Northern, with campuses in South Porcupine, Haileybury, and Kirkland Lake; Confederation in Thunder Bay; and George Brown in Toronto. Full-time enrolment in all colleges operating in 1967–8 was 11,202; in 1968–9 this figure increased to 19,801, and reached 36,936 in 1971–2. These figures do not include apprenticeship or manpower retraining programs. Expansion would have been even more rapid had sufficient places been provided in the larger urban centres. Although it was always possible for students to find places in colleges such as Northern, many were not prepared to go so far from home, and the desired programs were not necessarily available in the colleges that had unused accommodation.

GROWTH OF THE UNIVERSITIES

In view of the complex problems involved in the rapid expansion of universities and the creation of new ones, the development of the university system was at least as impressive as any other educational achievement in Ontario during the post-war period. Events were not clearly foreseen, particularly during the four or five years immediately after the war when returned veterans doubled what would have been considered under more normal circumstances a reasonable enrolment. This particular emergency tended to obscure the increased interest in university education among those emerging from the secondary schools. Even when the facts of the situation began to be recognized in the mid-fifties, the extent of the coming demand for places was consistently underestimated. By the early sixties the doubters were proclaiming that it would take a miracle to build facilities and to find staff quickly enough to accommodate all qualified candidates. Yet year after year the crisis was met, and provincial authorities could state with satisfaction that, although applicants could not always gain admission to the exact courses they wanted, no deserving candidate was turned away.

It is not very appropriate to look to 1945 as the base point from which to appraise post-war university expansion, as it is with other aspects of the educational system. Just before that time, enrolment was depleted by wartime concerns, and immediately after the end of hostilities the influx of veterans began. Looking back to 1939, we find about twelve thousand full-time undergraduate students attending McMaster University, the University of Ottawa, Queen's University, the University of Toronto, and the University of Western Ontario. The first two of these were still private institutions, while the other three received sums in public financial support that, in comparison with grants made thirty years later, appear to have been mere tokens. The University of Toronto was by far the largest, with about seven thousand undergraduate students. It was also the only one that offered any substantial opportunities for graduate study, although the University of Ottawa demonstrated a relatively venturesome attitude toward the establishment of graduate programs, and the others had a range of programs for the master's degree. All five, along with three-year pass or general and four-year honours courses in arts and science, had some form of arrangement for theological education. Engineering was offered at Toronto and Queen's, medicine at Toronto, Queen's, and Western, public health at Toronto and Western, and architecture, dentistry, education, forestry, pharmacy, and social work at Toronto.

The University of Toronto was noted for the complexity of its structure, which consisted of a nucleus of federated colleges and certain affiliated institutions. The other universities, except Queen's, had affiliated institutions, some of which were located at a considerable distance from the parent campus. Of particular significance were two affiliates of the University of Western Ontario, Assumption College in Windsor and Waterloo College. The first of these developed through successive steps into the University of Windsor and the second provided the nucleus for the University of Waterloo and Waterloo Lutheran University, which developed into separate institutions. St Jerome's College, originally an affiliate of the University of Ottawa, also had a role in the creation of the University of Waterloo. Sacred Heart College, which was at first affiliated with the University of Ottawa and later with Laval, evolved into the University of Sudbury, the major component of what became Laurentian University.

Enrolment in the existing universities almost doubled immediately after the war, and then receded until a post-war low point was reached in 1952–3. During that year there were estimated to be 18,840 full-time students, of whom 17,588 were in undergraduate and 1,252 in graduate programs. The increase over the following two-year period was only 1,590, but some of the trends that would become pronounced in later years were beginning to be in evidence. At the annual meeting of the National Conference of Canadian Universities in November 1956, E.F. Sheffield, at that time an official of the Dominion Bureau of Statistics, presented a paper, "The Expansion of Enrolment, 1955–1965," in which he predicted that enrolment in Canadian universities would double during the ten-year period referred to in the title. At the same conference C.T. Bissell, then president of Carleton University, speculated that, unless restrictive measures were adopted, enrolment in British Columbia and central Canada would increase by well over 100 per cent by 1964–5. In actual fact, enrolment in provincially assisted universities in Ontario (which was considerably short of total enrolment) increased from 15,727 to 42,022, that is, by 167.2 per cent, between 1955–6 and 1964–5.

Official notice of the emerging problem was taken in February 1956 when the minister, W.J. Dunlop, called a meeting of the heads of the Ontario universities to consider measures that might be taken to deal with the increasing enrolments that were then being observed. According to information available to Dunlop, the problem was "not a tide of increasing enrolment" but "a plateau" which would be reached in 1965.[2] Although he saw the matter as urgent, it is obvious in retrospect that he had no idea of the magnitude of the challenge. He felt that matters were being considered very carefully by the university authorities, and appeared to expect that further discussions would produce a satisfactory solution.

A good many spokesmen for the universities at that time speculated seriously about the possibility of deflecting a substantial number of potential applicants by raising entrance requirements. The determination of standards of admission was a well-recognized prerogative of the universities when they were largely sustained by fees and private philanthropy, and seemed to be a device that remained at hand if it became necessary to defend scholarly pursuits against mobs of mere degree seekers. In fact, the universities did not have all the options they sometimes seemed to assume were open to them. They could not have stood against a public that was determined to make them responsive to the needs of the province as these were coming to be seen. An institution that established admission requirements which were sharply at variance with those of the others, or that tried to adhere to a rigid quota of students, would soon have found itself by-passed when provincial funds, on which it depended increasingly for its welfare and ultimately for its standards of scholarship, were distributed. After several new universities had been created, representatives of the existing ones became convinced that it would be more beneficial for them to try to absorb the increased numbers of students themselves rather than let the process of proliferation go any further.

There was some particularly effective planning done after the mid-fifties in the University of Toronto by men such as Professors B.A. Griffith and G. de B. Robinson, who traced enrolment trends on the basis of assumptions about the rising proportion of attendance in the relevant age group. Some of their relatively high projections were not realized, not because they were defective, but because policy decisions by the provincial government resulted in the diversion of much of the subsequent growth to other universities. For the University of Toronto, the growth of an Ontario university system meant a steady decline in its proportion of the total provincial enrolment.

In 1960–1 total undergraduate and graduate enrolment in all Ontario universities reached 32,100, consisting of 29,501 undergraduates and 2,599 graduates. This increase of more than 70 per cent over the total in 1952–3 was largely the result of a higher percentage of attendance, since the number in the relevant age group had not yet been affected by the post-war rise in the birth rate. Prime Minister Leslie Frost was still citing unrealistic figures in forecasting an enrolment of ninety thousand for 1980, although he conceded that these might be too modest.[3] He was prepared to defer to C.T. Bissell, who in 1959 had foreseen an enrolment of 92,000 in all Ontario universities by 1975, a figure that was actually exceeded before the end of the 1960s. Bissell thought at the time that at least 46,000 of the total would be in Metropolitan Toronto. He was prepared to see the University of Toronto accommodate 23,000 students by 1965, after which the surplus would have to be provided for elsewhere.[4]

In 1962 the Committee of Presidents found reason to revise its estimate of the 1965 undergraduate enrolment from 42,000 to 49,000, and of the 1970 enrolment from 58,000 to 74,000. The actual figures for these two years were 52,124 and 103,593, although the totals in the provincially assisted universities, with which the Committee of Presidents was chiefly concerned, were of course somewhat less. In summary, total full-time enrolment increased by about 50 per cent between 1955–6 and 1960–1, and then by about three and one-half times in the next decade. Graduate enrolment rose from 1,452 in 1955–6 to 2,599 in 1960–1, an increase of nearly 80 per cent, and to 13,242 in 1970–1, about five times the figure at the beginning of the sixties. Part-time enrolment increased at a rate comparable to that for full-time enrolment.

The extension of university facilities during the post-war period followed definite stages. The first of these, apart from temporary measures of support for the education of veterans after the war, was one of neglect. Carleton University, which developed from an unimpressive program of part-time courses first offered in 1942, was a conspicuous sufferer from this policy. Although there seemed to be an obvious need for its services in the national capital, it existed for years under straitened circumstances, and at times faced the imminent prospect of collapse. Even after federal grants were made available in the early 1950s and provincial support began to be offered on a larger scale, there was a constant struggle to make ends meet, and in some years worrying debts were accumulated.

A second stage covered a period when a number of new universities appeared with substantial provincial assistance. Official attitudes toward them ranged from toleration to active encouragement. The strongest official approval was forthcoming where there was an obvious and imminent need for more accommodation, and the least enthusiasm was shown where there was a question about the ability of a particular area to provide the enrolment for a full-blown university. Throughout the period the provincial government maintained a consistent official policy of refusing to subsidize private, denominationally controlled institutions, although the federal government had no such qualms. This policy did not prevent the province from making grants for the establishment of facilities for specified purposes in denominational institutions: for example, the medical program in the University of Ottawa after the Second World War. For the most part, these institutions were under mounting pressure to meet the terms for general provincial support, partly because of their decreasing ability to meet rising costs and partly because of the danger that competing institutions would by-pass them.

York University is an example of a new university established to meet

CHART 2-4

Full-time enrolment in Ontario universities and colleges, 1951–70, with projections to 1975–6

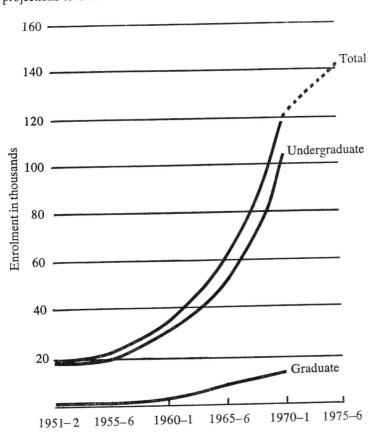

SOURCES: Dominion Bureau of Statistics (DBS), *Survey of Higher Education,* publication no. 81-204, and Economic Planning Branch, Policy Planning Division, Department of Treasury and Economics, *Education in Ontario,* Sept. 1971, p. 22

an obvious and compelling need. When steps were taken in 1958–9 to organize it as an affiliate of the University of Toronto, there was a clear understanding that it would assume complete independence within a period of four to eight years. Classes were begun in 1960 in facilities donated by the University of Toronto on what later became known as the Glendon Campus. In 1965 the university took over the responsibility of granting its own degrees, which it began to award the following spring.

The other universities which originated as affiliates of larger institutions assumed independent status in a somewhat less deliberate fashion. Assumption College, founded in 1857, was operated during most of its his-

CHART 2-5

Full-time enrolment in five senior provincially assisted universities in Ontario, 1960–72

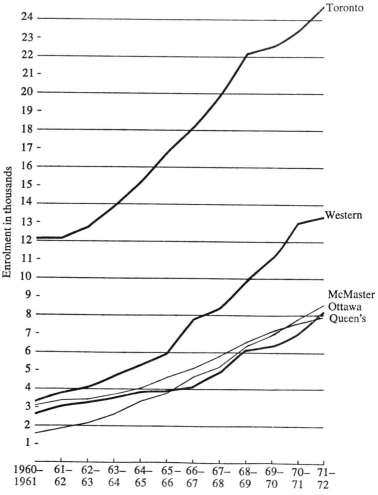

SOURCE: Reports of the Minister of University Affairs of Ontario

tory by the Basilian Order. Its affiliation with the University of Western Ontario, established by an agreement in 1919, was not considered to be a great source of satisfaction. Distance made it difficult for the staff or students to take advantage of the facilities and equipment at Western, while regulations and controls from that source seemed to place undesirable restraints on those who had the local responsibility. There was thus no great expression of regret when affiliation was ended. The main pressure for the change came from the realization that Windsor, a major centre of

CHART 2-6

Enrolment in nine provincially assisted universities in Ontario chartered in the twentieth century, 1960–72

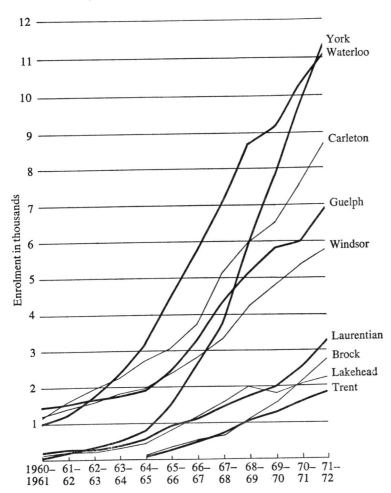

SOURCE: Reports of the Minister of University Affairs of Ontario

population, needed broader provisions for higher education than had been offered, and that provincial funds would be needed to help supply them. A first major step was taken with the transformation of Assumption College into the independent Assumption University of Windsor. Essex College was established under the control of a non-denominational board and became affiliated with Assumption in 1956. This college was to offer the more expensive programs in mathematics, science, business administration, and nursing and, by virtue of its status, could receive provincial

CHART 2-7

Full-time undergraduate enrolment in selected undergraduate programs in provincially assisted universities in Ontario, 1965–70

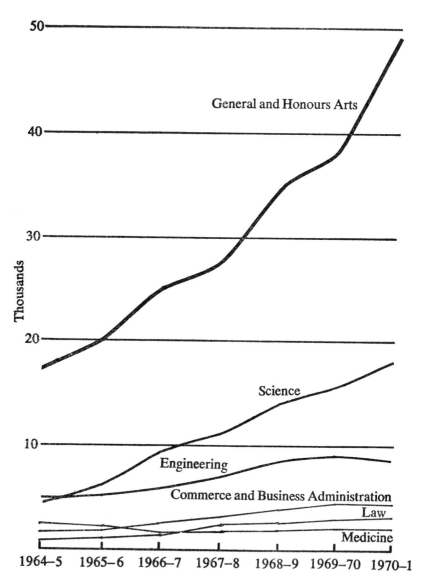

SOURCE: Reports of the Minister of University Affairs of Ontario

grants. For several years this arrangement persisted, although it was not always a completely harmonious one because those who had responsibility for the respective institutions did not always agree on objectives and priorities. It became obvious, however, that more provincial help was needed if the university was to expand sufficiently to provide for the enrolment projected for the area. In 1962 the process of secularizing control was completed, with considerable encouragement from the provincial government. Assumption College did not even maintain active degree-granting functions in theology. In a spirit of co-operation indicating considerable self-confidence, the Basilians decided to exert what influence they could by teaching in regular university courses. Affiliation agreements brought Holy Redeemer College, a Roman Catholic institution, and Canterbury College, founded by the Anglican Church and previously affiliated with Assumption, into the new university on a similar basis. A new Iona College, established by the United Church of Canada, was added later.

The two universities in Waterloo developed for the most part from the efforts of a dynamic group of local citizens, among the most conspicuous of whom were J.G. Hagey and Ira Needles, both influential members of the business community. In the early 1950s the flourishing Kitchener-Waterloo area was served by St Jerome's College, a small Roman Catholic institution, and by the conservative and rather somnolent Waterloo College, which was under the authority of the Lutheran Synod. Founded as the Evangelical Lutheran Seminary according to arrangements made in 1910, Waterloo College became affiliated to Western in 1925, but had somewhat the same unsatisfactory status as Assumption College during its years of affiliation. A drive for change became inevitable in 1953 when Hagey, a remarkable combination of idealism, promotional ability, and business sense, although not a scholar, was appointed as head of Waterloo College. Somewhat paralleling the development of Essex College, the so-called Associate Faculties were established to provide a program in science and engineering under conditions that would make possible the receipt of provincial financial support. In this way the notable University of Waterloo co-operative programs were begun.

It was intended that a single multi-faculty university would emerge after the ties with Western were cut. In preparation for such a development, the provincial legislature established Waterloo College, the Associate Faculties (as the University of Waterloo), and St Jerome's as degree-granting universities in 1959. The last two agreed on a merger, but there proved to be irreconcilable differences with Waterloo College. Objecting to the breach of a promise that it would have control of the arts program in the University of Waterloo, this institution continued separate existence as Waterloo Lutheran University under the control of the Lutheran Synod. At the end of the 1960s it remained the only provincial university under denominational control, and not eligible for provincial grants. Its enrolment necessarily had to be kept within bounds, and an effort was made to hold it to a figure below 2,500. In the meantime the University of Waterloo embarked on a program of vigorous expansion under Hagey's leadership, and had an enrolment of 11,195 by 1970–1.

Laurentian University provides a further example of the development of a non-denominational university from a small religious institution. Sacred Heart College, established by the Jesuit Order in 1913, won recognition for its graduates from the University of Toronto in 1935 and from Western in 1942. It was given a new status under *The University of Sudbury Act* passed by the provincial Legislature in 1957, and began to exercise degree granting powers. The transition to non-denominational status was brought about by *The Laurentian University Act* of 1960. Huntington University, founded by the United Church of Canada and incorporated by the Legislature early in 1960, entered the federation later in the year, suspending its degree-granting powers, except in theology, in the same manner as the University of Sudbury. A similar course of action was followed by Thornloe University, established by the Anglican Church in 1961 and accepted into the federation in 1963. The union appeared to work with reasonable harmony after that time.* The institution attempted to operate, with special provincial assistance, as Ontario's second bilingual university after the University of Ottawa. For a time this intended status looked extremely precarious, but the prospects brightened in the late sixties and early seventies as more French-language classes and schools were established, providing a better supply of bilingual freshmen.

Lakehead University grew out of a different type of entity, the Lakehead Technical Institute, which began classes early in 1948. The first program, in mining technology, was soon supplemented by others in forest technology and in arts and applied science. By arranging to meet requirements and standards of universities in the southern part of the province and of the University of Manitoba so that its arts and applied science graduates could obtain advanced standing there, the institute set itself on a course that differed fundamentally from that of the Ryerson Institute of Technology and of other similar institutions and paved the way for progress to university status. It operated two distinct divisions, one for the technology programs and the other for programs at the university level. In 1956 an act of the provincial Legislature placed the institute under the control of a board of governors as the Lakehead College of Arts, Science and Technology. Complete university programs were built up as degree-granting powers were bestowed by legislation in 1962 and full university status in 1965, when the institution became known as Lakehead University. Early steps were taken as a result of strong promotional activity on the part of local citizens who were largely inspired by faith in the future. Enrolment in the college was only 123 in 1959–60, although it grew rapidly after that time.

Before the period of major university expansion began, prominent members of the scholarly community often voiced the opinion that a proper

*A period of turmoil in 1970–1 found many faculty and students ranged against the Board of Governors, but did not imply conflict among the components of the university.

university had to have traditions established during a long period of growth. They refused to believe in the concept of the "instant" university. Yet two institutions, Brock University in St Catharines and Trent University in Peterborough, were established in defiance of this belief, and there is no reason to think that they had a less scholarly atmosphere than those which developed from parent bodies.

Brock University developed as a result of the generation of very strong community pressures, which were for a time contained by official scepticism about the need for an institution of that status in the Niagara Peninsula. The campaign was set in motion by Mrs Grover Egerter, who conducted an informal survey of high school graduates in the area and successfully introduced a resolution at a meeting of the Allanburg Women's Institute requesting the provincial government to give favourable consideration to the establishment of a university in the area. Support was obtained from other Women's Institutes and local organizations. The Minister of Education, W.J. Dunlop, responded unfavourably to the proposal, suggesting that it would be better policy for the government to support existing universities than to establish new ones which would be able to offer only a pass course in arts. When J.P. Robarts assumed the education portfolio, the official position was reversed. What became known as the Brock University Founders' Committee was recognized as the university's Board of Governors by letters patent in 1962, and the first classes were offered two years later, a few months after the passage of *The Brock University Act*.

Trent University was established on the initiative of the Peterborough City Council, the Board of Education, various associations, and industrial and commercial interests. Active promotion of the idea of setting up a junior college began with the formation of a committee in 1958. This group, like the Brock founders, encountered a discouraging response from Dunlop, but persisted until the atmosphere changed with the appointment of Robarts. Local enthusiasm was demonstrated by support for a fund-raising campaign, as was also true in the Niagara area in the attempt to establish Brock University. It did the Trent cause no harm to have the particular support of Leslie Frost, whose home was in the nearby town of Lindsay. The new university was established by an act of the Legislature in 1963 and a year of planning preceded the opening of classes in 1964. The particular hallmark of Trent was its attempt to avoid some of the disadvantages of large institutions by developing as a group of small colleges. The introduction of formula grants from the provincial government created difficulties in the maintenance of this policy.

A third stage in the extension of university-level institutions during the post-war period occurred when the provincial government, on the urging of the newly formed Committee of Presidents,* accepted the policy of establishing no more completely new universities. During this stage, press-

*This organization is treated more fully in chapter 4 of this volume.

ing needs in particular areas were dealt with by the creation of new colleges in affiliation with existing institutions. The best examples were Scarborough and Erindale Colleges of the University of Toronto. When new projections for the Metropolitan Toronto area were produced in 1962, it became evident, not only that York would have to expand to a far greater extent than had originally been intended, but that additional facilities would be needed. The University of Toronto was thus requested by government spokesmen to consider the necessary action. A favourable recommendation was made in 1963 by the Presidential Advisory Committee on Scarborough and Erindale. It was agreed that the new colleges would begin by preparing students for Toronto degrees in general arts and science. They would have the alternatives of remaining constituent colleges of the University of Toronto or of attaining ultimate independence. Scarborough College, which began operations in 1965, seemed at the beginning of the 1970s to be giving serious consideration to the possibility of seeking independent status. The relationship with the University of Toronto was thought to be hampering the development of a varied program without sufficient compensating advantages. Erindale, which offered its first classes in 1967, found more advantages in the association, although there were difficulties in having some faculty members divide their efforts between the college and the main campus.

The enthusiasm and optimism of local citizens in Sault Ste Marie and North Bay resulted in the formation of colleges affiliated with Laurentian University. Algoma College was legally incorporated in 1964 and began to offer first-year full-time classes in the physical sciences, the social sciences, and the humanities in 1967. Although ambitious to extend this program, it did not add a second year until 1971–2. Complete programs for Laurentian degrees were, however, provided in some areas of study for extension students. Members of the Board of Governors were given financial support for the college only after accepting the government's condition that they reach an affiliation agreement with an existing university. This action was taken reluctantly, and with the feeling that the institution could function as an independent university.

The attempt to establish a university at North Bay began with the formation of the Northeastern University Executive Council in 1958. This body, unable to secure a government charter, was incorporated under *The Companies Act*, and for the 1960–1 term offered classes with the co-operation of the Congregation of the Resurrection, which operated an institution at the secondary school level called North Bay College. When the latter withdrew support at the end of the year, the full-time classes ended, although instructors from Laurentian continued with an extension program. Nipissing College was established in affiliation with Laurentian in 1967, and began to offer full-time classes in the fall of that year. The future of the college was bound up with the proposed establishment of an education complex involving the North Bay campus of Cambrian College, a program of teacher education succeeding that offered by the North Bay Teachers' College, and a local school of nursing.

As of 1972 it appeared unlikely that there would be any substantial addition to the number of independent universities, in accordance with the official decision reached earlier in consultation with the representatives of existing institutions. The anticipated increase in student numbers would be largely handled by those already in operation. The lead in enrolment still maintained by the University of Toronto would continue to be reduced while the rapid growth of the smaller universities would presumably help to put some of their programs on a sounder basis and enable them to achieve economies of scale which were impossible during their "emergent" period.

CONCLUDING OBSERVATIONS

When all levels of the system are considered, the expansion in plant and facilities to deal with the growth in student numbers after the Second World War is extremely impressive, and constitutes a commendable social effort carried out with the obvious support of the people of Ontario. This verdict is not substantially changed by the fact that certain courses of action followed do not, in retrospect, appear to have been the soundest possible, and perhaps did not even appear wise in the eyes of perceptive critics at the time the decisions were made. Perhaps in a period of rapidly rising expenditure it is most urgent to consider whether or not "more of the same" is what is really wanted.

The most depressing part of the story is that dealing with the lowering of standards of teacher preparation. Those who wielded political power could certainly have done better, despite the obvious difficulty they faced, had they demonstrated more courage and leadership. Yet it remains a question how far the public would have permitted them to go had they tried to solve the problem of numbers by a more rapid improvement in the status and remuneration of the teaching profession. In the expansion of the schools, perhaps the most questionable actions were associated with the introduction of the Reorganized Program, including the expansion of vocational and technical education, during and after 1962. The mistakes that were made, however, were associated with the recognition of some very real problems, and with an attempt to solve these in a constructive manner. At the post-secondary level there was considerable criticism of the undoubted haste with which the colleges of applied arts and technology were established. If the assumptions on the basis of which they were developed were valid, they perhaps did not suffer unduly because of this fact. At the university level, no real evidence was presented that rapid expansion produced a lowering of standards. A phenomenon that caused a great deal of controversy was the large percentage of foreigners employed on faculties, with whatever that development meant for the contribution the institutions might make to Canadian life.

THREE

The quest for organizational efficiency in the school system

It is hard to quarrel with the proposition that every aspect of the educational enterprise should be carried out efficiently. Efficiency implies that the oganizational structure is logically and coherently designed; that powers are distributed so that they can be exercised effectively, with appropriate checks and balances to prevent arbitrary action and corruption, that optimum administrative talent can be marshalled and utilized to best effect. It means that legislation and regulations are flexible and subject to prompt change as new conditions develop, and general enough to allow for spontaneous and creative initiatives. It means that the activities carried out under the heading "education," whether in institutions set aside for the purpose or under less formal circumstances, are performed well according to some recognized standard, with a minimum of human effort, and at minimum cost. The concept of efficiency can be applied to the work of school trustees, officials, administrators, supervisors, consultants, teachers, and students.

When the businessman, according to the stereotype, looks at education, he is supposed to feel that it could and should be managed more efficiently. It is understandable that he should make this kind of generalization from his own experience, since his goals are usually sufficiently clearcut and the route to their achievement sharply enough defined that efficiency can be equated with effectiveness. Many an educator feels uneasy in the face of strong exhortations to efficiency simply because of the absence of these conditions. He tends to fear that efficiency, if stressed too much, may become associated with over-simplified goals or even become an end in itself in the absence of agreement on goals. The prescription of a single, all-sufficient textbook for all pupils may, for example, appear to be the acme of efficiency. Costs can be kept to the minimum through bulk purchases and distribution is relatively simple. In terms of teaching pupils to look upon the printed word as a fallible source of information, incomplete in coverage, subject to bias, and to be treated with scepticism, the approach is ineffective. The history of education is full of examples of means, well designed in terms of efficiency, that appear in retrospect to have been unrelated to the ends that were being confidently proclaimed.

This chapter is devoted to the quest for efficiency in the organizational structure of education in Ontario. It is only incidentally related to the question of effectiveness, although it would indeed be surprising – and lamentable – if the two concepts did not coincide a good deal of the time. A judgment as to whether they did or did not do so on any given occasion and with respect to any particular aspect of education depends on highly subjective factors. Perspectives can differ quite sharply, of course, within a relatively short period of time, and what appears to be the ultimate in common sense at one stage may take on the dimensions of a mass delusion a short time later. Attitudes toward external examinations constituted one of the best examples of this type of phenomenon during the 1960s, as will be shown later.

There are three major factors relating to the organizational structure for education, as for other human enterprises, that call for continuous effort and vigilance if efficiency is to be achieved and maintained. First of all, even if there are, as many believe, certain verities that should underlie educational pursuits in all ages, there are such frequent and substantial changes in the social, economic, and cultural conditions under which life is lived that constant adaptation of the process is demanded. Second, new knowledge about organization and administration at least holds out the possibility of refinements and improvements in technique. Third, there are destructive forces which, if not checked, tend to transform an efficient organization into an inefficient one. Habit, tradition, and the accumulation of precedent reduce the freedom, as well as the pain, of making choices. Innumerable practices emerge to enable officials to escape responsibility, since the consequences of making an unpopular or wrong decision are ordinarily worse than doing nothing. Matters are kept "under consideration" for indefinite periods, discussed by committees, or passed on to a higher authority for signature. Seniority plays an increasing part, and talent a lessening one, in determining promotion up the hierarchy. Operating procedures are defined in proliferating detail, and the emergence of a special jargon adds to their complexity, until eventually only a particular kind of expert can understand them. The prestige he gains in doing so has no essential relationship to the purposes of the organization. The personal interests of individuals, conflicting in varying degrees with one another, take increasing precedence over the objectives which the organization was designed to attain. A sound distribution of internal powers becomes distorted as unusually strong or weak individuals occupy particular positions and arrange matters to suit themselves or let things drift.

The distribution of powers over different aspects of the school system in Ontario has undergone profound changes since the first common schools were established. Considering the difficulties under which pioneer education had to be conducted at the beginning of the nineteenth century, the most efficient area of school administration was no doubt the school section, of which there were typically several in a rural township when municipal organization reached the stage of defining such a unit. It did not much matter that it took three trustees to manage the affairs of a single school, since their contributions cost nothing. In the early stages their main tasks were to see that a building was erected, usually by the efforts of local citizens; that a teacher was hired from among the least disreputable and cheapest of the available candidates; and that he was paid in cash or room and board in accordance with whatever agreement was reached. At first there was no teacher training, formal certification, or inspection to be looked after. There was no prescribed course of study, and textbooks consisted of whatever was available, often nothing but the Bible.

ESTABLISHMENT AND EVOLUTION OF THE
ELEMENTARY SCHOOL SYSTEM TO THE END
OF THE SECOND WORLD WAR

A brief review of the steps taken in the nineteenth century to establish an organized educational system will help to clarify the reasons for and the nature of more recent developments. The Common School Act of 1816 provided for the election of trustees and specified their duties. For the first time provincial grants were made to assist in the operation of schools with at least twenty pupils. The responsibility for administering the grants was placed in the hands of district boards of education, to which the trustees in the district were supposed to report every three months on the textbooks used and every year on the state of the school. In 1824 the district boards were given the power to certify teachers. A significant measure in the direction of centralization was taken in 1823 with the creation of a General Board of Education, which lasted for ten years. Its president, John Strachan, conducted a good many school inspections, thus establishing a precedent for supervisory practices that became general in later years.

For a number of years after the functions of the General Board of Education were transferred to the Council of King's College, which ceased to exercise them, there was a temporary trend back toward extreme decentralization. Elected township officials were given the right to choose texts, to decide on courses of study, and to determine the qualifications of teachers. As long as this situation existed there were great variations in practices, and standards were generally low. Where real freedom of action was possible, the officials lacked the ability and experience to make sound judgments. It was of vital importance to Ontario until at least the 1960s that the possibility of adopting the township as the smallest organizational unit was rejected in the mid-nineteenth century, and the school section continued in rural areas to be the basic unit. Had a different development occurred, the whole complexion of education would have been strongly affected.

The main contributions of the father of the Ontario educational system, Egerton Ryerson, who served first as assistant superintendent of education between 1844 and 1846, and then as superintendent until his retirement in 1876, were related to the creation of a strong central authority. An act passed in 1846 re-established the General Board of Education with strong powers, and a further act in 1850 replaced it with a Council of Public Instruction. This council gave way to a Department of Education when Ryerson retired, to be succeeded by a minister of education.

The creation of county boards of public instruction at the same time that legislation provided for a provincial council represented an intermediate step in the development of central control. These boards consisted of grammar school trustees and the county superintendent, almost all of whom were appointed by the governor. Their functions were to certify teachers and to select textbooks from lists approved by the provincial council. The first of these functions gradually declined in importance as normal schools were established and provincial certification became the rule. The second became less important as the list of textbooks from which a selection could be made was reduced in length.

Before 1871 supervision of schools was carried out by county superintendens who were appointed by county councils. In that year county inspectors with qualifications specified by the central authority were substituted for these officials. The measure represented a real increase in central control even though the inspectors were appointed in the same way as their predecessors.

Some of the inefficiencies of the school sections were obvious from the beginning. A School Act passed in 1841 represented a temporary and unsuccessful move toward the creation of larger units of administration. The district boards of education were abolished and their powers were transferred to the municipal councils of the districts, which were given the authority to divide the townships into school sections and to tax them for the construction of new schools. Provision was made for the election of township boards of trustees to be responsible for the common schools of their respective townships. Two years later these township boards were abolished and boards of trustees for individual attendance areas were restored. The system was reinforced in 1846, although an important modification was made in 1847 when all the schools in each city and town were placed under a single board. Urban boards were appointed by the city or town council until 1850, but elected after that date. This change was one of the most significant in the evolution of the pattern of local control.

Of major importance to the development of local provisions for education, and to the distribution of authority over education was the Baldwin Act of 1849. This legislation established the system of local municipalities, cities, towns, villages, townships, police villages, and counties in southern Ontario which was to endure without any serious effort to change it until plans began to be formulated for the development of regional government in the 1960s. Powers given to municipalities for the levying of property taxes did much to determine the pattern of local financing of public education.

A step was taken in 1850 toward placing the support of schools on a sound basis when municipalities were given the right to levy local property taxes. Two additional methods remained: voluntary subscription and the rate bill amounting to as much as one shilling and threepence for each child attending school. Although some municipalities supported their schools adequately under these conditions, many did not. In 1871 the next logical step was taken when the principle of compulsory local taxation was adopted and the common schools were made free. For the time being the high school boards could continue to exact fees, although an amount equal to half the government grant still had to be raised from local sources. Municipal councils were required to raise the sums that the boards indicated were needed. Local taxation in those days involved the taxation of both real and personal property, including personal income.

Ryerson hoped for and apparently anticipated a natural evolution toward the formation of township administrative units. School legislation in 1850 provided for voluntary amalgamation of the school sections but, since action could be taken only on the affirmative vote of a majority of the householders in every section of the township, it is hardly surprising that the strength of sentiment in favour of the existing arrangement prevented the formation of more than one township unit before 1871. During the 1860s Ryerson tried repeatedly to get the approval of county school conventions for legislation that would make mergers easier. He drew up successive bills that would have provided for the formation of a township board when the vote in a majority of the constituent sections was favourable, but failed to get them passed by the Legislature in a form acceptable to him. He then tried unsuccessfully to have county councils given the power to form township boards, and had to be satisfied with an arrangement whereby township councils could take this action on a favourable vote of two-thirds of the ratepayers.

The movement toward larger units was very slow in the decades that followed. A few union school sections, consisting of sections in more than one municipality, were formed in accordance with provisions of the Act of 1850. These developments were not, however, part of a deliberate effort to create larger units, but were rather designed to eliminate certain anomalies in municipal boundaries. Provision was made in 1919 for the establishment of consolidated school sections, which did not have to follow municipal boundaries. Consolidation proved unduly difficult under the requirement that action could be taken only on a favourable vote of the ratepayers in every section involved, and only a handful of consolidated school sections were formed.

In the mid-1920s, G.H. Ferguson, then minister of education, mistakenly concluded that the time was ripe to abolish the sections and make the township the basic unit. According to his scheme, a township board would have had from three to ten members, each with supervisory responsibilities for one of the areas into which the township was divided. Trustees in the existing boards put up such strong resistance to the scheme that the bill introducing it was withdrawn.

There were undoubtedly benefits during this period in having control of the local school so close to the community that the average voter could feel he had the means of making education responsive to his own desires. Keen interest in school affairs was a typical phenomenon. However, there was little chance that any great progress would be made. The trustees representing the rural community were unlikely to reach outside for teaching talent that might introduce new or disturbing ideas. In giving preference to Joe Smith's girl, fresh out of model or normal school, they would find it difficult to regard her as a professional or remunerate her to the point where her father would have any chance to give himself airs. Accounts of teachers' experiences in the annals of the Ontario Educational Association, at one time called the Ontario Teachers' Association, and of the Ontario Teachers' Union and the federations that followed it, are full of examples of petty, narrow-minded actions on the part of semi-literate trustees.

A major result of the long-continued local weaknesses was that the balance of power was strongly shifted in favour of the central authority. Weak or ignorant trustees required the exercise of firm control by the local inspector, who became recognized as the official agent of the Department of Education. He commonly had to explain how the business affairs of the board should be conducted, how the school laws and regulations were to be applied, and what the rights and obligations of trustees and teachers were. When economy was the main concern of the trustees, they acted as an obstacle to the improvement of teachers' qualifications. Teachers who were hired mainly because they would serve at or near the minimum salaries being paid at the time would not have been capable of exercising good judgment in the choice of course content, textbooks, or methods of instruction even if they had had an opportunity to do so. In an effort to raise standards, the Department of Education relied on specific regulation and on strict supervision to be sure that inexperienced, ignorant, or incompetent teachers did not go too far astray. The situation not only repelled many able people from teaching, but also produced a subservient mentality that prevented talented members of the profession from using their abilities to best advantage. The distribution of powers between the smaller elementary school boards and the Department of Education hindered educational progress in the 1930s and 1940s when a determined attempt was made to spur the development of township boards by voluntary amalgamation.

The basis for a new effort to form larger units by persuasion was established in 1932, when township councils were given the power to organize part or all of the township into a school area, thus abolishing the sections. Under the particular guidance and inspiration of V.K. Greer, chief inspector of public and separate schools from 1925 to 1944 and superintendent of elementary education from 1944 until his death a year later, a campaign was undertaken from 1938 on to bring about the maximum of reorganization in accordance with these condiitons. During this period local inspectors often competed to see which one could persuade the largest number of communities to form such areas. G.L. Duffin, wo ended his active career in 1969 as assistant deputy minister, was one of those who won particular distinction in this enterprise. When W.J. Dunlop became minister in 1951, official ardor for mergers was distinctly cooled, apparently because Dunlop saw considerable virtue in the existing system, and did not wish to see it too much disturbed. Inspectors were given to understand that they were to assist in the formation of township areas if asked to do so, but that they were not to press for further change. No matter how Dunlop felt, however, the greater part of the task had already been completed even before he took office. By the end of 1950, 536 township areas had replaced 3,465 school sections. Although the subsequent pace was slower, there were 601 township areas in September 1963, and 1,541 sections with boards of three trustees remained.[1]

The responsibilities of the trustee were greater in the township school area than in the school section, and he had more prestige. Since he was elected from a wider range of candidates, more satisfactory performance was to be expected. Yet there was no very pronounced improvement in the efficiency of school operation during the late thirties and early forties. After the war, however, dividends began to accrue in terms of a trend toward the abandonment of one-room schools in favour of central schools. With several classrooms, these schools could operate in some respects more economically, and were able to offer more satisfactory facilities. Teachers could concentrate their efforts more effectively, and found working conditions more pleasant. The necessity of travelling a considerable distance by school bus was a disadvantage for some children, especially the younger ones, but mostly proved to be a tolerable handicap. For the most part the new central schools retained their character as neighbourhood schools.

ESTABLISHMENT AND EVOLUTION OF
THE SECONDARY SCHOOL SYSTEM
The secondary school system was never under direct community control in the sense that the common or elementary schools were. The district schools, or grammar schools, as they came to be called, were at first managed by trustees named by the lieutenant-governor. Arrangements were made in 1853 for the appointment of boards of six trustees by the county councils. At the same time the councils were empowered to levy taxes for the support of the schools. An indirect form of control over schools at this level seemed appropriate at the time because secondary education was a matter of concern only to an elite minority rather than to the mass of the people. When a public secondary school system developed after 1871, the same principle of control was retained. High school boards, which were formed in every city and separated town and in such other high school dis-

tricts as the county councils might establish, consisted of varying combinations of appointees of county councils, municipal councils within the district, and public and separate school boards, depending on the type and composition of the district. Generally speaking, high school districts were large enough to provide a reasonable range of talent from which trustees could be chosen. Conditions resembling those in the school sections, and inviting the development of intensive supervision, did appear with the establishment of continuation schools, which evolved from the fifth classes added to public and separate elementary schools to enable bright pupils who lacked the opportunity to attend high schools or collegiate institutes to go beyond the regular elementary school program. According to an act passed in 1909, continuation schools could be established by elementary school boards or by county councils. In 1913 those in the latter category were recognized as a type of high school. When the high school program was offered by one or two continuation school teachers, strict departmental supervision seemed mandatory.

In addition to the prescription of courses and textbooks and the specification of teachers' qualifications, examinations were a major means by which departmental control was exercised over the newly established secondary school system. The grammar schools had not been organized originally as a distinct level beyond that of the common schools, but had provided overlapping services. During the 1860s the number of pupils in these schools who were studying at the elementary level was something of a scandal. In order to prevent the high schools and collegiate institutes from swelling their enrolments as a means of obtaining higher grants by admitting students who were not qualified for high school work, the Department of Education not surprisingly placed a good deal of emphasis on a high school entrance examination. It is also understanable that a brief attempt was made in the late seventies and early eighties to tie provincial grants in part to examination results. The widespread belief that examinations were an indispensable motivational device as well as a means of maintaining standards helps to explain why there were examinations at the end of lower school, upper school, and, when it was introduced somewhat later, middle school. Since the universities controlled the matriculation examinations, the department shared some of its regulatory power with them. Even after the school leaving and matriculation examinations were combined, this responsibility continued to be exercised in partnership. Until 1967 external examinations remained a powerful element of departmental control and one of the most important of the department's functions.

Some of the early vocational schools were placed under the control of boards appointed according to a procedure comparable to that applying to high school boards. It became common, however, to have the affairs of such schools managed by vocational advisory committees, which consisted of members of the high school board or board of education augmented by appointees of the board representing employers and, to a limited extent, employees in the area. This arrangement left the schools quite amenable to regulation and direction by the Department of Education.

A development of major importance in the evolution of school control was an act passed in 1903 authorizing the establishment of a largely elected board of education to administer both public elementary and secondary education. At first this provision was limited to cities with a population of at least 100,000, but in 1904 it was extended to cover cities, towns, and villages, and in 1909 to include any urban municipality where the municipal and school district boundaries coincided. According to legislation passed in 1911, a board of education could be set up only with the expressed approval of a majority of the ratepayers. In 1948 county councils were authorized to establish a board of education in any high school district on the request of the municipal councils involved without the necessity of securing ratepayer approval. As boards of education were created, secondary education in most of the larger centres came under the direct control of the electorate.

During the period after the First World War, there were two aspects to the drive for greater efficiency in the organization of secondary education: 1 / many of the units of local control, like the school sections, were too small to maintain a school with adequate facilities for a good education, and thus had to be enlarged, and 2 / many of the more sparsely settled areas of the province had to undergo an initial organization for secondary school purposes. Some rather minor success was achieved in the realization of both these objectives as a result of pressure from local ratepayers who found that the county rate, levied on county property not situated in a high school district, was higher than that levied on property of residents of such a district. More progress was made after 1937, when county councils were authorized to establish consultative committees consisting of three of their own appointees, a representative of the Department of Education, and the local school inspector.

Like the campaign for the formation of township areas, the attempt to create larger high school units was one of persuasion. Inspectors usually based their efforts on an objective review of the advantages and costs of the new arrangement. By 1950 most of the area in the counties in the southern part of the province was included in high school districts and by 1964, when legislation completed the process, little remained to be done. The situation was less satisfactory in the northern districts. Since provincial grants covered nearly all the cost of educating non-residents, there was no pressure comparable to that exerted by county rates in the southern counties. The sparse population and difficulties in transportation also militated against reorganization.

The district high schools formed all over the province provided much improved opportunities for high school education as compared with the continuation schools and the smaller high schools of the earlier period. As was true of the central elementary schools, there were objections to the long distances some of the students had to travel. Bus schedules made it difficult for them to participate in certain extra-curricular activities, and time spent on the bus cut into their opportunity for homework and for doing chores at home. Nevertheless, the new network of district high schools contributed a good deal to the increase in the proportion of young people remaining in school. One aspect of the organization of the high school districts led to later trouble: the fact that they could cut across county boundaries meant that they had to be disrupted when the county was used as the basis for reorganization in 1969. Another rather regrettable development in some areas, in terms of the desirability of co-ordinating elementary and secondary education, was that boards of education had to be disbanded when high school district and public school areas no longer coincided.

EVOLUTION OF THE DEPARTMENT OF EDUCATION
As these changes were taking place, the Department of Education expanded, as bureaucracies will do. A step was taken in 1906 that was to have implications at least into the 1960s. A superintendent of education was appointed to assist the minister in formulating suitable policies, while the deputy minister was expected to ensure that agreed-upon policies were carried out. The fact that neither official was clearly subordinate to the other ensured a continuing state of disequilibrium. A strong man with the responsibility of suggesting policy would chafe if he had no means of carrying it out, while a man with ideas would not be altogether happy merely to implement policy devised by others. The advisory position lapsed in 1919 with the death of John Seath, but was revived in 1923 when F.W. Merchant was appointed with the title of chief director of education. Both Seath and Merchant were strong men who played a dominant role during their respective terms of office.

An organizational initiative of another kind was also undertaken in 1906 with the creation of an Advisory Council on Education, with representatives from the universities, the public, separate, and secondary schools, the inspectors, and the trustees. Intended as a device by which the minister could keep in touch with opinion in various constituencies, it was limited by the fact that it could consider only those matters which the minister referred to it. The government abolished it in 1915 rather than accede to continued requests from the teachers, expressing themselves largely through the OEA, that its powers be extended. No comparable body was set up again, although the idea was suggested on various occasions, including the meeting of the Ontario Conference on Education at Windsor in 1961. It is understandable that a minister might be rather wary of repeating the earlier experiment, particularly if the constituencies represented were powerful in their own right. If he made a practice of deferring to the council's advice, he might eventually discover that, through the strength of habit and tradition, he had given up a good deal of the power that he exercised by virtue of his membership in the cabinet. The situation would also be awkward if he ignored the council so often that it came to be regarded as a nonentity. It would appear that a formal advisory council organized along the earlier pattern would have been out of tune with the leadership style characteristic of William G. Davis. The type of consultation which Davis seems to have preferred from the beginning was less formal, and involved direct contact with a very large number of groups. Despite his establishment of a Policy and Development Council, he would probably have felt cut off from many of his sources of strength and inspiration if he had been constrained to get his impressions through a council organized along the lines of the earlier body. Yet a council might well serve as a valuable link between the field and a minister with other personal characteristics.

The Ontario educational system reached a point of maximum centralization in the 1920s. The Department of Education exercised very firm powers over courses of study, textbooks, examinations, teachers' qualifications, and inspection. School boards could choose a teacher among qualified candidates, except where one could not be found, but had only the most limited powers beyond that. Although they could still get away with arbitrary dismissals, such action was becoming increasingly difficult, and could hardly be looked upon as a privilege of any great value. The teachers' organizations, the Federation of Women Teachers' Associations of Ontario, the Ontario Public School Men Teachers' Federation, and the Ontario Secondary School Teachers' Federation, all formed about the end of the First World War, were still labouring to get themselves established and to win a strong membership through persuasion, and were thus in no position to act as independent power centres.

The amount of real authority and influence exercised by school boards differed considerably according to their size and wealth. The smallest and poorest could afford no alternatives to a minimum departmental program, and had to lean heavily on the services the department would provide. As their resources were increased by more generous provincial grants after 1943, in some cases covering as much as 95 per cent of their total expenditure, they were inevitably subject to whatever regulations the department saw fit to impose. The larger and wealthier boards exercised much more freedom. Their control over the tax on real estate, which gave them their main income, enabled them to decide that the best interests of the community demanded extra facilities, equipment, and services such as health care and classes for the handicapped and the gifted. City school boards had the right to appoint their own supervisory officials beginning in 1847, and by the time the Royal Commission reported in 1950, twelve boards were exercising this right. Although these officials had to have departmental approval, and were responsible both to the minister and to their own board, they quite clearly felt that their main obligation was to the board that employed them.

A decentralizing step of major importance was taken in the 1930s when the external examinations for lower and middle school were permanently abandoned and the responsibility for appraising the success of students at this level was left entirely with the schools. Between 1935 and 1939 the school's recommendation was accepted for the better candidates for the Ontario Secondary School Honour Graduation Diploma awarded at the end of grade 13, and only those with less than second class standing had to write the departmental examinations. This privilege was, however, withdrawn, partly because some principals were accused of ensuring that no student got less than second class standing, and the system was left with external examinatons at the beginning and end of the five-year high school program until the former were dropped in 1949 and the latter in 1967. Curiously, the abandonment of the lower and middle school examinations does not seem to have been regarded as a healthy step toward decentralization as much as a means of saving money during the depression of the thirties.

The program of studies for grades 1 to 6 issued in 1937 had important implications for the actual exercise of power at the most vital point of all, in the classroom itself. A thoroughly progressive document prepared by Thornton Mustard and S.A. Watson, it owed a good deal to the so-called Hadow Reports produced in England,[2] which in turn owed much to American inspiration. By advocating a flexible school program built on a recognition of the child's fundamental needs and interests, it constituted a most vital attack on the whole system of detailed course prescriptions and specified textbooks, as well as on the kind of supervisory practices that made virtues of uniformity and conformity. It implied a weakening of administrative power at both the provincial and local levels in favour of a teaching body with more freedom and discretion. Unfortunately the possibilities inherent in such an approach were not realized, mainly because too many teachers lacked the training, experience, and attitudes to rise to the occasion.

When the Conservatives formed a minority government in 1943, George Drew became premier and minister of education. One of Drew's earliest acts which resulted in a significant change in the balance of power was to support *The Teaching Profession Act*, passed in 1944, which established the Ontario Teachers' Federation and provided for automatic membership through the appropriate affiliated federation for all practising teachers. The powers acquired through the implementation of this act enabled the teachers to press successfully for improved salary levels, for the adoption of salary scales, for greater security against unreasonable school board action, and for more satisfactory welfare benefits. Neither the Drew government nor its successors showed signs of yielding control of teacher certification or other major powers to the teachers' federations.

Drew consolidated his power in the election of 1944, partly on the appeal of his twenty-two points, one of which was an ambiguously worded promise that was interpreted to mean that a government headed by him would relieve local school systems of half the cost of education. Although that promise was kept for only one year, and even then only according to the most favourable interpretation of the facts,* the government did indisputably bear a much larger proportion of a rapidly growing burden of taxation for education than had its Liberal predecessor.

A very significant action on Drew's part was the appointment in 1945 of a Royal Commission on Education, commonly called the Hope Commission after its chairman, Justice J.A. Hope. This step was a popular one for several reasons. The war had demonstrated new needs for education and training, and wartime prosperity suggested the possibility of fresh progress after the period of retrenchment of the 1930s. At this time there was a reaction against the reputation for anti-intellectualism that the Hepburn government had acquired, and evidence of a new willingness to invest in education.

Drew began with a department headed by a chief director and a deputy minister with ostensible functions resembling those of their predecessors in 1906. The chief director, J.G. Althouse, was, however, soon placed in the ascendant position, and he dominated the department until his death in 1956. Althouse wrote and spoke in enthusiastic support of strong local authorities, but seems to have overestimated the share of power they actually exercised in relation to the department. The departmental machinery at his disposal was mainly designed for the exercise of supervisory functions. The officials with the greatest responsibility at the level next to that of the deputy minister were the superintendents of elementary education, secondary education, and professional training, and the registrar. A number of others, responsible for such areas as the public libraries and the archives, also reported, at least in theory, to the deputy minister.

By this time the department had supplemented its regulatory activity by the assumption of responsibility for a number of direct services. In addition to the pre-service preparation of teachers, it offered correspondence courses, supported railway car schools for remote areas in the northern and north-western parts of the province, maintained the first institutes of technology, provided citizenship training for newcomers, operated the Ontario School for the Blind and the Ontario School for the Deaf, circulated travelling libraries, co-operated with the CBC in radio broadcasting, and provided various other services. Immediately after the war, the Physical and Health Education Branch began to sponsor summer camps for leadership training and camp counselling. The Community Programs Branch was established in 1948, combining services in recreation and adult education previously provided by the Physical and Health Education Branch and the Ontario Adult Education Board. The new branch assisted community

*See ONTARIO'S EDUCATIVE SOCIETY, volume II, chapter 8, for a fuller discussion of this controversy.

agencies to develop their own activity programs and co-operated with other government departments working toward the same end.

The late 1940s were marked by increasing impatience while the Royal Commission on Education laboured over its report. The government hesitated to make any drastic changes in policy lest they conflict with the recommendations of the commission. Finally the minister, Dana Porter, who served between 1948 and 1951, would wait no longer, and announced a program of curriculum decentralization. This scheme constituted an attempt to enlist local initiative in the construction and adaptation of curriculum, particularly at the newly recognized intermediate level consisting of grades 7 to 10. It flourished for a brief period and then petered out in the absence of continued support from the top. Had it become a permanent part of the system, it would have reduced departmental responsibility very substantially, but in a way that would not have been strictly comparable to that implied by the program of 1937. Instead of placing more onus on every individual classroom teacher, it would have transferred responsibility to leading teachers working with inspectors. These would have constituted an intermediate level of responsibility between the department and the individual teacher.

The Royal Commission made some recommendations with respect to the distribution of powers, mostly favouring greater decentralization. There is little evidence of any fundamental actions being taken as a result of such proposals. The 1950s were largely characterized by reactions to the overwhelming increase in enrolment, requiring rapid increases in expenditure, the recruitment of large numbers of additional teachers, and the construction of hundreds of new buildings. W.J. Dunlop was called from retirement to serve as minister of education from 1951 to 1959. Although he perhaps had reason to admire many of the graduates of the little red school houses that had been so common in his youth, and had as yet far from disappeared, there is no evidence that he wanted to recreate the educational organization of earlier days. Yet he is certainly on record as favouring the eradication of every trace of progressivism from the schols. There was, in Ontario at least, comparatively little progressivism to eradicate, in large measure because the schools, in an effort to cope with rapidly rising enrolments, were very often staffed by teachers with too little training to comprehend or implement progressive principles. Dunlop's views were greatly reinforced by a book entitled *So Little for the Mind*,[3] full of polemics but short on evidence of actual acquaintance with schools, written by Hilda Neatby, a professor of history at the University of Saskatchewan. Many Ontarians, impressed by indications of poor performance in the schools, bought the notion that this situation resulted from a wholesale adoption of progressivism.

The most important organizational changes of the decade in the Department of Education occurred in 1956. In view of the attempt a few years earlier to establish the intermediate division as a meaningful unit, it seemed a retrograde step to move the elementary-secondary dichotomy one more level up the hierarchy and to have a deputy minister responsible for each level instead of a single deputy co-ordinating the work of the superintendents of elementary and secondary education. Other important changes of 1956 were the creation of the offices of superintendent of curriculum and of special services. In 1957 separate Teacher Education and Professional Development Branches were instituted, giving greater emphasis to in-service teacher training.

Some of the leading figures in the department at this time were recruited during an era when service at that level was regarded as an honour and a privilege. They were often notable for mingled idealism and competence, and gave Dunlop plenty of reason to admire the earlier educational system from which they had emerged. One official of the period, in an action that was undoubtedly rare but perhaps not unique, declined a promotion because he preferred not to be elevated above the rank of his current superior, and chose instead to serve in a lesser role while the latter received the appointment.

The department managed to hold most of its pool of high-level talent during the 1950s and early 1960s, and to recruit a number of new officials of high ability as well. Yet trouble was developing because of certain local trends. As a result of the serious teacher shortage and the efforts of the teachers' federations, teachers' salaries were rising rapidly, and with them the salaries of local administrators and supervisors. Since civil service salaries were chronically slow to respond to such a development, the department found it increasingly difficult to compete for top talent. Bureaucratic rigidities which increased apace under Dunlop, particularly after the death of Althouse, also reduced the department's ability to attract those with initiative. As an instrument for the implementation of educational policy, the department underwent a period of decline. Much of the trouble was directly attributable to Dunlop's method of operating. When departmental officials had to bear the brunt of criticism because of the unpopularity of certain policies, he was unable to see that they needed stronger support from the top, and tended to leave them to their own devices. Thus they were inclined to draw inward, to shroud as many as possible of their activities in secrecy, and to reflect the typically negative ministerial attitude. The more they adopted these approaches, the more severe the criticism became. Bascom St John, the noted *Globe and Mail* columnist, was always at hand between 1958 and 1964 to deliver a blast at secrecy for secrecy's sake and action without consultation. His reasons for unhappiness diminished somewhat, however, after John P. Robarts assumed the education portfolio in 1959 and undertook to open the windows and let in some fresh air.

Many of the features that reduced the department's effectiveness resulted from a kind of drift into practices that could only have been prevented by a fundamental shake-up at regular intervals. Responsibilities became more personalized as new duties were assigned to individuals because of their particular interests rather than being allotted according to principles of efficient operation. There were examples of officials carrying certain of their functions with them after they were promoted to some new sphere of responsibility. The system might work fairly well as long as the same officials remained on the job and remembered all the intricacies of the operation. A sudden death, like that of Althouse, however, threw matters into a great deal of confusion. At the best of times, also, it was unduly difficult for an outsider seeking information, advice, or direction to know whom to approach. Another serious defect in the organization was the inefficiency in the process of making decisions. In some cases no action could be taken on a matter until the last of a series of signatures had been obtained after a process that was usually very time-consuming. Much of the decision-making was too centralized in that matters of relatively minor importance had to be approved at a high level. The structure was poorly designed to enable fresh ideas to rise to the top. Protocol prevented a minor official from by-passing an immediate superior with any suggestion for change in procedure or policy. Some officials did, of course, manage to act constructively within the complexities of the system, but to do so required an inordinate amount of skill, tact, and effort.

Matters were brought to a head in the early 1960s when continuing increases in the obligations and work load of the department created a need for an expanded staff. Tradition called for experienced educators to perform all kinds of tasks, including many that might better have been assigned to accountants or others with various types of business training. Competition with local boards made experienced and competent educators increasingly expensive and, to fit the civil service salary schedules, they had to be appointed at high levels. Thus there was a proliferation of assistant superintendents of elementary and secondary education in particular. This distortion of the organization, along with repeated requests for salary increases, aroused an adverse reaction in the Treasury Board. A study made by T.I. Campbell, who had served briefly in teaching and civil service positions, and who was appointed to the newly created position of personnel director in 1963, and another by J.S. Stephen, at the time executive director of the Department of Civil Service, and later assistant deputy minister of education, identified the chief problems and pointed the way to change.

This review of developments in the school system, with attention to some of the most obvious deficiencies, has provided a background for the organizational aspects of the Davis reform program. This program was not entirely confined to the period after Davis was appointed as minister in October 1962, since his predecessor, Robarts, had been well aware of the need for change, and had introduced such major reforms as the Reorganized Program in the secondary schools and the Ontario Foundation

Tax Plan, which was not actually unveiled until 1963. Yet Davis deserves credit for initiating and guiding most of the sharp departures from tradition that characterized the decade. The organizational aspects of the program were not based on a tidy blueprint, worked out beforehand in such detail that its implementation was practically automatic. There were some hesitant steps, a certain amount of unproductive effort, and a few false moves. It sometimes seemed to an observer that important decisions were made and actions taken with little advance planning. Yet there were certain clear principles underlying and tying together the major elements of the program. Among the most easily identifiable were the following. 1 / Local control over certain aspects of education was to be strengthened and made more effective. 2 / Choices relating to the so-called interna of education, that is, over those matters affecting curriculum, techniques, evaluation, and equipment were to devolve increasingly upon local officials and teachers. 3 / Teachers were to be better prepared to handle increased responsibilities. 4 / As a complement to the decentralization of power in favour of school boards, the Department of Education was to give up much of its regulatory power and concentrate on service functions. 5 / The department was to be reorganized and streamlined for more effective implementation of policy. 6 / The increase in service functions meant that new dimensions of departmental activity had to be added as others were allowed to wither. 7 / Methods of financing education had to be devised to fit the new balance of powers and responsibilities. 8 / There had to be a major investment in research and development activities to provide a stream of fresh ideas that would constantly invigorate the system.

In the process of reorganizing the department, Davis had the services of a dynamic and iconoclastic executive assistant, C.H. Westcott, former executive assistant to Robert Macaulay who had retired from politics after losing the contest for the leadership of the Progressive Conservative party to J.P. Robarts. Also close to Davis were such youthful reformers as T.I. Campbell, already mentioned, and C.H. Williams who, unlike Westcott, was counted as an educator. Having the obvious confidence of the minister, these men exerted much more influence than their formal positions implied. They were by no means universally popular within the organization, especially among those who placed high value on certain traditions and were well aware of the contributions made by outstanding men during earlier periods. It seemed something of a humiliation to have these newcomers marking little empires for oblivion. Yet they played an essential part in the process of reform. Westcott in particular was constantly at Davis's elbow during his entire career as minister of education. Perhaps no one except those two will ever know how many of the reformist ideas of the period originated with Westcott, but there is no question that Westcott's vigour and enthusiasm placed an indelible mark on the entire program. His engaging informality did much to counteract the image of stuffiness that the department had had in earlier years.

Before the major reorganization which took place at the beginning of 1965, certain significant changes were made in the departmental structure as a response to new needs in the system. A Technological and Trades Training Branch was created in 1963 to give more attention to the institutes of technology, the institutes of trades, and the vocational centres, and to supervise the advanced technical evening classes, programs for training the unemployed, training in industry, the academic component of apprenticeship, and other programs involving co-operation with the federal government and with other provincial agencies. The particular leadership talents of L.M. Johnston were very much in evidence in the development of this branch, which in 1966 was renamed the Applied Arts and Technology Branch and expanded to deal with the system of colleges of applied arts and technology. Another departmental official, N.A. Sisco, later made important contributions in directing the branch.

A Youth Branch was created in 1963 under the temporary direction of W.F. Koerber, a noted specialist in special education and a prominent school administrator, who was seconded for a year from the Scarborough school system. The particular area of concern of this branch was the welfare of young people who were not in full-time attendance at an educational institution. Early emphasis was placed on studies of ways in which this group might be helped to deal with problems arising from automation, increased leisure, urbanization, and changes in social and family patterns. The creation of the branch was in a sense an alternative to pressure from the opposition in the Legislature for the establishment of a separate Department of Youth. In 1968 it seemed a logical development to combine the branch with the Community Programs Branch to form a Youth and Recreation Branch, since both units had focused their attention on the work of community agencies.

An attempt was made in 1963 to increase the internal efficiency of the department by establishing a Personnel Branch with T.I. Campbell in charge, as already mentioned. A more conscious effort was made to study and define job requirements and to match individuals with their responsibilities. Financial savings presumably resulted as it became possible to guard against the employment of people who had inappropriate educational qualifications for the work they had to do.

What was eventually known as the Policy and Development Council was established in 1964 under the chairmanship of J. Bascom St John, who had long played a leading part as a journalist and editor in expressing and shaping public opinion and in acting as the department's chief gadfly. The council seemed to represent a new attempt, reminiscent of the restoration of the position of superintendent of education in 1906 and the appointment of chief directors of education in and after 1923, to separate advisory functions, to some extent at least, from administration. Davis was the kind of strong leader who might have made such a system work if he had really wished to do so. It was clear, however, that he regarded the new council only as an *extra* source of ideas; he also expected the whole department to act to some extent in the same capacity. This was the implication of his determination to transform the department from a primarily regulatory to a service agency. In his search for a candidate for a redefined deputy ministership to head the departmental hierarchy, he looked not simply for a good administrator, but for an outstanding leader in every sense of the word. When he settled on Z.S. Phimister, he had a man who, on the basis of a reputation acquired earlier, was not going to stand back and await the advice of a council that was separated from the administrative machinery. The same could be said of Phimister's successor, J.R. McCarthy.

The Policy and Development Council was joined by a number of outstanding men who had played an important part in departmental affairs, but none of them stayed very long. They seemed to feel that the council was a kind of backwater where they had lost their power to influence events. Some returned to positions in the administrative hierarchy while others abandoned the department altogether. By the end of the decade St John was left alone as an adviser to the minister. In this role he was thought to be valued, since he had not lost his talent for analysing a situation nor his lack of hesitation in offering a frank and often pungently worded opinion. Unlike so many other public servants, he never developed a propensity for telling the minister what he thought he wanted to hear. It would be difficult to say to what extent his views influenced Davis, since the latter, in his characteristic reluctance to reveal his own inner thoughts, seldom gave much indication of the sources of ideas that influenced him most.

In announcing the departmental reorganization in 1965, Davis mentioned three guiding principles: integration, reallocation, and decentralization. The first of these covered the abolition of separate sub-structures for elementary and secondary education in the light of the growing tendency to regard the two levels as part of an unbroken process. A second aspect of integration involved bringing together the functions of supervision, curriculum, and examinations in a single Program Branch. These functions were handled by what were called divisions until 1967, when they were renamed sections. A third aspect of integration was the merging of small units for the supervision of subjects such as music, art, and guidance with the Supervision Division, since they were now regarded as part of the regular program. Reallocation of functions meant the abolition of the position of chief director in favour of a single deputy minister, as already mentioned. Reporting to this official would be three assistant deputy ministers responsible respectively for instruction, provincial schools and further education, and administration. The general set-up is shown in

CHART 3-1
Organization chart for the Ontario Department of Education, 1965

SOURCE: Ontario Department of Education

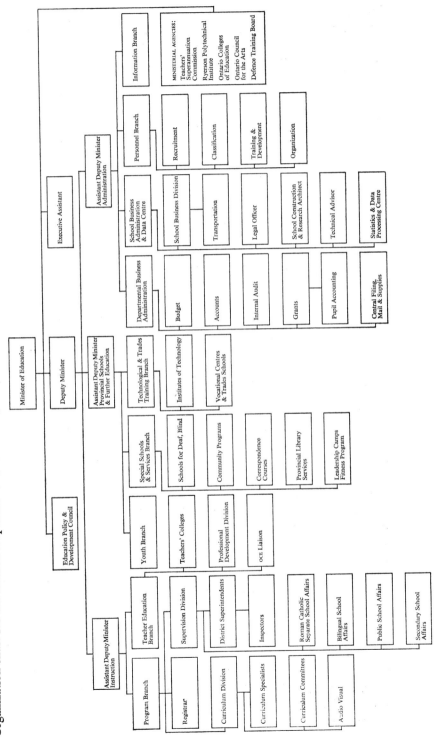

Chart 1. A second aspect of reallocation involved relieving many assistant superintendents and school inspectors of business and legal advisory functions which were to be exercised henceforth by officials in the School Business Administration Branch. Decentralization was to be carried out gradually as the existing organization evolved in that direction. Davis foresaw the establisment of "districts" in various parts of the province where superintendents and local inspectors might operate in close contact with local needs and respond quickly when assistance was required.

Although some concessions were made to vested interests, the new structure was well designed to alleviate many of the difficulties that had existed previously. It could only be an effective instrument for carrying out the minister's program, however, if sympathetic officials held the key positions. A major obstacle at the time was F.S. Rivers, who was promoted to the position of chief director in 1961 after serving in a number of important positions such as that of superintendent of professional training and that of deputy minister with responsibility for elementary education. Rivers had achieved brilliantly as a student and had performed outstanding service for the department in earlier years, particularly as a member of the Royal Commission in 1945-50. He was not, however, in sympathy with the extent of the reforms Davis wished to make and the speed with which he intended to carry them out, and his departure seemed a necessary preliminary to the implementation of the Davis program. After his resignation, he agreed to remain with the department in an advisory capacity, but his early death prevented him from serving for long in this role. Some of the retirements that occurred during the next few years reduced the ranks of those who doubted the soundness of the new policies.

During his brief career as deputy minister, Phimister did not make a particularly impressive mark. He had grown accustomed to certain procedures in dealing with school board members and officials in his position as director of education for Toronto, and found it hard to adapt to departmental protocol. He had a difficult time discovering how to wield power effectively in the new organization. Some of those who worked closely with him felt that his outstanding qualities were beginning to emerge by the fall of 1966, when he died suddenly after little more than a year and a half in active control of his office. He was succeeded by J.R. McCarthy, who had had long experience in operating in accordance with the bureaucratic subtleties of the department. McCarthy had stood unequivocally for progressive educational principles during the period when these were anything but popular, and thus seemed a good choice to implement the minister's policies. During his term of office, which lasted until early 1971, when Davis became prime minister and Robert Welch succeeded him as minister of education, McCarthy saw at least the partial implementation of many of his ideas. A balanced appraisal of his term of office would have to take account of some of the controversial aspects of his administrative style.

The process of decentralization began in 1965 with the establishment of five of what were known as area offices and, from 1967 on, as regional offices, in Port Arthur, Sudbury, North Bay, London, and Waterloo. Five others were added the next year, one in each of St Catharines, Kingston, and Eastview, and two in Metropolitan Toronto. The superintendent, who was eventually called the regional director, in each these centres, was expected to co-ordinate the work of all provincial school inspectors and to maintain close links with municipal supervisory officials. Inspectors and school officials were expected to communicate with the department through him.

The role of the regional centres evolved rapidly. Of major importance for them was a drastic change in the nature of provincial supervision. In 1967 all subject inspectors became program consultants with the responsibility of assisting individual teachers or groups, but not of appraising or reporting on teacher performance. District inspectors became area superintendents, answerable to the regional superintendent, and were expected to shift their emphasis from inspection to improving the quality of the program. At the end of 1968 provincial responsibility for supervision was abandoned entirely, except for private schools, and most of the area superintendents had to seek other employment. Such supervisory activities as remained were left in the hands of school principals, department heads, and locally appointed officials. Although program consultants remained attached to the regional centres, and were joined by educational television consultants and those with other specialized roles, the effect of the whole development was to reduce the importance of the centres. A second event that tended to have the same effect was the school board reorganization of 1969.* The smaller number of larger boards were better able to provide their own consultants and business advisers, and were thus less dependent on departmental assistance. Although some of the new boards were not so self-sufficient that they would not have welcomed whatever help they could get, it was government policy to encourage them to stand on their own feet. A third influence that inhibited the centres from assuming a major role was the appearance of field development centres of the Ontario Institute for Studies in Education which, although created with the understanding that they would co-operate closely with the centres, promised to fill some of the local need for certain evaluative activities.† Finally, new centralizing forces developed within the department, reflecting McCarthy's particular leadership style.

The Program Branch, one of two main units (the other being the Teacher Education Branch) in what was called the Instruction Division

*The school board reorganization of 1969 is explained later in this chapter, and more fully in ONTARIO'S EDUCATIVE SOCIETY, volume II, chapter 5.
†The founding and operations of the Ontario Institute for Studies in Education are discussed in chapter 7 of the present volume and in ONTARIO'S EDUCATIVE SOCIETY, volume V, chapters 13 and 14.

beginning in 1967, was under the direction of L.M. Johnston between 1965 and 1967. In the latter year, Johnston succeeded W.R. Stewart as assistant deputy minister for provincial schools and further education, and was replaced in his former position by M.B. Parnall, whose untimely death in 1968 again left a vacancy. Co-ordination of the components of the branch was thereupon left at the level of the assistant deputy minister for instruction, a position held in succession by H.E. Elborn, G.L. Duffin, and J.F. Kinlin. Shortly after the reorganization there were substantial shifts in the relative importance of the various units within the Instruction Division. After the abandonment of the supervision function by the successive steps already mentioned, the former inspectoral staff largely disappeared, most becoming either program consultants or finding supervisory positions with local boards. Relatively speaking, only a remnant of the former supervision group remained, either at departmental headquarters or in the regional offices. In 1969 A.H. McKague retired from the position of superintendent of supervision, to be succeeded by G.H. Waldrum. The Registrar's Section, from which C.A. Brown retired in 1965 to be succeeded by A.W. Bishop, also declined in importance after the last grade 13 departmental examinations were given in 1967. It thus became unnecessary to augment the permanent full-time staff with large numbers of examination markers, clerks, and others during the summer. There remained a surprising number of tasks, however, relating to the necessity of issuing certificates and diplomas for successful completion of programs in schools, teachers' colleges, colleges of education, and summer school for teachers, and such other matters as scholarships and the issuing of Letters of Standing and Letters of Permission.

The Curriculum Section soon overshadowed the other units in the Program Branch. It began by absorbing the directors of former branches responsible for music, art, guidance, physical and health education, and audio-visual education. The subject inspectors who became program consultants were attached to it. In 1967 it was reorganized into four areas: humanities, mathematics and science, social sciences, and a general group, consisting of art, commercial subjects, home economics, music, physical education, and technical and industrial arts. A chairman was appointed to co-ordinate the work in each area. The responsibilities of the section included the provision of new courses, the revision of existing courses, the promotion of sound teaching methods and useful equipment and materials, and the continuous revision of curriculum publications. The department relaxed control over school programs and encouraged experimentation, usually asking only that variations from standard procedure be in the hands of competent people and conducted under acceptable conditions. Although an essentially permissive policy was still retained, there was a definite tendency by 1970 to curb some of the more extreme initiatives. One reason for this development seemed to be that there was an apparent threat to standards in some schools; departmental officials also seemed aware of the possibility of awkward political repercussions if experiments in certain touchy fields went too far. The department could not, of course, backtrack too far without creating the impression that the liberty granted to local systems was really something of a sham.

In one respect the expansion of the Curriculum Section was curtailed. The major thrust in the field of educational television which began in association with curriculum in 1965 was continued in a separate branch beginning in 1967. Although there were obvious advantages in a close organizational link, it was felt that the new development could not be pushed adequately without a separate identity. T.R. Ide was appointed as director of the Educational Television Branch in 1967. Almost from the beginning there was criticism of an arrangement that seemed to tie the production and dissemination of television programs too closely to official policy. The universities in particular were wary of working intimately with an organizational unit of the Department of Education. Davis dealt with these apprehensions by setting up an Ontario Educational Communications Authority in 1970, which took over the functions and staff of the branch.

The bill to establish the communications authority was not passed in the Legislature without severe criticism from the opposition parties and a negative vote by the Liberals.[4] The essence of the Liberal argument, presented by the education critic for that party, Timothy Reid, was that a body of thirteen members appointed by the Lieutenant-Governor-in-Council, which in actual fact meant appointment by the minister, would differ little in status from the departmental branch which it was designed to succeed. The fact that the minister would appoint both the chairman and the vice-chairman seemed to emphasize the likelihood of government control. To Reid, the proposal seemed a denial of the principle of dispersing decision-making power throughout the system. He would have had at least half the members chosen without appointment or veto power by the minister.

The departmental Television Branch and its successor, the Ontario Educational Communications Authority, won plaudits for the quality of their productions, and none of their critics suggested seriously that the possibility of political intervention for partisan purposes was more than an unrealized threat. The fact that the programs were not more widely viewed was generally recognized as a condition that was to a considerable extent beyond the power of the agency to remedy, depending on such factors as the availability of broadcasting and viewing facilities and school organization. Some critics were of the view that a large central agency was in danger of stifling local initiative in the television field. In this writer's view, while the importance of local concern and participation cannot be exaggerated, only a well-financed and equipped central agency can produce the excellent models which alone can win acceptance of television in the education field.

The Teacher Education Branch was another unit that faced a role of diminishing importance in the 1970s. The implications of Davis's acceptance of recommendations contained in the report of the Minister's Comittee on the Training of Elementary School Teachers, completed in 1966, was that the universities would assume the responsibility for devising and implementing programs of pre-service teacher education. The existing colleges of education were also being encouraged to draw closer, organizationally and functionally, to the universities. When the process of integration was completed, the Teacher Education Branch would have little to do but ensure that certain agreed-upon conditions were being met. Even before the University of Ottawa Teachers' College and Lakehead Teachers' College were absorbed by their respective universities in 1969, and Windsor Teachers' College by the University of Windsor in 1970, many of the traditional apron strings were being cut. In 1968 the departmental course prescriptions were reduced to certain guiding principles and the staffs were expected to assume the responsibility for content selection. The central controls once exercised through uniform departmental examinations no longer existed. Although the colleges still had to get official authorization for certain rather routine matters such as the expenditure of funds for visiting speakers and co-operation with outside bodies, the director of the branch, G.L. Woodruff, was following a consistent policy of decentralization. To all appearances, the program of departmental summer courses was flourishing and the enrolment continuously rising. It was the intention, however, that the universities should assume an increasingly important role in this area. While the departmental summer courses might be phased out in view of the universities' assumption of further responsibility, however, it seemed probable that the teachers' federations and local school boards would assume an increasingly important role in the same area.

During the period after the reorganization, the activities of the Provincial Schools and Further Education Division increased in number and scope. The Applied Arts and Technology Branch had a major task in guiding the very rapid development of the system of colleges of applied arts and technology. Although certain matters of major importance were handled by boards of governors, and the Council of Regents was assigned an advisory role, it was clearly the minister's intention to retain enough control in the department to ensure that there would be adequate co-ordination and a minimum waste of funds through duplication of courses. The colleges were to be administered as a true system in a sense that the universities were not. The Council of Regents relied on the Applied Arts and Technology Branch to act as a secretariat for it. The establishment of three main power centres controlling the colleges was defended on the grounds that a certain degree of tension should be healthy. Some members of boards of governors expressed the view that those bodies ought to have more power if they were to respond sensitively to community needs. Members of the college staffs tended to express dissatisfaction because they could not settle questions of salary and working conditions through negotiations with their boards. The transfer of the Applied Arts and Technology Branch, with responsibility for the colleges, to the Department of University Affairs, renamed the Department of Colleges and Universities, in mid-1971 was expected to result in changes, but at the time of writing the nature of these could not be predicted.

During this period the scope of the manpower retraining program continued to expand. When this program was transferred from the larger school boards to the colleges of applied arts and technology, the obligations of the department were not noticeably diminished. A Business Management Program by which small industries conducted short courses for their employees with departmental and federal governent assistance grew rapidly after 1963. Supervisory courses and basic upgrading courses were also sponsored under similar conditions. While these programs conducted in co-operation with industry seemed to operate with reasonable success, they were on too small a scale to produce a major impact.

The Special Schools and Services Branch, which succeeded the Special Educational Services Branch in the reorganization, consisted of the Blind and Deaf Division, the Schools for Retarded Children Division, the Community Programs Division, and the Correspondence Courses Division. There were two influences, closely interrelated, that tended to limit the functions of the first two of these divisions, or sections, as they were called from 1967 on, and led to the dissolution of the second in 1968. First, the creation of the enlarged school boards in 1969 was intended to make it possible to provide locally for the needs of most groups, including the handicapped, in the regular program. The divisional boards were given the immediate responsibility, for example, of maintaining schools operated up to this time by the Retarded Children's Education Authorities. Second, most experts in special education were advocating that the physically handicapped, as well as those with other disabilities, be isolated in special schools only as a last resort. The disadvantages of residential schools such as the Ontario School for the Blind and the Ontario Schools for the Deaf were being increasingly recognized. In contrast the Community Programs Branch, which became the Youth and Recreation Branch in 1968, found an almost unlimited demand for its services, and was prepared to expand as far as financial and staff resources would permit. Similarly, although there were increasing opportunities for part-time instruction, and the nature of the demand for correspondence courses changed, the popularity of the courses remained at a high level.

There was a strong hint in the Speech from the Throne delivered in February 1970 that the Youth and Recreation Branch might be transferred to a reorganized Department of Citizenship. Certain responsibilities for offering language and citizenship training for newcomers had already been transferred to the Department of the Provincial Secretary and

Citizenship a decade earlier. The new proposal was to concentrate a wide range of community services in a single department in order to enrich the quality of life in the province. Although the session of the Legislature passed with no specific action taken, the branch was transferred to the Ministry of Community and Social Services in the reorganization of the spring of 1972.

The Provincial Library Service entered the new organization in 1965 under the direction of W.A. Roedde with very little change. An event of major importance was the report of Francis R. St John Library Consultants, which was released during the same year. Although this report found the number of staff in the unit much too small to provide the consultative and advisory services needed throughout the province, and recommended a substantial increase, no major action was taken. As increasing responsibility devolved on the larger school boards after January 1, 1969, centrally administered services were reduced. In April 1971 the Teachers' Reference Service was abolished.

A Departmental Business Administration Branch was responsible for preparing budget estimates, with the related task of studying current and planned program costs. It also established and maintained internal controls and accounting procedures, and ensured that various units adhered to government regulations in the receipt and disbursement of funds. In addition, it exercised certain functions relating to the educational system, such as discharging provincial responsibilities with respect to federal-provincial training agreements. Until 1966 the branch included the Grants Division, which was responsible for calculating and distributing grants to school boards, public libraries, Retarded Children's Authorities, municipalities, and non-profit camps. At that time this division was transferred to the School Business Administration Branch where it more logically belonged. The School Business Administration Branch had such responsibilities as conducting research into school planning, designing facilities for schools, developing procedures for allocating financial assistance for school building projects, administering data processing facilities, and dealing with matters affecting school boards such as transportation agreements and boundaries. An Education Data Centre was established in 1965 under the direction of J.A. Keddy, and rapidly developed means of improving statistical services. In 1968 this centre absorbed the Regional Data Processing Centre which was set up in the Ontario Institute for Studies in Education. The combined operation continued with Z.R. Patterson in charge.

The Division of School Planning and Building Research was an unusual unit in the organization in that it was not only expected to conduct research into a certain area, but even included the term "research" in its name. Generally speaking, policy applying to the Department of Education at this time was to leave research to other agencies such as OISE. Where the activity could not be avoided, it was preferably called something else. The unit was established in 1964 after an outstandingly successful and highly praised Minister's Conference on School Design held the previous year. During a period of high and rising expenditure on buildings, trustees and administrators in particular were concerned about obtaining the most economical materials and equipment and in using building designs that would ensure the most effective use for a variety of community purposes as well as for school education. As a result of its studies, the division produced a number of publications describing and illustrating buildings for various purposes. These received worldwide circulation and made Ontario education known to many people who had no contact with any other facet of it. S.T. Orlowski, who took charge of the division, or section, in 1967, placed strong emphasis on consultative services for school boards, boards of governors of colleges of applied arts and technology, and other such agencies.

A School Plant Approvals Unit was given the responsibility of examining all school building projects on behalf of the department and, during the time when federal grants were being paid to assist with the construction of vocational training facilities, for the federal authorities as well. The forms submitted for approval were extremely detailed and specific. With respect to this type of activity, there was little sign of decentralization of responsibility as there was in so many other aspects of education. The danger of waste was thought to be too great to give free rein to local agencies.

A novel feature of the reorganized department was the Information Branch, later renamed News and Information Services, first directed by C.H. Williams and later by Arnold Bruner. Considerable care had to be taken in establishing such a branch lest it be seen as a propaganda agency designed to present all departmental operations in an artificially favourable light. Newspaper reporters are typically suspicious of material provided to them in the form of official handouts. The branch attempted to escape severe criticism by concentrating on objective, factual information unless something more was demanded. Services were available, not only to the media, but also to individual inquirers. The branch played a very important role by improving communication within the department itself through publications and other means. Such measures were badly needed in an organization that was scattered over many different locations in various parts of the city of Toronto and of the province.

When certain programs such as the development of the colleges of applied arts and technology and the organization of the divisional school boards were undertaken, there was a considerable amount of criticism that the cost implications had not been studied in enough detail. There was said to be insufficient application of modern principles of planning. While such planning would not have reduced decision making to a mechanical process without consideration of human values, it would have made it easier to devise suitable financial measures well ahead of time, and would have facilitated the regulation of the pace of development to ensure that it did not get ahead of the taxpayers' ability or willingness to pay, or unduly upset the government's priorities in the whole range of service and welfare fields. A significant development occurred in 1969 when the deputy minister and the assistant deputy ministers, who met regularly as a planning committee, were provided with the services of a planning unit directed by T.I. Campbell. This group commissioned certain studies by such agencies as the Department of Educational Planning of the Ontario Institute for Studies in Education, and assembled information to enable top officials to explore the consequences of alternative policy decisions as they had not previously been able to do. The planning operation was closely tied in with program budgeting, which was being required of all branches of the provincial government.

Modern governmental bureaucracies do not decline; they merely grow at varying rates of speed. It is possible, of course, that certain units or branches may disappear, but a decline in one place is almost certain to be accompanied by expansion somewhere else. The phenomenon should cause no particular surprise in view of the popular demand for consistently expanding public services and benefits. The chief effect of automated processes for handling data seems to have been an increase in the number of operations undertaken rather than a decrease in the number of people required. Despite the general trend, there have at times been grounds for hope that the process of decentralization would enable the Department of Education to reduce its staff. In fact, as far as professional staff were concerned, it just about managed to hold the line in the latter part of the sixties. The numbers in this category for 1965, 1969, and 1970 were respectively 1,133, 1,202, and 1,163. Between 1965 and 1970, however, the number of non-professional employees grew from 1,021 to 1,947.* The total of all departmental staff, professional and non-professional, more than doubled between 1960 and 1970. In view of the huge increase in the educational enterprise during that period, as registered by such indices as expenditure, such a rate of growth may be regarded as reasonably creditable.

The Hall-Dennis Committee, which worked out many of its recommendations before the implications of some departmental changes were completely clear, made a strong plea for a reduction in the central bureaucracy in favour of more local responsibility. It speculated that a great deal of energy must be spent in keeping the organization going rather than in meeting the needs of children in the schools. The old problem that had brought matters to a head in the early sixties, the inability of an organization tied to the civil service to pay competitive salaries, was thought to be still preventing the department from obtaining its proper share of the best talent. The committee was not very favourably disposed

*These figures were supplied informally by the Department of Education.

toward the regional offices, which were regarded as an additional administrative layer. If the appraisal had been made a short time later, it would
probably have been considerably more positive, since the offices tended
to become the kind of service centres that the committee thought they
should. There were some criticis, however, who maintained that they were
an undesirable obstacle to the process of delegating power and responsibility to local boards, individual schools, and teachers. It is not the writer's
view that they had this effect, at least up to the early 1970s. For the time
being they were providing services to some of the smaller boards that
would not otherwise have been available at all.

The committee recommended a new departmental structure devoted to
three categories of responsibility: 1 / legislation, 2 / planning, research,
and development, and 3 / systems evaluation. The second of these would
be the most important. The section concerned would conduct long-term
planning involving all areas of education, engage in short-term research,
identify particularly important research areas, contract for research with
the Ontario Institute for Studies in Education and other agencies, develop
demonstration centres in local school systems, interpret new processes
and procedures from other parts of the world, and assist school boards
in undertaking new development projects.[5] All three sections would have
supporting services involving statistics, grants, data processing, information, and building guidance. It would appear that much of what was proposed was in essential harmony with the ideas that Davis had expounded
when he introduced the reorganized departmental structure in 1965, even
though there were substantial differences in the way the committee
thought his aims might be accomplished.

The Hall-Dennis Committee had some further recommendations affecting the Department of Education that did not seem to meet with any great
favour in official circles. One was that there be an advisory council,
reminiscent of the one which existed between 1906 and 1915, but with
more authority. Consisting of representatives of public and professional
interests, it would report to the Legislature through the minister of education and to the public at large in a manner similar to that adopted by
the Economic Council of Canada. It would evaluate the effectiveness of
existing facilities, propose the establishment of new institutions or programs and the extension of existing ones in accordance with social and
economic trends and the demands of public opinion, study proposals made
by individuals or groups, and give the government and other bodies a
judgmental basis for their decisions. Its relative independence of operation would be reinforced by a separate budget. This type of council would
no doubt have considerable advantages. Yet to the extent that its advice
would be difficult for a minister to reject, it would be taking away some
of the accountability of the government to the electorate. That is, it would
have to be evaluated as a move toward increasing the influence of the

expert at the expense of democratic control, which sometimes seems extremely tenuous in the complexities of a modern society. To say that under a weak or passive minister it would restrain the arbitrary and insensitive actions of departmental officials is beside the point.

There were some similarities between the Hall-Dennis proposals and certain suggestions made by R.S. Harris in *Quiet Evolution* a short time earlier.[6] These suggestions were based in part on a recognition that the ramifications of education go considerably beyond the responsibilities of the Department of Education, and involve other government agencies as well. Harris would organize education at all levels on a regional basis, and would have regional councils to co-ordinate the entire process. These councils would report to the government rather than to the minister of education. If such a scheme were adopted, there would have to be some very definite way of fixing responsibility for the implementation of policy. Further, the councils could not move from an advisory to an executive role without in effect becoming a branch of government. It would be easy for them to emerge finally as a form of regional school board. If they retained only advisory functions, they could easily be relegated to a position of impotence.

CHANGES FOLLOWING DAVIS'S ASSUMPTION
OF THE OFFICE OF PRIME MINISTER

The end of a most significant period in education came in March 1971, when Davis became prime minister and the portfolios of education and university affairs were assumed by R.S. Welch and J. White respectively. J.R. McCarthy subsequently retired as deputy minister of education to undertake a comprehensive study of the costs of education, and was succeeded by E.E. Stewart. H.H. Walker assumed the position of deputy minister of university affairs vacated by Stewart. Plans were announced in the Speech from the Throne at the beginning of the new session of the Legislature to reconstitute the Department of University Affairs as the Department of Colleges and Universities, with responsibilities, not only for universities, but also for colleges of applied arts and technology, Ryerson Polytechnical Institute, and manpower development programs; most of these involved activities of the Applied Arts and Technology Branch of the Department of Education. L.M. Johnston, who had been assistant deputy minister of education, assumed corresponding duties in the Department of Colleges and Universities. The change, which was implemented later in the year, seemed logical in the sense that it unified government responsibility in the post-secondary education field. It also provided a somewhat more even balance between the two departments concerned with education in terms of the scope and extent of their operations. There was always the question of how well the two empires would co-operate under the direction of separate ministers. The Ontario Secondary School Teachers' Federation saw a serious threat to effective liaison between the secondary and post-secondary levels, and called for a merger of the departments in a single Department of Educational Affairs.[7]

Welch came to his new portfolio after serving for a number of years as provincial secretary, where he had had responsibility for certain educational programs mainly involving new Canadians. During the campaign for the Conservative leadership, he had demonstrated an eagerness to make his mark in provincial politics. He faced certain problems in placing his own individual stamp on the educational system which had not confronted his predecessor. After the many Davis initiatives in the reorganization of the department and the local school boards, some aspects of which would still take several years before their full implications were clear, the range of possible innovations was somewhat restricted. Further, the public and the press were now demanding financial retrenchment rather than the ability to discover ingenious new ways of spending money. A successful campaign to reduce expenditure, or at least to reduce a rising rate of expenditure, is not usually the kind of contribution upon which a spectacular political career is based.

In the government reorganization of early 1972, which was accompanied by a reshuffle of the cabinet, Welch became provincial secretary for social development, a position which involved the formulation of policy for education and related areas, and T.L. Wells was named minister of education. Only time would tell how much influence would be exercised by the provincial secretaries, and how the role of ministers in charge of departments would evolve. There was always a possibility that the former, without the backing of departmental bureaucracies, would be mere figureheads.

Wells had considerable experience in education, having served as a school trustee and having assumed various educational responsibilities as minister without portfolio before his appointment as minister of health in 1969. He had been active in the Select Committee on Youth of the Legislature, which reported in 1967. Like Welch, he found himself with the task of defending the government's policy of restraining the rising costs of education. Although this policy had broad public support, there were vigorous protests from teachers' groups and from some school boards, particularly in Metropolitan Toronto. It would require a good deal of skill to placate the public while at the same time ensuring that the educational system was not damaged in any essential respect by false economies.

In April 1972 a major reorganization of the Department of Education was implemented as a result of recommendations by a task force consisting of departmental officials, consultants appointed by the Committee on Government Productivity, and staff members of the latter organization as well as of the Management Services Branch of the Treasury Board. The new plan was designed to carry further the principle of delegation of responsibility to local agencies. The minister outlined the intended role of the department in the Legislature.

The conducting and sponsoring of research and planning relating to the short and long range needs of education in Ontario.

The formulation of government policies consistent with these plans.

The development of educational programmes and activities appropriate to these policies, and where practicable delegation of their implementation outside the department.

The establishment of measurable programme delivery guidelines.

The evaluation of programme delivery effectiveness against these guidelines.

The provision of assistance necessary to improve the capacity of school boards to carry out effectively their responsibilities for educational administration.[8]

The plan involved the organization of the department into three major functional areas: educational development, educational administration, and support services. Under the co-ordination of the deputy minister, E.E. Stewart, these three areas or divisions were to be headed respectively by J.F. Kinlin, J.S. Stephen, and G.H. Waldrum, each with the title of assistant deputy minister. The educational development division was to consist of branches responsible for planning and research, curriculum development, facilities planning, and teacher education, along with a group of delivery services, including provincial schools, such as schools for the deaf and blind, correspondence schools, and hospital schools, as well as Provincial Library Services and Youth and Recreation. Branches of the administration division were responsible for the ten regional offices, curriculum services, supervisory services, school grants and finance, and educational exchange. The departmental services division included branches dealing with such matters as departmental accounting and administration, personnel, education data processing, education records, library information services, and the budget office. The change involved greater recognition of the educational needs of the Franco-Ontarian community, with the establishment of a standing committee on French language schools. At the time of writing the scheme had just been announced, and was subject to modification in the process of implementation.

CONSOLIDATION OF SCHOOL BOARDS IN THE 1960s
While the department was undergoing the changes recounted briefly in the past few pages, local school systems were being subjected to corresponding modifications. The need to replace the smaller units by larger ones became increasingly evident as the provincial government attempted to employ the school grant system to iron out some of the more extreme discrepancies in educational facilities and make some progress toward the equalization of educational opportunity. Provincial grants were, generally speaking, distributed in inverse relationship to local resources, with the wealthier boards raising most of their funds locally and the smaller boards being carried almost entirely by the province. But equalization of

opportunity could not be brought about by any conceivable distribution of funds while very small boards existed, even if the province had been prepared for a waste of resources on a colossal scale. There were not even enough specialists for programs for the handicapped, for example, to serve the larger systems where they could be put to the most efficient use.

It represented a significant change in provincial government policy to resort to compulsion to eliminate the remaining school sections. Those who were most attached to the traditional set-up were regarded as predominantly supporters of the Conservative party. Yet Davis could not afford to placate them at the expense of his plans for modernizing the school system. In 1964 he introduced an amendment to *The Public Schools Act* declaring that, as of January 1, 1965, every township would constitute a township school area. Also, all village, town, or city districts with a population of less than 1,000 or an average daily attendance at school of less than 100 were attached to the adjacent township school area. The ease with which the measure was put through was a tribute, not only to Davis's political skills, but also to the fact that public acceptance of the necessity for the action overrode any profound attachment to tradition. There was some criticism because the measure, introduced only a few months after the previous election, had not been mentioned in the campaign. However, although he noted that the reorganization would have to take place against the wishes of many of the people concerned, Robert Nixon announced that the Liberals would vote in favour of the change. While local control would move a step away from the immediate area, he felt that local autonomy was not in any real sense removed.

The reorganization abolished more than 1,500 rural school boards and reduced the number of public elementary boards in the province from 2,419 to 1,037. Yet there was no intention that the situation would remain static. Provision was made in 1964 for the appointment of consultative committees by the county councils and of corresponding bodies in the territorial districts to study all matters affecting education in their counties or districts and, in effect, to facilitate the establishment of county school areas or their territorial district equivalents. The county councils or, in the districts, the municipal councils would take the appropriate legal action. The responsibilities of the consultative committees were later extended. It was the policy at this time to encourage the formation of county school areas for public school purposes that would have boundaries corresponding to those of high school districts. Such a development would facilitate the formation of boards of education to administer both public and high school affairs. An attendance area with a minimum of three thousand pupils was regarded as desirable, although not practical in all parts of the province. Where there were this many pupils, it was considered possible to operate a composite school with a satisfactory range of options, to maintain senior public schools with specialists in key areas, to offer certain specialized services, and to ensure adequate supervision of instruction.

Within the comparatively brief period in which they were allowed to operate, the consultative committees seemed to be achieving reasonable success. Davis commented in the spring of 1967 that consolidation of school districts was proceeding rapidly. Composite high schools were replacing numbers of very small high schools that could not have expected to achieve composite status. Although costs were increased, there seemed to be a general appreciation of the educational advantages of larger units.[9] One can infer that Davis was beginning to believe that the next stage of compulsory amalgamation could be achieved without an unmanageable amount of opposition.

The idea of further amalgamation was encouraged by the Ontario Committee on Taxation (the Smith Committee) which advocated that a school administrative unit be established in each of its twelve proposed county regions. Such units would unquestionably have been large enough to provide a full range of services, but it is hard to see how any remnant of a feeling of community responsibility could have remained. Although the recommendation had no chance of being implemented, it presumably had some influence on the kind of thinking and planning that was going on. In 1967 a group in the Department of Education was given the task of examining alternatives and working out draft legislation. Yet when the announcement came in November of that year, it was not obviously related to much of this preliminary work. The circumstances surrounding the announcement seemed peculiar, since it was made by Prime Minister Robarts while Davis was out of the country. While the change seemed quite in accord with Davis's thinking and previous actions, the precipitous nature of the announcement, without specific consultation with educational bodies, was not.

According to Robarts's announcement, the government intended to introduce legislation in the forthcoming session of the Legislature to reduce the number of administrative units for public and secondary schools to approximately one hundred boards of education. Except for Metropolitan Toronto and a few major cities, where the existing boards would remain undisturbed, the county would be the basic unit in southern Ontario, including the cities and separated towns within its borders, while suitable units would be designated in northern Ontario. Consideration was also being given to the establishment of larger units for separate schools. The new scheme would come into effect on January 1, 1969.

Although the work of the departmental committee studying the next step in the enlargement of administrative units had apparently not exerted much direct influence on the plan, this committee had concluded that the county was the most satisfactory school board unit. Robarts gave four reasons for the choice. 1 / The county was a recognized and understood unit of administration. 2 / Existing school boundaries for both public and separate schools were established or altered by county councils. 3 / The Select Committee of the Legislature on The Municipal and Related Acts (the

Beckett Committee) had suggested that the counties be accepted as the basic unit as a practical start toward larger units of local government. 4 / The Smith Committee had supported the idea that taxes be levied on a base larger than the existing local units.[10] Robarts did not see fit to dwell on the fact that the county was not the larger unit that the Smith committee had in mind.

Initially there was considerable favourable reaction to the announcement. The government had made no secret of its intentions, and the public seemed generally to have accepted the fact that township school boards were too small to provide the range of services needed for a modern education. At the same time there was a good deal of adverse feeling, some of the reasons for which merit examination. 1 / It was said that insufficient time had been allowed for the measures permitting and encouraging further voluntary mergers to take effect. Although this point seems plausible and the area ultimately requiring compulsion would have been reduced if two or three more years had elapsed, the difficulties would hardly have been much less, since the voluntary approach would have worked only in the areas that were not disposed to offer opposition in any case. 2 / The political opposition felt that the proposals should have been presented as part of the Conservative platform in the previous election campaign. There seems to be a good deal of validity in this claim, although there was of course an opportunity to debate the proposed bills in the Legislature. 3 / The teachers' federations and various trustees' associations complained that they had not been consulted. Although the minister had to defend an action that had not been taken in the way he would have chosen had he been left to handle it in his own way, he pointed out that he had previously made the government's intentions reasonably clear; yet he could not dispell the air of arbitrariness that hung over the announcement. However, if various groups had been asked to offer opinions before the decision was made, there probably would have been a welter of conflicting suggestions to deal with, and the final outcome might have produced even more hard feelings than there actually were. On the other hand many groups used to leave Davis's presence feeling that he understood and sympathized with their position even if he was not won over to their cause. The same thing might have occurred in this case. Considerable opportunity was in fact provided for consultation when the legislation was being prepared, and some of the initial unhappiness was dispelled in the process. 4 / Considerable exception was taken to the choice of the county as the basic unit. It was pointed out that many of the counties were not real economic or sociological entities. They also varied tremendously in population; in September 1968 Haliburton County had the smallest enrolment, with about 2,100 students to the end of grade 13, while Waterloo County had over sixty thousand. Average assessment per student was another important factor on which the counties showed major discrepancies. Further difficulty was caused because high school districts did not necessarily follow county boundaries.

One alternative to using the counties would have been to designate an entirely new set of boundaries based on such factors as geographical features, transportation and communication, population, and assessment. The government was undoubtedly correct in assuming that such a choice would have led to endless dispute and ill-will, and that it was impractical under the circumstances. Another suggestion was that existing high school districts might have been selected. The problem was that public school units conformed to county boundaries, and it seemed more logical to adjust the high school district boundaries to these rather than the reverse. 5 / Many who agreed that in principle the county provided a suitable unit felt that there should have been some adjustments made to deal with particularly anomalous situations. There was bitterness in certain communities because natural and satisfactorily functioning units were broken up and convenience of access gave way to inconvenience because of rigid adherence to the plan. The minister dealt with complaints by insisting that the plan be allowed to stand for at least two years before changes were considered. If he had begun to agree to exceptions, it would have been very difficult to draw the line. 6 / It seemed to some people that the new units were too large for their voice or vote to make any real difference in the management of their schools. The fact that a very small proportion of eligible voters turned out in some divisions in the elections at the end of 1968 lent support to this impression. 7 / Even supporters of the move doubted that all the necessary changes could be made within the limited time allowed for the dissolution of the old boards and the formation of the new ones. Although there was a great deal of hasty work, and no doubt a certain amount of waste, the operation was conducted with reasonable success, and many of the worst apprehensions proved groundless.

The government released guidelines on February 1, 1968, indicating that, in addition to boards of education in the thirty-eight administrative counties of southern Ontario and the five existing boards plus the Metropolitan Toronto School Board in Metropolitan Toronto, there would be separate boards in Hamilton, London, Ottawa, and Windsor. The composition of the new boards was indicated and the means by which they were to be elected were explained. A supplementary document presented the results of the work of a larger unit committee which had been drawing the boundaries of the new units in northern Ontario. This work had been carried out in close consultation with regional directors, area superintendents, and business administrators in the areas concerned.

The legislation provided for boards consisting of between fourteen and twenty elected trustees, depending on the total population of the division. County councils would define the subdivisions from which these trustees would seek election. Ordinarily they would be based on existing municipal units, although it might be necessary to have a single trustee elected from more than one small municipality. Separate school representatives were to be elected at large except where there were more than four, in which case wards would be delineated. The boards in the defined cities, including Ottawa, where the reorganization was postponed until 1970, would continue to be elected according to existing procedures except that there would be a number of separate school representatives based on the ratio of residential and farm assessment for separate school purposes to the corresponding assessment for public school purposes. The minimum number of separate school supporters in any of these units would be two.

Certain small units in northern Ontario that were too isolated to be included in designated divisions were to remain under the control of local boards which would be concerned only with public school affairs. These boards would receive increased assistance from the department, including services from the Northern Corps of Teachers.* Boards operating schools on crown lands, in hospitals, and under other special circumstances would remain unaffected.

Vocational schools and vocational school programs in composite schools were to continue to be managed by advisory vocational committees according to the earlier pattern. The same principle was extended to cover two other types of schools: those at the secondary level where French was the language of instruction and schools for trainable retarded children. Non-board members on the French-language advisory committees were to be elected at a meeting of the French-speaking ratepayers while those on the advisory committees on schools for trainable retarded children were to be chosen by a local association affiliated with the Ontario Association for the Mentally Retarded.

The new grant scheme for 1969 placed more responsibility on the divisional boards for establishing priorities for expenditure. A long list of stimulation grants, designed to encourage the maintenance of various programs and special services, disappeared. Except for the boards in the five boroughs of Metropolitan Toronto, all divisional boards were given complete responsibility for capital expenditure, subject only to the approval of the Ontario Municipal Board. Tax bills for education were to be distinct from those for other municipal services, and were to indicate separately the rate and amount of tax for public and secondary school purposes. The municipalities, however, remained responsible for issuing the tax bills and for collecting the taxes, which they turned over to the boards. Members of municipal councils had long complained that the public held them responsible for the extravagance of school boards, and were not entirely mollified by the new arrangement, which still seemed to leave room for misunderstanding about their role. Some would have been satisfied only with a completely separate set of machinery for tax collection. Provincial authorities were not, however, prepared to agree to this kind of extravagance.

As a means of preparing for the difficult transition from the numerous small boards to the relatively few divisional boards, county councils were

*The origin and purpose of this group is explained in ONTARIO'S EDUCATIVE SOCIETY, volume II, chapter 2.

encouraged to set up interim school organization committees, with membership drawn for public school and high school boards and boards of education from the area. These committees could, in turn, set up *ad hoc* subcommittees consisting of trustees, officials, teachers, or parents to perform various specific services. Each committee was to prepare a report providing information about the existing school systems and indicating the administrative and supervisory activities that would have to be performed under the new board. Some very valuable reports were produced under this scheme, and undoubtedly did much to smooth the transition. Where the reorganization consisted, however, of the grouping of small boards about a large one in a major centre of population, the committees were in some cases given little attention.

Not all of the outgoing boards acted in an entirely responsible fashion. At one stage Davis complained that some of them reduced the mill rate, spent any surplus left over at the end of 1967, and even brought a considerable deficit into the new administrative set-up.[11] In certain cases the community received the parting gift of a new school or school extension that might not have been built had the decision been made in relation to the broader needs of the new division. These actions contributed to the financial problems that later occasioned considerable complaint.

A reorganization of separate school units took place in accordance with the comment made by Robarts at the same time that he announced the intended formation of public and secondary school boards. In this case the scheme was worked out in careful consultation with such organizations as the Ontario Separate School Trustees' Association and l'Association des commissions des écoles bilingues d'Ontario. Members of these associations were strongly in favour of the formation of larger units, feeling that, if appropriate action was not taken, the separate schools would be placed at a great disadvantage in relation to public schools. Several recommendations were made with respect to the way in which the amalgamation might be carried out. Legislation was prepared providing for the establishment by regulation of combined Roman Catholic separate school zones consisting of the existing zones and any new ones that might be established in the future whose centres were in a county or a combination of counties. Provision was made for the later alteration of boundaries within which a combined zone might be formed. Cities and towns were included in the combined zones except for Metropolitan Toronto, Ottawa, and Windsor, which retained their existing boards. Only those parts of a county lying within the three-mile limit of a zone were included in a combined zone. There was provision for the formation of combined zones in the territorial districts where there was a sufficient concentration of the original zones. A few scattered zones were left in their existing state.

Separate school boards were to consist of between eight and sixteen elected trustees, the exact number depending on the total population of the county or group of counties. Where the combined zones included cities or separated towns, their number of trustees was to depend on the ratio of their provincial equalized residential and farm assessment for separate school purposes to that of the entire combined zone. The number from each non-urban municipality or group of municipalities was to be selected in a similar way.

The reorganization had important implications for trustees, officials, and teachers. In theory, at least, the level of trustee competence might have been expected to increase substantially. There would be far fewer required, a wider range from which to choose, and more prestige attached to the position. However, many outstanding trustees were said to be unwilling to travel the extended distance required to attend meetings, and some of those who had previously been appointed to high school boards were not prepared to engage in campaigns to get elected. Some were also eliminated because the legislation forbade anyone connected with a firm doing business with the board from holding elective office. In the large school divisions the chance of a prominent businessman finding himself in this position was greatly increased.

It was a question how responsive to the voters' wishes the members of the new boards would be. Presumably the voter apathy that characterized Ontario municipal elections in general would ensure that, once trustees became known, it would usually take an obviously inept or scandalous performance to get them removed. There was little indication that fear of losing the next election acted as a major influence on the conduct of the trustees. If they could not or would not demonstrate responsiveness to their constituencies, the policy of decentralization might be eroded by a move back toward provincial government control. The imposition of maximum permissible amounts of per pupil expenditure in the fall of 1970 was a clear move in that direction.

Among the incentives for service on local school boards, financial rewards were never of great importance. As of 1954 *The Schools Administration Act* provided that a board of a township school area or of a high school district that comprised two or more municipalities or parts of municipalities might pay a trustee an honorarium not exceeding $5 for each of not more than twelve meetings attended in any one year, as well as a mileage allowance not exceeding seven cents for necessary travel to and from board meetings.[12] In 1964 arrangements were made for the payment to trustees of three-member boards of monthly honoraria ranging from $5 to $150, depending on the average daily attendance in the schools under the board's control. Trustees appointed to boards of education who were not entitled to vote on motions exclusively affecting public schools could receive up to half the corresponding amounts based on average daily attendance in secondary schools under the board's control.[13] In 1968 the maximum amounts were doubled, and the scales were related to enrolment rather than average daily attendance. Maximum payment was at that time made equal for the two categories of trustees.[14] The chairman of the board could receive an additional third of the amount due him as a trustee. In 1971 suggestions were heard from time to time that members of large city boards should receive sufficient remuneration to enable them to devote full time to the task, but for the time being at least the position of the trustee continued to be occupied strictly on a part-time basis.

There was, naturally, a substantial increase in the number of officials appointed by each of the larger boards. Considerable apprehension was expressed lest the systems be overloaded with their own bureaucracies. It seemed possible that, as certain regulatory functions of the Department of Education faded, a multitude of petty little imitations would spring up, and that neither the freedom of the teacher nor the welfare of the pupil would be enhanced. There was also considerable complaint about the high salaries offered to many officials. Although there were not enough of these officials to make a great difference in the total cost of the enterprise, there was a feeling that very large differences between administrative and teaching salaries would reinforce a false sense of values or else that an attempt to bring teachers' salaries up to these levels would produce a taxpayers' rebellion. At the time the divisional boards were established, the minister lacked any effective means of holding the line on administrative salaries. Decentralization of powers meant that the allocation of funds for specific purposes was under board control. Even when spending limits were imposed by the central authority in 1970, the establishment of priorities was left largely in local hands.

Administrative officials in the disappearing boards had to take their own chances when their jobs disappeared. In this respect they were unlike the staffs of the teachers' colleges, who were given a substantial measure of government protection as the teachers' college programs were taken over by the universities. There were undoubtedly injustices done and old scores settled during the period of fluidity in 1968. The new positions were desirable enough to arouse keen competition among the candidates. However, there were situations where the opportunity to bring in fresh talent was used to good advantage.

The reorganization promised to be beneficial for many members of the teaching profession in that it would speed up the elimination of the smallest and poorest schools and offer facilities and surroundings that would be more conducive to effective teaching. As proponents of the best of educational opportunities for all children, teachers could not do other than applaud the move. Those who were interested in pursuing some particular line of specialization would have more demand for their services. Those who were interested in rising in the administrative hierarchy would find more influential positions on which to set their sights. To some extent, at least, all these developments in fact took place.

There were also some threatening elements in the new situation. A smaller number of more powerful trustees in the province might show greater cohesion and act with increased decisiveness to tip the balance of power away from the teachers' federations. This development was very difficult for the federations to oppose openly. A second danger was that the freedom of individual teachers might be curtailed if boards exercised an unrestricted right to transfer them arbitrarily from one end of a county to the other. As long as the administrative unit was small, a transfer often meant that they need only drive a little further to reach their school. Now there was a possibility that their whole pattern of living might be disrupted. At worst the ruthless exercise of the power of transfer might bring the teachers back to the days when they had no security of tenure.

The Ontario Teachers' Federation advocated as a solution the establishment of transfer review boards to handle complaints from teachers who felt that they were being dealt with unreasonably. The Ontario School Trustees' Council took the position that there was no need for the boards, and made every effort during the period when the matter was under discussion to prevent incidents that would reinforce the teachers' case. The trustees were, as usual, opposed to any measure that they felt might reduce their ability to manage the affairs of the schools as they saw fit. Some of them envisioned what was intended as a protective device against a rare unreasonable decision becoming a serious obstacle to transferring teachers even when it was to the obvious advantage of the pupils. The minister expressed sympathy for the teachers' point of view, but would go no further than to support an amendment to the standard contract for permanent teaching staff providing that a teacher who was to be transferred from one municipality to another must be notified not later than May 1 before the school year in which the transfer was to take effect. Whether or not stronger measures would ultimately be taken seemed to depend on the amount of evidence the OTF could assemble to show that they were needed.

There was no official suggestion that the new set-up would help to reduce the costs of education. Davis warned, in fact, that despite certain economies resulting from operations on a larger scale the effect of attempting to equalize opportunity throughout the new divisions would be expensive. Robert Nixon agreed with this verdict and, in an analysis of his own, pointed out that communities in all parts of a new unit would insist that services previously available only to the most fortunate be made universal.[15] He insisted that a Liberal government, if elected, would make the burden more readily bearable by raising the level of grants to 80 per cent of the total cost.

When the tax bills went out in 1969 there were some very strongly adverse repercussions. The problem was not primarily in the size of the increase in the total amount to be raised locally, but in the change in the distribution of the tax burden. When municipalities with low cost educational services were combined with others where the level of expenditure had previously been much higher, they were immediately expected to make a greatly increased contribution. It was especially annoying when the costs skyrocketed before measures to equalize benefits had time to take effect. In some areas taxpayers, particularly farmers, began to threaten to withhold taxes for periods up to the three-year limit before action could be taken against their property.

For some time it was practically impossible for the provincial government to take any effective action to ease the situation. Audited financial statements were very slow in coming in from the large number of boards that went out of business at the end of 1968. Remedial measures awaited the collection of information, which took longer to assemble than might be expected in future years, on the proportion of costs among the municipalities, the applicable equalizing factors, the apportionment of local levies, and the establishment of mill rates. When the situation was reasonably clear, the department provided a special grant limiting the increase in mill rate on provincial equalized assessment in any municipality having a population of less than sixty thousand to one mill for elementary school purposes and one mill for secondary school purposes over the greater of the 1967 and 1968 mill rates. This special grant was to apply only to per pupil expenditure up to 115 per cent of that in 1969. Assistance was offered to boards to devise means of keeping their costs within reasonable limits. The amount of the extra costs came to almost $50 million. The opposition in the Legislature was critical of this outcome on the ground that it indicated a lack of proper planning. The matter proved to be less embarrassing for the government than early predictions indicated, since it turned out that Provincial Treasurer MacNaughton had been unduly pessimistic about the immediate financial problems facing the province.

Emergency measures helped to alleviate the immediate crisis, but they could not obscure the fact that many parts of the province were going to have better educational facilities, and were going to pay a substantial part of the cost whether the local population wanted to or not. In fact many citizens made it quite clear that they did not want to. They had not been persuaded that the advantages of greater educational opportunities were worth giving up a large chunk of their disposable income. Even though the opposition parties had promised no real alternative, some of those who ordinarily voted Conservative were expected to turn against the government in the election of 1971. Davis himself inevitably bore the brunt of a good deal of the criticism, and his popularity declined substantially. He was said, however, to have gained stature among his colleagues for the skill with which he blunted criticism and made the best of a difficult situation. His problems at this time were thought to have had a good deal to do with the narrowness of his victory in the contest for the leadership of the Conservative party in February, 1971, despite overwhelming cabinet support. They did not, however, prevent him from winning an overwhelming victory at the polls in October of that year.

Although the prevalent view is that the whole movement toward larger local units of administration has, despite possible faults in execution along the way, been conducive to greater efficiency, and thus to more effective education, there is a contrary view held strongly in some quarters. According to this position, the larger systems with their expanded programs, their multitude of options, their provision for special groups, and all the other amenities they can offer, inevitably produce schools that, because of their inordinate size, must be over-organized and run without enough attention to human sensibilities. They are thus thought to alienate young people to the point where they are incapable of appreciating or taking advantage of their opportunities. It would be far better, in this view, if some of the expensive equipment and the range of choices of areas of study were reduced in favour of the intimate atmosphere that could be developed in smaller schools where students would have a better chance of acquiring and retaining the thirst for learning that would lead them to seek out learning opportunities on their own. Even if large schools could be administered in such a way as to achieve these advantages, it is said that the large system generates a supervisory bureaucracy that demands power to exercise, and can find it only by taking it away from teachers and students, to their disadvantage. Moreover, a large system reputedly can have only attenuated contacts with local citizens. Even if these citizens are sometimes short-sighted, narrow-minded, and bigoted, the educational process, according to the argument, is invigorated when educators engage in an active interchange with them, and the ultimate results of educational efforts are likely to be much greater.

The possibility that large boards, despite the democratic processes by which their members were elected, might not be sufficiently responsive to various elements in the community was recognized in 1969 by legislation enabling boards of education to establish advisory committees consisting of three members of the board appointed by the board, the chief education officer of the board or his nominee, six teachers employed by the board and elected by their fellow teachers, and four residents of the area, appointed by the board, who were neither trustees nor board members. There was also provision, under certain conditions, for representation of the local Home and School Council and the Federation of Catholic Parent-Teacher Associations of Ontario. Such a committee could make reports and recommendations to the board with respect to any matter affecting the schools except for salaries and problems and policies relating to personnel. The measure was criticized because it was permissive rather than mandatory. It was said that the boards that most needed advice would be the last to set up machinery by which they would receive it. Even in the best of circumstances, recommendations which cost money could easily be ignored. Further, in some cases advisory groups were resented by school officials, who might interpret recommendations as indications of things they themselves should have brought before the board.

THE DEVELOPMENT OF AN EDUCATIONAL SYSTEM
FOR METROPOLITAN TORONTO
The story of the search for greater efficiency in the organization of administrative structures for education cannot be told without substantial reference to developments in Metropolitan Toronto. What happened there was important, not only because it affected something close to 30 per cent of the population of the province in the early 1970s, but also because it constituted a unique experiment in allotting local powers between two tiers of government. Lessons learned in the process have been of interest in other parts of Canada and far beyond Canadian borders.

The end of the war saw a central city, of quite moderate size by world standards, and with a relatively stable population, at least in numbers, although not in composition, with a group of adjoining suburbs. These included an inner ring, consisting of the township of East York, the village of Forest Hill, the town of Leaside, the village of Swansea, the town of Weston, and the township of York, all of which were at least partly developed, and an outer ring, consisting of the town of Mimico, the town of New Toronto, the village of Long Branch, and the townships of Etobicoke, North York, and Scarborough, the last three of which had hardly begun the extraordinarily rapid urbanization that occurred during the post-war period. These units were characterized by duplication of services, lack of co-ordination, and wasteful competition to attract the industry that would provide an adequate tax base. In the worst position were the dormitory suburbs, particularly the new ones, which had to provide education, water, sewage disposal, transportation, police and fire protection, and other necessities for people who earned their salaries and wages in adjoining municipalities which had the high assessment industries. Toronto itself faced the prospect of imminent decay, with increasing difficulty in reaching the downtown area encouraging industry and the more prosperous residents to flee to the suburbs, leaving the centre for the poor, the aged, the infirm, and those immigrants who were still struggling to establish themselves. The vicious circle would be accelerated as the welfare burden increased and revenues declined. Drastic action of some kind was obviously needed.

The area had a wide representation of school boards of different types providing services varying greatly in extent and quality. The Toronto Board of Education was the oldest and controlled by far the largest system in the province. It had an unusual concentration of highly qualified teachers and was noted for its innovations and special services. The Forest Hill board, which had a high assessment from which to raise taxes, was also noted for its progressive policies, including the introduction of a junior high school. The Weston board, along with that of Toronto, provided vocational facilities for students from surrounding areas as well as from its own vicinity. In 1951 the Lakeshore District Board of Education replaced separate boards for Mimico, New Toronto, and Long Branch.

Immediately after 1950 there were threats of an imminent breakdown in the system. It was becoming difficult or impossible to raise enough funds for capital expansion. The beginning of a steep increase in teachers' salaries promised to make the crisis even more acute. There were also serious obstacles to efficient provision of educational facilities because of the way municipal boundaries were drawn. Boards were unhappy about paying fees to have pupils attend under-utilized schools just on the other side of an artificial line. The willingness of the Toronto board to accommodate pupils from the suburbs in its special classes at cost did not ensure that such pupils would be satisfactorily provided for. Suburban boards were in no position to establish these services themselves.

Reorganization for educational purposes was closely dependent on that for other municipal services. The first steps were taken toward co-ordination by the establishment of the Toronto and Suburban Planning Board in 1947 and the Toronto and York Planning Board in 1949. By the time the latter recommended the amalgamation of Toronto and the twelve neighbouring suburbs, Toronto was prepared to espouse the cause, and the city council asked the Ontario Municipal Board to take the necessary steps. The authorities in the suburbs were almost unanimously opposed to such a step, although the attitudes of residents were never ascertained. The provincial government was and remained wary of the consequences of establishing a single large city, which would be difficult to keep in its place. As a result of the Toronto request, the Ontario Municipal Board, chaired by Lorne R. Cumming, undertook a series of studies culminating in the Cumming report.

The Cumming report recognized certain advantages in total amalgamation. It would be possible to provide a full range of municipal services of relatively uniform quality throughout the area, to distribute the tax burden equitably, and to raise funds at a reasonable rate in the capital market. The disadvantages would be that a sudden transition would create a great deal of administrative confusion, that the immediate equalization of tax rates in order to bring suburban services up to city standards would necessitate unacceptable increases, that a single monolithic administration might be insensitive to local problems, and that the hostility of suburban politicians might have undesirable consequences. The disadvantages were thought to outweigh the advantages, and the amalgamation solution was rejected in favour of a two-tier government, somewhat similar to the arrangement in the counties, where powers were split between county and local municipal councils. A Metropolitan Council would be responsible for the administration of justice, health and welfare, the supervision of children's aid homes, assessment, the distribution of water, main trunk sewers, and disposal plants. Existing councils would continue to exercise the powers that did not involve these matters.

For the most part the report was conservative in the sense that it advocated minimum departures from tradition. With respect to education, however, it recommended a definite break with precedent. The Metropolitan Council would include certain responsibilities for education along with its other functions. It would finance capital costs of sites, buildings, and equipment to bring them up to an adequate standard, assume all existing school debentures, receive all legislative grants on capital expenditures, select and purchase school sites, finance such portion of operational costs as it would itself determine, receive all legislative grants for operational purposes except those relating to books, milk distribution, and other special expenditures, require pupils in one municipality to attend schools in another municipality where it seemed in the general interest, and provide transportation for such pupils. In consultation with the Department of Education the Metropolitan Council would determine the minimum standards to be attained by area-wide financing, leaving the existing local boards free to raise additional funds to provide such services as the community desired and was willing to pay for. The proposal to give all these powers to such a body, particularly that of determining minimum standards of financing, caused widespread concern, especially among trustees. The provincial government heeded the protests and, in the legislation, which followed the report in most respects, introduced one significant departure by placing the educational powers, essentially as specified in the report, in the hands of a Metropolitan School Board, paralleling the Metropolitan Council. The relevant legislation was passed in 1953, with J.A. Long becoming the chairman for the first year and W.J. McCordic beginning a long period of service and influence as executive secretary.

The Metropolitan Toronto Act provided for boards of education in North York and Scarborough, thus making this form of school board uniform throughout the area. The Metropolitan School Board, according to an arrangement similar to that for the Metropolitan Council, consisted of equal numbers of members from the Toronto Board of Education and from all the other boards combined. Although such a balance was reasonable at the time in the light of the population distribution, it was bound to become less satisfactory as the suburbs grew and the city did not. From the beginning there were grounds for dissatisfaction in that suburbs differing greatly in size were each given one member. For 1954 and 1955 the act specified how much the Metropolitan School Board would pay the local boards in maintenance assistance grants per pupil, after which the Metropolitan Board itself would determine these amounts. This arrangement was another that contained the seeds of future trouble. During a period of rapidly rising costs, the grants would have to be increased to keep pace or else a growing proportion of the total cost would be shifted back to the local boards with their greatly varying capacity to raise revenue. Since the Metropolitan Board consistently had a majority of members from municipalities that stood to lose from greater equalization, the grants were raised comparatively slowly. Still other problems were inherent in the provision that, along with the assumption of all school debentures outstanding on January 1, 1954, the Metropolitan Board be responsible in future for the repayment of school debt only on the portion of the cost of school buildings recognized by the Department of Education. The recognized cost of $20,000 for both elementary and secondary school classrooms was already inadequate to cover the actual costs, particularly of the latter, and school boards began to accumulate new debts on the uncovered balance at a rate that accelerated as costs increased.

For the first few years after the act was passed some of the benefits were quite conspicuous. McCordic reviewed these in an address at the Ontario College of Education in 1958.[16] 1 / With uniform equalized assessment it had become possible to compare the tax burden in metropolitan municipalities by a direct examination of their tax rates. 2 / The sale of debentures had been centralized in competent hands, competition among the municipalities in the capital market had been eliminated, and the whole area had been provided assurance of the soundness of the debentures. 3 / The procedures for securing approval for building projects had been greatly improved, and much of the former haggling had been eliminated. 4 / The Metropolitan Board had been able to speak with a powerful voice for the special educational needs of Metropolitan Toronto in dealing with the provincial government. 5 / Maintenance assistance grants had helped to spread the financial burden more equitably. 6 / The establishment of attendance areas cutting across municipal boundaries had contributed to the full utilization of available space. 7 / The board's assumption of the full cost of auxiliary classes had ensured the fairest possible use of existing facilities. There were also important dividends of a less easily defined nature stemming from the opportunities members of the different boards had to work together.

Although the scheme was working at its best at that particular time, certain difficulties were definitely in evidence. In addition to those already noted as being inherent in the legislation and bound to develop as growth continued, McCordic observed that the removal of a large part of their responsibility for raising capital funds had made the school boards considerably less restrained in their demands. Now that metropolitan agencies were expected to look after capital expenditure, the municipal councils tended to reinforce the pressure generated by the school boards rather than trying to check them. There were also some local autonomists who tended to create obstacles to the interchange of pupils with claims for the superiority of the offerings in their own area. While it was undoubtedly true that some of these claims were specious, it is possible that in certain cases they were justified. Different communities had, after all, somewhat varying traditions of support for education.

Some observers were inclined to blame members of the Metropolitan School Board, who might theoretically have used existing machinery to prevent inequalities of financial status from becoming so pronounced. It is doubtful, however, that they could reasonably have been expected to act in a different way in view of their position. They were elected primarily to represent their own areas and to provide these areas with the best educational facilities that local resources would permit. It was thus difficult for them to vote for an increase in maintenance grants to benefit other systems that would have to come in part from revenues paid by their particular constituents. When the inclination arises to blame a whole category of officials for greed or lack of responsibility, the structure within which they operate can usually stand examination.

Concern over inequalities of resources among the municipalities led to the establishment of a committee of the Metropolitan School Board to study the matter. This committee concluded that even a substantial increase in the maintenance assistance payments would constitute only a partial solution. The levying of a uniform tax rate throughout the area was recommended as the best solution. At this stage the committee did not appear to feel that the measure would necessitate any drastic change in the existing school board set-up. In an extension of its work the committee later examined the implications of a uniform tax rate for the local boards, and decided that such a procedure would mean the end of local autonomy, since the old inequalities would soon return if local boards were permitted to raise extra amounts on the basis of their widely varying resources. The only way of allowing them any freedom of action would be to reorganize the municipalities so as to bring their tax bases close to equality. There would, of course, remain the alternative of total amalgamation. Another possible solution would be to establish a foundation plan by which the Metropolitan School Board would underwrite a minimum program in terms of administrative costs, capital expenditure, debt charges, teachers' salaries, maintenance and operation of plant, and supplies. Again, unless the municipalities were reorganized in order to equalize resources, differences would appear according to the extent to which boards varied in their expenditure on extra amenities and programs.

Some attempt was made to apply palliatives after the Ontario Municipal Board pointed out in 1963 that the amount of debt being assumed by local municipalities was threatening to get out of hand. It was suggested that the Metropolitan School Board exercise its legal right to recommend that the Metropolitan Council assume a greater share of this debt. The council and the school board thereupon set up a joint committee which proposed that, as of January 1, 1964, the council assume all existing school board debt and all new debt incurred thereafter up to a ceiling cost determined by a formula devised by the board and approved by the council. Only the second of these two recommendations was accepted.

The growing problems of education remained closely linked with those of municipal services in general. The inequality of representation among the different municipalities was becoming increasingly unfair as the big three on the outer fringes continued their rapid growth. By 1963 there were seven municipalities: Forest Hill, Leaside, Long Branch, Mimico, New Toronto, Swansea, and Weston, none of which had more than 1.3 per cent of the population of the whole area. Consideration began to be given to three possible solutions: total amalgamation of the whole area, a complete redrawing of the municipal boundaries to produce administrative units of approximately equal size, and a reduction of the number of boroughs by merging the smaller ones with their larger neighbours. The first solution still had strong support from Toronto officials, but little among their counterparts elsewhere. The provincial government remained apprehensive about the difficulty of controlling a single large city. Those with the power to do so did not seem to think it necessary to consult the citizens concerned. The second solution would have stirred up all kinds of adverse emotional reactions which no established government would have thought of arousing. Speculation was centred, not on whether the third solution would be adopted but on how many units would emerge and whether or not an even balance between the city of Toronto and all the remaining municipalities would be restored. Among educators, it was not universally assumed that new boundaries for educational units would necessarily follow those of the municipalities. In this respect some of the leaders seem to have been living in a theorist's paradise.

The deteriorating situation led to the appointment of H. Carl Goldenberg as royal commissioner in June 1963. His terms of reference involved a study of the structure and organization of Metropolitan Toronto, particularly of the Metropolitan Council and the Metropolitan School Board in terms of their functions, responsibilities, and relations with the area municipalities and local school boards respectively. He was to make recommendations on possible improvements in the way their objectives might be attained and on any boundary changes that seemed advisable in the light of recent experience. In view of his lack of knowledge of educational matters, he called in a group of reputed experts and turned over to them the task of working out a scheme of school area organization and school finance.*

*The advisory group consisted of J.R. Davidson, Toronto school trustee; G.E. Flower, Director of Graduate Studies, Ontario College of Education; D.W. Gilmour, Solicitor, Toronto Board of Education; R.W.B. Jackson, Director, Department of Educational Research, Ontario College of Education; W.J. McCordic, Executive Secretary, Metropolitan School Board; Z.S. Phimister, Director of Education, Toronto Board of Education; E.B. Rideout, Associate Professor of Education, Ontario College of Education; and D.L. Tough, Superintendent of Secondary Schools, North York Board of Education.

The scheme finally devised and presented by Goldenberg was said to offer a middle course between complete centralization and complete decentralization. There would be an elected central board responsible for school finance and for the development of an acceptable and uniform standard of education for the whole area. It would co-ordinate mutual services and provide services that were best offered on a metro-wide basis. A series of district education councils would complement its activities by administering and managing the school program on the local level. The boundaries of the districts would not correspond to those of the municipalities, but would be drawn on a more logical basis to take account of attendance areas, geographic features, and other considerations. They would be large enough to provide a full range of services but small enough for efficient and responsive administration. The district councils would consist of the two trustees elected to represent the district on the Metropolitan School Board, one appointed by the Metropolitan Separate School Board, and eight elected in the district.

The Metropolitan Board would have the responsibility of establishing salary scales and policies, suggesting recruiting procedures, and maintaining staff records, while the districts would handle recruitment, appointment, promotion, and definition of duties. Competition for the best teachers would have to be on the basis of factors other than salaries, availability of parking space, and buildings. Other functions of the Metropolitan Board would include the establishment of pupil-teacher ratios, the number of employees allowed for certain functions and services, and the allocation of funds for supplies and equipment. The board would also establish procedures by which the district councils would prepare their budgets. The districts would have discretionary power only over such items as the provision of special equipment, special services, and experimentation.

The chief executive officer of the Metropolitan Board would be a director of educaton, who would have a small supporting staff. His counterpart at the district level would be a superintendent, responsible for both elementary and secondary education. The role of this official would appear to be somewhat ambiguous, since he would report to the metropolitan director, presumably as well as to his own district council. There would be an advisory council consisting of the director, his central staff, and the district superintendents to advise the Metropolitan Board on policy.

Goldenberg's proposals with respect to education constituted the part of his report that was least palatable to the public and the provincial government. It was too radical in ignoring traditions, customary procedures, existing boundaries, and vested interests. It also had the disadvantage of being too difficult for the ordinary citizen to grasp easily. When the details came out, there was emphatic opposition from both large and small municipalities. It soon became obvious, if it had not been before, that the new school units would correspond with the boroughs. This meant that Toronto absorbed Forest Hill and Swansea, York absorbed Weston, Etobicoke absorbed the Lakeshore municipalities, East York and Leaside were combined, and North York and Scarborough remained unchanged.

The Metropolitan Toronto School Board, as it was now called, consisted of the chairman of each of the six local boards and five additional members from the Toronto Board, three from the North York Board, two each from the Etobicoke and Scarborough Boards, and three from the Metropolitan Separate School Board. In this way a very rough approximation of representation by population was achieved. The Metropolitan Board was empowered to require each area board to submit at regular intervals a statement of its accommodation requirements, with an indication of the approximate cost. Those proposals were to be combined to form a composite plan, which would be assembled in consultation with the local boards, the Department of Education, and the Metropolitan Council, and submitted to the latter at appropriate times. Attendance areas were to be defined, again in consultation with local boards. The local boards were to present their estimates to the Metropolitan Toronto School Board rather than to their own local councils. The Metropolitan Toronto School Board would then submit the combined estimates, of which the proceeds of not more than two mills on the dollar might be for capital projects for each of elementary and secondary school purposes, to the Metropolitan Council. As before, legislative grants were to be paid to the Metropolitan Toronto School Board with certain minor exceptions.

Budget-making was a flexible process requiring a good deal of give and take. In the exercise of its responsibility of co-ordinating expenditure in the whole of Metropolitan Toronto, the Metropolitan Toronto School Board had to ensure that the requests of the local boards were kept within reasonable limits. Although revenues for approved expenditure were to be raised by means of a uniform rate levied over the whole area, a board could exceed the sum obtained in this way by an amount raised on its assessment through a levy of up to one and one-half mills for public school purposes and one mill for secondary school purposes. The proceeds could be used for either operating or capital purposes. The board thus had some means to provide special services and to conduct experimental programs. If it was not willing to accept the Metropolitan Board's verdict on its budget submission, it could appeal to the Ontario Municipal Board, which could either rule against it or direct the Metropolitan Board to accept the budget and raise the necessary funds. It was obvious that impasses of this kind would have to be relatively uncommon if the scheme were to work harmoniously.

The local boards were no longer in a position to get into trouble over an accumulation of debt for capital expenditure, since the Metropolitan Board assumed the entire responsibility for all debt accumulated after January 1, 1954, and all that would be incurred in the future. After this, a local board had to secure the approval of the Metropolitan Board if it wished to discontinue the operation and maintenance of any school under its control or dispose of any building, site, or item of school property that had been paid for in whole or in part by the issue of debentures. The proceeds of an approved sale had to go to the Metropolitan Board, which was to use them for capital expenditure for public school or secondary school purposes depending on their origin. The Metropolitan Board itself could act to provide accommodation for pupils from an area covering more than one school district, and could have the Metropolitan Council borrow money to finance the expenditure. The property might subsequently be conveyed to one of the boards sharing jurisdiction over the area. Local boards could enter into agreement with municipal councils for the joint construction and operation of swimming pools provided as part of a school building.

The legislation establishing the new system left important areas of responsibility comparatively undefined. McCordic, who was named director of education for the Metropolitan Board, commented particularly on the lack of specific direction in what he considered to be the two most sensitive areas: school building standards and teachers' salaries.[17] A great deal of responsibility thus fell on the Metropolitan Board and particularly on the Advisory Council of Directors, which consisted of the six area directors of education meeting under the chairmanship of the Metropolitan director. The Committee of Board Chairmen, whose meetings were attended by the seven directors with a voice but no vote, became the effective executive of the Metropolitan Board. The teachers were initially determined to recognize the area boards as their employers in every sense of the word and to conduct salary negotiations entirely with them. It soon became obvious, however, that these boards had lost the power to make any substantial financial commitments on their own, and the teachers themselves requested that negotiations be conducted on a metro-wide basis.

The flexibility of the system and the lack of detailed regulations made it easier, given co-operation and good will on all sides, to look after the special needs of certain areas. Although the culturally deprived were to some extent scattered through the boroughs, by far the largest proportion were concentrated in the downtown sections of the city of Toronto. These pupils needed specially trained teachers, classes with a small pupil/ teacher ratio, and special equipment. There were also areas where the inability of parents and children to use the English language effectively constituted special problems.

The system established in 1954 called for a very small staff in the direct employ of the Metropolitan Board. This situation changed substantially after 1967. Since the appraisal of local budgets called for considerable understanding of the educational activities on which they were based, it became necessary to appoint a superintendent of academic programs. There was some initial criticism of the Metropolitan Board's undertaking to perform this function, since such action was seen as a possible threat to the exercise of local responsibility. In actual practice, however, this criticism did not appear to be sustained. A second major function, that of overseeing budgetary matters and of ensuring a flow of funds to the local boards for their day-to-day operations, was assigned to a comptroller of finance. A third function, working with local planning staff in the assessment of capital requirements, came under a director of capital programming and research. There were committees of the Metropolitan Board concerned with these functions and entitled respectively the Academic Committee, the Finance Committee, and the Building and Sites Committee.

Early relations between the Metropolitan Board and the Metropolitan Council were by no means smooth. The council exercised its right, subject to being overruled by the Ontario Municipal Board, to reduce the capital budget submitted by the Metropolitan Board. In 1967 and 1968 the respective reductions amounted to $6 million and $13 million. Since the board considered that its demands had already been pared to the minimum, this action seemed to constitute a deferment of essential expenditure. There was a feeling among some of those with a primary interest in education that the Metropolitan Board should have been given the right granted to the new divisional boards in 1969 to raise their own debentures without obtaining the approval of other municipal authorities. The advantage of the existing system was that a single agency, the council, could presumably look at capital needs for all municipal services, including education, in perspective.

Two of the major issues of 1970 involved relationships between the teachers' federations and both the Metropolitan Toronto School Board and the local boards. The local district of the Ontario Secondary School Teachers' Federation sought a voice in determining the conditions under which its members worked by asking the trustees to hire a specified number of new teachers in order to reduce the student/teacher ratio to a given point. The trustees were determined to retain what they saw as their responsibility to the electorate by refusing to yield on the principle. An uneasy accommodation was reached when the trustees agreed to hire more teachers than they had originally planned, but fewer than the teachers originally asked. There were differing interpretations of the nature of the precedent that had thus been set. Another challenge of a rather similar type was developing over teachers' demands for a share of the responsibility for choosing school principals. Here again, board members feared a loss of the power they exercised through appointed officials by virtue of their mandate from the voters. The other major issue was that of salaries. The trustees successfully resisted what they considered extreme demands of the teachers in 1970. They faced further difficult tests, however, with the teachers renewing their demands and the minister informing them that their expenditures per pupil must not exceed an amount that, however reasonable it might be for the province as a whole, seemed entirely inadequate for the metropolitan area. Although these issues may not have been directly related to the new administrative structure that came into existence on January 1, 1967, they put its effectiveness to the test.

By 1970 the re-organized two-tier system gave the appearance of operating successfully. Inequalities of opportunity had been greatly reduced, if not entirely equalized, throughout the area; the tax burden had been distributed evenly; and effective central planning and budgeting had been instituted. At the same time the local boards had retained enough authority to devise suitable programs for their own areas. They operated on a scale that enabled them to respond more effectively to the wishes of local citizens than a single all-powerful board could have done. Municipal government in the Metropolitan Toronto area would undoubtedly evolve to meet changing needs. There might well be strong arguments for a further centralization of some functions that remained in the hands of the mediocre politicians who so often won office in the boroughs. It was to be hoped, however, that no substantial change would be made in the educational set-up without convincing evidence that a superior alternative existed. As of 1972 such evidence did not seem to exist.

CONCLUDING OBSERVATIONS

The developments reviewed in this chapter indicate that, in the light of modern principles of organization and administration, the Ontario school system undoubtedly advanced toward greater efficiency of operation in the post-war period. Progress must be evaluated, of course, not primarily by comparison with earlier days when conditions and needs were different, but in terms of what present-day society requires. Given the widespread variation in views about the extent of those requirements, there is sufficient room for differences of opinion in evaluating the Ontario system.

Particularly notable among trends after 1960 was the attempt to decentralize a number of aspects of control over the system. This development ran counter to the general thrust of political development in most of the world. At the time of writing there was no certainty that it would in the long run succeed. There was always the possibility that the outcome would be the development at the local level of all the rigidities and inefficiencies of a highly centralized bureaucracy without compensating advantages. Much would depend on the continuance and strengthening of intelligent local interest and willingness to participate.

FOUR

Province and university come to terms

Some comments were made in chapter 2 about the effects on the universities of the rising demand for higher education during the post-war period. The rapid evolution of the relationship between the universities and the provincial government will be explored further in this chapter, although not in the detail to be found in various parts of *Ontario's Educative Society*.* On the whole, this evolution may be regarded as a successful one. However there were some major problems in the early 1970s relating to rising costs, which were continuing to demand maximum efficiency of expenditure and perhaps the curtailment of more of the universities' traditional rights and privileges. There was a continuing, and perhaps growing, danger that what appeared to be economy and efficiency to the public and to government officials might prove to be false economy in the long run.

The dangers inherent in government financing and the measure of government control that goes with it have often been stated. A government – any government – even though it may approve in principle the pursuit of knowledge for its own sake, has difficulty recognizing the value of certain literary or other cultural studies, or even of highly theoretical scientific investigations, when there seems to be only enough money to finance more immediately practical activities. Crash programs designed to produce more doctors, engineers, teachers, or whatever else is in short supply threaten to take precedence over everything else. Thus the institution tends to find its program bent and, by its own criteria, distorted. A second major problem area is that government representatives may easily persuade themselves that they are better judges of the way certain ends can be achieved than are university people themselves. There is always the possibility, of course, that they may be right. Some professors may be inefficient as teachers, wedded to outdated methods, and unshakeably biased against modern media which might be of great assistance to them in accomplishing their purposes. But the possibility that civil servants know more about university affairs than do university people themselves, who have often been intimately involved in such matters for many years, is not ordinarily very likely. Also, any change that has to be enforced by

*See volume II, chapter 12, and volume IV, chapter 2 of ONTARIO'S EDUCATIVE SOCIETY.

officialdom runs a serious risk of being misguided, and is certain to destroy the sense of responsibility that alone can ensure a productive relationship between teachers and students. A third danger is that the university may be destroyed as a centre of productive dissent and creative scholarship, both pure and applied. While it would be out of character for an Ontario government to demand the dismissal of university people who are too critical of its policies and actions, it is much easier to imagine that potential critics will adopt a softer line if their promotion and salaries have any direct relation to government favour.

There is a definite distinction between university autonomy and academic freedom. A university could in theory have relatively complete control over its own affairs and yet tolerate little internal dissent, whether it was governed by an autocrat, an oligarchy, or a democratically chosen body. Some recent demands by radical students that the university be dominated by faculty and students have caused apprehension, not so much because that form of government is in itself suspect, but because of the accompanying campaign for institutional commitment to political or social causes. Once there is a party line, dissenters are immediately put on the defensive, if they are tolerated at all. Conversely, it would be theoretically possible for a university to be administered as a department of government and still allow full academic freedom. Whereas there are tendencies for officialdom to suppress disagreement, to conceal sensitive matters, and to silence criticism, these inclinations can be resisted by inspired government leaders to whom the values of academic freedom are a reality. For the most part, despite the possibility of exceptions, academic freedom has been considered to be in the safest hands when the universities have been autonomous. This assumption is based on a long tradition stemming from the struggles of the mediaeval university against church and state.

Integration into provincial systems of education in a federal state presents the universities with special dangers in connection with their dual role of creating and disseminating knowledge. Provincial governments tend to feel most of the pressure from would-be students and parents for opportunities for study at the university level, and are most concerned with ensuring that the universities develop as teaching institutions. Operating from a somewhat more remote perspective, the federal government seems in a better position to support their research role. However, because of certain provinces' claim to exclusive jurisdiction in the educational field, the federal government has tended to play its part reluctantly and with constant apprehension over the constitutional controversies it is likely to arouse. Thus the universities are in constant danger of being starved for research funds.

During the period covered in this volume, most of the Ontario universities existed by virtue of provincial legislation. As an exception, Queen's had to appeal to the federal instead of the provincial government for an amendment to its charter. Whatever differences there might be in terms of the chartering authority, university acts were similar in that they outlined the structure in a fairly general fashion, without attempting, either in their own provisions or in the regulations approved under their authority, to define internal relationships in detail as was done with respect to the school system in the five major school acts consolidated in 1954.[1] This situation helped to safeguard the freedoms enjoyed by universities operating in the western tradition. Equally important was the fact that the acts did not give any outside authority the power to regulate programs, examinations, textbooks, or any other aspect of the educational process as the minister of education might do with reference to schools. Such powers of this nature that were mentioned were traditionally assigned to the senate of each university.

There was, of course, a certain amount of legislation passed to define the new relations developed in recent years. Far more important, however, were certain informal procedures designed to ensure the desired outcomes without the necessity of overt compulsion. The fact that major changes were brought about in this way did much to ensure the perpetuation of valuable traditions.

The nineteenth-century universities did not regard themselves as provincial institutions. They were established largely on the initiative of religious groups, although seeking legal and official status. The designation "the provincial university" which came to be applied to the University of Toronto thus distinguished that institution rather sharply from the others. It was apparently considered politically expedient for the government to offer small legislative grants to Queen's, Victoria, Trinity, Ottawa, Regiopolis, and St Michael's, which far from balanced the huge land grant set aside in 1797 for King's College, which was established many years after that date as the nucleus of the provincial university. It was also politically feasible for the government to announce the termination of these grants in 1867. All the institutions concerned were able to surmount the resulting crisis and to carry on with their meagre resources.

From that time on it was consistent government policy not to use public funds to support any institution under denominational control. Provincial subsidies became available, at first on a small scale, only to those that were prepared to place a lay board of governors or trustees in command. For a time the policy was even more restrictive, and support was provided only for institutions under direct government control, such as the Ontario Agricultural College and the School of Practical Science. Principal Grant of Queen's University secured some relaxation of this position in 1893 when he got a small grant for the School of Mining and Agriculture, established in Kingston the year before. Support was obtained on the same basis for the Faculty of Education, which was set up at the same university in 1909. More important were the regular maintenance grants which the University of Toronto began to receive in 1901, and which were extended to Queen's in 1907–8 and to the University of Western Ontario in 1910–11.[2] For many years these three institutions remained the only recipients of provincial subsidies, which by the early 1940s reached about $3 million a year. The amount given to each university was determined on an entirely arbitrary basis.

The immediate post-war period constituted an unusual interlude in which university operations were supported by large infusions of federal government funds. Not only did veterans receive substantial financial assistance, but the universities themselves were subsidized as well so that they could handle the emergency demands placed upon them. The arrangement was a kind of contractual one that left no particular residue in terms of precedents that might be followed later. By 1950 an increasing proportion of the depleted age group from which university students were drawn began to seek admission, and there was more talk of society's obligation to extend the opportunity for higher education to all qualified applicants, as well as of the beneficial effects of such a policy for the society that adopted it. The development of this attitude had major implications for university-government relationships.

As long as provincial grants were small, an erratic and inconsistent method of distributing them could be tolerated. When they began to reach substantial sums, however, some system of fair and effective apportionment had to be developed if charges of government favouritism, or even of corruption, were to be avoided. It was obvious by 1957 that this point was being reached. The provincial budget for that year projected operating grants of $9.4 million and a further $9.7 million to be added to the capital grants of $17.6 million made available during the previous five-year period.

There was no parallel between provincial assistance and the grants which the federal government began to make in 1951–2 for the support of provincial institutions. For the latter level of government it was possible to avoid the necessity and opprobrium of control by basing the amount each province received on its population. The mechanics of the procedure were taken care of by the National Conference of Canadian Universities. The universities received their individual allotments of funds on the basis of their proportion of the total full-time enrolment of all the universities in the province. The assumption that these funds would be properly spent actually depended on an implicit guarantee of the status of the institutions and the quality of their programs that the provincial governments would increasingly be expected to provide. Not even the federal government can spend large sums of money without eventually insisting on some kind of an accounting.

There was some hope in university circles during the 1950s that the continued autonomy of the universities could be safeguarded if they could successfully cultivate a variety of contributors. Major drives were mounted for donations from the general public and from corporate interests. Student fees were raised regularly and by fairly substantial amounts. Some spoke of policies of exclusion, which could not have held down most operating costs but might have kept capital expansion within bounds. It gradually became clear, however, that students had to be accommodated, that fees could not be raised without limit, and that private donors would not or could not provide a major part of the needed resources. There was no alternative to increased reliance on the provincial government.

Up to the early 1950s, co-ordination among the provincial universities was almost completely lacking. There was no provision for their administrators to meet regularly for consultation, much less for co-ordination of their plans. They were regarded in many respects as competitors, with no over-riding responsibility for the welfare of the province as a whole. There was thus a strong possibility that government funds might be used to subsidize overlapping or duplicated programs while areas of need, according to public criteria, would be neglected. Premier Frost took the first step toward co-ordination by appointing R.C. Wallace, retired principal and vice-chancellor of Queen's University, to act as an adviser. After his death, he was succeeded briefly in this capacity by J.G. Althouse and then by Dana Porter.

The next step, taken in 1958, involved the formation of a University Committee under the chairmanship of C.F. Cannon, chief director of education, with J.R. McCarthy, assistant superintendent of curriculum in the Department of Education, acting as secretary. The other three members were all senior civil servants, and the academic community was without representation. This situation caused a good deal of concern in the universities, but it was some years before there was a change. The committee began to take steps to improve the basis for university grants by collecting information from each university, including enrolment by faculty and year, salary scales for each academic rank, the number of instructors at each level, operating income and expenditure, and a projection of capital building programs. Such data were used in a process which remained somewhat mysterious to the universities, to say nothing of the general public, for the distribution of operating and capital grants. Each university in effect made the strongest possible plea for the funds it thought it could use, and hoped for the best.

The committee was renamed the Advisory Committee on University Affairs in 1961, and its membership was extended to include senior elected officials and members of the business community. J.P. Robarts, then minister of education, became chairman while J.R. McCarthy continued as secretary. Dana Porter succeeded Robarts when the latter became prime minister, and Leslie Frost joined the committee to fill the remaining vacancy. The academic community was still unrepresented. The increased membership made no basic change in the procedure for distributing grants, although greater amounts of information became available and the most seasoned judgment was brought to bear in the process of

making recommendations. It was inevitable that some universities believed that they did not receive their fair share in relation to the contribution they were making.

At this time there was a rising demand for the establishment of a body
somewhat like the University Grants Committee in Great Britain. Such
a body, standing between the government and the universities and completely independent of both, would apportion a lump sum provided by
the government in accordance with its appraisal of each university's
needs. The advantages of this type of arrangement were articulated with
particular effectiveness by J. Bascom St John. Another proposal, which
Claude T. Bissell outlined in his annual report as president of the University of Toronto as early as 1960, would involve the use of a grants formula based on an estimate of the costs of different types of programs ranging from three-year arts and science to expensive graduate work. There
would have to be special consideration for new institutions which had to
deal with low enrolment and unusual initial costs.[3]

In 1963 the newly formed Ontario Council of University Faculty Associations made a plea to the prime minister to adopt a more systematic and
consistent policy for supporting the universities, to be worked out in consultation with university spokesmen. It urged that both capital and maintenance grants be guaranteed for a period of several years so that each
university could plan its projects and facilities on a long-term basis. The
council reiterated Bissell's point that account should be taken of the varying costs of different programs. It expressed opposition to any attempt to
tie all grants to specific purposes, since such an approach would involve
the government to an unacceptable degree in the internal academic policies of the universities.[4] Many of the suggestions offered in the council's
brief actually foreshadowed arrangements that were made over the next
few years. The chief difference was that much of the discretion that the
council would have left in the hands of a grants committee like that in
the United Kingdom was eliminated by the nature of the grants formulas.

The Academic Advisory Committee recommended by OCUFA would
have been made up largely by people actively engaged in university teaching, research, or administration, supplemented by others, including government representatives. It would have had enough staff members and
resources to collect and publish statistics relating to the universities and
to undertake research studies. These were of course types of activities that
the existing Advisory Committee could engage in up to the limit of its
resources, which were not very great. OCUFA was asking both for a committee with a different composition and a much larger role.

The Advisory Committee did make some very useful contributions. Its
recommendations led to such projects as the Extended Graduate Program,
the Ontario New Universities Library Project, the Ontario Graduate Fellowship Program, and the expansion of teaching facilities for medical and
dental education. The initiative for most of such programs actually came,

however, from the Committee of Presidents of Universities of Ontario, as it eventually came to be called, which found means of commissioning a number of studies on which it based its recommendations. This body began to meet informally in 1962 to deal with problems confronting the whole university community. The first of these meetings was actually summoned by the Advisory Committee to discuss rapidly expanding enrolments. The immediate consequences were studies indicating the steps that would have to be taken to meet the challenge of the anticipated expansion. The work of the Committee of Presidents was supplemented by studies undertaken at the national level, such as the one leading to the publication of *Financing Higher Education in Canada*, a report produced under the chairmanship of Dean Vincent Bladen of the University of Toronto.[5]

By the end of the year the presidents decided to form themselves into a regular although informal organization with a chairman, a vice-chairman, and a secretary. For the time being they operated without a constitution and avoided formulating any statement of specific aims. Yet it was clearly their intention to attempt to co-ordinate some of the activities of their respective institutions, to engage in long-term planning, to prod the Advisory Committee to support certain lines of action, and in general to prevent the development of a vacuum into which the government might be forced to move. The organization was in a position from the beginning to commission research, since it was possible to make administrative arrangements for competent university people to work on needed projects.

The Committee of Presidents had a number of obvious limitations. It could not infringe on the prerogatives of boards of governors by committing individual universities to any particular course of action, despite the fact that its recommendations might be expected to carry a good deal of weight. On issues where the interests of a president's own university seemed to be in conflict with those of some of the others, or with those of the group as a whole, he could not be expected to act with complete impartiality. He was, after all, primarily a servant of his constituency, and was committed to helping it attain the highest levels of scholarship and teaching. There was still a good deal of the old competitive spirit among different institutions. The ambiguity of the presidents' position was particularly serious when provincial grants were awarded on an arbitrary basis. Individual presidents were considered quite capable of putting over a deal with the authorities behind the backs of their fellows, who thus had to be a little wary of one another, even though they handled the situation with gentlemanly equanimity. A further factor that militated against strong action was that all universities, whether large or small, had the same representation. A decision had to have unanimous approval. It was thus impossible to deal satisfactorily with such issues as whether it would be in the best interests of the province to concentrate graduate studies and large-scale research in a limited number of universities, or a single one, or to spread them more widely. As time went on, and Duff and Berdahl came and went, university faculties became less willing to let their chief administrators speak for them.* Yet it was not simply representation on a larger co-ordinating body that the "democrats" wanted. Too much co-ordination of any kind seemed to pose a threat to the kind of internal self-government that was developing.

A major development of 1964 was the establishment of the Department of University Affairs. Apart from the obvious task of relieving the Department of Education of the administrative tasks arising out of the activities of the Advisory Committee, there was considerable initial uncertainty about the nature of this department's role. Prime Minister Robarts clarified matters in an address to the Legislature by referring to the increasing complexity of problems relating to the growth of the universities and to the need to study them on a continuous basis.[6] Thus the new department became identified as the instrument for carrying out government financial policies with respect to the universities, for maintaining continuous liaison with them, and for engaging in a broad spectrum of research. Among its specific tasks would be to receive submissions for capital assistance from the Universities Capital Aid Corporation, which was set up in the same session of the Legislature, and to approve them in the name of the minister. Further, it would develop procedures for the detailed discussion of building plans with each university, maintaining consultation on a year-round basis; it would administer all major programs of government aid to students and try to co-ordinate them with those of other agencies in order to avoid duplication; it would review all proposed legislation affecting universities and make appropriate recommendations; and it would devise and recommend to the government special programs to meet particular needs. In the area of liaison with the universities, it would work with them in a non-prescriptive fashion to develop and co-ordinate plans for expansion in various faculties, schools, and courses. In actual fact, the legislation which established the department mentioned hardly any of the functions that Robarts outlined, thus leaving it without any substantial formal powers of coercion.

Some people felt that the creation of the Department of University Affairs would obviate the need for the continued existence of the Advisory Committee. University representatives, however, were apprehensive about the increase in direct government control that such a development implied. They were thus reassured when the government promised that the committee would be continued. A further step in the desired direction was taken in the fall of 1964 when Davis, as minister of university affairs,

*Sir James Duff and Robert O. Berdahl were commissioned in 1963 by the Association of Universities and Colleges of Canada and the Canadian Association of University Teachers to study the whole question of Canadian university government. They produced a report in 1966 called *University Government in Canada*, which had a great deal of influence on the development of faculty participation in university control and administration.

enlarged the committee by adding five members from a list supplied by the presidents and faculty associations, and renamed it the Committee on University Affairs.

There were now three bodies concerned to some degree with the need to develop a system of universities offering assurance that public money would be spent with a reasonable degree of efficiency and effectiveness and that a satisfactory range of provincial needs would be met. Yet no single one of them, nor all of them put together, could allocate specific roles, guarantee that needed programs were introduced and maintained, or take decisive action to prevent wasteful duplication. There were no strong incentives for particular universities to engage in critical self-examination with a view to eliminating unproductive activities. In fact, there was a distinct possibility that the reward for greater efficiency in operation would be a reduction in provincial grants.

The government seemed determined to avoid removing the essence of university autonomy. Yet at this stage a trend was developing that seemed likely to produce the very situation that no one wanted. Late each fall, each universiy submitted a summary of anticipated expenditures along with an audited statement of expenditures during the previous academic year. The civil servants who had to recommend the amount of individual grants studied these statements carefully. Since it was not at the time government policy to discuss the details of requests with university officials, there was a danger that errors might be made and that too much or too little money might be granted. It seemed inevitable that pressure to eliminate such errors would lead to government requests for more detailed information, for more careful checking, for more guarantees of accuracy, and for more adequate university justification. There would be steps to standardize the procedure for the sake of efficiency and in the name of fairness to all. Ultimately the universities' freedom of action would be gone and their financial affairs would be managed in a manner that would be indistinguishable from that of regular government departments.

There was considerable awareness among members of the university community of the dangers that lay ahead. The Committee of Presidents took a number of actions that may be regarded in whole or in part as evidence of such awareness. While there had been some satisfaction at the transformation of the Advisory Committee into a Committee on University Affairs with academic representation, and with an assurance from Robarts at one stage that it would have a role that would be substantially the same as that of a grants commission on the British model, performance fell disappointingly short of promise. The presidents therefore pressed assiduously for a full-time chairman and for more adequate means of carrying out the committee's objectives. They also made overtures, some of which were successful, for more co-operation between the two committees.

The government ended a period of apparent uncertainty by appointing

D.T. Wright to take office as permanent chairman at the beginning of 1967. This action placed the Committee on University Affairs on an entirely new level of influence. A second development that seemed to reflect the presidents' desire to defend university autonomy with more vigour consisted of measures to strengthen their own organization. They adopted a constitution in 1966 which, among other things, made provision for the executive vice-chairman as the senior paid officer. Increasing amounts of money were subsequently made available to maintain the activities of the secretariat. E.F. Sheffield and J.B. Macdonald served in succession as executive vice-chairman.

The minister took the opportunity at the Frank Gerstein lectures at York University in 1966 to express considerable dissatisfaction with the existing situation. He offered the view that university autonomy was not an inherent right or even essential in a democratic society. It was desirable only if the universities showed themselves able and willing to accept the responsibility that went with it. Such responsibility included not only fiscal accountability and economy of operation, but also a full recognition of the ways in which the universities could contribute to meeting the total needs of society. The situation demanded greater co-operation and co-ordination among universities than had ever been known before.

Davis proceeded to pose a number of questions, and to answer them in a way that did not show the universities in a very good light. He asked first whether the universities had given full recognition to the need for economy and taken steps to practise it. His negative answer was implied in a further series of questions relating to the use of research to improve teaching methods, the adoption of new techniques and devices, and the adjustment of old concepts about what was proper for higher education. He noted with a suggestion of disfavour the intention of the universities to reduce their student/teacher ratio in 1966–7 to a point definitely lower than that of the previous year, and substantially below that of reputable institutions in Michigan and California. Davis's second major question was whether boards of governors should launch new programs and projects without an assurance of the government funds needed to support them. During the previous four months, some of the major undertakings such as medical centres, new colleges of special types, and new faculties, departments, and programs had been announced without any consultation with the Committee on University Affairs. The third question was whether the universities could curtail the non-constructive aspects of competitiveness which then prevailed. Davis took particular exception to the attempt to use government money for student awards designed to lure students to particular institutions. Another aspect of the same problem was touched upon in the fourth question. All the universities were scouring the market for scarce library materials to augment their own collections rather than working out plans for sharing them. The development of graduate studies in general would also require careful co-ordination and the sharing of scarce resources, along with a willingness on the part of some universities to defer entry into certain fields until such action was clearly justified. In a fifth question, Davis wondered whether the universities could work in close co-operation with other institutions at the post-secondary level. He was thinking of the new system of colleges of applied arts and technology just being launched. An important ingredient in their success would be a realization on the part of university officials of their potential contribution.

At the end of the same year, the appearance of the *Report of the Commission to Study the Development of Graduate Programmes in Ontario Universities,*[7] commonly referred to as the Spinks report, suggested a way in which some of the problems involving co-ordination and efficiency of operation might be solved. Established on the joint initiative of the Committee on University Affairs and the Executive Committee of the Committee of Presidents, the commission's main task was to study graduate education and research in the universities of the province and to make recommendations with respect to future development in these areas. The commission did in fact make many specific and useful recommendations falling within its terms of reference in the narrower sense. These were that the provincial government adopt a method of determining operating and capital grants that would permit rational forward planning, that it take appropriate steps to ensure co-ordination and co-operation among the universities in the field of graduate studies and research, and that a number of centres of excellence be developed in Ontario universities. Because it found existing structures inadequate to implement these recommendations, the commission thought it advisable to go further. Comment was made on "the complete absence of a master plan, of an educational policy, and of a co-ordinating authority for the provincially-supported institutions."[8] Condemnation of an absence of co-operation and of wastefulness and lack of concern for the public interest was even stronger than that of Davis in the Gerstein lectures.

The commission saw a need for a strong co-ordinating agency to develop a rational fiscal policy and a sound academic policy. This agency would maintain common standards of admission and degree requirements, allocate capital and operating budgets, ensure the development of libraries on a provincial scale, and carry out other aspects of a master plan. The name suggested for the required agency was the University of Ontario. This entity would be headed by a president or chancellor who would preside over a board of regents consisting of the minister of university affairs, the minister of education, and the provincial treasurer serving *ex officio,* and about fifteen lay members. These lay members, representing such interests as industry, banking, management, labour, and communications, as well as the geographic regions of the province, would be chosen for their public prominence and their interest in and knowledge of higher education. They would be appointed by the Lieutenant-Governor-in-Council to serve for periods of at least five years. Subcommittees of the board would deal with such matters as long-range planning, graduate academic policy, budget and finance, libraries and buildings, and campus development. Direct contact would be maintained between the board and the universities through the Committee of Presidents, the Committee of Graduate Deans, the Committee of Librarians, and others as needed. An academic senate, consisting of three senior faculty members and a member of the board of governors from each of the fourteen provincial universities, would co-ordinate internal affairs. It would operate through committees dealing with graduate programs, departments, institutes, research centres, and schools. It would meet in plenary session about twice a year to vote on committee reports and prepare recommendations for transmission to the board of regents.

The commission minimized the extent to which the University of Ontario would interfere with or restrict the structure or activities of individual universities. Each of them would retain its board of governors, its senate, its executive and administrative officers, its alumni body, and its regional constituency. Each would make its own appointments and promotions and control its curricula and courses of study. The commission believed that the only powers that would be lost would be those that permitted unproductive competition. The academic community would be enabled to control its own affairs and forestall the imposition of government regulation.

University spokesmen did not place quite the same interpretation on the proposals. The implications seemed to be an unacceptable loss of autonomy which they had no intention of accepting voluntarily. The commissioners were criticized for being too much impressed by the co-ordinated system which had been developed in California, and for failing to realize the diversity in character that existed in Ontario universities. One president viewed with disfavour the new level of bureaucracy that would have to be created while another felt that the power of decision would be removed too far from individual members of the university community. The government appeared to be equally unenthusiastic, and was even accused in the Legislature of having information leaked about the key recommendations before the report itself was released so that a negative reaction would be built up ahead of time.

The plain fact was that the proposed development, whether or not it was logical and desirable in principle, was too drastic for Ontario, where "quiet evolution" was the rule. Despite the stern lecture that Davis had so recently delivered, the government was far from ready to abandon methods of persuasion to secure greater co-ordination and efficiency of operation. Adverse reaction to the costs of higher education had not yet reached the point where the public could have been counted upon to support what would certainly have been a challenge to most of the university community. There were suspicions also that the government was reluctant to create a structure that might have become difficult to deal with. Once in existence, the monster would have been practically impossible to destroy.

It would perhaps be an exaggeration to suggest that university leaders were frightened into a policy of greater co-operation. Yet coincidentally or otherwise, a series of developments occurred which removed some of the most obvious grounds for criticism of wasteful duplication. An Advisory Committee on Graduate Studies, originally established in April 1964, was transformed into the Ontario Council on Graduate Studies in December 1966, about the time the Spinks Commission report was creating such a furor. This council accepted the view of the commission that, while all the universities should offer honours and masters' programs in at least some of the central disciplines, doctoral programs should be limited to those institutions where adequate funds and facilities were available. It proceeded to develop an appraisals procedure by which a stamp of approval for proposed masters' and doctors' programs could be sought from an impartial panel of experts from the university community, both inside and outside the province. The fact that most of the verdicts proved to be favourable did not mean that the procedure was operated leniently, since most universities made a serious effort to ensure beforehand that they could meet the minimum requirements. The government added an element of seriousness which was not entirely to the liking of some academics when it made financial support of gradate programs dependent on approval obtained through the appraisals procedure.

A second proposal advanced at an early stage by the council was that the universities, through province-wide inter-university consultations within individual disciplines and professions, attempt to divide responsibility for specific fields of graduate work among themselves. Some apparent progress was made when a large number of disciplines organized themselves for discussion. There was agreement on a number of matters, such as that the special character of each discipline should be outlined, that an inventory should be compiled to indicate graduate programs in existence and in the planning stage, that consideration should be given to the feasibility of opening a limited number of graduate courses in one university in a region to graduate students in a nearby university, and that the disciplines should attempt to discover undeveloped areas of graduate studies research that ought to receive attention. The actual results were not very satisfactory, however, and independent or semi-independent program initiatives remained at the centre of the problem of university co-ordination. The Committee of Presidents circulated proposals in 1970 to deal more effectively with the matter by setting up an Advisory Sub-committee on Academic Planning. The Ontario Confederation of University Faculty Associations presented an unofficial working paper in September of that year pointing out the threat to the prerogatives of the senates of individual universities. It was suggested that, even though the academic policies that the Committee of Presidents worked out might be considered as purely voluntary, the government might make them coercive by withholding grants to universities that refused to accept them.[9] After offering a number of other criticisms, the working paper outlined an alternative that involved continued decentralization of the process.

A third area in which the council became involved was that of library co-ordination. As early as 1963 the Committee of Presidents sponsored a study which showed that a shortage of librarians threatened to impede the rapid development of university services. Several recommendations were made to the Advisory Committee on University Affairs and a Sub-committee on Librarianship was established. In 1965 a Committee on the Co-ordination of Academic Library Services undertook to study the matter suggested in its title. After the appearance of the Spinks report the Ontario Council on Graduate Studies took steps to develop a provincial library system for the universities. Central to this system was the proposed Humanities and Social Sciences Research Library at the University of Toronto, which ultimately came to be named after the retired Prime Minister, J.P. Robarts. Its bibliographic centre was to have an up-to-date registry in machine-readable form of all catalogue data from Ontario universities and other sources which would be at the service of any library in the system. The Ontario Council of University Librarians studied the feasibility of other co-ordinating measures. In April 1967 the Committee of Presidents accepted a proposal by the Spinks Commission that a transit system be adopted as a means of sharing the total library resources of the province for graduate study purposes. Under the management of York University, the scheme involved daily contact among the twelve universities in the southern part of the province. Arrangements were later made to transport graduate students and visiting scholars, as well as library materials, from one centre to another.

In 1968, under threat of a restriction on capital funds for library expansion, the Committee of Presidents asked the Ontario Council of University Librarians to estimate the university library facilities that would be needed by 1976. A preliminary report was submitted in April 1969 based on actual and current enrolment, current and projected numbers of staff and reader seats, and projected volume holdings. Later efforts resulted in an estimate of the total capital investment that would be required to meet expected needs during the period in question.

Major steps were taken in 1967 to co-ordinate admissions procedures when the Ontario Universities' Council on Admissions recommended the use of a common general application form. The scheme, as approved by the Committee of Presidents and put into effect in 1968, enabled a university to get a reasonable estimate of its student enrolment for a given year by eliminating multiple applications. Students were expected to list on the form the universities they were interested in attending in order of preference. The universities agreed to accept candidates, provisionally or finally, only after a specified date, and candidates were expected to accept an offer by another specified date. After the latter action was taken, the university in question notified the others. Measures were also taken to tie the award and acceptance of scholarships to the same dates.

Other areas of co-operation included television services and data processing. An Ontario Universities' Television Council was established in 1965 to advise and assist universities on request in the development and use of television for teaching purposes. This body exerted considerable influence toward the establishment of the Ontario Educational Communications Authority which began to function in 1970. An effort was made to provide some of the same services offered by the council to all Canadian universities through an AUCC agency. In the area of computer services, advice on the development, co-ordination, and financing of facilities was sought from a Subcommittee on Computer Services of the Committee of Presidents, established in 1967. A preliminary proposal was that there be computer facilities in each university to look after local needs, with supplementary regional centres to look after the more complex operations. Doubts about the desirability of investing in regional centres led in 1969 to the establishment of a Joint Ad-Hoc Subcommittee on Regional Computing Centres, consisting of members of the Committee of Presidents and the Committee on University Affairs. At an early stage this subcommittee advocated a regional computing centre in Toronto, with a large computer operated co-operatively by the universities. When it was realized that the capacity of such a computer would be inadequate to meet existing and future needs, reliance on commercial computer utility services was acknowledged as a superior alternative either to the establishment of a single large centre or to the further development of large centres at individual universities.

All these developments made a contribution to the moulding of the universities into a system in which their individual autonomy would be preserved. By far the most effective safeguard for autonomy, however, resulted from the development of formula financing. The essence of this approach, foreshadowed some years before it was instituted in suggestions made by various university spokesmen, was that each university's grants would be based on the size of its enrolment. Since costs varied by program, faculty, school, year, and other such factors, per student allowances would have to be weighted according to some rationale. Once each university's total allotment was calculated, it was, for the time being, at least, permitted to distribute the amount largely according to its internally-established priorities. There would be built-in incentives for efficiency, since money saved on one activity was available for expenditure on something else.

Although the government accepted the principle of formula financing as early as 1965, it took considerable time to work out the details. Some of the necessary work had actually been initiated earlier by the Presidents' Research Committee, which commissioned a study and a working paper early in 1964. A sub-committee of the Committee on University Affairs combined its efforts with those of the Presidents' Research Committee, and a report, acceptable to the CUA and the Committee of Presidents, was prepared. The formula which took effect in 1967 covered all maintenance costs, the purchase of books for libraries, the purchase of all equipment except that required for new buildings, and all ordinary costs of operation. The initial unit was based on a calculation of average costs, and was expected to be adjusted upward as these increased. It was no doubt inevitable from the outset that university representatives and government officials would disagree on the amount of the increase provided each year.

According to the scheme, most students were placed in one of eight basic categories with different weights to be multiplied by the unit value. A value of 1 was assigned to those in the first category, which included general arts, general science, pre-medicine, pre-business administration, pre-commerce, journalism, secretarial science, social work, first year honour arts and science, technology at Lakehead University, and undergraduate diploma courses. Higher categories had weights ranging up to 6 in category 8, which applied to PhD work except for the first year direct from the bachelor's degree. Part-time undergraduate students were initially given one-sixth of the weight of full-time students working toward the same degree, part-time graduate students doing course work were given one-fifth the weight of the full-time equivalent in the same category, and graduate students doing dissertations under supervision were given a weight of 1.

The need for modifications was soon apparent. For example, the practice of counting graduate students on a semester-by-semester basis was found to reduce the amount obtained on their behalf to a level below that intended. By 1969 it was evident that medical internship and residence, medicine, veterinary medicine, and dentistry had been assigned weights that were too low, and these were accordingly increased. Part-time graduate work was upgraded to receive one-third the weight of full-time work. Blurring of the distinction between general and honours courses at the University of Toronto had to be recognized in such a way as to avoid penalizing innovation. The process of examination and modification promised to be a continuous one.

Although a particular university could decide how it wished to distribute its funds over specific programs, broad control could of course be exercised by a manipulation of the weighting factors. The controlling agency could make it relatively profitable or unprofitable to offer general courses, honours courses, graduate work at a particular level, or anything else it wished to influence. Whether the universities were placed at the direct service of the economy, relatively speaking, or encouraged to add to the cultural resources of the province and the country would depend on what interests were paramount. Thus a great deal depended on the composition of the Committee on University Affairs, which made what were ostensibly recommendations, but in fact could be treated as decisions. The Committee of Presidents could of course bring pressure to bear for specific changes, which it did after the initial operation of the scheme revealed certain weaknesses.

There was one problem for which there was no easy solution. While individual universities obviously had to be prevented from offering substantially the same course to uneconomically small groups of students simply to round out their program, there was a strong case for some university to devise unique offerings which, although appealing to few students, would make an important contribution to the development of individual students and possibly of the discipline itself. Some courses had to be given on a trial basis in order to prove their interest or value before they could be expected to attract a reasonable enrolment. The formula approach tended to militate against such offerings in favour of those with proven attractions. There was a danger that the money-maker among university officials would be more highly regarded than the innovator. The formula system had been in use for only a short time before complaints were heard that this situation was acutally developing.

It was impossible to apply the formula without modification to the newer universities, since they had to operate under high cost conditions. In order to provide a reasonably attractive program, they had to offer courses that were initially only partly filled. These could be financed only with the assitance of extra-formula grants. Special allowances were also given to certain universities to help them launch expensive programs in such areas as medicine, dentistry, and library science, which were unquestionably needed for the welfare of the province. The normal expectation was that conditions requiring special consideration would ultimately disappear. An unusual situation existed in Laurentian University and the University of Ottawa, both of which were given a premium to defray the extra costs of operating on a bilingual basis.

Some of the problems involved in determining amounts of extra-formula support did not speak well for the ability or willingness of certain emergent universities to define their needs in a modest manner. When the Committee on University Affairs requested in 1967 that they produce their own financial projections, the results indicated that, when increased enrolments were taken into account, they expected a rising total in special assistance over the years. After holding a series of meetings with their representatives, the Committee on University Affairs produced its own recommendations, which would have ensured the phasing out of the grants within a definite time limit. The Committee of Presidents took the view, however, that the proposed rate of reduction was too harsh, and would cause unreasonable hardship. What followed was an example of the kind of give and take that characterized government-university relations during this period. The minister asked that a special study of the situation be made to establish the basis for a reasonable course of action. The committee formed to carry out this task, headed by M. Elizabeth Arthur, undertook a very thorough review of each university's program, giving consideration to details of course offerings, enrolment in individual courses, teaching loads, and other factors. The resulting report was critical of the inadequacy of the planning on which some of the claims for extra-formula support had been based. In certain cases there were no studies to show what could be accomplished with ordinary formula support. The committee urged such money-saving approaches as limitations on the growth of new courses and the addition of staff for undergraduate teaching, the elimination of some existing courses, and an effort to increase student numbers in others. An observation that caused some irritation in the universities in question was that there was too much copying of older universities and a lack of innovation.

While the search for a satisfactory method of making operating grants was in progress, attempts were also being made to solve the problem of capital grants. Certain administrative difficulties were overcome by the establishment in 1964 of the Ontario Universities Capital Aid Corporation, which enabled universities to escape the restrictions of appropriations from the Legislature covering a period of a single year, and facilitated long-term planning. There remained a number of difficulties which elicited expressions of dissatisfaction from the Committee of Presidents. Capital grants, which had to be approved by the Department of University Affairs without the intervention of the Committee on University Affairs, seemed, like operating grants, to be awarded on a somewhat mysterious and arbitrary basis. The absence of an over-all plan for expansion left individual universities in a constant state of uncertainty. A second cause for dissatisfaction was that the provincial contribution, which covered 85 per cent of the cost of approved academic facilities and 50 per cent of the cost of other approved projects, was proving inadequate. Donations from private sources were drying up as the government increasingly assumed financial responsibility. A third source of criticism was that student facilities tended to get eliminated from lists of approved projects, and a point was reached where some universities could provide few facilities except classrooms for their students.

The minister responded sympathetically to these problems in 1967 when he observed in the Legislature that he was looking forward to the development of a capital grant formula similar to that being introduced for operating grants.[10] An appropriate scheme had to provide for equality of distribution and for a method of control. The matter was studied by a Subcommittee on Capital Financing of the Committee of Presidents, which joined forces with the Committee on University Affairs and the Department of University Affairs. The complexity of the problem was indicated by the fact that the three overlapping phases of the program which this group outlined were to extend over the period from 1967 to 1975. A joint committee of the Committee on University Affairs and the universities arranged for studies of enrolment, available space, system resources such as libraries, computers, television, and residences, policies and practices for control of capital planning elsewhere, and the structure of the building industry.

While a preliminary formula was being worked out, a new capital grants policy was adopted for projects undertaken between 1964 and 1969. The government agreed to pay 85 per cent of the first $10 million for approved capital costs and 95 per cent of the remaining costs. The arrangement covered not only academic buildings and essential services, but also student unions, cafeterias, gymnasiums, and other such buildings. At the same time the Committee on University Affairs was given authority to review each university's plans as a whole and to assign priorities to its different projects.

For new construction, the basic formula approach involved the use of a "space standard" initially set at 130 net assignable square feet per full-time student. This figure could be multiplied by the projected enrolment figure to obtain an estimate of the total space requirement for all universities in the province in each year of a planning period. A cost estimate could be obtained, in turn, by multiplying this space requirement by a cost standard of a specified amount per square foot. The proportion of the total allotted to each university would be partially determined by the assignment of weights to various categories of enrolment reflecting their different space requirements. If each university was to be treated fairly, account had to be taken of existing usable space. This problem was very difficult because of the existence of widely differing styles of architecture and of varying amounts of decorative, nonfunctional, or unusable space. There seemed to be no way of dealing satisfactorily with replacements and renovations, land acquisitions, and general services and site development through regular formula methods, since these factors did not bear a linear relationship to the general development of capital facilities. They therefore had to be supported by special non-formula funds.

Like the operating grants formula, the scheme left room for the universities to determine their own capital spending priorities, and thus gave them a maximum of autonomy within a set of over-all restrictions. They had a powerful incentive to plan carefully and to spend parsimoniously in order to use funds to the best possible advantage. The effects of the new arrangement were almost immediately observable in the way in which internal administrative affairs in the universities were being conducted.

The remaining point at issue had to do with the total amount the provincial government felt the universities would need for capital expansion during the first half of the 1970s. In the fall of 1970 the Committee of Presidents, using certain enrolment projections worked out by the Dominion Bureau of Statistics, indicated that the intended capital grants would fall far short of enabling them to accommodate the expected number of students. The presidents felt that they would have no alternative to placing sharp limitations on admission. Their case was weakened by uncertainty about the validity of the enrolment projections they were using. There was some indication that the difficulty university graduates were experiencing in finding jobs would curb the future demand for university education. If it turned out, however, that students were merely diverted to the colleges of applied arts and technology, the government would face, not a lesser problem, but merely a different one.

A problem of an unfamiliar kind was encountered in the fall of 1971 when the most expansive enrolment projections proved to be over-inflated and actual enrolment showed a considerably smaller increase than had been expected. University officials, caught in some cases with excessive commitments for staff and facilities, blamed the Department of University Affairs for persuading them to rely on invalid projections. The new minister, John White, was unsympathetic to their plight, and proved unwilling to ease their financial problems to the extent they thought justifiable. There was a great deal of uncertainty as to whether the lower rate of increase in enrolment would be temporary, or whether a new trend was being established.

When all aspects of the co-ordinating machinery worked out during the 1960s were considered, the situation seemed more satisfactory than any alternative that had been suggested. There were criticisms, not unexpectedly, that the Committee on University Affairs had become almost indistinguishable from a government agency. This feeling was no doubt based on the fact that it had shown no hesitation in cracking down on the universities when their self-interest got too obviously in the way of their broader responsibilities. There was no evidence, however, that its members suppressed their better judgment in favour of some undesirable course of action that the government wanted followed.

The growing secretariat of the Committee of Presidents, renamed the Council of Ontario Universities, under the firm direction of J.B. Macdonald seemed to promise an expanding role for that body. There was, however, a potential threat to its continued effectiveness as a result of the growing power of university faculties and students operating through university government and through their own associations. The growth of university democracy placed increasing stress on participatory internal decision-making, and was thus essentially inimical to strong presidential action. The effects of having academic faculty members serve along with presidents on the councils was likely to reinforce this trend. Further, the growing power of the Ontario Confederation of University Faculty Associations showed signs of being exercised, not only against actions by the presidents that would in any way constitute commitments on behalf of their universities, but also against the collection of data and the conduct of studies that would provide the basis for such action. There was some apprehension that the leaders who were likely to be thrown up through the processes of internal self-government might fail to realize how vulnerable they would be to a government reflecting the attitude of a disgusted public if the universities themselves did not continue the moves toward self-co-ordination which in so many ways had been successfully began. There were grounds for apprehension lest staff and students concern themselves too exclusively with their own insitutions and lose sight of the fact that the universities must act as parts of a system.

In one major respect the co-ordinating structure was unable to deal effectively with important alternatives. It could only work toward increasing equality in standards, facilities, programs, and prestige among different universities. There was little possibility of dealing objectively with the question of whether the best interests of the province would be served by an official attempt to sustain a hierarchy of quality. Specifically, the University of Toronto, or perhaps some combination such as Toronto, McMaster, and Queen's could not be given financial assistance to achieve and maintain world-wide renown. If they did so, it would have to be by non-financial means. When there were protests from the University of Toronto in the fall of 1970 that existing tendencies were forcing it into a position of mediocrity, a common public reaction was that reprehensible elitist tendencies were being demonstrated, and should be counteracted without hesitation. This reaction may or may not have been sound, but the point is that no other could have been expected. The degree of public control attained in Ontario and the form in which it was exercised made levelling tendencies almost inevitable, although the strength of tradition might be counted on to ensure the continuation of substantial differences for many years to come. Existing methods of awarding research funds would do more than anything else to counteract equalizing tendencies. As long as the major grants went where there was the greatest concentration of expertise, certain centres would continue to attract the most highly qualified faculty members. The continued role of federal agencies in this field provided the strongest guarantee against change, since the main criterion for the award of grants by such agencies was the promise of success by the applicants.

DEVELOPMENTS AFTER DAVIS BECAME
PRIME MINISTER IN 1971

When he became minister of university affairs in early 1971, John White responded strongly to what was seen as the cost-cutting mood of the province. He promptly announced that he would make it his objective to reduce the number of staff in his new department by 10 per cent. On one occasion in the Legislature, he indicated that he planned to do so gradually during the following year.[11] At a meeting of the Committee of Presidents on March 12, 1971, he affirmed his belief that the previously favourable public attitude toward universities had to be regained. He felt, however, that costs could be controlled while the government at the same time continued its policy of widening accessibility.[12] In line with his objective, he announced at the beginning of the debate on the estimates of his department in the Legislature that he had reduced the amount of expenditure originally planned by $24.5 million. Particular attention was focused on the reduction of funds for graduate fellowships.

Speaking for the Liberal party, Tim Reid was pointing to what he saw as the failure of the Committee of Presidents to control duplication of expenditure, inefficiency, and under-utilization.[13] Among the examples he cited were facilities for educational television, which he believed could be productively shared among universities, colleges of applied arts and technology, and secondary schools. He also charged that there were no effective central review and control procedures in the field of library acquisitions. Further, he deplored the lack of a plan for the co-ordinated expansion of graduate programs in the universities as a group. He held the operation of the grant formula in part responsible for the difficulty. The solution Reid proposed on several occasions appeared to be a revival of the idea of the University of Ontario, as recommended in the Spinks report. If a co-ordinating body of that nature were established, and if the academics who formed a majority on it failed to perform according to a government's idea of efficiency, there might well be a temptation for the government to step in and run the machinery itself.

White was succeeded by G.A. Kerr in early 1972. Like Wells in education, Kerr was faced with the task of explaining the government's policy of financial restraints to various groups that would be adversely affected. There were particular protests over an announced increase of $100 per year in undergraduate student fees, the first general increase since 1964. Fees for graduate study rose by considerably greater amounts. It appeared that the government was attempting to reduce the surplus of recipients of graduate degrees by raising the financial barriers. The most serious objection to this policy was that arrangements for student assistance were not adjusted in such a way as to ensure that the added burden fell only on those best able to pay.

A major event of early 1972, as far as the universities were concerned, was the appearance of a *Draft Report* of the Commission on Post-Secondary Education in Ontario.[14] The substance of this report was presented in seventy-two recommendations, of which only the highlights can be presented here. A number of the recommendations centred around the principles of universal accessibility, openness of educational services, diversity of services, flexibility, and transferability from one post-secondary educational enterprise to another. These principles were based on the idea that every citizen should have the widest possible opportunity to continue his education beyond the secondary level, either on a full-time or on a part-time basis. This objective could be attained by appropriate funding policies on the part of the government, by flexible provisions for employment that would facilitate part-time study, and by the adaptation of formal programs to allow for more pertinent outside experience and for educational credit for such experience. Voluntary agencies would be given greater support in their efforts to offer opportunities for educational advancement.

One aspect of these proposals was that degrees and diplomas would be attainable, not only for work done within educational institutions, but also for evidence of comparable achievement under less formal circumstances. An "open university," the University of Ontario, would use communications media to reach members of the public who would otherwise be denied the necessary opportunities. There would also be a general evaluation service to examine candidates and award degrees on the basis of performance. By making degrees more readily available to those who could demonstrate the necessary competence, the commission hoped to reduce what it regarded as a common obsession with paper credentials.

At the same time facilities for formal education would be extended in a number of ways. In communities more than thirty miles from an existing university or a university-affiliated college, the colleges of applied arts and technology would offer university courses in affiliation with a provincially-assisted university. There would be satellite campuses in affiliation with existing universities where other facilities were not available. The establishment of small colleges in various locations throughout the province would be facilitated. Special grants would be made to libraries in communities beyond commuting range of a post-secondary educational institution so that they could provide materials for use in courses given by the University of Ontario.

The commission was opposed both to inflexible timetables and to fixed and rigid curricula. Courses were to be scheduled for both day and evening, and patterns of study where to be numerous and highly subject to individual choice. A student might even study at two institutions simultaneously while preparing for a degree at the University of Ontario.

As indicated in chapter 1, the commission was concerned over the temptation of the self-governing professions to erect artificial barriers to entrance in terms of formal educational qualifications that were not necessarily related to the skills needed in actual practice. Note was taken of the tendency to stipulate additional years of schooling or additional diplomas or degrees, often in any field at all. Doubt was expressed that many practising members of professions could pass the examinations now being set for entrants. The commission professed to believe that most of these practitioners were capable of reasonably adequate performance, and that the entrance qualifications were at fault. There was even more objection to the growing tendency of business organizations and government agencies to use formal educational attainments as criteria for job classifications and promotions when these had no obvious relationship to the skills required. The commission made the rather dubious recommendation that legislation should be enacted to prevent discrimination in employment because of attendance or non-attendance at educational institutions. It is hard to see how a legal distinction could be made between educational experiences that were relevant and those that were not.

Some of the most controversial recommendations had to do with financing post-secondary education. It was obvious that many of the commission's proposals would cost a good deal of money, and some means had to be found to square them with the public resistance to rising expenditure. The commission believed that one solution was a more assiduous search for economy of operation. Further, it proposed to separate the financing of research and other services from direct service to students and to charge the latter 50 per cent of the instructional costs incurred on their behalf. A more selective scheme of student assistance was recommended to ensure accessibility for poorer students. Those in better financial circumstances would have the opportunity to borrow from a fund maintained by the government.

The commission favoured open decision-making within institutions and supported the increased participation of faculty and students in the process. It also suggested that there should be adequate provision for public accountability. While it rejected centralized control as a means of attaining this objective, there was some doubt that the measures it proposed would have any other outcome. It recommended the establishment of a Senior Advisory Committee, with equal numbers of members from the public and from institutions of post-secondary education, to advise the minister on matters pertaining to post-secondary education, including the allocation of funds. There would also be three co-ordinating boards to deal respectively with the universities, the colleges of applied arts and similar institutions, and the open sector. Like the Senior Advisory Committee, the boards would have an even balance between public and institutional representatives. The board responsible for universities would have the power to decide where and when new undergraduate programs would be set up or abolished and what admission standards would be maintained. The other boards would have similar powers in their areas of responsibility.

The report was received, not unexpectedly, with mingled approbation and criticism. On the positive side, there was widespread approval of the commission's hope that educational opportunities could be spread more widely, and that society could be made more truly educative. Some of the means it proposed for reaching such objectives were applauded. A considerable number of academics felt, however, that the particular values of formal education were being underestimated. They feared that too enthusiastic an attempt to give educational credits for relevant work experience would be a blow to standards of excellence. It also seemed probable that the practice of awarding degrees and admission to the professions solely on the basis of success in examinations would have the same result. Many educators refused to concede that outcomes of education could be adequately measured by examinations. They also pointed out that, if an overwhelming proportion of those who sought educational or professional qualifications entirely by examination failed to meet a given standard, there would be tremendous pressure to lower that standard.

There was little disagreement with the view that degree worship had become a serious social evil, and should be effectively counteracted. Certain critics doubted, however, that the solution lay in making degrees more widely available. It seemed even less likely that effective results lay in legislating against discrimination in employment on the basis of paper qualifications. Ultimately the problem would have to be dealt with by a better public understanding of the real values of education and an increased ability to distinguish between appearance and substance.

A considerable amount of criticism centred around the cost of the proposed program. Some newspaper editorial writers suggested that the commission should have spent more time exploring means of financial retrenchment rather than in proposing schemes that would involve huge new expenditure. Other critics were concerned with the ways in which rising costs resulting from the implementation of the commission's recommendations would be met. Professors who believed that they could instruct effectively only if they had time for intensive preparation feared that the drive for efficiency would reduce their efforts to a routine, mechanical exercise. In their view, society would be better served if instruction of a high quality were provided for the few rather than dissipating scarce resources in attempting to educate everyone.

The proposal to exact a larger proportion of instructional costs from the student were received with considerable scepticism. Some were solicitous of the middle income group, whose children would receive comparatively little assistance from grants, and would have to supplement their own resources with loans. The commission seemed too sanguine in its belief that borrowing had become such a well established aspect of modern life that young people would not hesitate to incur debt against the hope of future earnings.

The plan for stronger government control over universities through a co-ordinating board aroused strong opposition from university spokesmen. It was feared that the board's proposed power to develop and abolish particular programs involved an intolerable amount of interference in academic affairs, and would constitute an unreasonable infringement on university autonomy. The chairman of the commission, D.T. Wright, was believed to feel, however, that the record of a number of universities in managing their own affairs had been so poor that some form of imposed co-ordination such as that proposed was inevitable. It was a question whether the final report of the commission, expected later in 1972, would involve any drastic change in the scheme.

FIVE

Educational agencies outside the formal system

A wide range of agencies apart from what was usually recognized as the formal educational system contributed to the process of education in Ontario during the period under review. Some of these had a primarily and others a secondarily or peripherally educational purpose. The total influence exerted by all of them together was very great. Brief consideration is given in the present chapter to four groups of such agencies: those operating under the jurisdiction or at least with the financial support of the Department of Education or the Department of University Affairs (reorganized in 1971 as the Department of Colleges and Universities), departments of the provincial government other than Education and University Affairs, federal government departments and agencies, and associations.

THE PUBLIC LIBRARY SYSTEM

The public library system, as already noted, was supervised by officials of the Provincial Library Service of the Department of Education. Local library boards, which exercised immediate responsibility, were a kind of counterpart to school boards, although appointed by other municipal agencies rather than being elected. The history of the public system was characterized by the struggle to replace inadequate private benevolence with substantial public support, to win recognition for the tremendous educative potential of public libraries, and to place libraries under the management of satisfactorily trained personnel. Although substantial improvements were made in the 1960s, a good deal remained to be done before these objectives were fully realized.

The first libraries in Ontario, apart from strictly private collections, appeared about 1800 on the initiative of local associations, which charged fees for their use. In the 1830s mechanics' institutes, which spread from the United Kingdom, began to receive government grants for their contributions to adult education and to the provision of library service. Those that survived in 1880 were placed under the supervision of the Department of Education. One of these became the central branch of the Toronto Public Library. Early library legislation included the Library Association and Mechanics Institute Act of 1851 and the Free Libraries Act of 1882. In the latter part of the nineteenth and the early twentieth centuries the population was served in part by association libraries and in part by tax-supported public libraries. Use of the former was restricted to subscribers, while the latter were accessible to local residents in general.

Legislation provided for the establishment of a public library on the passage of a by-law submitted to the electorate by the municipal council. Submission of such a by-law was mandatory on receipt of a petition from at least sixty qualified municipal voters in a city or town and at least thirty in a village. The controlling public library board consisted of three members appointed by each of the municipal council and the board of education and two by the separate school board, with the mayor or reeve as an *ex officio* member. The legislation required the council to provide funds at a minimum rate of 50¢ per capita. Larger cities established branches of the central or main library, and in some cases eventually extended their services by means of bookmobiles. Provision was made in due course for county councils to establish county public libraries, which also operated through branches and bookmobiles. County library co-operatives, to which association and municipal public libraries had the option of belonging, were a device for supplementing local efforts and extending service.

Since the establishment of public libraries was permissive rather than mandatory, much of the more sparsely settled part of the province was neglected. A submission of the Ontario Library Association to the Royal Commission on Education in 1945 indicated that about one-third of the population remained without service.[1] At that time over half the libraries were association libraries; since many operated on budgets of one or two hundred dollars a year, they were obviously in no position to act as a major educative force in their communities. There was an evident need for a co-ordinated organization, and the minimum level of public support, which had not been changed for decades, would have to be raised if adequate book stock, other materials, and trained librarians were to be provided. The Ontario Library Association advocated a whole series of reforms, including more adequate provincial supervision, larger provincial grants, and better provision for the training and certification of librarians.

An event indicative of increased official interest occurred in 1956, with the appointment by the provincial government of W. Stewart Wallace to study the need for a Provincial Library Service. Since Wallace's terms of reference were very limited, it is hardly surprising that he failed to recommend any drastic changes. His chief proposals were that the Provincial Libraries Branch of the Department of Education be renamed the Provincial Library Service, with an enlarged staff and role. It would provide interlibrary loans to small libraries and loans to people in areas without library service. Wallace failed to give a strong push to the formation of regional libraries, although he observed that, where these had been developed, far better service had been provided than could have been given by the smaller dependent libraries on their own.

The impetus for the formation of the regional library systems is said to have come from the work of a commission set up by the Canadian Library

Association in 1929. The development of these systems occurred gradually in successive years. By the end of the 1960s the whole of Ontario was organized into fourteen regional systems, most of them corresponding in rough terms to the ten economic regions. The minister of education determined which counties, cities, and towns would be included, with the restriction that each must consist of at least three counties and a minimum population of 100,000. The systems provided co-ordination and assistance to member libraries according to a variety of patterns and practices. Funds were obtained from provincial grants, fees from member boards, and sometimes from municipal councils.

The period immediately after the Wallace report was issued was one of very gradual expansion, greatly hampered by inadequate funds. Fresh attention was focused on the public libraries by a report of major significance, released in 1965, which resulted from the work of Francis R. St John Library Consultants Inc. of New York.[2] The study was commissioned by the Ontario Library Association and financed by the Department of Education. Among the recommendations were that a Provincial Library Council be established to advise the minister on the co-ordination of library development and to act as the Board of Trustees for a new Library Division which would co-ordinate responsibility within the Department of Education for all public, elementary school, and secondary school libraries; that the association libraries be eliminated and their assets conveyed to public libraries; that county library co-operatives be encouraged to change to county libraries, with the responsibility for providing service to all parts of the county; that regional library co-operatives be strengthened to enable them to provide a wide variety of services; that centralized ordering and cataloguing be adopted, with full use made of computers, and that bibliographic information be made available to libraries throughout the province; that each regional co-operative establish a regional reference centre; and that the Toronto Public Library act as a super-reference resource for the province, with provincial subsidies to support the function. A number of other recommendations, not of immediate relevance here, applied to school libraries.*

The Public Libraries Act of 1966 put many of the recommendations of the report into effect. Public libraries established by school sections and police villages were dissolved and their assets and liabilities transferred to public library boards set up by municipal councils. The councils of two or more municipalities were authorized to establish a union public library. Qualifications for librarians holding particular positions were specified. Fees for the use of publicly maintained libraries were abolished for local residents. An Ontario Provincial Library Council was established along the lines recommended in the St John report, although with different procedures for the appointment of its members. Conditions for the establish-

*Further discussion of these recommendations is found in ONTARIO'S EDUCATIVE SOCIETY, volume v, chapter 20.

ment of regional library systems were outlined, and the powers of regional boards were defined. The association libraries were dissolved and their assets transferred to the regional library systems. Provision was made for the establishment of county libraries and for the formation and operation of their boards.

Between 1965 and 1968 there were large percentage increases in provincial grants for public libraries, although they leveled out in 1968–9. The amount spent remained small in comparison with the total expenditure for education, and suggested that libraries still occupied a low place in terms of public priorities. In a sense, their status was an unflattering commentary on the success the Ontario educational system had had over the decades in inculcating a true regard for learning and a thirst for knowledge and aesthetic satisfaction that would continue after the termination of formal education. There were some who feared that exaggerated statements about the obsolescence of print had produced an unrealistic impression in the public mind about the importance of books. On the other hand, it seemed possible that concern over the high costs of education might produce a realization that library facilities and supplies gave some of the best returns for educational investment.

Although the St John report took a firm stand against combining public and school libraries, the idea continued to offer superficial appeal as a money-saving device. Most knowledgeable people seemed to feel, however, that materials collected for school use would not be of much interest or value to adults, that access to combined libraries would be difficult for adults during the daytime, and that there would be almost insuperable administrative problems. One of the recommendations of the Hall-Dennis report was that there be enabling legislation to place all libraries under the jurisdiction of a board of eduation where the board of education and existing library boards agreed on such action. Many of those whose interests lay primarily in the public library field objected to this proposal on the grounds that it would shift attention further toward school libraries.

THE PROVINCE OF ONTARIO COUNCIL FOR THE ARTS
An agency of recent origin receiving grants from the Department of Education is the Province of Ontario Council for the Arts. Created by an act of the Legislature in 1963, this body consisted of a ten-member council appointed by the government. It was originally expected to stimulate the creative arts by assisting music and theatre groups in particular to perform in small communities and by providing scholarships, grants, and loans for study or research in the arts.

For the first few years, the council dispersed its funds among a wide variety of groups and individuals. By 1968–9, however, a mood of disillusionment with this approach had set in because there were so many deserving causes and so few funds that it was impossible to give any group very much. Further, the effect of the donations was not as positive as had been anticipated. As a result, the council placed relatively less emphasis on this area of activity and began to concentrate more effort on fewer programs. One of these was a Co-ordinated Arts Service, which involved combined marketing of tickets, accounting, and publicity for many groups rather than leaving each one to handle its own operations. A second program was a Regional Arts Service which involved an initial concentration of efforts and resources to develop cultural and educational activities in pilot regions of the province. As experience was gained, the service would be extended to additional regions. A third program involved the establishment of a Centre for Arts Research in Education, where ranking professional artists and media experts would attempt to develop a systematic approach to education in the arts, including creative programs in music, drama, dance, film, and other fields for classroom use. The success of the agency in this enterprise during the period immediately after it was undertaken was not impressive.

Support for the Province of Ontario Council for the Arts notwithstanding, encouragement of activities in this field was not a major achievement of Ontario governments during the post-war period. The amount of financial subsidies was extremely small in comparison with educational expenditures. There was little evidence of an attempt to resist the powerful impression in North America that support for the arts should be left largely in private hands. This view was in part based on a fear of the potentially enslaving power that might devolve on a government that assumed regulatory power over artistic production. Yet a policy of neglect makes a vicious circle almost inevitable: if support falls below a certain level, the best artists and performers are forced to seek a more congenial environment, and the quality of creative expression declines. Mediocrity of production keeps private contributions low, and thus the possibility of improvement is denied.

Any attempt to develop the arts in Canada, in terms both of creation and appreciation, is undeniably extremely difficult in view of the cultural dominance of the United States. But unless Ontario finds more effective means of dealing successfully with the problem, it will continue to find that the attainment of the aesthetic aims formulated for its educational system is always difficult to reach, and that the undue predominance of utilitarian features remains characteristic of the educational process. There will continue to be an air of unreality about education for artistic expression until the highest levels are more frequently attained and more highly appreciated in Canada; similarly, it will be less than completely effective to teach aesthetic appreciation until there are more abundant examples of Canadian achievement to supplement those produced abroad.

THE ROYAL ONTARIO MUSEUM
Apart from universities and colleges, one of the major agencies receiving financial support through the Department of Colleges and Universities

was the Royal Ontario Museum. This institution was established in 1912 and was operated as part of the University of Toronto between 1947 and 1968. In the latter year it was placed under the control of its own Board of Trustees as a means of making it more readily recognizable as a public resource. Increased funds enabled it to improve its collections and to counteract threatened deterioration through lack of effective maintenance.

The Royal Ontario Museum has been particularly well known for its collections of Chinese art and archaeology, its artifacts of other ancient cultures, and its departments of mineralogy, geology, palaeontology, entomology, ichthyology, ornithology, and mammology. The McLaughlin Planetarium was opened as a part of the museum in the fall of 1968. A total attendance of 1,326,864 was recorded in 1969–70.

Unaided observation of the displays in the museum was an effective educational experience, particularly as a supplement to other activities. In addition, however, the museum maintained a series of positive educational programs for children and adults. School children were first permitted to visit the institution under the supervision of their teachers in 1914, and four years later staff members began to conduct groups on tours and to give instruction. In the 1920s the Toronto Board of Education arranged to appoint its own museum teacher to look after visting classes from the Toronto school system. The museum itself established a Division (later a Department) of Education consisting of a group of regular teachers and others providing occasional service. During the 1960s improved transportation, more flexible school administration, and events such as Canada's Centennial celebrations encouraged larger numbers of children from outside the Metropolitan Toronto area to visit the museum. The educational value of the visits was increased through the preparation of information sheets to be studied beforehand and through the compilation of related books and films. In 1969 skilled teachers began to present slides of objects to be seen in the galleries, with appropriate comment so that the visitors would be better prepared for perceptive viewing.

As a supplement to educational activities carried on within the museum, a considerable amount of service began to be provided in the late 1950s to groups in various parts of the province. Teachers carried exhibits to hundreds of elementary and secondary schools, and unaccompanied travelling cases went to many others. Visits were made to some of the most remote areas of the province for the benefit of both children and adults. These were especially appreciated because the local inhabitants had so few contacts with the outside world.

For many years a Saturday Morning Club, operated by paid leaders and volunteers, catered to scores of children during the fall, winter, and early spring. Activities involved art work, the study of alien cultures, and exchange programs with children in other countries. The wide variety of projects undertaken were characterized by a high degree of individual participation. Other special programs included special sessions for the blind and deaf. Artifacts, specimens, and films were transported to hospitals for the benefit of patients unable to visit the museum.

Adult education activities included extension courses offered in conjunction with the Extension Division of the University of Toronto. The themes of these courses were mostly of a cultural nature. Some were offered in locations in Metropolitan Toronto other than at the museum headquarters. Various university and professional groups were given a special reception, sometimes including lectures and conducted tours. Particular attention was directed in the late 1960s to the interests of student teachers and to teachers practising in schools within and outside the city.

THE ART GALLERY OF ONTARIO

The Art Gallery of Ontario had a status somewhat similar to that of the Royal Ontario Museum, and performed comparable educational functions. It received operating grants amounting to $550,000 through the Department of University Affairs in 1969–70. As early as the 1920s the gallery conducted an active educational program consisting of public lectures and gallery talks, study groups, and musical displays. Beneficiaries of this program included school and university students, teachers, members of associations and clubs, visitors from abroad, and members of the general public. Saturday morning classes gave a limited group of children an unparalleled opportunity to engage in creative artistic expression. Those with special talent were identified and encouraged to continue their studies.

In the late 1960s the educational activities of the gallery included conducted tours, seminars for staff members responsible for conducting tours, gallery talks, and special lectures. Junior art classes were offered for those ranging from five to nineteen years of age, and senior classes for adults. Exhibitions were circulated either directly or in co-operation with the Art Institute of Ontario or the National Gallery.

EDUCATIONAL ACTIVITIES OF PROVINCIAL
GOVERNMENT DEPARTMENTS OTHER THAN
EDUCATION AND UNIVERSITY AFFAIRS

It was commonly assumed that the provincial government's responsibilities for education were discharged almost entirely through the Department of Education and the Department of University Affairs (Colleges and Universities). In actual fact the evolution of modern government dictated that nearly all government departments be concerned with certain aspects of education. Most provincial ministers were in reality to some extent ministers of education. One major reason was that the quality of the work done in their departments was increasingly dependent on the kind of general and specialized preparation their employees had, and they had therefore to be concerned with training and upgrading. Another was that government functions tended to go far beyond regulation, involving the dissemination of knowledge and the shaping of attitudes designed to produce certain economic and social consequences. The same principles applied equally to organs of the federal government. If these agencies had really been excluded from every kind of educational activity, they might just as well have been abolished altogether.

Some provincial government departments were involved in the actual operation of schools and colleges, although this type of activity decreased in the 1960s. The best example was a control formerly exercised by what came to be called the Department of Agriculture and Food over the Ontario Agricultural College, the Ontario Veterinary College, and Macdonald Institute. Formal jurisdiction was abandoned when the University of Guelph was established in 1964, but the department retained a relationship that ensured that some of its objectives would continue to be met, including the offering of certain courses of benefit to the agricultural community and the conduct of agricultural research. The same department continued to administer what became known as the colleges of agricultural technology at Centralia, Kemptville, New Liskeard, and Ridgetown, formerly called agricultural schools. These colleges held out against the general tendency for institutions offering courses at the technician and technological levels to be absorbed into the colleges of applied arts and technology. The fate of the Forest Ranger School operated by the Department of Lands and Forests from 1945 on was somewhat different. In 1968 the technician-type course in forestry that had been given there was abandoned in favour of offerings at certain colleges of applied arts and technology, and the school was henceforth used for short staff training courses. Another department directly involved in the operation of educational institutions was the Department of Justice, which maintained the Ontario Fire College at Gravenhurst and the Ontario Police College at Aylmer. Both of these, as their names imply, were designed for the training of quite specific groups. The advantages of bringing them under the comprehensive umbrella of the colleges of applied arts and technology had not been considered overwhelming. In a somewhat different category were training schools for delinquent boys and girls operated by the Department of Correctional Services. While not strictly educational institutions in the usual sense, these schools attempted to rehabilitate through education. They followed provincial programs of study and employed the best qualified teachers they could attract. Still a different kind of involvement with schools, in this case quite indirect, was that of the Department of Energy and Resources Management, which had the responsibility of organizing and supervising conservation authorities. In 1963 the Metropolitan Toronto and Region Conservation Authority established the Albion Hills Conservation School with funds provided by the Metropolitan Toronto and Region Conservation Foundation. The Claremont Conservation Field Centre, completed in 1969, was of a somewhat similar nature. Programs offered in these schools, covering only a brief period, were co-ordinated with those of the user agencies such as school boards and certain associations.

Generally speaking, there seemed to be over-all advantages in bringing schools that tended to go beyond strictly technical training under the supervision of the Department of Education or the Department of Colleges and Universities. It seemed desirable to co-ordinate their entrance requirements and programs with other elements of the system, and to ensure a reasonable degree of transferability of students from one institution to another. A single school or a small group of schools operated by a department not primarily concerned with education tended to suffer from extreme isolation. The case for integration did not perhaps apply to programs of the Department of Correctional Services. Rehabilitation was intimately tied to education, and could hardly remain a tenable concept if the two were separated.

If there was a diminishing tendency for schools to be operated under the authority of departments other than education, the same could not be said of educational programs for particular groups. One of the best examples was the provision of language and citizenship training conducted by the Department of the Provincial Secretary and Citizenship beginning in 1961. Before that year the operation was supervised by the Community Programs Branch of the Department of Education. By the end of the 1960s, some of the main features of the program were the conduct of language and citizenship classes, the provision of summer courses in teaching English as a second language, the distribution of teaching materials, the administration of tests in English and in knowledge of Canada for applicants for citizenship and others, and the conduct of research into the program.

In addition to its training schools, the Department of Correctional Services maintained educational programs for adult offenders. The provincial assumption of responsibility for county jails in 1968 greatly increased the demand for such services. A major problem in the operation of these programs was that of motivation, which commonly meant identifying a highly practical and utilitarian objective. At the end of the 1960s it was becoming increasingly feasible to release certain inmates from strict confinement so that they could participate in educational programs in outside institutions. While some substantial successes were achieved, the unpleasant fact remained that a large proportion of the inmates did not benefit very much from the educational programs available to them and, on release, entered a suspicious society without good prospects of leading a law-abiding life.

The Department of Municipal Affairs encouraged somewhat informal programs designed to improve the quality of citizenship. Operated by the Ontario Conference on Local Government, these consisted of series of evening sessions designed for actual and potential elected officials and for those who were simply interested in voting intelligently in municipal elections. Short courses for such purposes were held in various centres. There were some informal indications that the participants subsequently took a more active role in local politics.

The Department of Labour had substantial responsibilities for the training of apprentices and for the upgrading of various occupational groups. Powers exercised under *The Apprenticeship Act* were designed to ensure that training met adequate qualitative standards and that the interests of apprentices were protected. In the performance of these functions, the department had to co-operate with the formal educational system, particularly with the Applied Arts and Technology Branch of the Department of Education, which had jurisdiction over the colleges of applied arts and technology, where formal aspects of training were given. The courses were formerly offered by the provincial trades institutes and vocational centres. In recent years the department became increasingly involved in short-term skill development for adult workers who did not need or were not prepared to take complete trades training. On-the-job training was assisted in co-operation with the federal government.*

The Department of Tourism and Immigration and the Department of Public Records and Archives were associated for many years under the same minister. They had the responsibility for a number of institutions and activities providing support for formal education or adding informal dimensions to education. Ontario's Centennial project, the Ontario Science Centre, which was opened in 1969, provides a major example. It was planned in close co-operation with the Department of Education and had unequivocal educational purposes. The provincial Archives, transferred from the Department of Education in 1959, contained material that served both cultural and educational purposes.† Somewhat related contributions were made through the program of restoring historical sites and erecting commemorative plaques. These helped school pupils to develop an interest and a sense of pride in the historical origins of the province.

Perhaps the most common type of educational activity in which government departments engaged was the promotion of economic, social, and cultural causes through publicity. The Department of the Provincial Secretary and Citizenship worked through the ethnic press to point out the advantages of citizenship and to encourage the economic integration of newcomers. Members of the staff spoke to interested groups on various aspects of citizenship and immigrant adjustment. The media were used to inform the public about government services open to them.

The Department of Tourism and Information engaged in the production of brochures, pamphlets, posters, maps, photographs, and films in order to extol the scenic attractions of the province and the opportunities it

*For a more complete discussion of these matters, see ONTARIO'S EDUCATIVE SOCIETY, volume II, chapter 13, and volume IV, chapters 13 and 20.
†The role of the provincial Archives is discussed in ONTARIO'S EDUCATIVE SOCIETY, volume II, chapter 13.

offered for recreation. This material was designed both to lure foreign visitors and to extend information among the inhabitants. There was increasing emphasis on the conservation of natural resources for the benefit of future generations. In this respect the department shared important interests with the Department of Lands and Forests, the Department of Energy and Resources Management, and others. The tourist was encouraged to search for and study rocks and minerals, and to engage in fishing and other such activities. The Archives staff helped to prepare materials illuminating historical events in their geographical setting. These were of particular use in schools, often as a means of preparing for excursions. Also of value in creating an appreciation of the past were such enterprises as Upper Canada Village, which depicted pioneer life in the nineteenth century.

In addition to promoting an appreciation of plant and animal life, the Department of Lands and Forests provided assistance for the pursuit of certain commercial ventures such as trapping and the cultivation of farm woodlots. The Department of Mines also promoted practical activities such as prospecting for minerals and claim staking. Various means were employed, in addition to publication, such as short courses, lectures, field trips, and visits to museums. One course dealt with such topics as drilling, handling explosives and blasting, claim staking, geological mapping, magnetic surveys, the use of air photos, and cross country travel. The Department of Mines made some effort to interest young people in careers in mining. Through its Junior Forest Ranger program and by other means the Department of Lands and Forests pursued similar purposes.

The Department of Transport assumed a major responsibility for the promotion of traffic safety. For this purpose it produced pamphlets, leaflets, and guides for motorists, pedestrians, school children, teachers, and driving instructors. Some of the material was designed for integration into the regular school program, where it would presumably have maximum effect in building up desirable attitudes. A Crusader Cycle Club program was intended to produce safe cyclists and to establish a foundation for safe driving. The assistance of various groups such as local safety councils, the police, service clubs, and Home and School associations was enlisted in maintaining the clubs. Attempts were also made to reach "senior citizens" through pamphlets, posters, coloured slides, and manuals, which might be used in locally organized groups.

Many departments were deeply involved in the training and upgrading of their own employees and of personnel who had to be counted upon to provide the services for which they had a responsibility. They relied to a large extent on institutions in the formal educational system such as universities and colleges of applied arts and technology. In some cases they played an influential part in designing appropriate courses of study, and they might be the means by which funds were channeled to support the programs. They conducted campaigns to enlist suitable applicants for training, whom they encouraged with scholarships, bursaries, and loans. Where no satisfactory training programs existed, they often organized and administered them on their own initiative. While there was a large amount of such training, most of it was of a short-term nature, consisting of isolated seminars, series of evening or week-end sessions, or courses lasting for two or three weeks.

One of the departments most concerned with the training of specialized personnel was the Department of Health. The names of some of the committees operating in the early 1960s indicate the range of occuptional groups in which the department had an interest: the Bursary Selection Committee in Public Health, the Bursary Selection Committee in Mental Health, the Committee on Sanitary Inspectors, the Committee on Laboratory Technicians, the Committee on Public Health Nursing, and the Committee on Nursing Education and Registered Nurses. Funds were granted by the Legislature for use in encouraging non-employees interested in advanced training in certain specialties such as psychiatry, psychology, bacteriology, speech pathology, and physiotherapy. Some examples of training programs offered for departmental employees were those for child care workers, hospital aides and attendants, laboratory technologists, occupational therapy assistants, pest control officers, registered nursing assistants, rehabilitation officers, and sanitary inspectors. The programs were conducted on premises controlled by the department or in institutions such as Ryerson Polytechnical Institute. Some were up to four years' duration. Less formal in-service training included courses in environmental sanitation for summer camp inspectors, refresher courses for sanitary inspectors, courses for local air pollution staff, refresher courses for representatives of regional laboratories, educational conferences for public health nurses, and worker conferences for local nursing personnel in administrative, supervisory, and staff positions. Employee upgrading involved sending people to outside institutions for courses in public administration, supervision, and data processing. Employees were encouraged, sometimes with bursary assistance, to take evening and correspondence courses offered by universities and colleges. They also attended innumerable seminars and conferences offered by these and other agencies.

The in-service training activities of the Department of Social and Family Services began in 1949 with courses of several weeks' duration for welfare field workers in Toronto. The program included a study of legislation relating to old age assistance, and allowances for the blind, the disabled, and mothers with dependent children. Some time later, courses with similar content and approach were offered for employees in municipal welfare departments. At the beginning of the 1960s, federal and provincial concern about the lack of an adequate supply of social workers led to the provision of funds for students in schools of social work. Efforts were also made to expand existing schools and to establish new ones. Through co-operation with Ryerson Polytechnical Institute, a Welfare Services course was introduced to prepare qualified personnel at the intermediate level. Similar courses were later offered at some of the colleges of applied arts and technology. The Advisory Council for Public Welfare Training helped to define suitable content for these courses, as well as offering advice to universities considering the introduction of undergraduate programs. Internal staff training included orientation, in-service training, and educational leave. There were short lecture courses supplemented by field practice, meetings, conferences, workshops, and institutes. In the educational leave program some employees were enabled to enrol in schools of social work or Ryerson Polytechnical Institute on full salary. Assistance was also given for attendance at summer school and for night school courses.

The peculiar nature of its operations compelled the Department of Lands and Forests to provide an unusually comprehensive program of in-service training. About two temporary summer employees were required for every member of the permanent staff to perform such tasks as stocking streams, planting trees, banding birds and animals, and acting as park attendants. They were prepared for their work in intensive courses lasting between ten days and two weeks and held in various parts of the province under the direction of the district forester. In-service courses were also offered for permanent employees, who had to have an increasing amount of knowledge about conservation, law enforcement, and other such matters. Because of the extent of the training program, it was a task of major proportions to prepare the necessary instructors. The efforts of the department were supplemented by reliance on university extension courses, which employees were subsidized to take.

The Department of Municipal Affairs offered an orientation course for new employees to familiarize them with the aims, operation, and structure of the department. More advanced training was provided by specific branches such as the Community Planning Branch and the Municipal Assessment Branch. The provincial assumption of full responsibility for assessment in 1970 was accompanied by a substantial increase in training obligations. The department worked closely with certain colleges of applied arts and technology to prepare the content for two-year programs, and provided instructional assistance from its own staff. It also prepared material of value in the courses as well as for the actual task of assessment. The department offered assistance in programs for municipal clerks and treasurers included in the extension program of Queen's University beginning in 1958, and one for municipal accounting trainees introduced ten years later.

During 1967–8 it was estimated that more than half the 6,654 employees of the Department of Highways took part in some form of training. Many took technical courses, involving qualifying examinations, at the department's Training Centre. Others enrolled in courses offered by the Department of Civil Service or by other outside agencies. Different types of training were provided for employees of the various branches. For example, employees of the Operations Branch took courses for survey technicians, construction technicians, highway inspection assistants, engineering office supervisors, contract administrators, municipal surveyors, concrete inspectors, grade inspectors, asphalt inspectors, landscape crewmen, and sign painters. A similar range and variety were offered in other branches and divisions. Training services obtained from outside agencies included evening classes and seminars lasting up to five days. Among such agencies were university extension departments, Ryerson Polytechnical Institute, school boards, the Society of Industrial and Cost Accountants, and various industrial corporations.

The Department of Civil Service maintained its own quarters and facilities for in-residence courses and seminars. Courses were offered on several levels, including those for senior management, line managers, supervisors, and those whose work involved the exercise of some specific skill. The supply of those in the latter category increased greatly with the expansion of the colleges of applied arts and technology. The training programs sponsored by the Department of Civil Service helped to supplement those given by many other departments.

EDUCATIONAL CONCERNS OF THE FEDERAL GOVERNMENT

If provincial government departments not primarily concerned with educational matters could not function effectively without engaging in some activities definable as education in the broad sense, the same was true of federal agencies. Like their provincial counterparts, some of them operated educational institutions for groups for which they had a special responsibility. Most of them were concerned in some way with the promotion of their objectives by influencing public opinion. They were in general becoming more dependent for their continued efficiency on in-service training of civil servants, whether provided internally or by outside agencies. An acceptance of federal responsibility for the promotion of cultural objectives had important educational implications. Of major importance, also, were direct federal involvement in manpower training and the diversion of federal funds to support post-secondary education programs administered by the provinces.

With about a third of the Canadian population, Ontrio was both a major contributor of funds for federal educational programs and a major beneficiary from them. Although possibly less important than provincial activities in similar areas, these programs were much too significant to be ignored. If they frequently received little attention as an aspect of education, the main reason was that it was politically advantageous to call them something else in view of the prerogatives of the provinces in the field.

Educational activities of provincial government departments had counterparts among many federal government agencies. Two departments in particular had a direct involvement in the education of school children: the Department of Indian Affairs and Northern Development and the Department of National Defence. The first of these executed the federal government's constitutional responsibility for the education of Indians living on reserves. The tendency was for the government, where practical, to purchase education for Indian children in conveniently located provincial schools. In isolated regions, the department had itself to assume the responsibility for maintaining suitable facilities. In 1968 there were approximately 7,500 children attending federal schools, some on a residential basis.

Indian education presented some very serious problems which had not been satisfactorily resolved. Where the population was widely scattered, and education seemed possible only by sending the children to residential schools for long periods of time, there was a danger that they might be alienated from their own community and unable to fit in when they returned home. At the same time, they were unlikely to have assimilated enough of the mainstream culture to succeed occupationally and socially off the reservation. Another difficulty was that of preserving the best of the Indian cultural heritage while preparing the young people to win a place in the economic life of the country. Certain features of the traditional outlook such as a lack of individual competitiveness and a disinclination to sacrifice and save for distant objectives were a stumbling-block in the way of adaptation to predominant Canadian values. Some observers noted that, where children from the reservation attended neighbouring schools, what passed for integration hardly went beyond outward appearances.

The Department of National Defence was responsible for the maintenance of the Royal Military College of Canada at Kingston, which granted degrees up to the master's level. The program was supposed to prepare young men for careers in the armed forces. The department also had a training program for the development of skills at all levels of the services.

The same department was responsible for the provision of schools for dependents of members of the armed forces. Some of these schools were actually administered by provincial departments of education or by local school boards. They were mostly rather small, although the total enrolment in all of Canada in 1969–70 was nearly twelve thousand. Schools were also maintained in association with army bases at several locations in Europe. The program up to the end of grade 6 was designed as a kind of composite of the curriculum in the various provinces while that for grades 7 to 13 led to Ontario certificates and diplomas. Teachers were employed by agreement between the Department of National Defence and local school boards with provision for continuing credit for superannuation and other benefits. There was a certain amount of friction between the department and the Canadian Teachers' Federation because of the latter's dissatisfaction over some of the conditions of service of its members. The schools were criticized for encouraging a ghetto existence for the children, who missed opportunities for a broadening form of education in return for the assurance that they would fit into the system when they got back home.

An example of a specialized educational or training institution was the Air Services Training School established under the authority of the Department of Transport in 1959. It provided programs for those preparing for careers in aviation as well as for employees of the department seeking advanced skills. In the late sixties, groups of courses were given in the three areas of air traffic control, meteorology, and telecommunications and electronics. Students spent part of their time in the classroom and part of it in practical work. The total training period might last up to several months. The courses differed from those offered in the colleges of applied arts and technology in being more highly technical and making no pretence at mixing general education with job training.

Federal educational programs for special groups included the work of the Canadian Penitentiary Service, which paralleled that of the provincial Department of Correctional Services among adult inmates. A beginning was made in instruction at the elementary school level as early as 1851, but the predominance of a punitive outlook kept progress at a minimum. A royal commission report, completed in 1938, recommended a major thrust in education, involving a program with academic, cultural, recreational, and physical components. An effort was made against serious obstacles to put the proposals into practice after the Second World War. Further progress was marked by the introduction of a ten-year plan of institutional development in 1963. In view of the level of schooling attained by the average inmate, a good deal of attention had to be centred on elementary school work. Despite every enticement, only a minority showed an interest in participating in formal courses at any level.

The educational interests of quite a different special group were served by the Canadian International Development Agency. This body, formerly called the External Aid Office, made arrangements and provided financial assistance for foreign students to study in Canada. The program began with the adoption of the Colombo Plan in 1950, and was extended to the Caribbean, Africa, and Latin America after 1958. The CIDA of course worked though provincially supported educational institutions, particularly universities. The training of foreign nationals was closely tied in with other aspects of aid programs.

A number of federal departments provide examples of educational activities designed to promote economic and social causes. Beginning in 1919 the Department of National Health and Welfare maintained a publicity service to supply health information to the press, the professional journals, and the public. Efforts were made to reach parents, professional health workers, teachers, and school children with material relating to general health, prenatal and child care, mental health, dental health, and the dangers of smoking and drug abuse. Training films were produced for the use of teachers and television programs were broadcast to schools. The educational programs of the department were supported by research into various questions such as the effects of tobacco. The federal department was able to undertake more ambitious production of promotional materials than was possible in provincial departments. The latter co-operated closely in their distribution.

The major branches of the Department of Fisheries and Forestry conducted programs that bore a close resemblance to those of the Ontario Department of Lands and Forests and the Department of Mines. These branches attempted to increase public understanding of the value of forest and fishery resources through the publication of educational aids, brochures, and films. Much of this material was made available for use in schools. The National Film Board produced films and filmstrips to encourage forest conservation and to provide information about careers in forestry. Technical films demonstrated how the products of the forests might be used for commercial purposes. In the area of fisheries, efforts were made to assist those who depended on various aspects of the industry for a living. Material was prepared to encourage the consumption of fish by dealing with methods of handling, preparing, and cooking, and was sent primarily to home economics teachers in educational institutions.

The Canadian Government Travel Bureau was concerned with the same matters as the Ontario Department of Tourism and Information. With its travel promotion offices in a number of different countries, however, it concentrated somewhat more on enticing foreign tourists to visit Canada. Materials were supplied on request to teachers and students to assist in geographical studies. The bureau collected information about summer courses offered in Canadian universities for the use of students in Canada and in some other countries. As a means of encouraging the development of the tourist industry, the bureau co-operated with tourist agencies in the training of employees involved in providing tourist services. These included restaurant and hotel employees, gas station attendants, taxi drivers, and store clerks. This aspect of the program was not on a scale large enough to produce very obvious results.

The Meteorological Service of the Department of Transport was involved in the preparation of materials for study in school in the form of weather maps with explanatory information, along with exercises enabling the student to make simple forecasts. These were intended for use in general science or as a means of interesting students in the study of meteorology in its own right.

Some federal government departments had programs of employee training comparable to those maintained by provincial departments. Of particular interest were those of the Public Service Commission of Canada. As of the end of the 1960s the Treasury Board was responsible for the development and regulation of policy while the Public Service Commission operated central programs and offered advice on departmental programs. In accordance with its first role, the commission provided courses in executive development, in administrative trainee development, and in particular professional, managerial, and occupatinoal areas. Assistance to other departments involved planning, evaluation, and research. The department kept an inventory of resources, including its own staff, qualified people from other departments, and available outsiders. It also had the responsibility of preparing professional trainers and resource personnel for special training assignments.

The federal government assumed the chief responsibility for encouraging and financing various forms of scientific and cultural research and production. These activities were important for education because they enlarged the available resources of study materials for use in educational institutions. A large proportion of those whose work was subsidized were directly involved in such institutions, either as students or as teachers.

The National Research Council, established in 1916, awarded grants-in-aid for research in universities, supported seminars and conferences for research scientists, co-ordinated research, operated research laboratories, published scientific journals and other materials, maintained a library and documentation centre, and exchanged information with other countries on scientific research. Grants and scholarships were awarded to students for graduate study, including that at the post-doctoral level, in science and engineering. Some were tenable at foreign universities as well as in Canadian institutions and in the council's own laboratories. Grants to university faculty members were for the purchase of special equipment and supplies or the employment of assistants. Publication activities included the production of eight scientific journals at the end of the 1960s. An offshoot of the National Research Council, the Medical Research Council, was formed in 1960 to develop medical research and to support medical researchers in Canadian universities. Its activities closely paralleled those of the parent body. A particular effort was made to develop the research programs in university medical schools.

The Canada Council for the Encouragement of the Arts, Humanities and Social Sciences, established in 1957, represented an effort to balance support for the natural sciences with encouragement for the arts and letters. It began with two funds of $50 million each, and thereafter received further government grants and substantial private donations and bequests. The first fund was intended for comparatively prompt expenditure to develop university capital resources, and was largely exhausted by the mid-sixties. Substantial amounts were used each year for scholarships and fellowships and for the exchange of scholars. Another major category of expenditure was designed to assist organizations concerned with music, theatre, ballet, opera, and the visual arts. Smaller amounts went to individual and special projects in the same areas. Encouragement of the humanities involved assistance to libraries and grants for research, conferences, and publications. Aid for publication was designed to encourage the production of scholarly books and articles. Efforts were made to stimulate creative writing and to make Canadian writers known abroad. Translation grants were awarded to help make the works of the two major linguistic groups in Canada known to each other.

The National Film Board, an agency responsible to the secretary of state, performed important educational functions by increasing the cultural resources of the country and by acting as a major source of audio-visual aids for schools in all provinces. Interest in the production of educational films in the narrow sense developed rather slowly after the establishment of the board in 1939. An important milestone was the formation in 1950 of an advisory committee involving the Canadian Education Association. During the 1950s and 1960s major efforts were made to work closely with provincial departments of education and to involve educators in such activities as writing scripts, directing photography on location, taking photographs, preparing art work, and editing material. Summer institutes for the study of film and television were begun in 1966 to enable administrators and teachers to engage in media study. Members of the staff gave lectures in teacher training institutions on the production and use of media in the classroom. Special films were also prepared for use in programs of teacher education. By the end of the 1960s the board was in a slump as a result of waning enthusiasm on the part of the federal government, the increasing role of private film producers, and the growing tendency on the part of provincial governments to assume responsibility for the production of educational material. If it were allowed to disappear, there was no prospect that an agency of comparable value would replace it.

Certain institutions maintained by the federal government constituted important educational resources. The National Library of Canada contained a comprehensive collection of books, government documents, and periodicals published in Canada, as well as books relating to Canada published in other countries. It also accumulated books published outside Canada in the humanities and social sciences, including literature, history, economics, religion, philosophy, and art. Other items were selected foreign documents and Canadian recordings. A location service, based on a National Union Catalogue, provided the basis for interlibrary loans of books, serials, and documents. The National Museums of Canada, consisting of the National Museum of Man, the National Museum of Natural Sciences, the National Museum of Science and Technology, and the National Gallery, had educational functions as well as those of collection, preservation, and research. The educational function, of increasing importance in recent years, was carried out through exhibits, publication, and other programs. Lecture series were provided both for adults and for children, and less formal instruction was offered, in some cases enlisting the help of university students. An answering service was maintained for the benefit of teachers and pupils across the country. Responses sometimes involved the supplying of free material or the identification of specimens sent in for the purpose.

In a special category was the semi-official Canadian National Commission for UNESCO, which promoted the attainment of UNESCO objectives within the country. It brought together a large number of government and voluntary agencies, with particular support from the Canada Council. Of special concern to education was the Associated Schools Project, begun in the 1950s. Topics of international interest were studied and special efforts were made to encourage the development of respect for justice, the rule of law, human rights, and fundamental freedoms. The topics were particularly related to history and geography, but also had implications for language, art, and other subjects. Extra-curricular activities were in some cases organized around the chosen themes.

THE COUNCIL OF MINISTERS OF EDUCATION
It was obvious during the 1960s that an increased exchange of information and an effort to co-ordinate educational activities in certain fields would contribute both to the effectiveness of provincial systems and to the attainment of certain national objectives. Some educational leaders called repeatedly for an extended and strengthened role for the federal government. The realities of the political situation, however, practically ruled out such a development unless the remaining provinces were in effect to invite the departure of Quebec from the union. Another approach had to be found, and the obvious solution was voluntary interprovincial co-operation.

The Canadian Education Association for many years provided opportunities for provincial education officials and other leading educators from across the country to meet and exchange views. At the annual meeting of that organization in 1960, J.P. Robarts, then minister of education for Ontario, took the lead in forming a Standing Committee of Ministers of Education, and became its first chairman. For the next few years, this committee operated quietly and there is little indication that it exerted much influence in provincial or interprovincial affairs. On succeeding Robarts, however, Davis showed considerable interest in expanding its field of operations.

In 1964 the ministers played a rather negative role in the movement to establish a Canadian council on admission to college and university, offering the view that the issue required further consideration before definite action was taken. Of a more positive nature was their decision to form an *ad hoc* subcommittee called the Minister's Information Systems Committee, which would study the possibility of setting up an educational information service for the entire country. The scheme failed to live up to its promise, partly because the provinces varied greatly in their ability to collect the necessary data in the form required. Responsibility for the task remained in the hands of the Dominion Bureau of Statistics.

For some time before any definite steps were taken, there was discussion of the possibility of establishing a secretariat for the Standing Committee which would act as an interprovincial office of education. A major problem had to do with the relationship the secretariat would have with the CEA. For a time there appeared to be an expectation that it would provide service for the latter, but it was eventually decided that the CEA would continue its independent existence.

An *ad hoc* committee of the ministers formed in 1966 met early the following year and recommended the formation of a Council of Ministers with the primary objectives of collecting and exchanging information and facilitating effective consultation with the federal government. In some matters the second of these objectives meant, in less diplomatic terms, putting collective pressure on the federal government to adapt its course of action in the light of provincial interests. The formation of the council would not limit the powers of the provincial departments of education, since these would not be obligated to accept or to act in the light of council decisions. In accordance with the recommendations of the *ad hoc* committee, the council was formally established in September 1967 with Davis as the first chairman.

During the next few years, interprovincial committees consisting of experienced officials from the departments of education became active in various areas. Three committees formed at an early stage were the Instructional Media Committee, the Post-Secondary Education Committee, and the Manpower Committee. Their work provided a basis for provincial dealings with the federal government, which had an interest in all three areas.

It is possible that the major achievement of the council was the relatively intangible one of promoting understanding and a sense of common purpose, not only among the ministers themselves, but among the officials who served on various committees as well. Of greatest importance, perhaps, was the contribution to bridge building between Quebec and the English-speaking provinces. Further, the development of a power centre to negotiate with the federal government was probably desirable during the late 1960s, although there was always the possibility that the kind of tension involved might become destructive.

Between the spring of 1969, when the Liberals overthrew the Union National in Quebec, and the fall of 1971, the portfolio of education changed hands in most of the provinces, and the membership of the Council of Ministers consisted largely of relative newcomers. As a result the organization played a less prominent role than it might have done under other circumstances. Perhaps this was the time, however, when the value of the contacts provided was greatest.

ASSOCIATIONS CONCERNED WITH EDUCATION

A final area of significant educational activity outside the formal educational system is that of associations. These may be divided into two broad categories according to whether they had a primary or a secondary interest in education. The total of their contributions was greater than most people realized. In recognition of this fact, the whole of volume VII of ON-TARIO'S EDUCATIVE SOCIETY is devoted to an account of the efforts and influence of a representative group of associations.

A number of the most important associations were those consisting entirely of people who were involved in some capacity in the operation of the educational system. In certain cases the purpose was almost exclusively the improvement of the educational process through the professional development of the members or the advancement of knowledge in a discipline or in some field of education. Conspicuous among associations of this type was the Ontario Educational Association, which provided an umbrella for many sections and councils with particular subject, service, or administrative interests. Objectives were achieved mainly through meetings and conferences involving addresses, the presentation of papers, and discussion and through the publication of specialized journals and other material. Although the OEA encouraged participation on the part of those engaged in post-secondary education, it was largely identified with elementary and secondary school affairs. At the university level, most of the comparable activity was conducted by learned societies, which were ordinarily national in scope. Because of their small potential and actual membership, many of them had to struggle along on limited funds and pursued quite modest objectives. They nevertheless managed to add to the prestige of their disciplines and to give their membership a certain *esprit de corps*. Among the associations concerned with a range of scholarship beyond a single discipline were the Royal Canadian Institute, the Royal Society of Canada, and the Royal Canadian Academy of the Arts. One of their contributions was to identify conspicuous achievement in particular areas of scholarship.

The name of the Canadian Education Association suggested a closer parallel to the Ontario Educational Association than was actually the case. The difference was mainly attributable to the peculiar constitutional provisions for education in Canada. The main functions of the national organization were to promote contacts and exchanges of information among provincial educators, particularly officials, administrators, and supervisors. It exerted an important influence in favour of co-ordination of educational policies and thus of national unity.

A large number of associations combined efforts to improve education with measures to protect the power, security, or financial position of their own members. They often made a very plausible case for regarding these two sets of objectives as different aspects of the same thing. In a society determined to retain the maximum element of democratic control, they were under a continuous obligation to demonstrate the validity of their claims. The most active and important of the associations in this class were the teachers' federations, consisting of the Ontario Teachers' Federation and five affiliates: the Federation of Women Teachers' Associations of

Ontario, the Ontario Public School Men Techers' Federation, the Ontario Secondary School Teachers' Federation, the Ontario English Catholic Teachers' Association, and l'Association des enseignants franco-ontariens. These organizations were among the most powerful of their kind in the world, sharing with their counterparts in other provinces a provision for compulsory membership dating from 1944 when *The Teaching Profession Act* was passed. When the first three of the affiliates were organized immediately after the First World War, their main interests were in raising the deplorably low level of salaries and in securing their members against arbitrary dismissal. Other protective concerns that got immediate or ultimate attention were superannuation, life insurance, health insurance, and loan funds. The broader professional activities of the federations included the formation of committees to study various aspects of education, the compilation of reports and other documents of assistance to their own members and to the general community of educators, the conduct of in-service educational activities such as short courses, seminars, and conventions, and the preparation of briefs on educational issues for submission to government agencies. They helped to ensure that their members acted ethically and that minimum levels of competence were maintained. Unlike some other professional groups, they did not have the privilege of controlling admission to their ranks.

There was increasing criticism of the teachers' federations because the affiliates exercised a disproportionate amount of power, sometimes worked at cross purposes, and tended to leave the Ontario Teachers' Federation without sufficient authority to speak and act for teachers as a unified profession. The separate organizations at the elementary and secondary levels were held in part responsible for the difficulty in integrating the elementary and secondary school levels to produce a continuous educational process. It seemed possible that the substantial upgrading in qualifications for admission to elementary school teaching planned for the 1970s would help to remove the barriers to greater unity.

At the national level, the Canadian Teachers' Federation concentrated on the exchange of information among teachers' organizations in the various provinces, on the performance of certain service functions such as research, and on giving voice to certain points of view that characterized the teaching profession in general. It exerted pressure on the federal government in favour of teachers' interests and in support of worthy educational causes. Protective concerns were left largely to provincial organizations.

At the university level the first counterparts to the organizations of teachers at the elementary and secondary school levels were the faculty associations in individual institutions. They usually presented the interests of their members to the administration in a gentlemanly and dignified fashion, but did not attemtp to exert a significant influence on the process of education. For the first few years after its formation in 1950, the Canadian Association of University Teachers concentrated on efforts to improve faculty salaries. During the 1960s it assumed increasing responsibility for defending academic freedom and tenure, a role that grew in importance as universities expanded and the proportion of relatively new and untried faculty members rose at an unprecedented rate. At the same time certain informational services were provided and influence was brought to bear on university development. The Ontario Council (later Confederation) of University Faculty Associations, formed in 1963, immediately staked out a claim to a voice in the shaping of university development in all its aspects by presenting a brief to the prime minister of the province. A stream of documents of this type followed in succeeding years. The organization pressed for the right to deal directly with provincial agencies in defence of the interests of its membership. After an initial rebuff from the Committee on University Affairs, it was formally received by that body in 1969. There seemed little doubt that provincial faculties would insist on a way of presenting their views on salary levels to those who controlled the purse strings, and would not be content to work through presidents and boards of governors.

In the early years of the operation of the colleges of applied arts and technology the question of faculty representation was a matter of dispute. The Labour Relations Board of Ontario ruled in 1967 that the colleges were Crown corporations, and thus subject to *The Public Service Act* of 1966. As a result, the Civil Service Association of Ontario claimed the right to represent the faculty members. Although this arrangement would have been acceptable to many, particularly those who had served earlier in the institutes of technology, the institutes of trades, or the vocational centres, there were others who were determined to establish the newly formed Ontario Federation of Community College Faculty Associations as the agency with the recognized right to represent the faculty. While a judicial decision was sought, the provincial government gave an undertaking to permit various categories of Crown employees to select their own bargaining agency. Under this arrangement, an umpire was named to judge among the claims of associations that could offer evidence that they had enrolled at least 35 per cent of the eligible membership in the colleges. Since the Civil Service Association of Ontario was the only one that could meet these terms, a vote was held to determine whether or not it would be recognized by the Council of Regents as the official bargaining agent. This vote resulted in the recognition of the association. College faculties were in a particularly difficult position to negotiate over their salaries and conditions of service in view of the division of powers and responsibilities among the local boards of governors, the Council of Regents, and the Department of Education (later the Department of Colleges and Universities). While the Council of Regents outlined status categories and salary scales, its functions were officially only advisory.

School principals organized largely or exclusively according to level.

During the 1950s and 1960s, principals of the larger elementary schools participated in what was known from 1966 on as the Ontario Principals' Section of the OEA. In the late 1960s membership included principals of various types of public elementary schools, junior high schools, and private schools. The secondary school principals formed the Ontario Secondary School Headmasters' Association as a section of the OEA. In 1964 this agency gave way to the Secondary School Headmasters' Council, which constituted part of the Ontario Secondary School Teachers' Federation. There was continued debate over whether principals should be associated with teachers in the same protective organization when school trustees generally felt that they should be treated as management, paralleling the situation in labour relations. The OSSTF preferred to regard them as part of the same professional group with a special type of responsibility. Principals' associations provided an opportunity for the exchange of information, the adoption of common approaches to certain problems, and the development of fraternal relations. Some consideration was also given to professional standards, training, and protective matters. Much the same might be said of organizations of locally employed school superintendents and directors. During the post-war period three of such organizations emerged: the Association of Secondary School Superintendents, the Association of Directors of Education of Ontario, and the Ontario Association of School Superintendents and Directors. Under the impact of the school board reorganization of 1969, these gave way to the Ontario Association of Education Officials. Also included were members of the Ontario Association of School Business Officials.

School trustees have been even more noted than teachers for their propensity to organize on the basis of a particular interest. In fact the main reason for the formation of the Public School Trustees' Association in 1939 was to combat some of the objectives of the Ontario Separate School Trustees' Association. For many years the lack of a united effort did not matter greatly. However, the passing of *The Teaching Profession Act* in 1944 called for a strengthening of the trustees' capacity to resist what many of them saw as excessive or unjustifiable teacher demands. After a first unsuccessful effort in 1945–6, an Ontario School Trustees' Council was formed in 1950. During most of the fifties and sixties it co-ordinated some of the activities of the member associations which, in addition to the two mentioned, included the Ontario School Trustees' and Ratepayers' Association (later the Ontario School Trustees' and Municipal Councillors' Association), the Ontario Urban and Rural School Trustees' Association, the Associated High School Boards of the Province of Ontario, l'Association des commissions des écoles bilingues d'Ontario, and the Northern Ontario Public and Secondary School Trustees' Association. As a result of initiatives begun in 1967, all but the northern, separate school, and bilingual associations united to form the Ontario Public School Trustees' Association. Contributions of the various associations included the holding of conventions to exchange information and ideas, the publication of journals, the submission of resolutions and briefs on educational issues to government officials, the study of certain problems, often in co-operation with the teachers' federations, and the establishment of standard hiring practices.

By far the most important organization of university administrators was the committee of Presidents of Universities of Ontario, dating from 1962. During the remainder of the decade it played a leading part in the transformation of the role of the provincially assisted universities, taking particular responsibility for the protection of university autonomy. These matters have already been discussed in chapter 4. In 1971 the committee adopted the name Council of Ontario Universities to reflect its enlarged membership from the university community and the corresponding change in status. At the national level, the chief organization was the Association of Universities and Colleges of Canada, a body largely expressing the point of view of university administrators. Under various names, it contributed to the exchange of information and the development of common policies across the country and acted as the official voice of the universities in dealing with the federal government. It performed a significant role in conducting research into problems of higher education. Also worthy of note was its provision of a channel of communication between Canadian universities and colleges on the one hand and foreign governments and organizations on the other. Additional associations of administrators operating at the national level included deans of various faculties or schools and officials responsible for such aspects of university work as extension and student awards.

Some associations, involving professional educators, members of the general public, or both, attempted to promote a specific aspect of the school program. Most of the provincial groups concerned with a particular school subject operated as part of the OEA. There were also national counterparts to some of these such as the Canadian Council of Teachers of English and the Canadian Association for the Social Studies. Reaching a stage beyond the national was the International Reading Association. Certain organizations devoted themselves to aspects of the school program other than the teaching of school subjects: for example, the use of programmed learning materials and television. Another group of associations with close links to the schools consisted of those attempting to promote the interests of individuals requiring special attention or methods of treatment such as the physically handicapped, the mentally retarded, and the emotionally disturbed. Besides arousing public interest in the needs of children, and sometimes adults, with special problems, these groups in some cases financed programs for such individuals.

There were certain organizations working at the local, provincial, and national levels which provided broad support for formal and sometimes informal education. These included the Ontario Educational Research

Council and the Canadian Council for Research in Education, which attempted to disseminate information, to bring researchers together to report their activities, and to stimulate research. Organizations designed to facilitate the work of the school in somewhat different ways were the Ontario Federation of Home and School Associations and the Federation of Catholic Parent-Teacher Associations of Ontario. Perhaps their main contribution was to promote understanding among the diverse groups with an interest in education. They were characterized by a certain looseness of organization, and had widely varying success from one community to another in their efforts to elicit the active concern of teachers.

The professional associations were one of the most important groups with major educational concerns. Some of them, usually with the word "college" or "institute" in their title, were authorized by provincial legislation to control admission to the profession. In certain professions such as medicine and dentistry, this privilege meant fairly complete control of practice. In others, such as nursing, where it would be unrealistic to attempt to reserve all the functions performed by nurses to a specific group, the profession controlled the award and use of a particular designation, which stood for a recognized level of training and competence. As indicated in chapter 1, control of admission to a profession might involve one or more of a number of responsibilities: the granting of licences, the setting and marking of qualifying examinations, the offering of part-time or full-time courses as a preparation for qualifying examinations, and co-operation with universities or other educational institutions in establishing and offering programs of study with the same objective. In addition to the associations with the right to award licences to practice, there were many others at the provincial and national levels which published professional journals, held conferences, organized in-service programs to upgrade the competence of their members, raised and distributed funds to enable promising young people to prepare to join their ranks, and in some cases attempted to educate the public with respect to causes to which they devoted their efforts.

Youth organizations such as the Boy Scouts of Canada, the Girl Guides of Canada, Boys' Clubs of Canada, the Canadian Girls in Training, and others attempted to supplement the work of schools by providing opportunities for the development of certain skills and by promoting character development. Some of them originated with a consciously religious orientation which they might or might not have maintained. The YMCA and the YWCA were good examples of associations that did not particularly concentrate their efforts on youth, as their names implied, but provided educational, athletic, recreational, and cultural programs for all age groups. In addition, they maintained impressive training programs for various categories of staff.

A large percentage of the associations with educational concerns were primarily or exclusively involved with adults. Co-ordinating and stimulating roles were assumed by the Canadian Association for Adult Education and its provincial counterpart, the Ontario Association for Continuing Education. The first of these especially maintained an active program of information dissemination and the promotion of educational and cultural causes through meetings and short courses. It also attempted to exert a constructive influence on public authorities and private agencies. Many organizations devoted their efforts to the education of specific groups such as immigrants with language handicaps and people in remote areas with few cultural amenities. It was usual for associations of particular linguistic, cultural, and religious groups to include education as a major objective or to attempt to realize other benevolent purposes through education.

It was generally felt that church services were a combination of worship and education, and that a form of education suffused most of the other activities in which the churches were involved. There were well-known programs designed to help particular groups of members such as adolescents, those contemplating marriage, and those encountering marital difficulties, to solve characteristic problems. There were recent attempts to improve the quality of Sunday schools and to slow the decline in membership by increasing and improving training of voluntary teachers.

Service clubs and associations involving both men and women played a particularly important part in the field of student assistance before government agencies entered the field on a large scale in the 1960s, and continued to make selective awards to help individuals meeting certain criteria. They often raised funds to provide amenities for schools beyond the standard equipment and supplies furnished by the public authorities. Not least important were the educative effects of some of their activities on their own members. For example, meetings of Women's Institutes were customarily planned as educational experiences, involving presentations by informed speakers followed by discussions.

A multitude of different associations were organized to promote a particular political, social, or cultural cause. In the health field there were groups concerned with most of the major diseases. They made use of the media to elicit support for research into causes and treatment, to publicize methods of prevention, and to appeal for understanding for the victims. Sometimes they helped to provide the special equipment and facilities needed for the education of the latter. Other causes inspiring the efforts of voluntary associations included conservation, safety, the humane treatment of animals, and the preservation of parks.

Voluntary association for worthy objectives is a good indicator of a healthy society and a strong democracy. One of the chief problems, however, is that such organizations must achieve their educational and other purposes through a limited number of channels. As the media become overloaded with messages, a substantial degree of public apathy is inevitable. The recipient of floods of brochures, pamphlets, and newspaper and television appeals cannot be counted on to take the trouble to sort out what is important and ignore the irrelevant. At the same time, the vital quality of voluntary effort could easily be lost by too many ill-advised efforts at co-ordination.

CONCLUDING COMMENTS

This chapter represents an effort to cover, in very brief form, the same ground that receives a large amount of attention in ONTARIO'S EDUCATIVE SOCIETY. The necessity of extreme condensation invites the charge of superficiality, a defect that could hardly be remedied in such a way as to satisfy every reader's particular interests without running headlong into serious problems of another kind. In any case, perhaps the highlights selected are sufficient to make the point that Ontario society, like that in the remainder of Canada and in other parts of the world, was characterized, during the period covered, by a very wide range of educative forces of varying degrees of formality. It was a realization of this fact that has prompted critics of the organized system of schools and colleges to suggest that the young individual who, wherever the responsibility lay, had lost the ability to profit by further attendance at these institutions, could be permitted to withdraw without being cut off from a multitude of aids to intellectual, emotional, and aesthetic growth. This point of view was expressed with particular effectiveness by Walter Pitman in his role as education critic for the New Democratic party in the provincial Legislature.[3] Pitman usually coupled the observation with an assertion that the formal educational system must become increasingly open so that the drop-out could return at any age when he perceived a need.

SIX

New practices and procedures
in the educational process

The inhabitants of Ontario were willing to support schools even when they were living close to the subsistence level and the contribution they had to make meant considerable sacrifice. The same inclination persisted down through the years. Strong psychological forces obviously underlay public confidence in the value of schooling. This chapter traces some of the changes in educational practice and procedure involved in that schooling, with particular reference to curriculum, textbooks, examinations, and the use of media.

SOME UNDERLYING FACTORS

There have been human societies at various stages in history where individuals have had no evident drive for power in relation to their fellows. But Ontario society, like others in the predominant tradition of the modern era, was highly competitive. The urge to growth meant to excel, or at least maintain status, in relation to others. Ambitious parents always sent their children to school primarily so that they could get ahead, while the less ambitious wanted theirs to keep up. Those who did not accept this dominant value system were looked after by compulsory education.

The existence of competitiveness as a prime force supporting schooling had a characteristic effect on curriculum content. Most elements in the curriculum originally won their place because there was some plausible justification for them. That is, they could be related to a definable and socially acceptable objective. As time went on, however, they seemed to acquire a value of their own apart from the original purpose, and might persist long after such a purpose had clearly become irrelevant. This tendency has commonly been ascribed to the strength of habit and tradition – to a fundamental human antipathy to change. Although such a theory probably has some validity, the more convincing explanation is that the material continued to serve the purpose of competition. That is, it continued to sort out the able, the persistent, the energetic, the ambitious. Up to a point, the more difficult it was the more effectively it did these things.

Even in a society where the concept of free enterprise historically had a good deal of currency, people were not prepared to admit that the school system existed to gratify competitive drives. As a result the strength of this motive was underestimated or even ignored, and a pretence was maintained that the schools were completely devoted to other more "worthy" aims. It is of course quite legitimate, and perhaps highly desirable, to formulate aims in terms of developing intellectual powers, cultivating aesthetic tastes, and producing the skills and attitudes that characterize good citizens, workers, parents, worshippers, and whatnot. It is futile, however, to attempt to understand the actual operation of schools in the light of such aims alone.*

What often happened in schools was that content originally introduced for a completely functional purpose and perpetuated mainly because it continued to be an effective sorter was justified as if it were a means of attaining idealistic aims. Thus claims were made that it trained the intellect, uplifted the character, or developed the personality. Educators did not readily turn to thorough research or to rational thought to satisfy themselves that means were really related to ends. The fact that their faith might be entirely misplaced was one of the major reasons why a study of stated aims is often of so little help in understanding reality. Some would argue that this situation is not really strange or remarkable, since aims need not do more than reflect the values to which society expects education to aspire.

The strength of the powerful but relatively unacknowledged competitive factor had a bearing on method as well as on content. It was plausible to suggest, as it was of curriculum, that particular methods of instruction were reasonably effective when they were first introduced. The classical example was the lecture, which characterized instruction during the Middle Ages when books were scarce and there was no other convenient way of transmitting information. Although a number of attractive justifications were offered for modern adaptations of the lecture method, thousands of students could attest that professors still used the procedure in its original form and forced students to accept it, if not by compulsory attendance, which declined in institutions of higher education, then by examining them on the content covered. If the lecture designed to transmit information was really as obsolete as it appeared to be in terms of such idealistic aims as teaching students to think, it would have been rooted out long ago. It persisted because it was not at all antithetical to the concept of education as an obstacle course to sort out those with certain qualities that enabled them to excel in competition. In fact, a bad method of instruction might even be considered an advantage when education was treated as a sorting process.

There may be a good deal to say in favour of competition in economic affairs, provided that it is encouraged or permitted under controlled conditions to prevent the undue exploitation of the weak by the strong. It is also possible to make a case for it in education as long as individuals are

*Volume III, chapter 1, of ONTARIO'S EDUCATIVE SOCIETY is devoted to a discussion of educational aims.

expected to compete on the basis of relatively equal capacities and with comparable opportunities for exercising their powers. But the tacit acknowledgment that the school system was to be regarded as in large measure a proving ground did a tremendous amount of damage in Ontario as elsewhere. As already suggested, it tended to perpetuate obsolete content and ineffective methods, and thus stood in the way of a real attempt to attain the commendable aims and objectives so commonly formulated by theorists. Since the true situation was sensed, although not necessarily articulated, by students at all levels, the process of schooling had to be maintained by rules and regimentation. The resulting atmosphere tended to kill healthy growth trends in the individual which would impel him to seek knowledge and understanding to gratify his impulses toward growth rather than as weapons in the struggle for status or prestige. Educators finally recognized the ill-effects of flaunting differences among children with unequal abilities by entering their relative standing on report cards. The real problem went much deeper, permeating the whole structure and operation of the school.

The historical development of schooling in Ontario cannot be interpreted in relation to a single theme without a great deal of over-simplification. It is nevertheless helpful to look for evidence of the waxing and waning of the role of education as an instrument of social competition. The habit of concealing this concept under idealistic verbiage makes the situation at certain times somewhat confusing, but not completely incomprehensible.

A second major theme that must be kept in mind in interpreting the historical development of Ontario education has to do with the trends of philosophical thought among officials, administrators, and teachers. The overwhelming proportion of such educators could not have explained where they stood in relation to the positions outlined by leading pilosophers. Many did not know enough about the major philosophical systems or analyze their own feelings with sufficient clarity to be able to state the nature of their allegiance. Yet their behaviour and actions usually reflected a distinguishable orientation.

The two basic positions, the traditionalist or essentialist and the progressive, contain contradictions which cannot be glossed over. From the first of these two points of view, there is a basic conflict between the individual's natural drives and full participation in the cultural milieu into which he must be integrated before he can realize his highest human potentialities. Education must bridge the gap by imposing control and discipline, which eventually become internal. The content of education consists of carefully selected items chosen from among the highest intellectual and cultural achievements of man. The effect of studying them assiduously is to ennoble and uplift. If the student can approach them with interest and enjoyment, so much the better, but he cannot expect that the process will always be pleasant, and he must not be allowed to abandon his efforts because of boredom or whim. The process of struggle will help him to build character.

To be called an elitist is seldom considered a compliment in an age when people everywhere reach out for the word "democratic" to describe almost any social or political practice of which they approve. Yet the traditionalist has difficulty escaping some such descriptive label when he observes how his theories work under conditions of mass education. His prescription often seems to be reasonably effective with a minority, while the remainder fail to catch the vision of high cultural achievement, and react by rebelling, dropping out, or perhaps more commonly by going through the motions, particularly if they accept education as a necessary although unpleasant sorting process. The recommended solution for those considered unable to measure up is typically to teach them some marketable skill so that they may become part of a contented proletariat. This is not, of course, to suggest that the traditionalist necessarily recognizes himself as an elitist. He may insist idealistically that sufficiently competent teachers operating under favourable enough circumstances could make his approach widely applicable. Without this hope, he would have had considerably more difficulty in surviving than has been the case.

The progressive believes, not that the individual must be introduced to civilization as a somewhat recalcitrant alien, but that he may be expected to find his cultural surroundings a comfortable environment for growth. If his deep-seated drives are encouraged and cultivated, he will find increasing satisfaction in exploring, acquiring skills, and learning. The teacher's task is to provide opportunities for gratifying his natural impulse toward self-development. Every infant is regarded as a natural learner, although his ultimate level of achievement will depend to some extent on his inherited capacities. If he arrives at school, or reaches a particular stage of schooling, with an attitude of indifference or of active hostility, it is because his healthy inclinations have been thwarted by unsympathetic or ignorant treatment. In the progressive view, any apparent successes achieved by imposing material on the uninterested or resistant pupil are illusory. He learns superficially, and sloughs off what he has learned as soon as the external motivation has been withdrawn. The progressive has no confidence that external motivation will become internalized.

The progressive feels that his approach, if properly applied, will lead every individual to the limit of at least some of his capacities. The implications of such a belief are that progressive education provides maximum assurance that the cutlural treasures of civilization will continue to be augmented. This is one of the points on which the traditionalist and the progressive most sharply part company. The traditionalist insists that the natural impulses of the child are too uncertain and ephemeral to provide a foundation for really oustanding achievement. To cater to them is to ensure uncritical adaptation to mediocrity. In common with the progressive, he believes that only the application of his own distinctive approach will enable the individual to realize his full potentiality.

The traditionalist-progressive dichotomy, if considered in the broad sense rather than being defined in terms of the ideas of particular philosophers, does not provide a clear-cut guide to a person's views about the relative emphasis to be placed on the individual as contrasted with society. Rousseau, one of the earliest philosophers in the progressive line, was regarded as an extreme individualist who seemed at times to believe that social organization was nothing but a reprehensible restraint on human liberty. John Dewey, who formulated his theories during a period when American society was noted for extreme individualism, is thought to have been trying to redress the balance, and is often accused of placing too much emphasis on social adjustment. The traditionalist is easier to identify with respect to this issue than is the progressive. He believes that, while the road to high achievement is hedged in by discipline, intellectual and aesthetic contributions are individual, and not emanations of the masses. Thus he is apprehensive about conscious efforts at socialization in the educational process.

In practice the chief enemy of the progressive in the real Dewey tradition is not the outright traditionalist as much as the supporter of the extreme permissive approach. Although Dewey's writings do not leave him open to any charge of confusion on the matter, he may perhaps be legitimately accused of failing to demonstrate sufficient vigour in disowning some of his self-proclaimed disciples. The interests of the child on which Dewey's educational process were to be built were not whims of the moment which had to be worshipped and followed along whatever ridiculous paths they might lead. Inherent motivational forces might have to be discovered through persistent and searching self-examination with the guidance and sympathetic assistance of an understanding teacher. Part of the process is a prior exploration of the long-term consequences of specific actions, which must be assessed in terms of the accepted values of the society in which the individual lives and functions. The learner does what he wants to do, but only after he is sure he wants to do it, and understands, to the limit of his capacity, why he wants to do it. There is no room in this approach for the teacher contemplating chaos with equanimity, or for a class that disregards every rule of order.

Despite the fact that progressives see no educational value in the exercise of physical force or arbitrary intellectual domination, and traditionalists are more inclined to support such measures as corporal punishment, there is no fundamental basis for a distinction between the two in terms of humane concern for the learner. They may be equally committed to his ultimate good, equally willing to exert themselves on his behalf, and equally distressed over his failures. It cannot be denied, however, that teachers with sadistic tendencies are inclined to gather under the traditionalist banner, and can be as much of a trial to the thoughtful, humane adherent of that school as are the fuzzy-minded, sentimental camp-followers of the progressives.

A view that seems to have had its part in shaping Ontario education consists of a kind of compromise between the two basic orientations. According to this position, progressive principles are appropriate for the infant and the child in the early stages of schooling. The urge to learn, unless it has been clearly obstructed, is an obvious factor on which to build, and full advantage should be taken of it. As adolescence approaches, however, the whole motivational pattern changes. The individual becomes lazy, apathetic toward study and application in general, preoccupied with his emotional changes and developing sexual drives, and, generally speaking, a poor student. At this stage, external pressure must be exerted to keep him at his books. While his natural interest may lag, he can continue to store up the mental building blocks which he will be able to appreciate and use to good advantage later. Possibly by the time he is ready for university, he is over the slump and prepared to become a voluntary learner once again. Those who see no validity in this theory put the entire blame for adolescent lassitude on external factors. They insist that the student's advancing maturity enables him to perceive the irrelevance of much of the content imposed on him, the arbitrariness of many of the rules which he must obey, and the wide gap between idealistic aims and mundane practice. In schools where real efforts to correct these conditions have been made, students' interest in learning has continued unabated. Some of the voluntary enrichment programs offered by larger school boards on Saturdays and in the summer have demonstrated beyond doubt that adolescent reaction against study is at least not a universal phenomenon.

It is even less productive to try to sustain a position between the traditionalist and progressive orientations in dealing with one particular age group than it is to try to apply different philosophies to different age groups. The teacher who pretends to base the program on the child's interests but stands ready to use compulsion if persuasion fails is likely to produce a sense of insecurity. He would probably be better to make known the real terms of the educational contract in the first place and at least win respect for consistency.

CHARACTERISTICS OF CURRICULUM
IN PIONEER SCHOOLS

In order to gain some insight into the characteristics of education in modern Ontario, it is desirable to give brief attention to its historical antecedents. In dealing with pioneer days, it is necessary to distinguish between the common schools, later known as elementary schools, and the district schools, dating from 1808, which were renamed grammar schools, and evolved into high schools and collegiate institutes. The three RS of the common schools had a practical purpose from early times, although they were taught before they had an obvious and necessary relation to making a living on the pioneer farm. As a money economy developed along with specialized production and trade, there were evident practical advantages in being able to read labels, price lists, reports, and other items, to know how to calculate, relate measures of weight and quantity, and to possess the skill to write legibly. The fact that the curriculum acquired a good deal of content that was not of immediate use is evidence that learning was considered to have inherent value in itself, and that it served a means of acquiring personal prestige. For example, the ability to spell very rare and difficult words could only be regarded as an intellectual ornament, since it had little functional value. The same could be said of skill in performing complex operations with fractions. Attention to writing went far beyond mere legibility to the point where it became an artistic achievement. The whole educational process in elementary schools during this period demonstrates an unabashed cultivation of competitive impulses in a curriculum taught according to traditionalist principles. Subject matter that could not be demonstrated to be useful was presumed to have value in character building.

The curriculum in the district or grammar schools was largely imported from the old world. Strong emphasis on the classics was a tradition inherited from a period centuries earlier when such studies had a highly practical purpose in enabling one to gain access to the storehouses of knowledge passed down from the ancient world and in opening the doors to participation in diplomatic affairs. What Upper Canada needed for the administration of a colony according to aristocratic principles was a group of young gentlemen who could be readily distinguished from the rest of the population. The administrative skills they needed could be acquired in practice. Thus it did not really matter much what they learned beyond the basics as long as it was reasonably difficult and out of reach of most of their fellows. Naturally no such crude opinion was expressed at the time. Lofty values of a type that could not be derived from a study of English or other contemporary languages and their literatures had to be assigned to the classics. Some of the snobbish attitudes that were prevalent at the time persisted, and may be held responsible for preventing the Reorganized Program of the 1960s from achieving complete success in terms of equalizing prestige among alternative areas of study.

There was little sign of progressive attitudes at either level of schooling in the early nineteenth century. The chief virtues expectetd of the child were diligence and obedience. To give evidence of an inquiring mind and a curiosity about the nature of things was to demonstrate irreverence or impudence, and a child who revealed such propensities invited punishment. What were regarded as the essentials of the curriculum, replete with maxims and exhortations to espouse good and shun evil, were taught with an air of certainty that left no room for questions. Because of a complete confidence in the close relationship between verbalization and action, it was assumed that the child would learn to be good by memorizing and copying long passages of elevating material. Subject matter was organized according to the adult's concept of logical order, without any concession to the psychological characteristics of the learner.

Since the interests of the average child were so completely trampled upon, he was inclined to resist in one way or another. Misbehaviour and seeming inability to learn were often regarded as almost equally objectionable, and were both subject to punishment. Since the economy provided enough unskilled labour for the failures, a large amount of wastage could be regarded with equanimity. There were always enough children whose growth urge persisted in the face of discouragement, and real scholars managed to emerge from the system. Moreover, although it was regarded as natural to dislike school and to pine for release from the classroom, the general acceptance of authoritarian social relationships prevented any real rebellion against the inhumanity of the school.

As time went on, new subjects were added to the curriculum. According to a description of a school in Toronto after the middle of the nineteenth century, boys in the senior division studied reading, scripture, sacred geography, history, political economy, dictation, science, writing, drawing, bookkeeping, arithmetic, grammar, composition, geography, map drawing, algebra, geometry, singing, and recitation of poetry. The list for girls was comparable, although their program was somewhat lighter to allow for their supposed weaker mental powers.[1] As each item was introduced, it was apparently evaluated in isolation, rather than as part of a whole. It had only to satisfy the judgment of the authorities that it consisted of material that children should know, either because such material had practical uses or because their minds and characters would benefit from grappling with it. Thus the curriculum was overloaded and fragmented.

Egerton Ryerson, the superintendent of education, ran into some resistance in his effort to extend the number of subjects even further to include agriculture, mechanics, and chemistry. He was evidently inspired by the need to prepare young people for certain occupational opportunities in the expanding industries of the province. The Toronto teachers objected in part because many of them were unprepared to teach such subjects, but also because they could see the futility of trying to cram any more information into the minds of the children. For a time the number of subjects was somewhat reduced, but it rose to nineteen in 1871 with the introduction of natural history and natural philosophy. Fortunately individual pupils were not required to take all the subjects.

Another effort was made in 1884 to restore the subject load to a tolerable level, when the program was reduced to twelve subjects: reading, writing, arithmetic, history, geography, composition, grammar, music, drawing, temperance, drill and calisthenics, and agriculture. Once again, but to a more limited extent than before, the list was subsequently length-ened as physiology and later manual training and domestic science were introduced. A more urban orientation was reflected in the decision to make agriculture optional as Canadian history became compulsory.

During the second half of the century there was a gradual shift toward more humane practices in the elementary schools. Although it would be unrealistic to suppose that many teachers actually read the works of such philosophers as Comenius, Rousseau, Pestalozzi, and Froebel, the idea of building on the child's innate capacities began to gain some headway. While the development of character remained a major objective, there was more stress on example as compared with precept. Teachers began to ob-serve the harmful effects of too many examinations, and to realize that there were more constructive kinds of motivation. The change reflected emergence from some of the crudest aspects of pioneer life. The majority of elementary school teachers, instead of coming from the dregs of the community, were now young women of good moral character who met at least modest educational requirements.

Before the middle of the century, Latin and Greek remained predomi-nant in the grammar school curriculum, although English, mathematics, history, geography, writing, drawing, and vocal music won increasing im-portance. An attempt was made in 1854 to give the program a more prac-tical orientation by shifting the emphasis from classics to English. The schools were so steeped in tradition, however, that this attempt had little initial success. The list of subjects was lengthened at the same time by the addition of natural philosophy, which consisted of physics, chemistry, geology, and physiology, and of the optional subjects of bookkeeping and French.

The move to make the grammar schools a distinct stage in the educa-tional system between the common schools and the university, following the pattern of the American high schools, forced the educators of the 1860s to attempt to deal with the needs of students preparing for different types of careers. They instituted a course substituting English and French for Latin and Greek for those wishing to take civil engineering in the Uni-versity of Toronto. Since provincial grants were based on the number taking the classical course, it is hardly surprising that the innovation failed. A change that produced more lasting results was the admission of girls, although at first they were not permitted to study Latin and Greek or to be counted for grant purposes.

A milestone in the movement to democratize the secondary schools was reached in 1871 with the passage of the Act to Improve the Common and Grammar Schools of the Province of Ontario. The first serious effort was made to institute a program that would appeal to those who were not bound for the university. Such students were expected to attend the high schools, which would offer a general course consisting of English, com-mercial work, and natural science. The collegiate institutes, in contrast, would offer a university preparatory course with emphasis on classical and modern languages. Other attempts to relax the grip of Latin and Greek on the curriculum were counteracted by the initial requirement that a school could maintain collegiate institute status only if it had at least sixty boys studying these subjects. The intended distinction between the high schools and collegiate institutes might have developed in a highly urbanized province or country with more towns and cities capable of maintaining schools of both types. It was inevitable, however, that high schools would yield to the demand for the classical program where collegiate institutes were not accessible. The collegiate institutes also contributed to blurring the line of demarcation by offering the general course.

The high schools and collegiate institutes at first demonstrated the same curricular tendency as the common schools in offering a long list of compulsory subjects. From 1871 on, however, there was a reduction in the number of these, and by 1897 the total in the first form had declined from eleven to seven and that in the third form from twelve to six. The larger schools also provided an increasing range of options. These were apparently intended more as a means of enabling students to prepare for different vocations than to pursue individual intellectual interests for their own sake. Thus their introduction did not represent a weakening of the form of traditionalist education that dominated nineteenth-century secondary schools.

OTHER ASPECTS OF SCHOOL OPERATION IN THE NINETEENTH CENTURY

Three developments in the schools of the nineteenth century are particularly illustrative of the search for efficiency in operation: the standardization of textbooks, the appearance of the grade system in the common schools, and the emphasis on examinations. All of these demonstrated the typically traditionalist outlook of the time, and all in some measure continued as obstacles to the advance of progressive practices in the twentieth century. Yet in the light of conditions during the preceding era, they seemed to constitute substantial advances.

Graded schools depended on two basic conditions: sufficient pupils to make a class of acceptable size for each grade, or form, to use the earlier term, and a supply of uniform textbooks so that each child in the class could keep in step with his fellows. The first condition existed in larger centres of population, but not in many rural areas. Although children in one-room schools progressed through forms, there remained an element of flexibility there that tended to be lost in the schools that could properly be called graded. While grading reduced the burden of lesson preparation for the teacher, and thus offered the possibility of superior instruction, it contributed to the impression of schooling as a mechanical process rather than one of uninterrupted growth. The familar practice developed of examining the pupil at the end of the year, and of forcing him to repeat the whole year's work, including what he had learned as well as what he had not, if he failed. The second condition for the development of graded schools was largely achieved during the Ryerson era. The adoption of the Irish National Readers was a particularly important step in this direction. Ryerson also helped matters by establishing his "Depository" from which books could be distributed at nominal cost. The Council of Public Instruction maintained a short approved list from which a selection could be made by local authorities. The use of a single textbook as the supreme authority supported the view of education as a process of obedient absorption of prescribed material. The fact that teachers were often ill-informed and relatively helpless without the text reinforced the same impression.

Examinations developed into a formalized part of the system as a means of elevating and maintaining standards of achievement. Stories about the old-fashioned spelling bees demonstrate how effectively they could appeal to the competitive spirit. It became common to award prizes of books to those who were most successful in bringing honour to themselves or to their schools. The external high school entrance examination was instituted as a reaction against the grammar schools' practice of swelling their enrolment with pupils working at the elementary school level in order to get higher provincial grants during the 1850s and 1860s. Examinations were also introduced at different levels of the secondary school and as a device for determining fitness for admission to normal school as well as university. Between 1876 and 1882 an attempt was made to tie provincial grants in part to the examination results obtained by secondary school students. Although the experiment was soon ended, it is said to have helped to make the Ontario educational system examination ridden for decades thereafter.

The introduction of the first kindergartens into the schools of Toronto in the 1880s was significant in that for the first time there was an attempt to base a program on a progressive view of the child's nature. According to the theory formulated by Friedrich Froebel, the infant personality unfolded in a definite pattern which educators could discover and facilitate with the proper treatment. Later proponents of the kindergarten movement differed with Froebel on the educative value of particular objects and activities, but the essentials of his approach remained. It is questionable whether many teachers, let alone parents, really understood the theoretical justification for kindergarten practices. Undoubtedly kindergarten was often looked upon as a period of play before the child was old enough to begin the real business of learning.

STATUS OF CURRICULUM AND SCHOOL ORGANIZATION
IN THE EARLY TWENTIETH CENTURY

The first three decades of the twentieth century were a period of relatively minor change in the elementary school curriculum. What were regarded as fairly substantial reforms were made in 1904, although these did not indicate any alteration in basic approach. More emphasis was placed on cultural subjects such as art, music, and "constructive work," and on nature study and physical culture. At the same time, manual training, domestic science, and agriculture were put on the optional list, to which were added elementary science, stenography, and typing for fifth form students. English, mathematics, geography, and history still occupied a central place.

The secondary schools of the period showed some of Herbart's influence in that subject matter was arranged and presented in accordance with his views about how the mind apprehended and assimilated information and formed concepts. This type of departure from the earlier practice of considering only what appeared to be the inherent logic of the discipline represented a definitely humanizing influence. The change was said to be most evident in revisions of textbooks between 1908 and 1910.

Attempts were still being made in the second decade of the twentieth century to distinguish clearly between those who sought a terminal education at the secondary school level and those who planned to attend an institution of further education. In 1911 the general course was supposed to serve the first of these purposes, while the special courses included those for university matriculation and the preliminary examinations of the learned professions, the courses for admission to teacher training institutions, and a series of others with a vocational orientation. The distinction, however, was largely fictitious and the universities dominated the entire program. An effort to invigorate the general course in 1913, when two-year programs were installed in each of lower, middle, and upper school, had no greater success.

Growing dissatisfaction with the situation led to the abandonment of the distinctions among the general, university preparatory, and normal school entrance courses in 1921. The burden of the secondary school program was lightened by the reduction of upper school from two years to one and by a decrease in the number of obligatory subjects in lower and middle school. The list of optional subjects remained substantially the same until the 1960s. Such additions as were made until that time attracted only a small number of students. University-bound students could not afford to depart from the set of options prescribed for admission to a particular course.

The range of subjects offered in the secondary schools depended on geographical factors. A major proportion of the population lived outside the towns and cities where high schools and collegiate institutes were maintained. As a means of providing further instruction beyond the fourth form for those who wanted it, teachers gradually began to offer fifth form work, at first in a rather casual fashion. Regular provision was made in 1889 for public and separate school boards to set up fifth classes in any municipality where there was no high school. Some of these classes evolved into continuation schools, which commonly had one or two teachers, possibly with First Class Certificates. When such schools offered the complete program up to matriculation, as many of them attempted to do, they had to stick to a minimum range of subjects. This was the kind of secondary education that a great many Ontario residents obtained, including a considerable proportion of the prominent educators of the post-war period. Quite a number of them averred that the self-reliance they learned under a system that gave the teacher so little time for each subject stood them in good stead in later years.

THE EARLY DEVELOPMENT OF VOCATIONAL EDUCATION

Secondary schools in Ontario did not espouse the cause of vocational education with any great haste or enthusiasm. During the last three decades of the nineteenth century most of those who sought formal preparation for mechanical or commercial occupations had to go to private institutions. There was little opportunity for preparatory training for jobs requiring a lower level of skill. After the reforms of 1871, commercial work began to be offered in the high school program. The bookkeeping option was made compulsory in 1882, and a Commerical Diploma was offered from 1885 on. A two-year commercial course provided in the 1890s gave way to a three-year course during the following decade. Expansion of vocational aspects of the high school program around the turn of the century included the recognition of manual training, household science, art, and agriculture as regular subjects and the introduction of a two-year course in agriculture at certain schools.

Toronto began to offer technical night classes in 1891, and followed these in 1901 with day classes consisting of drafting and industrial design, physics, chemistry, commerce and finance, mathematics, and domestic science.[2] School boards were authorized to establish vocational schools in 1897, a development in which Toronto and Hamilton pioneered. For the next few years, however, technical schools were regarded more as a curiosity than as a fundamental part of the system. John Seath, superintendent of education, presented the whole subject of vocational education in a new light in his study of 1911 entitled *Education for Industrial Purposes*.[3] He offered fairly detailed prescriptions for suitable programs for learners between the elementary school and adult levels. He had to allow, of course, for the fact that whatever formal industrial education many individuals would get had to be at the elementary level, since they would not normally plan to attend high school. His technical high schools would prepare students for positions in industrial life on a higher level of skill and responsibility than those held by skilled mechanics.

A good deal of progress was made following the publication of the Seath report. The Industrial Education Act of 1911 authorized municipalities to levy taxes to establish and support day and evening industrial and technical schools as well as commercial and agricultural high schools or such departments in ordinary high schools. Within two years there were twenty-nine evening technical and industrial classes and six technical and industrial day schools.[4] Progress was impeded by the First World War, but resumed under the stimulus of the federal Technical Education Act of 1919, and by 1921 there were thirteen vocational schools in Ontario. The Seath report also inspired the extension and improvement of commercial education.

THE RISE OF THE PROGRESSIVE OUTLOOK IN THE 1930s

The 1930s were notable in Ontario education, not only for the effects of the depression, which touched practically every aspect of society, but also for the first determined effort to implement progressive principles. John Dewey, who had already made most of the contributions of a long life to the elaboration of educational ideas originating years before, was at last acknowledged. It was not that many were prepared to identify themselves as his disciples, perhaps because of the lack of appeal in his pragmatic philosophy. In this respect C.E. Phillips, who for many years until his retirement in 1962 directed the program of graduate studies at the Ontario College of Education, was almost an isolated figure among leading educational thinkers. But a significant force in the Department of Education, apparently supported by a number of teachers, accepted Dewey's view of the child's nature and attempted to introduce an educational program consistent with it.

The new curriculum introduced in 1937 was attributable largely to the efforts of Thornton Mustard and S.A. Watson of the Department of Education working with a committee of teachers. They borrowed heavily from the reports of the Consultative Committee of the Board of Education in Great Britain, commonly known as the Hadow reports, which between 1927 and 1934 had outlined programs with a progressive orientation. Progressive ideas were evidently more palatable when introduced in this indirect fashion than if they had been taken directly from American sources. The main theme was that the child developed through purposeful activity. The teacher was to take advantage of his inquisitiveness, his delight in movement, his pride in performing small tasks with deftness and skill, his interest in the character and purpose of the material objects around him, his absorption in creating his own miniature world of imagination and emotion, his keen powers of observation, and his pleasure in reproducing his observations by speech and dramatic action. The school was to stimulate him through his own interests and to guide him into experiences that would help him satisfy his own needs.[5]

The fact that the child was a growing organism dictated strong emphasis on his physical welfare and on the development of his physical powers, which he was to learn to use and control. He was to acquire desirable attitudes by an orderly management of his energies, impulses, and emotions. In recognition of his need to function as a member of civilized society, he was to learn to live with others and to gain their approval. Although the approach to the curriculum was to be modified, the actual content was not to be basically different. Language and numbers would be taught as means of thought and communication. Reading would bring the child in contact with other minds and reveal that life had a past and a future as well as a present. Information about the physical environment would help to create an understanding of the earth as the home of man. Participation in a variety of aesthetic activities would develop the capacity to create and appreciate beauty. Although adult standards of performance would not be demanded, the child would be expected to acquire habits of thoroughness and honesty in his work.

Instructions were provided on the teaching of individual subjects, and a specified amount of time was suggested for each. Distinctions might, however, be considerably blurred in actual practice. The enterprise method was particularly recommended for social studies, where it might be appropriate to follow the implications of some problem or theme. In developing it the children might have opportunities for oral and written communication, the expression of aesthetic interests, and the like. Similarly, a starting point for broader activities might emerge from nature study.

In accordance with the views prevailing at the time, the schools were to be pervaded by a Christian atmosphere. Although the program was to include hymn singing and the teaching of the parables and Bible stories, religion was not to be offered as a distinct subject, but to be introduced incidentally as a means of developing Christian attitudes. However enlightened the framers of the curriculum were in other respects, they were evidently not prepared to acknowledge that non-Christians had a right to attend public schools without being exposed to the fundamentals of an alien faith. Nor did they recognize the difficulty in teaching even Bible stories in a completely non-sectarian manner so as to avoid giving offence to the adherents of any Christian group.

Although the whole approach implied careful attention to individual differences, there was no recommendation that the graded system be completely abandoned in favour of a program specially tailored to suit the capacities and interests of each child. The structure was to be relaxed so that some particularly bright children could cover the six grades in five or four years, while enrichment would meet the needs of others. Another possible arrangement was the combination of two or three grades through which children might pass in cycles. Whatever system was used was to avoid the mechanical processing of children, since the elementary school had no business with uniform standards. For the most part, promotion in the junior grades was to be by age rather than by achievement. While the average child would be expected to handle the regular program, there would be special provision for the slower learners. There would be reduced emphasis on examinations, although numerous informal tests might be given in the skill subjects including reading, writing, arithmetic, spelling, and language. In social studies and natural science, there was to be less testing in favour of encouragement to read, explore, discover, record, and create. Reporting to parents was to be in terms of the child's capacity rather than according to some presumed absolute standard.

The new approach conflicted with any policy of insisting on strict adherence to a prescribed textbook. In order to implement it, teachers and pupils had to be free to seek information from any appropriate source. There were, it is true, certain changes; the Department of Education ceased having books prepared under its supervision and instead appointed committees to choose those acceptable for authorization. In some cases teachers might make a selection from a list of two or more books, subject to the approval of the school board. This amount of freedom did not, however, go nearly far enough to enable them to carry out the spirit of the new program. It is idle to talk about meeting the child's individual needs and preferences when the work to be covered is presented in a uniform manner for all.

Textbooks of this period did show an improvement in that they demonstrated a better understanding of what would be beneficial and interesting for most children to learn. They dropped a considerable amount of relatively useless material such as involved arithmetic calculations and unusual words to be spelled. A good deal of formal grammar was eliminated in favour of exercises in English usage. More care was taken to present certain concepts, vocabulary, and arithmetical operations at a stage when they could be properly understood rather than parotted by rote.

The period was characterized by evidence of strong feelings both for and against the changes that were instituted. The enthusiasts sometimes spoke as if they had for the first time discovered the child as a human being, and looked forward to the removal of old antipathies to schooling as well as to a sounder type of development in line with psychological realities. The efficacy of the project or enterprise was propounded in some circles with the fervour of a religion. The doubters, on the other hand, saw the old standards of achievement crumbling, and feared that the schoolroom would become simply an extension of the playground. They could find examples among early experimenters with the revised program to confirm their worst apprehensions.

The results of the attempted reforms were on the whole disappointing. The Department of Education made only a very modest effort to explain what was intended and how it was to be carried out. Many teachers were too poorly educated and insecure to abandon familiar landmarks in favour of the original and flexible approach required. They lacked the skill and ingenuity to seize upon a valid expression of pupil interest and to develop from it a set of constructive educational activities. In their hands the enterprise method often produced little more than tepees in a sandbox. They were not, of course, entirely to blame for the relative lack of progress. As was demonstrated clearly in the 1960s, the approach they were supposed to follow required access to library and other supportive materials that could not be supplied in the final years of the depression or in the midst of the exigencies of the war period. Further, the attitude of many inspectors, who are frequently considered to be the most conservative element in any school system, was often unsympathetic. Thus the subjects listed in the program of studies often continued to be taught in a traditional fashion.

RECOMMENDATIONS OF THE ROYAL COMMISSION
ON EDUCATION, 1950
The report of the Royal Commission, which appeared in 1950, probably came close to reflecting the prevailing views of the time. It presented a reasonably adequate statement of the traditionalist/progressive antithesis, although perhaps displaying some misunderstanding of the progressives by claiming that "they would allow the learners to discipline themselves" instead of indicating more accurately that discipline, from the progressive point of view, is inherent in the learning situation.[6] The commissioners tried to compromise to some extent by suggesting that progressive principles had considerable validity in the early school years. For the high school student, however, their prescription was largely traditionalist. He was expected to be too busy learning subject matter arranged in order according to an adult criterion to have time for such nonsense as following his own interests. There were certain things that individuals of all ages had to learn regardless of personal inclinations. If these things could not be accepted voluntarily, compulsion might be required.

A major aspect of the work of the Royal Commission was a recommendation that the school system be restructured on the basis of a 6–4–3 plan, corresponding to elementary school, secondary school, and junior college. Communities that were unable to provide the full program might offer only two years at the third level. The commission suggested the subjects that might be taught at each level and in some cases the methods of instruction it considered appropriate. It did not, however, go so far as to indicate the topics that should be covered in each subject. It proposed, rather, that courses be developed through co-operative effort by all who were concerned with the educational development of the child. Its set of guidelines for nursery school and kindergarten were in reasonable harmony with the program of 1937, stressing activities that met the psychological and social needs of the child. For the higher grades of the elementary school, it recommended the subjects already prescribed and gave a good deal of support to the methods that were supposed to be in use. Rather sharp criticism was directed at the existing secondary school program, which was accused of providing little more adaptation and selection of courses than there had been in the grammar schools of the previous century. The program was said to be dominated by university entrance requirements and to be failing to meet the needs of students who were not headed for university. For the proposed secondary school, which would cater to the needs of students between the ages of twelve and sixteen, there would be a common obligatory program for the first two years consisting of a basic core of English, social studies, physical and health education, and religious education or ethics. Options in the last two years would introduce specialized academic training and exploratory vocational courses. No great promise was seen in work-study programs, which had been difficult to operate where they had been tried because of the problem of co-ordinating the efforts of school authorities, organized labour, and employers. The junior colleges would have a range of offerings including university preparatory work and terminal technical courses. In some respects they were to follow a pattern that was consciously rejected when the colleges of applied arts and technology were established.

THE PORTER PLAN

The next event of major importance in the development of curriculum after the appearance of the elementary school program of 1937 was the introduction of the Porter Plan in November 1949. This scheme, named for Dana Porter, who was minister of education at the time, had implications both for the structure of the system and for curriculum. An effort was made, following the abolition of the high school entrance examination, to bridge the gap between the elementary and secondary school levels by treating grades 7 to 10 as a single intermediate division for curriculum purposes. This change would have obvious parallels to the Royal Commission's recommendation for high school covering grades 7 to 10, but a less drastic reform was envisaged. The new plan was worked out by those who knew what the commission was going to recommend. There were plans to reduce the number of obligatory subjects and increase the number of options in the upper years of the junior division and to provide terminal courses at the end of grade 10. At the same time there was to be an attempt to redistribute part of the grade 13 program through grades 11 and 12.

The most important aspect of the plan was that it represented a serious effort to decentralize the process of curriculum building and to place unprecedented responsibility in the hands of groups of teachers and local supervisory officials. Under the general direction of curriculum co-ordinating committees, these groups might revise earlier courses or adapt new departmental courses to meet local needs. If they preferred, they might decide to use departmental courses in their original form. The procedure did not leave the individual teacher free to make his own decision as to what to teach, since he was expected to follow a locally devised or revised course just as if it had come from the department.

For two or three years there was a great flurry of activity as elementary and secondary teachers gathered to pool whatever combined knowledge and wisdom they had. The experience of working together undoubtedly had beneficial results as those from the different levels gained an opportunity to understand one another's point of view. The process also constituted an excellent type of in-service training for those who were forced to think about their subject matter in a new light. The courses of study produced did not, however, break much new ground. It was too much to suppose that local conditions called for radically different treatment of most subjects from one geographical area to another. While varying approaches to geography and some of the sciences may have been in order, it was not to be expected that algebra should differ much in content or method of presentation between Ottawa and Windsor. In addition to the inertia that sets in after the novelty has worn off any new scheme, there were two chief influences that killed the Porter Plan. The first was that the Department of Education used its resources of expertise to such good effect in producing courses for the intermediate division that local groups often failed to see any great advantage in introducing their own variations. The second was the official policy of indifference, if not actual disfavour, that accompanied the appointment of W.J. Dunlop as minister of education in 1951. Although the plan was not completely disowned, there was relatively little activity after the mid-fifties.

MAJOR CONCERNS OF THE 1950s
The 1950s were a period of concern about education in the United States which reflected a fear of the expansion of international Communism. The Russians, besides breaking the American monopoly on nuclear weapons, had demonstrated their belligerence by attempting to force the western allies out of Berlin and by instigating an attack on South Korea. The Chinese, under a newly established Communist government, seemed to be part of the expanding monolith. When the Soviet Union gave evidence of superiority in space technology in 1957, the Americans looked to their educational system for a scapegoat. Some of their reactions were no doubt justified. There were many schools where standards had deteriorated badly in an overly permissive atmosphere, and many others that were not being run competently by any criterion. There was also a need to upgrade curricula, particularly in mathematics and science. To some extent, Canadians also began to wonder about the validity of their curricula.

Canadians were inclined to be uncertain about the reasons for their dissatisfaction. This uncertainty enabled Hilda Neatby, a professor of history at the University of Saskatchewan, to set up the straw man of progressivism, which she proceeded to belabour with great vigour and sarcasm in *So Little for the Mind*.[7] A good deal of the difficulty was actually attributable to the fact that many of the teachers produced by the emergency training courses were unable to perform competently in accordance with any philosophical theory, although their general approach owed most to the traditionalist school. That Neatby's unscholarly book was widely praised demonstrates clearly that the mood of the times was blindly rather than perceptively critical.

W.J. Dunlop denounced progressivism and declared that every trace of it would be rooted out of the schools. Perhaps his major initiative in this direction was his attempt to have the teaching of history and geography as separate subjects replace the broader social studies approach. His policy did not prevent S.A. Watson, one of the key framers of the 1937 program of studies, from heading the Curriculum and Text-books Branch, or J.R. McCarthy, an official with unusually strong progressive views, from serving as Watson's assistant. For the most part, however, the atmosphere in the department was one in which Dunlop could be reasonably comfortable.

TESTS AND EXAMINATIONS

There was a growing interest in testing in the schools, although nothing like the mania that existed in certain parts of the United States. The most popular types of tests were group intelligence tests or tests of learning capacity and survey tests of achievement in basic elementary school subjects such as reading, spelling, and arithmetic. The main purpose of testing appeared to be to categorize the pupils rather than to help them reach higher individual levels of attainment. When the writer undertook to produce a revised set of survey tests in arithmetic fundamentals in the Department of Educational Research of the Ontario College of Education in 1955, he discovered that there was a satisfactory demand for the product. There was, however, too little interest to justify a similar effort in the area of diagnostic tests designed to assist teachers to identify specific weaknesses and to help pupils overcome them.

The development of testing was closely related to that of guidance, which grew quickly, largely in the secondary schools, after the Second World War. During the early period a considerable number of the teachers who entered the field were not considered to be of the highest calibre, at least partly because the greatest prestige was accorded the academic specialists, who were graduates of honours courses in the universities, while those who assumed responsibility for the guidance program were mostly graduates of pass or general courses. As a result of the rather inadequate nature of their preparation, the latter often administered tests too uncritically and failed to show sufficient skill in interpreting and applying the results. A lack of confidence in their activities on the part of other teachers may well have had something to do with the rather pronounced reaction against testing demonstrated in the late 1960s.

There were backward looks at the external high school entrance examination, abolished in 1949, and a number of secondary school teachers called regularly for its reinstatement. They felt that the effort to prepare for it was a salutary influence on the pupils who were not recommended for promotion on the basis of their year's work, and that it screened out a certain number of those who could not measure up to existing secondary school standards. In fact, however, the secondary school could no longer be a selective institution, but had to devise programs to suit virtually all needs. As indicated in chapter 1, the demand for higher educational qualifications for most occupations was making the future look bleaker year by year for those who dropped out of school at the elementary level. The school was perhaps the most acceptable, although not necessarily the cheapest, form of welfare for young people who could not have found a job. The feeling grew that, if education was to be compulsory for all but a few until the age of sixteen, there was more chance that those who were not academically inclined would benefit from a specially designed secondary school program than they would from being forced to repeat one or more elementary school grades until they could legally withdraw.

For a time there was no attempt to find a satisfactory solution to the problem at the secondary school level. Technical and commercial schools and the technical and commercial wings of composite schools suffered from a reputation as dumping grounds for those with no talent for academic work. Such students often had no more talent for or interest in technical or commercial work. Attempts at streaming during the 1950s often involved a mere separate treatment of groups of students who were all appraised at the end of the year by the same examination. Some secondary schools tried to maintain high standards of achievement by failing large numbers of students at the end of grade 9, while others regarded entrance to grade 11 as the main sorting stage.

At the end of grade 13 the departmental examination system was firmly ensconced. The universities counted on the examination results as almost the sole criterion for admission, and prescribed patterns of subjects as preparation for specific courses. The examination system was administered by the Department of Education in a co-operative relationship with the universities. According to this arrangement, carefully selected university professors had the responsibility of setting the examination papers. Fellow faculty members did not on this account refrain from criticizing the quality of the grade 13 graduates who gained admission to the university. The chief complaints were that too many weak candidates got through and that the average student was inadequately prepared to think independently and intelligently about his material. Outstanding educators such as Sidney Smith, president of the University of Toronto, and P.A.C. Ketchum, headmaster of Trinity College School, were critical of the examination system itself, feeling that it placed a premium on cramming, conformity, and the learning of isolated facts. As a means of making grade 13 a more truly educational experience, they advocated the use of objective tests of scholastic aptitude and achievement similar to the College Entrance Examination Board tests administered widely in the United States as at least a supplement to grade 13 examination marks for university admission purposes. Their interest in the matter led to the Atkinson Study of Utilization of Student Resources, which was undertaken by the Department of Educational Research of the Ontario College of Education with the assistance of grants from the Atkinson Charitable Foundation. Although the results of this study did not support the hope that objective test scores could be used as a satisfactory substitute for examination marks for university admission purposes, interest in testing was enhanced to the point where the departmental grade 12 objective testing program was introduced and objective test items found a place in some grade 13 papers.

The departmental objective testing program, which became firmly established by the end of the 1950s, was administered principally as a means of regulating standards in the secondary schools. The teacher shortage meant that some remote areas could not obtain qualified teachers who knew what to expect of their students. There were said to be schools where practically every student who was promoted from grade 12 and proceeded to grade 13 failed the departmental examinations at the end of that year. The provincial tests provided over-all indicators of the aptitude and achievement of the students in a particular school, and presumably enabled the staff to bring their marking standards into line. Departmental officials had to resist the efforts of many principals and teachers to adjust individual students' school marks to their test scores, a procedure which would have denied the independent value of the school marks. The teachers of the day generally approved of the testing program and the uses to which it was put. When certain departmental officials considered abolishing it in the early 1960s to make way for essay-type examinations set centrally and marked in the schools, they were dissuaded by an expression of opinion that was strongly in favour of the existing arrangement. For several years both objective tests and essay-type examinations were given, although not in the same subjects.

NEW CURRICULUM INITIATIVES BEGINNING
IN THE 1950S AND EARLY 1960S
Concern over obsolete curricula, particularly in mathematics and science, was demonstrated by the Ontario Teachers' Federation in 1957 when a Committee on Mathemtics and Science was formed. This action led to the establishment of the Ontario Mathematics Commission, which became an independent organization while continuing to receive financial support from the federation. The commission brought together some of the leading university scholars and school teachers to prepare new sequences of subject matter. Its activities led to the preparation of textbooks in "new" mathematics and to the organization of various in-service programs to enable teachers to keep up to date. Participation of Department of Education officials in the work of the commission represented a significant break from past practice, when the department had preferred to operate in relative isolation.

Curriculum changes initiated by the department during the late fifties and at the beginning of the sixties were numerous enough in one sense, but they tended to be of a rather minor nature. The lack of emphasis placed on this phase of the work was demonstrated by the fact that a much larger proportion of staff time was devoted to supervisory activities than to curriculum development. New courses of study were often assembled in a very brief period of time and with no pretence at the kind of research or development work that might have led to real innovations. It was not to be expected that many radical ideas would sneak into the system through the textbook route, since a textbook that did not follow the course of study rather closely had little chance of being accepted. In his column in the *Globe and Mail* on February 14, 1964, Bascom St John denounced procedures that characterized the period then coming to an end.

> A pedantic curriculum committee sits down in a dusty office and decides what historical facts Ontario children should know, and this comprises the history course. It then becomes necessary by a sort of jig-saw puzzle procedure to fit together a large number of sentences which include the facts that are in the course.
>
> The result is called a textbook. The marvel is that some of them are as good as they are.[8]

A somewhat broader extra-departmental initiative than that of the Ontario Mathematics Commission had its roots in a Joint Committee of the Toronto Board of Education and the University of Toronto. That development owed a great deal to two Toronto trustees: Roy Sharp, a prominent lawyer who won a reputation as an educational reformer, and Robin Harris, a university professor who was interested in building bridges between the academic world and the school system. During the summer of 1960, committees met under the ægis of the Joint Committee and with the financial support of the Atkinson Charitable Foundation to study certain aspects of the school curriculum. The results of their studies were later published in *Design for Learning* with an introduction by Northrop Frye, who acted as editor.[9] Areas of initial concentration were English, science, and the social sciences. It is slightly ironical that the Social Science Study Committee could find no more appropriate name in view of the fact that the two chief disciplines with which it dealt, history and geography, are somewhat uneasy members of the group, the former frequently being claimed by the humanities and the latter by the natural sciences.

The procedure adopted by the study committees was to have groups of university professors and teachers from the elementary and secondary levels of the school system assemble to consider existing courses of study and methods of instruction and to suggest appropriate adaptations of the relevant disciplines to meet the needs of children and young people at various levels. Perhaps because of the relative novelty of the approach, a number of outstanding people were induced to offer their services. The pattern established continued on a broader scale in the Ontario Curriculum

Institute, which grew out of the Joint Committee.* Although much depended on the personal characteristics of individual participants, there was said to be a tendency for the secondary school teachers to defer to the professors and for the elemenary school teachers to defer to both. This proclivity would account for the strongly subject-centred approach that permeated the committee reports. One group did not hesitate to recommend the extension of subject specialization among teachers down into the elementary school grades. Such a proposal was at complete variance with the spirit of the 1937 reforms, and conflicted with the views of the Royal Commission, which advocated the avoidance of teacher specialization until as late as possible in the secondary school.

The guiding spirit of the Joint Committee and of some of the early committees of the Ontario Curriculum Institute was Jerome Bruner, who contributed two ideas that had a particular appeal for the participants. One was that it was important in education to recognize the structure of certain disciplines and to adapt to this structure in order to facilitate maximum learning. The other was that the curriculum should be based on the great issues, principles, and values that a society considered important for its members, that a child could at a very early age be introduced to these fundamentals in some intellectually honest form, and that the process of education thereafter should involve a growing understanding of them through an exploration of more complex and sophisticated manifestations. The curriculum could be conceptualized as a spiral in that the learner came back repeatedly to the same basic elements, but each time at a higher level of understanding. Research into the psychological characteristics of children, and particularly into the nature of the learning process, would have to guide the selection of the most suitable learning materials for any particular stage of development. This latter aspect of Bruner's approach gave some cause for gratification to the progressives, while at the same time he made a considerable appeal to the traditionalists.

Ontario progressives such as J.R. McCarthy tended to be suspicious of Bruner, since the process of selecting the basic issues, principles, and values seemed to overemphasize the importance of the culture at the expense of the individual. There was also apprehension lest the concept of structure be carried too far and applied inappropriately to disciplines such as English, where some leading scholars saw little place for it. However, Bruner's emphasis on the discovery method had a strong appeal for the progressives.

The work of the study committees of the Joint Committee revealed some serious weaknesses in teaching even in Toronto schools with a reputation for high standards of instruction. High school history classes, for example, were often conducted with obsessive attention to the coverage of

*A more detailed account of the origin and early development of the Ontario Curriculum Institute is found in ONTARIO'S EDUCATIVE SOCIETY, volume v, chapter 11.

factual material for examination purposes. Opportunities were neglected for arousing interest in contemporary issues and for relating the events of the past to them. Students were seldom encouraged to conduct serious independent studies of their own or in any major way to stray off the beaten track. Although teachers did not escape criticism for the dullness of the subject as it was presented, a good deal of the blame was placed on the network of expectations within which they operated. The rigidity of the grade 13 program exerted an undesirable influence down through the earlier grades, and departmental prescriptions made it difficult and frustrating to adopt a really innovative approach.

Through the early and middle sixties, the study committees of the Ontario Curriculum Institute covered all important areas of the curriculum between kindergarten and grade 13. Most of their reports were written in a lucid style and demonstrated a high level of competence among those who produced them. As expositions of purposes and principles of teaching various subjects, they were highly regarded far beyond the borders of Ontario. However, almost every one of them suffered from a tendency to advocate that more time be spent on the subject in question if the students were to obtain maximum benefit from it. Given the limits of the school day, such advice could obviously have been followed only to a limited degree. Another group of committees set about, with varying degrees of success, to study some of the underlying factors affecting curriculum. Their work was hampered in certain respects because of inadequate facilities for research.

Evidence of the extent to which the work of the institute influenced educational practice in Ontario is largely circumstantial. It could be coincidental that the operations of the Curriculum Branch of the Department of Education began to expand and become much more comprehensive, that the influence of energetic and progressive officials including M.B. Parnall, J.K. Crossley, J.F. Kinlin, and a number of others became more pronounced. It was perhaps inevitable that a strong emphasis on curriculum reform would be part of the Davis program when the new minister got his bearings after his appointment in the fall of 1962. Yet, although these developments might have occurred anyway, it is not hard to believe that departmental initiative was strengthened by the threat that an independently controlled agency (on which the department had minority representation) might usurp too many official responsibilities. It is true, of course, that a plausible line of demarcation was drawn: the OCI was to work out basic principles of curriculum and conduct only limited experiments to test the feasibility of certain ideas, while the department was to retain the sole power to prescribe courses of study and to determine when, where, and to what extent an innovative procedure was to be adopted. The line of demarcation was, however, thin, and to some officials the department seemed in danger of being reduced to a position of issuing prescriptions in a mechanical sort of way. Departmental officials made sure that this danger did not materialize by performing their functions in a much more thoroughgoing manner than had characterized any previous period.

EDUCATIONAL MEDIA

While these developments were occurring, considerable attention was being given to the possible role of certain methodological contributions. During the 1950s the acute teacher shortage turned some minds toward the possibility of using the products of the technological revolution to better advantage. Such ideas for the most part issued from theorists and promoters who were more successful in attracting public attention than in influencing the actual practice of education. They never made a convincing case that any of the new techniques or devices would achieve the traditional educational objectives at reduced cost. It was also very difficult to show that education, conceived essentially as a process of absorbing knowledge from books and notes, could be greatly facilitated by the interposition or support of some non-human intermediary. Demonstrating this kind of thinking in the early 1970s, certain boards of education declared their opposition to any more expenditure on educational television facilities until there was some research evidence that there were practical results from the approach. It took a long time to make headway with the concept that modern life was acquiring new dimensions that education should recognize and incorporate in order to remain live and relevant.

Radio quickly became a regular feature of life in the twenties and thirties. From the beginning its role was educational as well as informative and entertaining. There was no great haste, however, to give it recognition in the formal educational system. From the time of its formation in 1936, the Canadian Broadcasting Corporation was prepared to place network facilities at the disposal of provincial departments of education, but not until 1943 did it secure the co-operation of all nine of these departments in order to begin a series of national school broadcasts. Up until that time the Ontario Department of Education had been notably unresponsive to any suggestion that it enter actively into the field.

After that time a School Broadcasts Department engaged in a rather ambitious program of broadcast production and evaluation, with the assistantce of a National Advisory Council on School Broadcasting. The number of children who heard certain broadcasts appeared reasonably impressive. In actual fact, however, radio did not occupy a vital part in the educational process in the schools. A broadcast was something special, a unit in itself, unrelated to the rest of the program. In order to listen to it the pupils had to set something else aside, to postpone a regular activity, to experience an interruption in the ordinary schedule. It was regarded more as a diversion or as an occasion for relaxation from regular work than as a basic learning experience. Even when teachers were able to use guides to prepare the pupils beforehand, and engaged in prescribed follow-up activities, the broadcast did not lose its special, extra-curricular quality.

By their nature, national school broadcasts cannot accommodate individual schools, teachers, or pupils. They can only dictate their own terms and require that they be used accordingly or not at all. From time to time, local radio stations co-operated with schools to enable students to go beyond this limited experience with the medium. Facilities and time were made available for the production and broadcast of programs giving students, writers, actors, and directors full scope for the exercise of their talents. In certain cases radio itself was the subject of study as a medium of communication. Examples of this kind of activity were, however, sporadic and unusual.

Toward the end of the 1950s the concept of programmed learning caught the imagination of many educators who were on the look-out for a real educational innovation. The approach had several promising features: it was based on a plausible, although not necessarily universally acceptable, psychological theory; it was down-to-earth – easily described and understood; it produced tangible and measurable results; and it held out the possibility of substantial savings. While a good deal of attention was focused on the box or machine that tended to be used in the earlier stages to house the contents, this feature proved to be of relatively minor importance, and usually quite dispensable. The main significance of the programmed learning movement was that it focused attention on the organization and analysis of content for ready assimilation by the mind of the learner. In a sense, it was merely an extension of what teachers had always tried to do with their material.

If there had been a desire to develop the full potentialities of programmed learning, one can envision a serious effort to identify all the major content areas where students might have wanted or needed to acquire information, concepts, or verbalizable skills, and some of the best available minds might have been assigned the task of reducing these to programmed form. After the major task had been completed, a smaller corps of such people might have continued with the task of revising the existing programs and adding to them as additional material was identified as being worthy of inclusion. With such an arsenal of devices, teachers might have concentrated entirely on the tasks that could not be standardized, such as guiding, motivating, encouraging, inspiring, and evaluating. They might have devoted themselves to what only humans could do and ceased to involve themselves in what programs could do better. There would have been no impromptu, ill-prepared, incomplete explanations of something the student wanted to know. He could always have had the help of an inanimate expert whose material was thorough, complete, and accurate.

Of course nothing of the kind ever happened. The programs failed to appear at the teachers' elbows, ready for service at the first sign of need,

Nor would most teachers have known what to do with them if they had. Neither the provincial department nor local school systems proved willing to commit any major resources to the production of programs or to teacher preparation for their use. The field was left to commercial producers, who moved in eagerly enough, but could not escape certain overwhelming handicaps. For example, they lacked access to pupils in classrooms, where adequate developmental work would have had to take place. Also, under the competitive conditions of the marketplace they typically put their products on sale without the proper assurance of quality, and left trails of disillusionment behind. Thus what might have been a powerful weapon in the arsenal of the teacher continued to be a mere fad.

There had always been an awareness of the possibility of misusing the programmed learning approach. Those who emphasized the humanizing aspects of education were afraid that programmed learning might be relied on for a greater contribution than it was capable of making. Many feared that it might give the student the wrong impression of the nature of problem solving, which did not always include a neat answer on the other side of the page. It seemed antithetical to discovery learning in which the child followed his unique path to whatever surprise there might be at the end. These apprehensions were not, however, the main reason why programmed learning was not seriously tried. The approach failed to make headway chiefly because educational systems do not have inherent incentives and rewards for efficiency. Thus it was not even used for the acquisition of routine skills which are an essential part of education.

In view of their peculiar advantages, programmed texts and similar devices made the greatest appeal exactly where one might expect – in industrial and commercial enterprises. The subject matter which the employee had to cover in order to better himself tended to be particularly amenable to analysis and logical organization. The approach was especially suitable for a person who had to work on his own time and at his own speed. Unlike the program in the formal school system, upgrading courses were not compulsory, and there was no need to worry about the ways in which the employee might defeat the objectives of the process through boredom or lack of interest. While many programs were used without an adequate evaluation of their effectiveness, employers were prepared to gamble that it was cheaper to have the material prepared carefully once and have successive employees use it in printed form rather than have a live teacher go over it innumerable times.

Advancing technology soon made the earliest programmed learning techniques look old-fashioned. The computer was utilized to show how the approach could be made vastly more flexible and capable of adaptation to the individual's peculiarities. Enthusiasts looked forward to the day when the eager learner could address the machine in a normal voice and receive back in the same manner an answer to any question he might put to it. For those to whom that was not miracle enough, there was always the realm of thought transference. The great problem was, of course, cost. What was likely to happen was that certain items of content would gradually be made available in the highest cost programs such as those for executive training or medical education. While ordinary school learning would not soon be strongly affected, there might be occasions when the individual pupil researcher would discover that a desired sequence of material was accessible on some computer terminal.

By far the most important among the technological contributions to education was television. Like radio a short time earlier, it became a major educative influence in society before its existence was seriously acknowledged by formal educational systems. Nothing could better demonstrate the compelling urge of such systems to remove themselves to the sidelines rather than seeking a position in the mainstream of social and cultural life. Some of the first reactions of educators to the medium were highly defensive and negative: children would ruin their eyes watching it; they would have no time left for reading, which was obviously the only real way to learn and to acquire cultural values; their physical powers would remain undeveloped or atrophy if they sat passively for hours a day watching programs. The school-teacherish reaction was to advocate regulations and prohibitions. When television began to win a place in school education, the tendency was to try to fit it into or around a process of which the outlines were already fixed and relatively immutable. Thus it might serve for enrichment, which usually meant that it was a diversion, a relaxation, an alternative to serious effort, or just a plain frill. When a more serious role was sought for it, it was viewed as a means of extending the image of the teacher to more classrooms with more children sitting at desks. Only gradually did educators begin to realize that they had a potentially new means to some of their old ends. It was a still slower process to recognize that television implied new means to new ends, a message that lay within some of McLuhan's mystifying verbiage.

Homes in cities close to the American border began to sprout television aerials shortly after the Second World War. It was not until 1952, however, that the Canadian Broadcasting Corporation began to exercise prerogatives conferred upon it by the federal government by offering a few hours of programs a week from Montreal and Toronto. After that time the amount of service and coverage expanded rapidly to include a large part of the country. As early as 1954, experimental school telecasts were prepared with the assistance of the National Advisory Council on School Broadcasting, and from then on these constituted a regular service. Some of them were evaluated at the national and provincial levels, and for the most part they were considered to be of commendable quality. However, for the same reasons that radio broadcasting failed to win a vital part in the school system, television watching remained a strictly peripheral activity. There was an additional handicap in that the equipment was much more expensive than that required for radio reception. Thrifty school boards hesitated to purchase it until there was some prospect of fairly regular use, while no agency could be expected to undertake elaborate and expensive production until there were adequate means of reception.

Local initiatives were evident long before the Ontario Department of Education entered the field. A unique organization called the Metropolitan Educational Television Association was formed in 1959 by a group of school boards from Metropolitan Toronto and the adjacent area, the University of Toronto, York University, the Royal Ontario Museum, the Art Gallery of Toronto, the Toronto and Scarborough Public Libraries, the local branches of the teachers' federations, and other organizations, each contributing financially in accordance with its resources. This association was able to prepare many broadcasts of interest to its member groups, either alone or in co-operation with the CBC or local broadcasters. Some of these broadcasts were closely related to various aspects of the school curriculum and, as time went on, were increasingly accompanied by explanatory and supplementary material that could be used by teachers and student viewers. META had no broadcast facilities of its own and consequently had to purchase them from the CBC and private interests. While school hours were not prime time, there were relatively serious problems with adult education programs, which tended to be pushed into awkward hours in the early morning or late at night. It became a persistent cause for META supporters to attempt to have ultra high frequency channel 19 made available for educational purposes. Ironically, the organization passed out of existence when this objective was achieved in 1970.

Entry by the Department of Education into the area of educational television on an almost unique scale was one of the most conspicuous achievements of the Davis era. From a number of points of view the venture was bold and controversial. The early 1970s were much too early a period in which to estimate the degree of success achieved, although there were a good many portents of the way things were going.

There were, first of all, certain issues of jurisdiction between the federal and provincial governments. While the province was constitutionally responsible for education, the federal government claimed the right to control and regulate communication. On the face of the matter, it appeared necessary only for the provincial government to secure approval for the use of broadcast facilities to meet its educational purposes. The problem which developed, involving prolonged discussion between the two levels, was one of definition. The federal authorities were very much aware of the fragility of the cultural links that bound the country together, and were determined not to give up any prerogative that might serve as a means of strengthening national unity. They were apprehensive about the possible development of provincial cultural centres in the guise of educational facilities, particularly if the programs were designed to reach adult audiences. A related fear was that provincial premiers and their political parties might help to ensconce themselves with the aid of pervasive propaganda machines. Ontario was not, of course, seen as a potential centre of separatist sentiment, but if such tendencies were to be curbed in Quebec, Ontario could not be allowed to establish damaging precedents. From the provincial point of view, education via television could not be restricted to a formal, dogmatic, didactic process with exercise books and examinations closely paralleling what went on in the traditional classroom if it was going to add something vital and up-to-date to the curriculum. Nor were the provinces prepared to admit that only those in the same age ranges as those ordinarily found in educational institutions such as schools and universities were capable of being educated.

There were some who felt that it would be dangerous to permit either level of government, federal or provincial, to assume a major educational role through such a pervasive and influential medium as television. The possibility of twisting and distorting attitudes and values seemed almost unlimited. There was said to be no comparison with the textbook, which could be examined, criticized, and revised repeatedly before it was ever placed before the eyes of students. The television program might flash across the screen and disappear, its subtle message left in the unconscious before anyone realized what had happened. Adults had a certain degree of protection, since they ordinarily had a range of broadcasts from which to choose. The circumstances under which pupils watched programs might not, however, give them such a choice.

A third controversial aspect of the venture was that of cost. No matter what the particular combination of facilities chosen, these and the equipment required for reception were bound to stand out as highly visible items of expenditure in provincial and local budgets. The vastly more expensive aspect of the enterprise, the production of programs, would run into many millions of dollars a year if highly qualified professional talent were to be used in order to ensure good quality in the finished product. Children were a sophisticated audience, unlikely to tolerate the kind of performance provided by local talent at the old-time social evening in the church hall. Expenditure would be subject to criticism if research failed to demonstrate that television made a measurable contribution to the traditional processes of education, a piece of ground upon which it ought not, stictly speaking, to have to stand and fight at all. But the fact was that the public would take a long time to accept the idea that television had to be a part of formal education if formal education were to be a vital part of life.

The major provincial effort began in 1965 when an ETV section was organized in the Curriculum Division of the Department of Education under the direction of an assistant superintendent. At that time it was the intention that such an arrangement would be permanent, since there were thought to be substatial advantages in tying program construction closely to other aspects of curriculum development. Not least important would be that educational interests would be in control, and technical concerns would remain subordinate. Davis expected that a relatively routine request would lead to the granting of a licence by the Board of Broadcast Governors to establish a broadcasting station. Assuming that such a licence would be granted by mid-1966, he hoped that transmission in Metropolitan Toronto and the surrounding area would begin from channel 19 within a year of that time. The granting of further licences would make it possible to set up a network of stations to serve exclusively educational needs in all parts of the province.

Production of a limited number of programs was promptly begun with the assistance of the CBC and the private stations and, like META, the department found these agencies prepared to sell transmission facilities under certain conditions as well. Before long, internal administrative arrangements proved inadequate, and plans were made to set up an Educational Television Branch. A new director, T.R. Ide, assumed responsibility for the operation on July 1, 1966. An application went to the federal Department of Transport in March 1966 for approval for the use of channel 19. There it remained while the department awaited a ruling on whether the federal government was prepared to grant such authority to provincial governments. By the middle of the year the federal government indicated its intention to create a new licensing agency which would presumably be able to carry out the desired functions and enable the provincial government to get on with its task. In August the Board of Broadcast Governors opened hearings on the use of the ultra high frequency band and the Department of Education made a submission to it the following month. The flames of controversy were perhaps somewhat fanned by the departmental assertion that no one could doubt the necessity for an informed and intelligent public.[10] The federal government was certainly not at that time prepared to see a provincial department of education assume the responsibility for informing the public. Nevertheless, matters seemed to be going reasonably well in November when the Board of Broadcast Governors announced that it would recommend to the federal government that channel 19 be reserved for educational use and that manufacturers be required to make all future sets capable of both very high frequency and ultra high frequency transmission. The fact that some of the department's additional requests were rejected did not seem too serious a matter, although there were objections that the failure to make very high frequency facilities available in the Toronto area demonstrated a questionable set of values.

The subsequent period was one of almost unbroken frustration. The federal government took no action on the positive recommendations of the Board of Broadcast Governors. By November 1967 the only definite move was a resolution by the House of Commons referring the matter to the Standing Committee on Broadcasting, Films and Assistance to the Arts. This committee produced a definition of educational programs that included some exceedingly restrictive terminology. Such programs were, for example, to be only for the acquisition or improvement of knowledge, and were to involve the registration or enrolment of participants, their examination on the content of the programs, and the granting of credit toward a particular educational level or degree. At this stage the federal government planned to have a Canadian Education Broadcasting Agency which would operate facilities for the broadcasting of educational programs for provincial authorities and other agencies. Action was again delayed when the federal Parliament was dissolved and elections were held in June. The new Secretary of State, Gérard Pelletier, promised legislative action the following September, but found it necessary in the meantime to set up a task force to look into certain aspects of the problem.

By April 19, 1969 an arrangement was made whereby channel 19 would become available for the broadcasting of educational television programs. During the same period various aspects of a broader plan were being worked out. In the fall the Council of Ministers of Education arranged for discussions with the Secretary of State over the contentious definition of educational programming and over the question of how broadcasting facilities would be financed. Earlier federal plans to establish a Canadian Educational Broadcasting Agency were dropped and instead the CBC was given the responsibility of making facilities available where the provinces were willing to pay for them. The federal government also required that all existing and future cable TV licences set aside at least one channel for educational programming. It was under the first of these two arrangements that the CBC agreed to build and operate a transmitter for broadcasting on channel 19.

Direct government control over the provincial educational television scheme was ended in 1970 with the transfer of the departmental Educational Television Branch to the jurisdiction of the Ontario Educational Communications Authority. This body consisted of thirteen members appointed for fixed, renewable terms by the Lieutenant-Governor-in-Council; they were intended to be broadly representative of the civil service and a variety of educational interests such as school boards, universities, teachers, adult education, and the general public. Under the supervision of this agency, the work of producing programs and of evaluating their effects continued much as before, although now there was supposed to be a satisfactory safeguard against the government's subversion of the process to suit its own purposes. The universities were more favourably disposed toward the arrangement than they had been toward an operation conducted by a branch of the Department of Education.

Educational television faced a time of real testing in the 1970s. The departmental Educational Television Branch had already demonstrated that it could produce programs of excellent quality, on some occasions winning prizes in international competitions, and normally obtaining high ratings from teacher and student viewers. The problem of availability was gradually being solved through more frequent and convenient broadcasts, the use of video tape and cassettes, and the introduction of devices for quick selection of programs that might serve a useful purpose. But would the material be used? Would it find its way into the instructional process as an integral, indispensable, daily feature? Or would it remain a special, rather atypical adjunct to be resorted to occasionally when it seemed desirable to depart from the usual routine? The answer had to be provided within the larger context of how successfully the educational system could break many of its traditional routines. As long as classroom practice consisted largely of coverage of prescribed material with a uniform test at the end to see that each student retained a desired minimum, television was not going to win a place. Its hope lay in a situation where teacher and student together surveyed the landscape to select those educational experiences that might add up to a useful learning program. Under such conditions the student might select a series of broadcasts for purposeful viewing, with a direct relationship to other activities. Meaningful viewing might almost be regarded as an individual activity, although there would be many occasions when the interests of large numbers of students would converge on a single program.

In certain communities the availability of local television facilities provided valuable educational experiences for students. A special significance was given to literary or artistic expression when the objective was a television broadcast. There were accompanying opportunities to study the characteristics of the medium and of techniques by which it could be effectively utilized. In some schools it was possible to introduce some of the relevant technologies into the technical program.

NEW SECONDARY SCHOOL PROGRAMS OF THE 1960s
While teaching aids and educational media were receiving considerable attention, important developments were occurring in curriculum selection and organization. Reference was made in chapter 1 to the Reorganized Program or Robarts Plan as a response to the need for higher levels of education to prepare young people to fit into a more sophisticated economy. That purpose was pursued by improving offerings in the Business and Commerce and the Science, Technology, and Trades Branches, which succeeded the older Commercial and Technical courses, and by developing the Occupational program as a means of fitting students with slight academic talents and interests for occupations chiefly in the service field. The four-year program was to feed a certain number of graduates into the institutions for technological and trades training and ultimately the colleges of applied arts and technology, while others went directly into employment. The departmental curriculum builders declared their intention of making the four-year program in the Arts and Science Branch a stimulating educational experience. Rather than simply watering down the content of the five-year program, they attempted to work out several innovative courses designed to make a strong appeal to the students' interests. In this effort they attained what many observers felt was a rather

limited degree of success. Much of what was actually presented in the schools was a rather uninspired version of material already familiar to teachers. The new and innovative courses constituted a minor part of the program, and took some years to win a place. Nevertheless, some of the new courses were promising initiatives.

The course that received the most attention was called Man in Society, which was available in all four-year programs. Cutting across the traditional social science disciplines, it involved a study of the way in which some of the forces in contemporary life influenced man's behaviour. Attention was to be given, in historical context, to such institutions as the family, the state, the courts, and the government; to such social issues as adjustment to cultural change, freedom and responsibility, emotions and thinking, propaganda and the transmission of ideas, changes posed by technology, community planning, minority groups, and the welfare state; to such psychological topics as hereditary and environmental influences, learning, remembering, conditioning and habit formation, reasoning, and problem solving. Students would be encouraged to base their conclusions on thorough investigation of problems and on hard, critical thinking. A second innovative course called World Politics was designed to create an interest in important national and international affairs, to make students better informed about them, and to cultivate the practice of basing conclusions on sound evidence. Courses in speech arts were to produce cultural, social, and economic benefits by enabling students to listen with understanding, to express themselves effectively, to develop their creative talents, to exercise powers of leadership, and to fit successfully into social and economic life. Classroom time devoted to the study and practice of the effective use of the voice, platform behaviour, types of addresses, logic and argument, debate, rules of procedure, and evaluation would be supplemented by experiences at public meetings, in the Legislature, in the law courts, and elsewhere, and by the use of radio and television. In another course going beyond the compulsory one in English, students with a particular interest in modern literature might study contemporary drama, novels, and other forms.

Some of the severest critics saw the four-year program in Arts and Science as nothing more than a mistake. One complaint was that, although the choice of a program was a parental prerogative, guidance services were inadequate to provide a basis for sound decisions. Although there was supposed to be provision for transfer from the four-year to the five-year program for those not properly placed at the beginning, few students were ever actually transferred. It was also claimed, no doubt validly, that all four-year programs carried a social class stigma which the teachers had much to do with maintaining.

It is possible to acknowledge these weaknesses without altogether accepting the conclusion. The four-year program must be evaluated in the light of the alternatives. Although it may have been regrettable that many students could not cope with the academic demands of the five-year programs, it was a fact that they could not. For the most part, they were much better dealing with content that they had some prospect of assimilating than struggling in frustration where they had little chance of success. Further, if snobbish attitudes existed among teachers, parents, and the community at large, there was no way of eradicating them in a year or two. Even if teachers had had more adequate pre-service preparation, they would not necessarily have broken more quickly through traditional prejudices to adopt more egalitarian attitudes. On the other hand, better preparation would have enabled new teachers to deal more successfully with the complex demands made upon them in reorganizing course content. The government of the day can justifiably be criticized for not taking measures to remedy the inadequacies of the special summer course.

EXAMINATION REFORM

Innovations attempted as part of the Reorganized Program portended drastic changes in the secondary school program that were promoted in the latter part of the sixties. When teachers and students who were confined to the more traditional curriculum of the five-year program became aware of the experimental courses, they began to express a desire for something similar. Real change, however, awaited the abolition of the external examination system in grade 13. The necessity for new examination approaches was clearly foreseen in the late fifties, when projections of school population showed that the large numbers of students to be expected in the sixties could not be handled under existing procedures – not, perhaps, the most commendable reason for change. The registrar of the department, C.A. Brown, was very much aware of that prospect when he visited centres in the United States and Great Britain in 1958–60 in search of ideas that might be adapted to meet Ontario needs. The adoption of objective-type items on many of the papers was originally designed to reduce marking time, although it never made any great contribution in that respect.

More than one committee functioned during the early 1960s to study the role of external examinations in grades 12 and 13, particularly the latter, and to make suggestions for improvements. Consisting of various combinations of university representatives, departmental officials, and prominent educators from a cross-section of the system, these committees went far beyond administrative problems to consider the proper role of external examinations as a safeguard of achievement standards and as criteria for university admission. A committee established by the University Matriculation Board under the chairmanship of President G.E. Hall of the University of Western Ontario decided, in fact, that it could not fruitfully discuss such matters as the number of papers required for university admission without first expresing its views on what it regarded as necessary reforms in the secondary schools. Its prescription was in substance that teachers and students work harder in grades 9, 10, and 11 so that the existing thirteen-year program could be covered in twelve years. With a uniform external examination blocking the academically untalented from going beyond grade 12, grade 13 could become a really superior year of pre-university experience. A smaller number of subjects might be offered at that level and treated in greater depth. This suggested solution had an elitist tone that did not go over in some quarters. Although the department did begin to set essay-type examination papers in some grade 12 subjects, there was no chance that it would move toward making this system fully uniform by undertaking centralized marking at a time when grade 13 papers threatened to become too numerous to cope with.

The most important work was done by the Grade 13 Study Committee, which was set up and reported in 1964. According to its terms of reference, this committee was to inquire into and report on the nature of the grade 13 year in the light of responsible opinion that it was a cram year with too much emphasis on the memorization of factual information and on preparation for the final examination; that it should provide for a richer experience for all students, whether or not they were preparing for university; and that it should be a better liaison between the programs of the schools and those of universities and other institutions of post-secondary education.[11] It was thus made clear, among other things, that the minister would not particularly welcome a proposal that grade 13 be made an exclusively university preparatory year. Other clauses of the terms of reference asked for suggestions that would help to alleviate immediate problems as well as for an ideal long-term solution, with steps by which it could be implemented. The fact that an examination of the structure of the whole school system was not requested occasioned some criticism at the time.

The committee managed to look considerably beyond grade 13 to recommend that the school system, not including kindergarten, be ultimately reduced from thirteen years to twelve. University-preparatory work, which would in the interim continue to be offered in grade 13, would be moved to the twelfth or matriculation year when the long-term solution was implemented. There it would be an alternative to courses preparing students for admission to other institutions such as community colleges, teachers' colleges, and polytechnical institutes. In the meantime it would be improved by a reduction in teaching time, more student initiative, the increased use of the library, and a less rigid prescription of courses. As a means of allowing for different levels of achievement in the most important subjects, work would be given at general and advanced levels.

A General and Advanced Committee was set up to study the implications of the last of these recommendations. Early in 1965 it proposed that further committees be appointed to draw up tentative course outlines to serve as guides for experimentation and to let the universities know what to expect from students working at each level. A good deal of careful work was done in this project leading to the printing of attractive course outlines. The courses recognized the principles recommended by the Grade 13 Study Committee – that rigid prescriptions be avoided and that wider reading and independent study be encouraged. Different methods of distinguishing between the two levels were explored, and a flexible approach recommended, with variations depending on the size of the school and other factors. External examinations might be required for work at the advanced level, while the school might be responsible for evaluating work at the general level. A pattern of credits was suggested for university admission, although the universities would of course be expected to make the final decision in the matter.

In accordance with the committee's recommendations, the scheme was to be introduced gradually, with a few schools undertaking experiments in 1965–6 and an increasing number following in later years until all were involved by 1969–70. This and other aspects of the plan were to be carried out under the guidance of an Implementation Committee. Before any action could be taken, university and other authorities would have to give assurance that students in experimental programs would be eligible for admission to institutions of post-secondary education and for scholarships and bursaries. What happened when the universities were asked to express an opinion of the value and feasibility of the whole scheme is evidence of the powerful influence they exerted over the school curriculum as well as of their reluctance to see any fundamental change. In response to a request from the minister, the president of one university after another expressed opposition to the proposal and since the schools were also giving evidence of lack of enthusiasm, the plan was dropped. University opposition was based on several arguments: 1 / that it would be a good idea to digest a number of changes already under way, including the recently announced abolition of the grade 13 departmental examinations, before undertaking any more; 2 / that the students would lose some of their flexibility of choice by having to make an early decision about their ultimate university course; 3 / that increased specialization was contrary to the general trend to broaden rather than narrow the first-year university program; 4 / that it would be administratively difficult to provide two levels of instruction at the university during the first year; and 5 / that there was doubt that enough properly qualified teachers could be found to teach at the advanced level. There may have been some validity in the first point. The second could have been dealt with by permitting students who were not yet prepared to make a choice to gain admission on the basis of a wide range of subjects on the general level rather than a narrow combination of general and advanced subjects. Such an approach would also have answered the third objection unless the universities intended to prevent specialization in the first year rather than merely avoiding an insistence on it. The fourth objection suggested an obvious response. If the students who entered the university were prepared for work offered at a more advanced level than that of first year, why could they not have been admitted to second-year courses? As to the fifth point, the colleges of applied arts and technology were soon to find high school teachers capable of handling up to three years of liberal arts courses beyond the grade 12 level.

The abolition of the grade 13 departmental examination system in 1967 was one of the landmarks of the twentieth century in Ontario education. The announcement that the change was coming took most of the province by surprise, since there was little advance warning that anything that drastic had been contemplated. The Grade 13 Study Committee, although advocating a reduction in the number and importance of external examinations, had nevertheless seen a continuing role for them in some form. In any case, most of the newspaper and public response to the minister's action was favourable, demonstrating that the adverse reaction to the undesirable effects of the system was widespread. There was a less enthusiastic response from the Ontario Teachers' Federation, which continued for some time to press for the use of final examinations set by the Department of Education and marked in the schools. Many teachers felt that such an approach would help to guard against the collapse of provincial standards of achievement. In the universities, a considerable number of professors saw the barriers crumbling and deplored the consequences. Registrars were concerned about the extent to which they could rely on marks supplied by the schools.

Part of the original expectation was that standardized testing programs would to a considerable degree take over the function of screening or selecting candidates for university admission. The provincial government was prepared to give interim support to the Ontario Admission to College and University (OACU) program, which was administered by the Ontario Institute for Studies in Education, until the nation-wide Service for Admission to College and University (SACU) program was in full operation. Under these programs, candidates would write a scholastic aptitude test in two parts and objective achievement tests in basic subject areas such as English, mathematics, and science. Although the universities planned to take the scores into account, departmental interest in the programs proved to be slight. Some officials may have been aware that earlier research such as the Atkinson Study of Utilization of Student Resources had given little hope that the scores would have very high predictive value, an apprehension that was well sustained, as it turned out. The main factor was, however, that the department was now dominated by officials who were determined that the educational process would not again be stultified by any form of external assessment.

The department took some immediate steps to ensure that the schools realized the extent of their opportunity to experiment and innovate. While it continued to publish courses of study for grade 13, it encouraged the principal and staff to adapt these as they saw fit. The services of members of the Program Branch, insufficient as their numbers were, helped to ease the transition. Initial teacher doubts soon gave way to approval, and often to enthusiasm. While some continued to miss the final examinations as a motivating device, many found that other measures such as frequent short tests and appraisals of classroom work were more effective. Although some students were unhappy about having to sustain a high level of performance throughout the year rather than being able to make up for a butterfly existence with a few weeks of cramming at the end, most felt that they were getting a better education. Certainly the teacher who had the capacity to make the work more interesting found increasing opportunities and encouragement to do so.

An inevitable question was whether or not standards of marking went down. The relevant statistics suggested that they did, since the number of students who received Ontario Scholarships in 1968 on the basis of their record was almost double that in 1967, while the failure rate in the major subjects was halved. It did not seem conceivable that students of equal calibre and quality of preparation were given comparable treatment in the two successive years with such drastically different results. Yet any close comparison was impossible to make in view of the difference in the two situations. If the essential purpose of the change was actually realized, the standards of 1967 depended a good deal on learning in order to forget, while those of 1968 reflected a more valid educational experience.

NEW SECONDARY SCHOOL PROGRAMS OF THE LATE 1960s
The end of the departmental examinations was followed by a fundamental change in the organization of the high school program which involved the scrapping of some of the most basic features of the Reorganized Program or Robarts Plan. The effect on curriculum content and methodology was also pronounced. The essence of the change was that students would not be confined to a few standard programs that had to be taken as complete entities, but could build up individual programs which included courses at different levels of difficulty cutting across the Arts and Science, Business and Commerce, and Science, Technology and Trades Branches. The approach was introduced experimentally in 1967–8 in six secondary schools: Parkside High School in Dundas, Newtonbrook Secondary School in North York, Oakville-Trafalgar High School, Fisher Park Secondary School in Ottawa, Sir John A. Macdonald Collegiate Institute in Scarborough, and Malvern Collegiate Institute in Toronto. With the assistance of departmental officials and some members of the staff of the Ontario Institute for Studies in Education, each school worked out its own individual approach.

In the new approach, most subjects were offered at different levels of difficulty, or in different phases. In the five-phase system, the first phase usually consisted of remedial work for those who were not prepared for serious study at the secondary school level. At the other extreme, work in the fifth phase called for a good deal of student initiative in conducting studies at a comparatively advanced level. The basic unit of achievement was the credit, which was awarded for work covering five periods a week throughout the school year. As the pattern became established, the student qualified for the grade 12 diploma by obtaining twenty-seven credits in a combination of compulsory and optional subjects, while the grade 13 diploma required seven further credits in phase three or higher. The student who aspired to attend university made sure to obtain enough credits in the higher phases, while one who was less ambitious could accumulate his credits at a lower phase. The scheme was flexible in that the student was not required to study at a common level in all subjects. He no longer had to repeat any courses which he had passed simply because he had failed others at the same level. If he failed a particular course, he was ordinarily faced with a series of choices: he could drop it, repeat it in the same phase, or continue it in a lower phase.

Guidelines in the departmental Circular HS1 for 1969–70 indicated that, in order to get a balance of basic education in certain broad subject areas, each student was to choose a minimum number of courses from each of communications, social sciences, pure and applied sciences, and arts. Beyond that, he could choose from whatever options the school was able to provide. Some schools extended the range of possibilities by offering courses in two- or three-year cycles. Another approved procedure, first implemented by Thornlea High School in Thornhill, was the trimester system, which enabled students to change levels in mid-year and to choose different subjects each term. It also became possible to offer some work for credit in summer school blocks.

This non-grading scheme, as it could justifiably be called, was made possible by advances in computer technology, which enabled administrators, even in large schools, to prepare the necessary individual timetables. Effectiveness in operation also depended on adequate guidance services to make students fully aware of what possibilities were open to them. They had to be prevented from discovering, after several years' attendance, that their credits were at too low a phase to enable them to proceed to their chosen careers. Although guidance services were improving, there was considerable evidence that they were by no means yet equal to the new demands placed upon them.

In an address to the Ontario Secondary School Headmasters' Council in March 1969, the minister indicated some of the reasoning underlying the new program. He presented it as a natural development arising out of the Robarts Plan, from which certain guiding principles had emerged. One was the idea, at the very core of the progressive approach, that the choice of experiences for the student should depend on his needs and interests. These were judged to be best served by a balance of basic education over certain broad subject areas and a choice outside these areas. Concentration on narrow areas of study was assumed to belong to later years of schooling. The scheme thus failed to please those who felt that the system should provide for students with highly specialized talents, but with little interest in or aptitude for activities outside their specialty. In this respect, a considerable element of the essentialist position was retained.

Davis emphasized measures that would enable the schools to improve the learning environment. Requirements based on forty-minute class periods would be dropped and periods of different lengths would facilitate the use of seminars, variable group instruction, individual research, concentrated group projects, and excursions. Limitations on requirements for departmental diplomas would further facilitate the devising of individual programs.

Davis did not emphasize the degree to which the report of the Provincial Committee on Aims and Objectives of Education in the Schools of Ontario (the Hall-Dennis Committee) influenced the developments he was describing. Yet some of them strongly reflected the thinking that went into that report, and the possibility of their successful introduction into the system as a whole owed much to the discussion that ensued.

Although the new scheme represented a long step forward in Canadian terms, it was not at all radical in comparison with what had been done for decades in American high schools. Not only had something like the Ontario credit system been in use there, but many schools were much less restrictive about the options they permitted students to take. The widespread tendency to choose a combination of easy subjects had provided a basis for campaigns by such critics as Admiral Rickover to have standards raised. Unless restraints were further relaxed, there was little chance that the situation would be duplicated in Ontario. Nevertheless, under a system allowing a wide range of options at different levels of difficulty, teachers faced an obligation to point out to students that their ultimate interests might demand a choice of some of the tougher courses.

SPECULATIONS ABOUT THE OPERATION OF A MORE HIGHLY PROGRESSIVE APPROACH AT THE SECONDARY LEVEL

It is tempting to speculate about what might happen in a school system where nothing was asked of a secondary school student other than that he engage in worthwhile study requiring the full exercise of his learning capacities. The situation would not be synonymous with one where every individual did "exactly as he pleased," to use a favourite expression of the critics of the extreme permissive approach. There would be room for adult society to exert the full weight of its influence to ensure that students operated within a defined framework.

Boundaries between disciplines would not be regarded as rigid or inviolate, but rather as guides to clear and orderly thinking, just as they are in university circles. The student would be encouraged to learn why they are drawn in certain ways and for what reasons they are sometimes altered or ignored. He would acquire an understanding of the structure imposed on various areas of knowledge by the best minds working on them, and would come to realize how this kind of activity contributes to the further extension of knowledge. His freedom to choose which aspects of knowledge he might explore would not involve the notion that he could ignore all existing concepts of order and regularity in favour of some completely new organizing principles of his own.

In the completely individualized approach the student would map out his own program for a short or long period, depending on the degree of clarity with which he was able to define his interests. He would need to have access to teachers, librarians, and perhaps other students in order to make realistic and valid plans. These consultations would continue as he encountered unforeseen conditions or as he perceived a need to modify his goals. His actual studies might be conducted largely in isolation in the library, in the learning resources centre, or, under controlled conditions, in excursions outside the school. On the other hand, he might find a good deal of benefit from work in groups bearing a strong resemblance to regular classes. For the most part, regularly scheduled classes with adult-selected content and extending over periods of weeks or months would be confined to skill areas such as mathematics and certain aspects of foreign languages. These might be offered at different levels of difficulty or with different degrees of intensity to correspond to variations in learning capacity. Apart from classes of this type, most group work would have to be organized more or less spontaneously as a number of students realized that they had a common interest in certain themes or topics. When this situation arose, they might seek out the teacher who was best able to conduct the desired classes and, through participation in prior planning, ensure that their needs would be met. If the course proved to be a disappointment to them, they would have to have legitimate ways of making known their displeasure, including the right to withdraw without penalty apart from any adverse effect a mistaken decision might have on their own program.

If standards of work were to be maintained, every student would have to answer to a particular teacher for the execution of his plans. If he were to receive maximum assistance, his assignment to a teacher could not be arbitrary, but would have to depend on the nature of his program. Impressionable students might very well be tempted to devise programs that would give them an opportunity to work with a teacher of outstanding reputation. Since there would be no captive audiences, poor teachers would tend to be eliminated. Those who could not establish rapport with students would not be consulted or approached for help. Those who could not present material in an interesting and effective manner would have no students, particularly if programmed learning materials or educational television on demand were available as alternatives to classes in basic skills. Every teacher would operate in the open, with his successes and failures obvious to all. If he could find no way to play a constructive part in the operation of the school, but yet attempted to cling to his position, it would be relatively easy for the principal to make a case for his dismissal.

There would be insuperable administrative problems if hundreds or thousands of students swept through the doors of the school the first week in September, all ready to make a fresh beginning and all looking for assistance to draw up a learning program. If the traditional vacation period were retained, there would have to be much more continuity between one school year and another so that the majority of students could continue from where they had left off while a manageable number of initiates were devising new plans and getting a large share of the teachers' attention. The best arrangement might well be to run the school continuously and to stagger vacations for students and teachers. Students might be permitted to study continuously, if they so desired, and to cover the high school program in the minimum period of time, or they might opt for a more leisurely pace.

The question arises: would not students concentrate their efforts in such narrow areas that they could hardly be considered educated in the usual sense of the word? A modern stereotype of the educated man consists of two sets of conditions, one superimposed on the other. He must first have a broad grasp of the essentials in many fields of knowledge along with the capacity to integrate and comprehend the whole. Then he must build some type of expertise on the broad foundations so that he may know the true nature of excellence and gain an insight into the character of all specialties. He is a combination of the well-rounded citizen of the Greek city state and of the expert slave whom that citizen despised. Such a man appeals as the kind of leader who is badly needed in modern society where new solitudes constantly appear to separate one individual from another, and where the forces of fragmentation and disintegration threaten constantly to get out of hand. But society does not in fact expect the individual to be that type of person. In every sphere of life, people win security, prosperity, prestige, and fame solely because of their success in specializing. That the winning athlete reads, that the outstanding actress is an expert on sea molluscs, that the scientist plays the violin – these are mere curiosities that have nothing to do with whether the world ever hears of them. The supremely successful man does not lose a whit of general acclaim when he admits that he has no interest except in his narrow field of work. If the educator is not aware of these things, the student certainly is. That is why it is so difficult to give him a "balanced" education – a process that can be achieved only by making certain subjects compulsory. He fights this process by lassitude and indifference, getting by with a minimum of effort while he reserves his energy for what is really important to him.

The student who pines for a chance to explore an area of interest while he suffers through some unrelated prerequisite may eventually become disillusioned with the whole learning process and end up without either a broad base of knowledge or specialized expertise. Paradoxically, if he were allowed to pursue his own set of priorities, acquiring a measure of competence in an area of particular interest, and with it a sense of self-confidence and of harmony with the conditons of real life, he might just possibly be prepared to turn his attention outward and explore various fields of knowledge on a broad scale. There is no guarantee that he would follow this line of development, and the educational system could hardly attempt to insist upon it, as it now tries to insist on the reverse. The answer to the question with which we began, in so far at it is reasonable to give one, is that the scheme might well produce some very narrow specialists indeed along with others with both breadth and depth of knowledge and interests. In both cases, there is reason to think that something of lasting value would be acquired.

We may attribute a second question to the sceptics: would not the suggested scheme lead to the destruction of all standards of intellectual achievement? The answer is that, if the scheme were competently handled, standards should reach the highest possible level. After all, that presumably supreme intellectual challenge, the PhD dissertation, calls for much the same conditions as the proposed individualized program. The standards the student would have to meet would depend very much on what his teachers demanded of him. The fact that he was pursuing a matter of vital interest to himself should ensure his willingness to work much harder than he could normally be expected to do. There should be much more frequent examples of some of the mental feats that psychologists say are possible under optimum learning conditions, which include optimum motivation. There would be no necessity under the scheme to tolerate laziness or indolence. The atmosphere might be one of high – although constructive – tension and of serious purpose.

All teachers have encountered students who are thrilled at the opportunity to devise and follow their own program. They are also very much aware of the stolid, unimaginative type who seems to prefer to be told what to do and is merely bewildered by too much freedom of choice. How would such an individual who through temperament or training had become dependent on external direction fare under the proposed scheme? The answer is that the right to follow an individual program need not be imposed like an incontrovertible article of faith. For those who were not ready for it, there might be a variety of pre-designed programs from which a selection might be made. True, the work done under such conditons might not be very educative, but at least it would be no worse than much of the routine drudgery of the systems that have existed hitherto, and the student could escape at any moment when he became prepared for something more vital. Teachers would have a major responsibility for fanning the spark of creative interest, realizing the degree of waste in whatever was done without it.

How would the scheme provide for the needs of the economy? In a democratic society, there are really only two major steps that can be taken to ensure that individual interests and social needs are harmonized; there must be strong enough financial and prestige incentives to ensure that sufficient candidates are attracted to essential occupations and there must be adequate educational and training opportunities to give these candidates the right preparation at the right time. The proposed scheme would not in any way increase the difficulty in meeting these conditions. In fact, the chief source of complaint would probably be that too many young people would opt for strictly practical courses with a direct bearing on occupational preparation, at the same time scorning the liberal element which should theoretically help them prepare for the job mobility that increasingly characterizes the modern economy. One can only respond that liberal studies are of little value unless chosen voluntarily. The student who takes them because he is forced to invariably makes certain that he derives as little benefit from them as possible. The only way to ensure that they are beneficial is to create an awareness of a need for them.

A tax-conscious public would make haste to inquire how much the scheme would cost. The very hint that high school students might be handled in a manner somewhat comparable to PhD candidates is enough to conjure up visions of skyrocketing budgets. There need not be undue apprehension, however, if it is kept in mind that the students would be working, not at the PhD but at the high school level. There would undoubtedly be rather high expenditures for library and other learning resources, and there might have to be a greater space allowance per student than in most existing secondary schools to permit dozens of impromptu meetings and sessions, as well as quiet individual study. At the same time there would be great potentialities for saving. As already pointed out, teachers who were not serving a useful purpose could be readily identified and eliminated and their salaries used to better advantage. Educational media would also be put to the kind of test that is impossible when education is at least partly a process of imposition. A school board would not need to put a television set in every classroom because someone speculated that it was desirable. It could begin with whatever number the students demonstrated an interest in using to capacity, and could add as many more as were needed according to the same criterion.

People with different attitudes toward recent trends in institutional control might ask: would it mean that the students would run the school? While there is no question that the operation of the school would have to be in harmony with the students' true interests, there would be no reason whatever why adults, in a flood of unmerited guilt and mistaken humility, need turn over their authority to a gang of inexperienced and ignorant adolescents. While the student's integrity would have to be given the most complete respect, he would not lose his need for example, for guidance, for admonition, and in certain respects for regulation – all of which would have to come from self-confident and self-respecting adults. The atmosphere might in many respects be democratic, but it could still be controlled. Students who demonstrated a capacity for leadership could be given ample opportunity to exercise it. Those who refused to respect the rights of others might be isolated or excluded.

How would teachers fare? They would have to work very hard, as the best always do. They would be constantly challenged to devise new and more productive ways of meeting student needs, a familiar activity for the most vigorous and imaginative. They would always be on trial, with no chance to rest on laurels earned during earlier and more idealistic years. Such a fate would be difficult for those who feel that the reward of advancing years should be to claim a few prerogatives. However, it must be kept in mind that schools are not operated for the welfare of teachers but for that of students. For teachers who excelled in understanding the motives and aspirations of young people, the atmosphere would be extremely rewarding. For those driven by a desire for intellectual growth, there would be the constant stimulation of young people reaching out toward every imaginable field of specialization and demanding the assistance of an informed adult.

The scheme as outlined here was one toward which the Ontario secondary school system seemed in the early 1970s to be evolving. By 1971–2 the old organization, which had for a time been allowed to persist in certain schools, had been largely phased out. There remained a considerable amount of uncertainty among students and teachers, but it seemed probable that the problems would gradually be solved. As yet it was still generally felt that each student should distribute his efforts over the basic subject areas, and his preferences were thus not allowed full sway in determining his program. Class organization and the assignment of teacher responsibilities remained quite formal and structured. Yet the system had changed sufficiently within a few years to suggest the possibility of radical transformations to come.

CURRICULUM DEVELOPMENTS IN ELEMENTARY SCHOOLS IN THE 1960s
At the elementary school level, particularly between kindergarten and grade 6, the 1960s did not witness changes in the actual content of the curriculum as drastic as those at higher levels, although the publication P1J1 superseded the 1937 curriculum. Perhaps the main reason that the change was not as striking was that, after thinking the matter over, the authorities decided that work done in earlier decades was not as outmoded as the passage of years suggested, and that the main improvement needed was a more determined effort to achieve objectives already set out. The most important changes were in classroom organization and in instructional techniques.

During the period of the Robarts ministry, there were discussions of the possibility of revising the K–6 curriculum. On succeeding Robarts, Davis indicated that any action would be preceded by thorough consultation among departmental officials, teachers, inspectors, and teachers' college staffs. There appeared to be a good many different views at the time about the direction that the reforms should take. Many of the criticisms of the existing program suggested that it was not sufficiently challenging, and that children were capable of learning more than was being demanded of them. Robarts himself expressed such a view, urging that elementary school pupils be more adequately prepared for the stiffening programs that awaited them at the secondary school level. For many people, the implications of the knowledge explosion were that humans at every stage of development would have to become more efficient learning machines. The participation of professors on the Joint Committee of the Toronto Board of Education and the University of Toronto and on the early committees of the Ontario Curriculum Institute for the most part generated pressure in favour of more intensive learning experiences at the elementary school level. On the other hand there remained those who felt that the progressive implications of the 1937 program had never been adequately realized.

Some active steps were taken in 1964 to bring about the desired revision. The Curriculum Branch was augmented by a group of inspectors and teachers' college masters who assembled information on aims, organization, methods, and content from a variety of sources. By 1966 some interim statements were ready for mailing to the schools, indicating for the most part only relatively minor changes in existing procedures. It was suggested that the adoption of any drastically new approach would await the report of the Provincial Committee on Aims and Objectives of Education in the Schools of Ontario. In fact, the concepts outlined in *Curriculum Bulletin No. 5*, issued in January 1967, in many respects anticipated the spirit of that report. While there was an attempt to outline the fundamental concepts of each discipline, the teacher was urged to adjust and modify these to meet the needs of individual pupils. Courses were to be adapted to grades, units, levels, or non-graded organization. The prescription of uniform levels of achievement was to be avoided, and no excessive attention was to be directed toward average levels of achievement lest the practice lead to unwarranted judgments about children. The course was not to be used, and indeed was not of a type that could be used, for detailed daily planning. The teacher was expected to find appropriate content in textbooks, films, television, field experiences, and elsewhere. Warnings were issued against the use of achievement tests that were not related to the objectives of the course and against the use of learning capacity tests in such a way that the results became expectations.

The essential purpose of the school experience was said to be to give the child an opportunity to grow physically, mentally, and emotionally through a series of individual and group experiences. If he was to develop self-confidence and gain recognition, he should be encouraged to excel in some phase of the work. Teachers were to seek opportunities to offer encouragement. There was said to be sufficient time for the child to engage in the necessary activities during the day, and thus no additional school work need be done at home, although out-of-school pursuits might arise from interests originating in school.

By this time a strong interest had developed in the possibility of breaking down the grade system in favour of truly individualized instruction. Some systems such as that of Hamilton had long before countered the rigidities of annual promotion by breaking the year into units and enabling the pupils to proceed at different rates of speed according to their success in mastering different units. Thus a bright pupil might cover certain ground in four years while an average pupil took five years and a slow pupil six years. Within a unit, however, the pupil received essentially the same kind of treatment as his fellows.

A thoroughly individualized program worked best in a large open classroom area with space for a variety of different individual and group activities at different levels of difficulty. Several teachers and possibly teachers' helpers were available at various strategic points ready to offer assistance and consultation, to demonstrate various procedures, and to exercise general supervision. Groups of children were formed for various purposes as the need arose and dissolved when their objectives had been met. A particular child could work at different levels in arithmetic, reading, art, and physical education depending on the particular level of competence he had reached in each. The whole procedure depended on a great deal of careful planning both by teachers and by pupils. Without intelligent and sensitive management it was easy to produce complete chaos. Where the scheme was well organized and the teachers had a thorough understanding of their roles, the pupils found unprecedented opportunities for enjoyment in their work and learning became a really vital experience. New heights of achievement were observed and many of the usual types of discipline problems disappeared.

The individualized approach was strongly advocated in departmental circles. In the teachers' colleges, student teachers were taught to think of themselves as facilitators of learning rather than as holders of the centre of the stage so that they would be prepared to handle the new system if the opportunity arose. Most large school systems organized some classes or schools on the new plan. Yet an organizational and methodological change that called for so many new attitudes and practices would obviously take a long time to implement. There was always the possibility that an indiscriminate reaction against "permissiveness," a term frequently used as a synonym for lack of control, would provide an excuse for a campaign to suppress children's creative initiative and subject them to new authoritarian repression. Even if such a reaction did not occur, it would be a truly massive task to persuade thousands of teachers to abandon the familiar models and acquire the delicate touch required to reinforce the individual initiative of each of a large and confusing group of children.

THE REPORT OF THE PROVINCIAL COMMITTEE
ON AIMS AND OBJECTIVES

The idea of individualized instruction, at both the elementary and secondary school levels, was given very strong reinforcement by the appearance of the report of the Provincial Committee on Aims and Objectives, or the Hall-Dennis report, in 1968. The original idea was that the committee should define objectives for the program between kindergarten and grade 6. Before long it began to seem desirable to look at the entire sweep of the school system to the end of grade 13, and the committee's terms of reference were defined accordingly. Since the mere definition of aims and objectives tends to be a sterile task in isolation, the committee devoted its main attention to the problem of suggesting how worthy aims and objectives might be achieved. The report brought progressive ideas to the centre of the stage as few would have thought possible five years earlier.

The spirit of the Hall-Dennis recommendations for elementary schools was in keeping with those for the same level contained in the report of the Royal Commission eighteen years earlier, although presented in a much more lyrical style. There was, however, a great divergence in the treatment of higher levels, for which the Royal Commission reverted to what was largely a traditionalist prescription, while the Hall-Dennis report suggested the same set of progressive principles throughout.

The report was several things: an adoring tribute to the nature of the child; a statement of limitless faith in his potentialities if developed in an ideal educational environment under the guidance of inspired teachers; an assertion of his claim to an ideal education; a description of the ideal learning environment; a powerful condemnation of rigid, inflexible, outmoded, and unproductive activities and practices found in schools and school systems in Ontario; a set of proposals for the organization and administration of schools; an outline for the handling of educational programs for different types of handicapped children; and various suggestions for improving structural and operational aspects of the system, including the Department of Education. Its style was a mixture of the inspirational, the hortatory, and the descriptive. Numerous and colourful illustrations gave it the kind of attractive appearance that ensured widespread distribution. For an educational document one can probably assume safely that it attracted an unusually wide readership.

The kind of school the committee envisioned was a happy place where each child found gratification and fulfilment in his own unending search for truth. He would work essentially for the rewards inherent in the process itself, and not because of extrinsic motivation. There would be no pressure to induce him to try to measure up against unrealistic group standards, and he would have no sense of failure if he could not match someone else's performance. Thus the report represented the strongest reaction against the atmosphere of competition mentioned at the beginning of the chapter which has characterized the schools of Ontario through most of their history. The committee seemed to feel that the school could insulate itself against the outside world and persuade the child that his best achievement could be appraised independently of external standards and expectations. That is, if he proved no match for arithmetic, but developed passable talent in art, the world would not attach any stigma of failure to him. Some critics of the report felt that the committee was holding out unrealistic expectations in this respect. Others took the view that the report was attempting to portray an ideal school in an ideal society.

Many passages in the report put strong emphasis on the importance of discovery learning. In doing so they portrayed the learner as an active, seeking organism, constantly reaching out for the elements of his own growth. He was anything but a passive receptacle into which the teacher was responsible for pouring facts, ideas, concepts, and attitudes. Some psychologists insisted that the committee's view of the learning process was an over-simplified one. While they agreed that discovery was an important learning principle, they insisted that there were many things the child should know that could not be acquired very conveniently or efficiently in this way. They reserved a much more active role for the teacher in selecting content, in organizing suitable learning experiences, and in planning strategies that would successfully overcome resistance to learning.

Most of the newspaper editorials that followed the report were favourably disposed toward it, and hailed it as a blueprint for education in the space age. Some of them saw it as a severe indictment of the past policies of the Department of Education. Others, more perceptive of the nature and purpose of recent changes in curriculum, examination practices, and central influence on the learning environment, realized that it was a reflection of the most advanced departmental thinking. That it should demonstrate such tendencies was not surprising, since a number of the members of the committee were departmental policy makers. Generally speaking, responsibility for the faults it identified was applied diffusely. There was no specific set of villains that had to be rooted out, but, rather, certain survivals of the inhumane and obtuse traditions of the past. If there was an object of attack, it was really society itself.

The committee based its assessment of what went on in the schools on a large number of briefs and hearings, which should have provided it with some very up-to-date insights. Yet there were educators who saw little relationship between the situation it professed to find and conditions as they knew them. Presumably the difference was mainly one of interpretation. For a person who believed that young people learned to become orderly, law-abiding citizens by the practice of adhering to regulations and following an orderly pattern of living, there might be a good deal of cause for satisfaction in appraising the existing system. On the other hand, one who felt that discipline ought to arise out of the conditions of learning itself could only object in the face of abundant evidence of regimentation for its own sake, and could not help but feel that children were given rules and empty forms instead of human sympathy and understanding.

Editorial comment was not slow to identify the implications of increased costs. Some of these implications had already been accepted in the favourable reception given to proposals such as those of the Minister's Committee on the Training of Elementary School Teachers (the MacLeod Committee). It was easy to conclude that, if every child were to be taught by a well prepared teacher in a school supplied with every modern learning device, and that if every special individual need were to be provided for, educational expenditure would have to continue to rise rapidly. Some said that, apart from normal increases, the implementation of all the recommendations in the report would require a doubling of existing educational expenditure. This prospect did not shock the editorial writers as it certainly would have done three years later when a more penurious mood had settled over the province. In fact, some were quite prepared to say that the results should be well worth the extra cost. There was very little evidence that the same writers were thinking along these lines in 1972.

The minister never got around to giving the report a really ringing endorsation, let alone declaring that future government policy would be based on its recommendations. It perhaps would have done no violence to his own ideas and views if he had welcomed the spirit of the document with more enthusiasm. In his address of March 1969 already referred to, when he outlined the changes taking place in the secondary schools, he demonstrated much of the same type of thinking. However, he could not have accepted 256 recommendations, some of them advocating quite specific changes in the school system, without severely limiting the government's freedom of action. No government can afford to go further than considering such recommendations as a guide to be taken into account when specific changes are made. In some cases the government would not have wished to exert too much initiative or pressure to bring about a suggested reform. If the teachers of the province, for example, thought it was time to eliminate the federations affiliated with the Ontario Teachers' Federation in favour of one large organization, a move in that direction might be expected to come from them.

The minister did take steps to ensure that the report would be given the maximum of publicity and that the points it raised would be thoroughly debated in all parts of the province. He employed the co-chairman, Lloyd Dennis, for most of the year following its release to ensure that it was properly explained. Dennis, who had a very dynamic speaking style and a flair for the dramatic, delivered hundreds of addresses to educational and lay groups. Other members of the committee also offered their services freely for the same purpose. Never before had the province been so involved in an examination of the issues affecting public education.

Where the audiences consisted of elementary school teachers, the reception of the message was said to be predominantly favourable. Teachers at this level had long been exposed to progressive currents, which had not been determinedly countered even during the 1950s, and by 1968, as has been noted, the leadership from the Department of Education was unequivocally in progressive hands. Audiences of secondary school teachers were reported to be a good deal more critical. A substantial proportion of their members were doubtful that young people would learn much of anything if external pressures were removed. They were also apprehensive lest they be called upon to abandon a clear-cut organization of subject content in favour of some chaotic smorgasbord of material from which each student would be expected to fashion an individual program. Some doubts were cast on the supposition that elementary and secondary school teachers were sharply divided on the report by a survey undertaken by the Ontario Institute for Studies in Education and the Ontario Teachers' Federation in 1969. The researchers asked carefully selected groups of teachers, identified by the level at which they served and the length of their experience, to express their opinions on the committee's recommendations. On most points, elementary and secondary school teachers showed surprising little difference in their views. There was overwhelming support for most recommendations, which was perhaps not to be wondered at since few of them were as controversial as the main thrust of the report.

In one respect the survey cast serious doubt on the extent to which the essence of the report was acceptable to the educational establishment. The majority of teachers were opposed to the idea of abolishing corporal punishment. If there was anything that epitomized the punitive approach of the bad old days in the eyes of members of the committee, it was the strap. Its use was absolute proof that a teacher had failed to catch the vision of the shining-eyed youthful idealist seeking for truth. The educator with the Hall-Dennis report in one hand and a strap in the other was the most flagrant anomaly. It was small comfort that few now believed that adult-administered torture was a positive instrument of education, and that most of those who wanted to retain the strap saw it as an ultimate instrument of control.

CHANGES IN THE UNIVERSITIES

There will be many efforts to assess the ultimate significance of the Hall-Dennis report. It will be seen in the context of a larger move toward the humanizing of education, manifestations of which were numerous, as we have seen, in the curriculum and structure of elementary and secondary education. A similar movement developed in the universities during the 1960s, showing itself in many different spheres of university life. A brief reference to a few of its major features will suffice to show that the movement there was all part of a broader whole.

The "humanizing" drive produced its most obvious curricular effects in the arts and science faculties, while programs in the professional schools continued to be shaped more by the changing demands of the occupational fields for which candidates were being prepared. In the former, attitudes toward the traditional honours courses underwent a remarkably rapid transformation. Some of the very spokesmen who had defended the value of early and intensive specialization in a narrow discipline suddenly discovered that the whole approach was undemocratic, unfair, and of doubtful educational validity. The investigations that led to the production of the Macpherson report in the University of Toronto uncovered strong support for the idea that the student should be permitted, or even encouraged, to range widely over different courses and fields during his first year, without being confined to prescribed patterns of subjects, and that he should take his time about specialization, if that approach was even desirable at all before the graduate level.[12] What would have been called an unacceptable hodgepodge of subjects a few years before might now be regarded as the result of an imaginative and fruitful search for broader meaning in knowledge. The changes introduced in the University of Toronto in 1969, although accompanied by some warnings that standards were being dealt an irretrievable blow, were approved by faculty members who would have given them short shrift at the beginning of the 1960s.

A second evidence of the same trend was demonstrated by growing evidence of student impatience with poor teaching. Instructors were not so readily tolerated if they stood in a remote position in the front of a class droning through hackneyed material and dictating notes for examination purposes. Some perceptive students felt that the whole university system conspired to deprive them of a vital learning experience. The professor won tenure, promotion, and salary increases through his scholarly contribution to knowledge. That often meant that he wrote in mystifying language for obscure journals that only a small and specialized group ever read. By scratching one another's backs, professors were said to be keeping themselves insulated from any real pressure to perfect their teaching skills and be of service to students. It was rather easy for students who came to see the institution in this light to demand commitment on the issues of the day, and to work for such commitment through the acquisition of student power.

The period saw the effective demise of the idea that the university ought to act *in loco parentis*. As parental authority was weakening in all spheres of behaviour, it became increasingly ludicrous to think of the institution in terms of some great big Victorian super-parent, prescribing what the inhabitants of residences might do at certain hours, dictating how students might dress on particular occasions, exacting penalties for missing classes, threatening suspension for those who brought liquor on the campus. Most universities acted in a more liberal manner than the rules and regulations in their calendars implied that they did. Even the suggestion that they had a right to exercise authority over many aspects of conduct, however, created an unnecessary impression of paternalism which was bound to build up a certain amount of hostility. Some of the same issues were being raised in the high schools, where numbers of students became eligible to vote in the election of 1971, when the voting age was lowered to eighteen. The fact that the high schools were responsible for an age group that included children as well as adults of course gave the problem a different dimension.

For some university students, the only way of ensuring that student interests would be adequately recognized and safeguarded was to gain a substantial share of power.* That meant a large representation on the controlling body. Most were willing to share representation with the faculty, the public at large, and perhaps also that group who earned their living by helping to maintain university operations but without pretending to understand the essential business of the institution. The essence of the view was that power should be the prerogative of those whose interests were involved rather than of those who demonstrated particular expertise for the task. There was a kind of naive faith that a "democratic" controlling body would enlist the services of those with the necessary skills to carry out the minimum of administrative responsibilities.

CHANGES IN UNIVERSITY GOVERNMENT
Changes in many aspects of university life have been dealt with at length in volume IV of ONTARIO'S EDUCATIVE SOCIETY. It is impossible in a book of this kind to touch on more than a few of these changes, let alone explore any of them thoroughly. One development, however, demands a certain amount of attention, since it was more or less closely related to the others – that of university government.

At the beginning of the 1960s, as remained true a decade later, the ultimate *de jure* power rested in a body typically called a board of governors or a board of trustees. At the University of Toronto, the members were all appointed by the provincial government, while at other institutions a variety of methods of selection prevailed. Appointment by the existing membership, or self-perpetuation, was a common procedure. In accordance with their origins, private colleges and universities were typically controlled by religious organizations. In 1960, as far as public institutions were concerned, the most suitable candidate for board membership seemed to be the successful businessman, who was presumed to be the best qualified to raise funds and to ensure that the institution was kept under an effective administration. The board seemed to be no place for an academic, who could not be expected to have the necessary practical talents, even though he might be advising governments on economic policy. There

*For a more detailed discussion of the student power movement, see ONTARIO'S EDUCATIVE SOCIETY, volume IV, chapter 11.

was also a strong feeling that a professor who received a salary from the university could not properly act as a member of the employing body.

The faculty did, of course, have control of many aspects of internal policy making. The senate was a legally defined body responsible for academic matters such as admission requirements, programs of study, and the award of degrees. Although in some cases they were cluttered up by a considerable number of appointees from the community who had no particular claim to academic expertise, all university senates remained essentially academic bodies. A virtue was often made of the senate's lack of direct contact with the board of governors. A major responsibility of the president of the University of Toronto, for example, was to provide liaison between the two entities. In addition to their activities in the senate, faculty members exerted varying amounts of influence in the formulation of policy through their participation in faculty and departmental councils and committees and in faculty associations. Of prime importance was the informal power they were able to exert through their common views of the rights and privileges of the academic community. Thus there were certain things that no board or administration would have thought of imposing on them collectively, since to attempt to do so would have meant certain failure.

There were certain factors that prevented the voice of faculty members from being felt effectively in the management of internal affairs. One of these was that presidents, deans, department heads, and other officials were usually appointed without any time limit on their tenure of office. Too complete and too long removal from research and teaching were often conducive to the development of a special administrative mentality that conflicted with that of the scholar. A related factor was that recommendations for appointment were often made exclusively by administrators, without adequate consultation, or even any consultation at all, with the appointee's future colleagues. Thus a department head might shape his department largely according to his own tastes. A further influence that seemed to militate against faculty interests was the practice of conducting more university business in secret than could be logically justified.

This situation was changed in a number of fundamental ways during the 1960s and early 1970s. Some of the changes were traceable to the influence of the Duff-Berdahl report, already referred to, which appeared in 1966 under the title *University Government in Canada*. Among the most important underlying factors was the rapidly growing size and complexity of the universities, which would inevitably concentrate increasing power in the hands of professional administrators unless strong countermeasures were devised. Another development with somewhat similar impact was the increasing co-ordinating and regulatory power of the provincial government, which would have to be balanced by the mobilization of internal strength if the autonomy of the universities, and ultimately the academic freedom of their faculty members, were to be preserved. Also, there was a growing realization that it was incongruous to deny a primary role in the management of their own affairs to leaders of and participants in vital aspects of the life of the community.

Most of the changes came without undue fanfare. Administrative appointments were increasingly made in the light of recommendations of representative search committees, and were held for a specified period of time, possibly with provision for a single renewal. Meetings of a type once held in camera were thrown open to observers. Faculty associations and associations of the teaching staff became increasingly active in performing a kind of watchdog function over the operation of more formal organs of the university. The Ontario Council (later Confederation) of University Faculty Associations, formed in 1963, became an effective supporter of faculty interests, as did its national counterpart, the Canadian Association of University Teachers. One of the most fundamental reforms was that faculty representation on boards of governors began to be accepted, although such representation continued to be of a minority or even token nature.

The increase in internal participation was not, of course, without its dangers. One of the most serious of these was that, in their desire to ensure that administrators were responsive to the academic community, faculty members might inadvertently weaken them to the point where they were incapable of effective policy implementation at all. The result might well be chaos that would invite outside intervention. It was also questionable whether the practice of assigning the responsibility for executing (as opposed to formulating) policy to committees in certain areas could produce effective action in view of the difficulty of providing for accountability. Yet this approach appealed to considerable numbers of faculty members. There was also a danger that the large investment of time required for participation might repel considerable numbers of faculty with pressing professional obligations, and that control might fall into the hands of a particularly undesirable type of campus politician. Yet there was an overwhelming conviction among the university community that the risks were worth taking.

While these developments were taking place, the status and role of students were changing in a somewhat more dramatic manner. Students decided rather suddenly that they were entitled to share in the control of the universities, and a rather substantial share of control at that. Although by their own standards many students were dissatisfied at the amount of success they had achieved by 1972, the change, looked at from the long-term point of view, was really quite remarkable.

As the decade of the sixties progressed, there were alarming reports of student violence on a number of American and a few Canadian campuses. Up until 1972 at least, Ontario had been spared any extreme example of

228 Education: Ontario's preoccupation

this type of phenomenon. There were examples of student strikes and sit-ins at various universities, some resulting in success from the students' point of view, but none of these could have been called in any real sense destructive. Whatever their nature, however, they were far from being the most important aspect of the students' drive for power. What mattered more was the steady pressure for student representation on councils, committees, senates, and ultimately, boards of governors, or on whatever unicameral governing body might emerge.

Up to and including the level of the senate, most faculty members tended to favour and support student representation as long as it did not threaten their own predominant position, and as long as students were not given a voice in recommending faculty promotion, tenure, and salary increases. The majority, however, resisted the principle of parity on the bodies in question. A struggle over students' attempts to get this principle accepted in the council of the Faculty of Arts and Science drew a good deal of attention at the University of Toronto in 1970–1. At stake was the issue of whether power should be exercised primarily by those with special training, expertise, and experience, and with a long-term commitment to the university, or whether it should be shared on the assumption that students' welfare and interests were matters which they deserved an equal voice in determining. A corollary of the second proposition was that non-academic staff members and employees of the university had a right to participate in shaping their own working environment.

Student representation on boards of governors was a principle that encountered considerable resistance. Some of the bitterest exchanges in the Legislature occurred over a bill to reform the governing structure of the University of Western Ontario in 1967. Constituencies such as the board, faculty, and students had apparently agreed beforehand by an overwhelming margin on a clause by which the students would elect a non-student representative to the board of governors. Some students appeared before the legislators in committee, however, and persuaded a majority of them that student opinion had not really been presented accurately, and that what was desired was that students be represented by one of their own. The government took the position that the officially expressed views of the university community should be followed, and passed the bill as originally drawn up. As a result of this action it was severely criticized by opposition members as being against student representation. This charge was refuted by the government's later actions in approving such representation on other boards where the recommendation was made through recognized channels.

One type of student representation was that tried at Carleton, where students might be elected to successively higher levels of responsibility through department and faculty councils, the senate, and ultimately the board. The relevant legislation did not make it mandatory that students should have top-level representation, but the faculty did in fact make every effort to ensure that elective positions would be filled by students. The scheme did not work very well in practice, in large measure because too few students could be found who were willing to work their way up, so to speak. Those who favoured direct election by students of their own representatives at each level felt that the scheme was designed to ensure that only Uncle Toms got to the top. Faculty members felt that students should be willing to earn responsibility just as they themselves had to do.

Both student and faculty representation were involved in the issue of unicameral versus bicameral government, which began to assume some importance. Although it appeared for a time that the University of Waterloo would be the first to petition the provincial government for the abolition of its senate and board of governors in favour of a unicameral governing council, the plan developed in 1969 and 1970 was held up because of internal changes, and finally abandoned, and the University of Toronto was the first to adopt such an arrangement by an act of the Legislature passed in 1971. Much of the work of the new council would be conducted by committees consisting of appropriately qualified members, augmented by others from outside that body. There was a certain amount of scepticism on the part of the minister, John White, about the effectiveness of the scheme, although he felt that there was no alternative but to proceed in view of the strength of the pressure for reform from the university itself. White promised a review of the situation in five years. The opposition members for the most part supported the principle of unicameral university government with greater confidence in its success than the minister seemed to feel. A final assessment would await the implementation of the plan in mid-1972.

The debates in the Legislature indicated general agreement with the government's policy that half the membership of the university governing body should be from the lay community. There was strong opposition, however, to the arrangement, following the recommendations of a university-wide committee formed the previous year, whereby the faculty was given greater representation than the students. The fact that there was considerable protest by the students against the rejection of the parity principle demonstrates how far they had come within a few years in claiming a strong voice in controlling their own destiny.

CONCLUDING COMMENTS

The pressure for greater freedom and more humane treatment for the learner at every educational level was a development of great importance in Ontario society, as it was in other parts of the country and of the western world. It might best be regarded as a manifestation of human determination not to be overwhelmed by the modern advance of technology. There were more and more effective ways of identifying the individual, of measuring his abilities, talents, and attitudes, of fitting him into an occupational slot and moving him around at the dictates of some superior authority. The complexity of government operations made it increasingly difficult to understand his rights and defend them against administrative convenience. Advertisers studied his attitudes and reactions in order to manipulate him more effectively. There was a constant threat that he might slip irretrievably into one form of slavery or another. Trends in education were one sign that he was determined to defend himself against dehumanization in any way he could.

SEVEN

Early research efforts and the development of the Ontario Institute for Studies in Education

THE STATUS OF EDUCATIONAL RESEARCH UP TO THE 1960s

At the beginning of the 1960s, research was the orphan child of education, despite some improvements made in the 1950s.* Since the contributions of scientific research to the advance of technology were well known, it was commonly assumed that educational research had something positive to contribute to education. Those who wanted to be considered forward-looking and ready for change counted themselves in favour of it. There was general agreement, however, that only a pittance was being spent on it, and that substantial results could not be expected without a much larger investment.

The generally favourable attitude was rather fragile and superficial. The average educator had an underlying conviction that the best way to improve education was to follow the example of great teachers or to put more successfully into practice the ideals and beliefs expounded by the great educational philosophers, all leavened by a generous measure of common sense. He was not conscious of being beset by a host of researchable problems, the solutions to which would immediately enable him to perform at higher levels of competence and skill. If he were asked to name a subject for research, the chances were that he would identify something entirely beyond scientific definition and control or else something too trivial or obvious to merit serious study. Very often his ideas of what ought to be included in a definition of research were vague or inaccurate. Research had acquired some unfavourable connotations because its chief practitioners, graduate students seeking higher degrees, were considered to be addicted to two types of themes: those that were so abstract that they could not have any conceivable bearing on the current or future practice of education, and those that were so narrow that the results could not possibly matter. In short, the educator was all too often neither conscious of any urgent need for research in relation to his own immediate concerns nor aware of any circumstances where it had made any major

*Research and development activities of various agencies during this period are described at some length in ONTARIO'S EDUCATIVE SOCIETY, volume v, chapters 11 and 12.

difference to practice. Yet he was for the most part prepared to believe that it had unrealized potentialities and thus justified his support.

The Davis program for educational reform may be said to have rested on four main pillars: the extension of the system at the post-secondary level, with particular reference to the universities and the colleges of applied arts and technology; the overhaul of the administrative structure, including the reconstitution of the Department of Education and the amalgamation of the small school boards; the establishment of procedures for continuous curriculum renewal; and the improvement of teacher education. At one stage, plans seemed to call for a fifth pillar, provision for the continuous leavening of practice in all spheres by a process of research and development. By 1971, despite the fact that various individuals and groups were dissatisfied with specific aspects of the set-up, and there was indisputably room for improvement, the universities were flourishing and the colleges of applied arts and technology were, within their own frame of reference, an undoubted success. The administrative restructuring of the Department of Education had been carried out as planned, and several functions, formerly centralized at Toronto, were now performed locally. Although critics claimed that the school boards had been amalgamated too precipitously, and there was unquestionably a great deal of protest and unhappiness about the financial repercussions, no substantial body of opinion took essential issue with what had been done. In the area of curriculum, the department assumed a role of enlightened guidance, providing models and materials for the use of teachers, but making it clear that the latter must assume a degree of freedom and responsibility that they had not known in earlier decades. Considerable improvement had been made in teacher education within existing structures, and a substantial part of the program of elementary teacher preparation had been transferred to the universities. The intended transfer often seemed to move at a glacial pace, but the prospects were good that it would eventually be completed. Only the hope of making research and development an integral and vital part of the educational process was still to be realized.

This is not to deny that there was a phenomenal increase in research and development activity, nor is it to disparage the quality of much of the work that was done. The fact is, however, that Ontario education, by the end of the sixties, had not begun to bear the imprint of any specific research programs. Ontario educators still showed no substantial sign of seeking research evidence as a basis for the bulk of their decisions. The educational system had not become research oriented. The researcher as an adviser, consultant, or guide was not conspicuously relied upon or respected in the corridors of power. Research was still commonly looked upon as an exercise in statistical manipulation for the graduate student or as an esoteric pursuit for the professor. The efforts of the classroom researcher were praised, but the results had no great currency among the teaching body.

All this was true despite the fact that, considering the size of its school population, Ontario had made one of the greatest efforts to promote the cause of educational research and development ever undertaken anywhere. Why were more satisfactory results not achieved? Was the whole effort badly conceived and hopelessly mismanaged? Were the original aspirations of the promoters of the cause inflated beyond all reason? Were the forces of indifference and even of open hostility too great to be overcome? Was the initial degree of success all that could be hoped for, and were the real triumphs still in the future?

EARLY DEVELOPMENT OF RESEARCH IN ONTARIO

The roots of educational research and development do not go very far back in Canada, or anywhere else, for that matter. The word development as an aspect of innovation in education began to acquire currency only in the 1960s when people sought a term to describe the process by which abstract concepts or principles were adapted to practice through the construction of textbooks and teaching aids, the devising of instructional or administrative procedures, and the like. Research itself became a practical possibility earlier in the century as a result of two major advances: the progress of the testing movement and the elaboration of probability theory. The first of these made it possible to measure human phenomena with a minimum acceptable degree of precision and the second provided a means of applying findings based on a sample of variable observations to a larger group or population from which the sample was drawn.

By the 1920s tests were being constructed in the United States to measure every imaginable aspect of human achievement and many psychological characteristics as well. Many of these tests were spilling across the border and attracting interest among Canadian educators. It was mainly a feeling that Canadian schools would be best served by the use of instruments of indigenous origin that led Professor Peter Sandiford of the Ontario College of Education to secure a grant from the Carnegie Corporation to establish the small unit in 1931 which came to be known as the Department of Educational Research. In modern terminology, this department might better have been called the Department of Test Development, since that remained its only significant activity for several years, and the centre of its concern for considerably longer. New dimensions were added by Maxwell Cameron's studies of educational finance later in the 1930s. The arrival toward the end of the decade of R.W.B. Jackson, who studied abroad under the leading statisticians of the day, resulted in theoretical contributions of considerable importance. John A. Long, a psychologist who succeeded Sandiford as director of the department, encouraged a continued emphasis on test development.

Another root of educational research is to be found in the initiatives of William Blatz who, after conducting studies in association with some of the leading figures in the United States, became director of St George's

School for Child Study in 1925–6. Attention was centred on the investigation of mental hygiene problems of school children. Assistance was at first obtained from the Rockefeller Foundation, and the sponsorship of the Department of Psychology of the University of Toronto was secured. Later the enterprise was taken into the university as the Institute of Child Study. A good deal of valued and influential work was done at the institute in the area of child development but, although graduates of institute courses proceeded into the school system, the agency itself remained rather remote from public education. A major reason was that it relied heavily on experimentation with its own private school children rather than undertaking projects in the public system.

After the Second World War, the Department of Educational Research of the Ontario College of Education moved toward the *de facto* position of a service organization for the provincial government. The report of the Royal Commission on Education suggested that it act as an educational research bureau for the province, and that it be given the financial means to assume that role by regular departmental grants.[1] A suggestion of this kind was in accordance with the views of R.W.B. Jackson, who served as secretary of the commission and was destined to be appointed as director of the Department of Educational Research after the death of J.A. Long in 1957. The assumption by the organization of a semi-official position was not altogether compatible with the recommendation that the organization co-ordinate, supervise, and assist in the work of outside agencies on their request. Teachers' federations, trustees' associations, organizations of teachers' college masters, and groups of school administrators were somewhat hesitant to appeal for assistance to an arm of government, especially during a period when the results of their findings might be construed as hostile by a rather defensive and touchy Department of Education.

On the national scene, both the CEA and the CTF demonstrated an interest in the possibility of encouraging, co-ordinating, or conducting research. During the Second World War, the former supported a rather short-lived Canadian Council for Educational Research. For a number of years, assistance was mainly directed toward specific projects rather than toward the maintenance of a continuous program. In the late fifties, however, a large grant from Imperial Oil made possible the appointment of a research director, who combined a program of service studies with many activities designed to stimulate and co-ordinate projects undertaken by other agencies. In 1953 the Canadian Teachers' Federation appointed its first full-time research director. At about the same time, a small group of people, several of whom were located at the Ontario College of Education, took steps to establish a Research Section in the OEA. This section sponsored the compilation of some material on research and organized a program each year at the OEA convention. It had difficulty, however, in securing enough paid-up members to safeguard itself against compulsory dissolution. Before long it was dissolved in favour of the larger and stronger Ontario Educational Research Council, which was formed in 1958 largely as a result of the initiative of members of the OTF, with support from the staff of the Ontario College of Education and interested individuals such as Robin S. Harris. For the OTF, this development removed the possibility of establishing its own research staff and program, a possibility that had been considered on a number of occasions. The Ontario Educational Research Council drew support, much of it more moral than financial, from a wide range of educational organizations throughout the province. It did not have enough funds to become an actual centre of research activity, but concentrated instead on promotion, stimulation, and co-ordination. It is doubtful that the oncept of research that it promoted really did much to enhance expectations of major progress by the research approach.

In the meantime the Department of Educational Research at the Ontario College of Education was continuing to expand. Its professional staff were mostly part of the nucleus of a rather anemic Department of Educational Theory in the University of Toronto, which was mainly in the business of offering summer courses to enable Ontario teachers to secure graduate degrees in education. The staff of the Department of Educational Research was enlarged to carry out major longitudinal studies of student progress entitled the Atkinson Study of Utilization of Student Resources and the Carnegie Study of Identification and Utilization of Talent in High School and College, which were financed with the assistance of grants from the Atkinson Charitable Foundation and the Carnegie Corporation of New York respectively. Certain other functions were also assumed, such as the administration of the departmental grade 12 objective tests, including machine scoring and reporting the results. As time went on the facilities of the department were also employed to mechanize certain operations related to the administration of the departmental grade 13 examinations. A major responsibility throughout the period was that of assisting the Department of Education in the devising of schemes for making financial grants to school boards and for studying their effects. This basic program, much of which was not research at all, but rather service, was supplemented by test construction and a multiude of minor studies and advisory functions conducted in association with or on the request of outside agencies. While the Department of Educational Research may never have demonstrated the full power of research as such to improve education, it did a great deal to facilitate certain administrative operations. Perhaps it was guilty of promising more than *bona fide* research could deliver.

In form the Department of Educational Research remained strictly a part of the Ontario College of Education, and its finances and the academic appointments of its members came through the University of Toronto. Thus a certain distance was maintained that kept it from functioning as a part of the Department of Education. That degree of distance was perhaps unfortunate from the latter's point of view, since officials never developed the habit of requesting research services freely as they might otherwise have done, and thus continued to rely on unsupported opinion for decision making in doubtful areas. With the Department of Educational Research reasonably close at hand, they were prevented from developing their own research facilities and resources. The situation was perhaps also less than ideal from the point of view of the Ontario College of Education. It would have been desirable to have active research being conducted in close association with the instructional activities of members of the teacher training department. Instructors would have benefited if they had been able to suggest research, to participate actively in it, and to take the results into account in their work. One must assume that a reasonable proportion of them would have welcomed the opportunity to do these things, but they were not in fact given a chance. The Department of Educational Research never operated as a research bureau for the college as it did for the government, and its college ties were easily severed in 1965. The legacy it left was one of complete separation between educational research and teacher preparation in the college.

THE FOUNDING OF THE ONTARIO INSTITUTE
FOR STUDIES IN EDUCATION

When William G. Davis was appointed minister of education in 1962, R.W.B. Jackson soon established a close association with him. Jackson had long experience as adviser to ministers and prime ministers, and also possessed an innovative type of mind that made him a fruitful source of new ideas. These were qualities that Davis particularly valued and was able to use in devising some of his reforms. It is easy to see how Davis might be impressed by the potentialities of research, and might decide to get the fullest possible value from it.

There appeared to be a close association in the mind of the minister between educational research and development and the improvement of administrative efficiency through information systems and data processing techniques. The latter were being applied innovatively in the Department of Educational Research. Davis was also said to be in close contact with Frederick W. Minkler, director of education for North York, who was actively promoting the cause. The founding of the Ontario Institute for Studies in Education occurred at a time when ambitious efforts were being made to improve the collection and interchange of educational data across Canada by the Ministers' Information Systems Committee, a subsidiary of what became known as the Council of Ministers of Education.

While the nucleus of the Ontario Institute for Studies in Education was found in the Ontario College of Education, another major component of the new organization was the Ontario Curriculum Institute. Although this independent organization was a very positive force in Ontario education, its establishment could be looked upon as a manifestation of dissatisfaction with official inertia in the face of a need for major changes in school curriculum. It represented an attempt by grass-roots forces to seize the initiative and carry the Department of Education along in a great reform movement. At the centre of its approach was the idea that the best human resources should be mobilized in the work of curriculum development. That meant a co-operative effort on the part of elementary and secondary school teachers, university professors, informed officials, educational researchers, and the like. Although the term research was used rather freely in the planning stages, educational research in the strict sense did not play a fundamental part. The founders were interested in curriculum development, which meant assembling the best available information in the form that might exert the most effective influence on what was taught in the schools.

The success of the initial venture encouraged the idea of creating an organization on a provincial basis to continue the work in a more comprehensive fashion. Sharp, the Toronto trustee who played an active part in the initial stages, secured promises of financial support from a group of the larger school boards and from the Ontario Teachers' Federation. In due course the Department of Education gave assurances of financial contributions and of assistance in kind. The initial program was heavily subsidized by the Ford Foundation, although it was made clear that help from this source could not be relied upon on a permanent basis. When the organization was first formed, a great virtue was made of the practice of securing funds from a variety of sources so that none of the sponsoring agencies would be in a position to dominate the enterprise. Just what kind of domination the institute had to beware of was never specifically defined, although the usual implication was that undue influence from the Department of Education had best be avoided.

The institute was under the control of a board of governors consisting largely of representatives of the sponsoring agencies. The members went far beyond the caretaking role that is characteristic of such agencies, and actually planned and supervised the institute's program of activities. The permanent staff consisted only of a director and a small administrative and clerical group with the responsibility of carrying out the mandate of the board of governors. Most of the work was done by teachers, professors, and other educators acting on a part-time basis or seconded for limited periods to participate in committee work. It was assumed that the kind of contribution that was wanted could best be made by those who did not stray too far from the classroom, the lecture room, or some other sphere of regular educational responsibility. This approach was feasible as long as the institute did not undertake any comprehensive research program, which would have demanded a long-term commitment on the part of a specialized staff.

The first full-time director of the Ontario Curriculum Institute, J.R.H.

Morgan, did not assume his responsibilities until January 1964, although an ambitious program of committee activitiy was under way considerably earlier. Morgan immediately threw himself energetically into a campaign to raise the funds required to implement the plans already agreed upon, and to make the institute self-sustaining after the contributions of the Ford Foundation were exhausted. He soon concluded that he faced an impossible task. The amounts that industrial enterprises, for example, were willing to contribute to such a cause were clearly inadequate to sustain a continuing and comprehensive program.

Seen in perspective, the Ontario Curriculum Institute was a small interruption in the movement toward the assumption of more complete government responsibility for education. The educational enterprise was simply getting too large and expensive for a combination of voluntary groups to acquire a major share of control over any part of it. Further, while the institute was operated with the co-operation and support of the Department of Education, it was unrealistic to expect the department to let itself evolve into a state of undue dependence on an outside agency.

Having decided that the kind of dynamic educational system he envisioned required a large and continuous research and development contribution, Davis faced a number of possible alternatives. There were three which had little appeal for him. First, he might have created a departmental agency, either by making a completely fresh beginning or by arranging for the transfer of the Department of Educational Research to the governmental structure and adding to its staff and other resources as needed. Second, he could have chosen to build up the Department of Educational Research within the College of Education. Third, he could have encouraged the establishment of a number of counterparts to the Department of Educational Research in other universities of the province. The first of these courses of action would have ensured that research facilities were close at hand, and officials might have got into the habit of calling upon them as a normal part of their administrative operations. It also would have been relatively easy to ensure a continued balance between studies with an immediate practical value and those offering the possibility of more remote benefits. There was the disadvantage that educational researchers ordinarily thought of themselves as scholars, proclaimed the need for a high level of professional training, and asserted that they needed to work in close association with various university departments. It was feared that the most competent researchers could not be recruited to work within the civil service. If the Department of Educational Research had been moved into the Department of Education, the graduate Department of Educational Theory of the University of Toronto would have been weakened at a time when it badly needed to be built up. The minister's second possible course of action was unappealing because the main business of the Ontario College of Education was to prepare teachers, and a major expansion of its research and graduate studies appendages would have distorted it out of all recognition. It seemed administratively advisable to leave its main functions undisturbed. The third possibility was unattractive because there seemed to be a need, at least initially, for a substantial concentration of resources to allow for adequate specialization and for the massing of forces in an attempt to deal with some of the major educational problems. The development of such resources in other parts of the province might come later.

The minister was actually attracted to a fourth possibility, which would have involved the establishment of an independent research and development agency, unattached to any university, and with no responsibility for a program of graduate studies. Presumably it would have been operated in close association with the Department of Education but, in controlling its own program, would have been able to demonstrate more initiative and vitality than a departmental branch. Davis was persuaded by his advisers that active participation in a program of graduate studies would not only be an important contribution in itself, but would also constitute a major source of strength for the research program. The most obvious way to achieve these objectives was to have the new institute incorporate the graduate programs in education of the University of Toronto.

Research programs conducted by graduate faculties of education had not proved to be major sources of strength for public education systems anywhere in the world. Students had a way of demanding first priority in terms of staff time and effort. Although faculty members were often accused of neglecting their teaching in favour of other activities, there was something compelling about an assembled group of students waiting to be taught. Further, although students were supposed to be a great source of cheap labour as research assistants, they were seldom well enough trained or able to detach themselves from their own pursuit of a degree for long enough to enable them to make a contribution of high quality to another project. The professor, who required a large amount of freedom for the adequate performance of his teaching duties, tended to engage in small, independent research studies as a sideline. Since there are innumerable ways of defining almost any problem in education, the results obtained by different individuals very seldom added up to anything important. Moreover, unless he was released from his regular duties in order to carry out a particular commission, the professor was inclined to be unreliable as a party to a contract. Because of the basic security of his position, he could not effectively be called to account if he missed a deadline or in some other way failed to meet his obligations.

The writer, who had the main responsibility for devising the structure of the Ontario Institute for Studies in Education during 1964–5, felt that some of these disadvantages could be overcome within an academic framework. A number of features were designed to ensure such an outcome. 1 / Control of the institute was vested in a board of governors with wide representation from the university community, the Department of Education, the teacher training institutions, the Ontario Teachers' Federation, school trustees, and other groups, including members of the institute staff. Although the graduate studies program would be under the jurisdiction of the senate of the University of Toronto, the board would have a strong influence in shaping the institute's program of research and development. While it would not be able to manage operations in detail in accordance with the practice established by the board of governors of the Ontario Curriculum Institute, it would be in a position to assure itself that the OISE program was broadly acceptable to the educational community. For this purpose, it would have to have a decisive voice in the determination of priorities. 2 / The internal structure was supposed to be such that administrative power could be exerted to ensure that certain objectives could be achieved. For example, if a contract were drawn up with an agency such as the Department of Education to conduct a particular study and report the results by a certain date, there had to be a means of carrying out the specified conditions. As the institute was first set up, the director had the unrestricted right to recommend the employment of certain personnel for limited periods to perform specified functions. He was also in a position to secure the board's approval for the assignment of funds to meet defined obligations. The administrative structure included three coordinators whose responsibilities roughly corresponded to the three basic functions of the institute – graduate studies, research, and development – and who were originally in a position to contribute a good deal to the effective operation of the institute as a coherent entity. The division (later department) heads were also supposed to have sufficient authority to ensure that balanced programs were developed within their own spheres of operations. Provision was made for an academic council, consisting initially of all faculty members with the status of assistant professor or higher, and later somewhat broadened, which might consider any matter relating to the institute's functions and welfare, but which could do no more than advise the director.

FURTHER ORGANIZATIONAL AND STRUCTURAL DEVELOPMENT OF THE ONTARIO INSTITUTE FOR STUDIES IN EDUCATION

After little more than a year's operation, it became evident that a large proportion of the faculty were determined that the institute should develop into a kind of internal democracy. Some of the assumptions that underlay the evolution that followed were clearly articulated and others were merely implied. Most fundamental, perhaps, was the idea that the soundest decisions would result from the fullest possible participation on the part of those who qualified for membership in the Academic Council. It was necessary, therefore, to give this council *de facto* powers to cover every important aspect of the institute's operations. The major organs created for this purpose were a series of standing committees. Perhaps it was inevitable, in view of the rapid initial growth of the faculty, that a resolute stand was taken against "status hierarchies." This meant that the most junior and inexperienced council member had the same potential influence as the distinguished scholar, of whom there were a few among the early recruits. As time went on, there was at least superficial acceptance of the idea that all employees of the institute, regardless of training or function, had a right to a voice in the basic decisions affecting the organization. Thus in the fall of 1970 all students and employees, including research assistants, librarians, finance officers, and stenographers, were assembled to discuss priorities among the institute's operations.

The dictates of the earlier concepts of internal democracy demanded faculty participation in practically all important aspects of the administrative process. The kind of participation that the faculty were determined to have meant going much further than the privilege of having representative faculty members advise the director or other administrative officials. It had to be established in practice that the director, except in unusual circumstances, acted upon the advice of advisory bodies. If the matter in question had to be referred to the board of governors, he would be expected to take the recommendation to the board as a matter of course. The director, R.W.B. Jackson, was rather readily persuaded to act in the desired fashion. Thus most of the powers that he was entitled to exercise according to the act and regulations were soon in abeyance. When he stepped out of line during the summer of 1968 by recommending the reactivation of the position of assistant director without full consultation with the Academic Council, there was such a storm of protest that this type of independent action on his part was never repeated. Naturally, with the director rendered incapable of significant initiative, the role of subordinate officials became largely one of presiding over the democratic decision-making process.

It was during the 1966-7 academic year that the Academic Council established the procedures by which it subsequently for a time dominated the affairs of the institute. Until that time, it was the prerogative of the coordinator of research to nominate candidates for department headships. Such nominations were actually made after extended informal consultation with other officers and faculty members. Similarly, department heads engaged in consultation with members of their departments before recommending appointments. After that time, recommendations for coordinators, assistant coordinators, department heads, and other officials were made by formally constituted search committees, the decisions of which were not questioned. The position of department head was made subject to renewal after four years. Although there remained some question about whether an incumbent would be allowed under any condition to serve beyond a second term, the extraordinary turnover among department heads suggested that the matter was likely to remain academic. Symbolic of the reduction of the authority of department heads was the establishment of a secret committee named by the director to review recommendations having to do with salaries and promotion. This committee had, of course, a very commendable purpose in that it was in a position to ensure that no faculty member was subject to arbitrary and unfair treatment.

In the early stages of the institute's operations, it was customary for the coordinators, the department heads, and two or three other officials to meet under the chairmanship of the coordinator of research to deal with various administrative problems and to attempt to develop the institute program as a coherent whole. Naturally, in view of the need to formulate new operating procedures, there were many policy matters to be considered. Results of the deliberations of this group, which came to be called the Administrative Council, were customarily conveyed to the director in the form of recommendations. Leading members of the Academic Council, apart from those with regular administrative responsibilities, became convinceed that the influence of this body must be neutralized. After a first abortive attempt, they got it established that the Administrative Council must stick to matters of routine administration and might not make recommendations to the director on policy issues. From that time on, the Administrative Council exerted little visible influence on the development of the institute.

Much of what was happening at the institute was comparable to developments in Ontario universities as a whole. As indicated in chapter 6, the Duff/Berdahl report, which appeared in 1966, gave a strong impetus to the democratization of internal university organs.[2] The powers of deans and department heads to act against the wishes of the faculty were being sharply curtailed, in part by placing limits on their terms of office. For the most part, the regime that was being established gave the individual faculty member the maximum opportunity to exercise his freedom and initiative as a teacher, and to conduct the usual type of individual research leading to scholarly publication. A strong case could be made for the principle that the best leadership was the least leadership, or at least the exertion of a kind of unobtrusive influence that depended mainly on providing an outstanding example of scholarly excellence. University teachers were confined and disciplined in many ways by tradition and by the expectations of colleagues and students. The last thing they wanted was a boss to organize and direct operations as was commonly done in industry and in the civil service.

There were two main reasons why the university model, as it was developing during the contemporary period, was inadequate for OISE. 1 / The organization was not set up with the expectation that it would carry out a role already fairly well established in the mind of the public and of the academic community, as was true of the universities. It was expected to assume unique functions which would best be defined in full consultation with responsible educational interests and agencies outside the institute, rather than exclusively by internal debate. 2 / If the individual faculty member had the final decision about the research projects in which he would engage, it would be difficult to avoid having only a collection of separate fragments, and not an organized program directed toward the attainment of a limited number of larger objectives. Those faculty members who were in actual control of the development of the institute through their influence in the Academic Council recognized the existence of these problems, and made some attempt to deal with the second, at least, through the establishment of internal committees and boards, with some members elected by the faculty and others appointed by the director.

With respect to the first question, it was quite clear that the faculty were determined that they would exert relatively complete control over the program and would define the institute's developing role. It thus seemed necessary to leading members that the board of governors, despite its absolute *de jure* authority, should in fact perform only caretaker functions and put the stamp of approval on policies that were actually formulated through internal democratic processes. From the beginning, board meetings were filled up with matters of routine business, while requests for the discussion of policy were repeatedly postponed. In this way potential friction between the board and the faculty was avoided and the faculty continued on its way without serious interference. The establishment of board committees to deal with the essential business of the institute, as opposed to finance and various aspects of staff welfare, was carefully avoided. The main concession to the need for outside consultation was the formation of advisory committees for research and development. These committees could only propose activities, and exerted little influence, since most faculty members preferred to formulate and carry out their own individual projects.

The question of how to bring outside influence to bear on the process of developing a program for the institute was undoubtedly a difficult one. There was no doubt that the board of governors could not come to grips with the problem during meetings covering part of a day every second month, or even once a month, according to later practice. If the members had been prepared to act through committees, they would have had to invest substantial amounts of extra time in acquiring background information and formulating policies. If they had been lured into matters of methodology, the results might well have been unfortunate. There were many faculty members who were prepared to assert quite unequivocally that board members lacked the training to pass judgment on the suitability of specific research and development projects, let alone offer opinions on the appropriate methodology. Such a view, if valid, did not obviate the importance of a major effort to arouse the interest and to secure the understanding approval of the educational community through the board for whatever was undertaken. If the OISE faculty defined its own role in isolation, without ensuring that board members were sufficiently informed of their activities and sufficiently sympathetic toward them to support them with some enthusiasm in public, it invited almost certain rejection of much of its work. Considerations of this kind had a major influence in the abolition in 1971 of the Academic Council in favour of an Institute Assembly, where board members and elected representatives of various constituencies within the institute began to meet together to formulate policy.

There were special reasons why the institute in its early stages was soon alienated from much of the provincial educational community. Because of the long period of neglect of graduate studies in education in Ontario, a large enterprise could be quickly staffed with qualified people only by securing the services of individuals from other provinces and abroad. Among Canadian provinces, Alberta was the most conspicuous source of recruits, while many others came from the United States and farther afield. The situation demanded that such people quickly establish a network of local contacts and determine how they might best meet the needs of the province. While some did so, often in the face of considerable difficulty, others followed the line of least resistance and engaged in abstract studies without obvious provincial significance. There was a strong temptation to seek international prestige by producing articles for publication in leading journals, particularly those produced in the United States. While this type of activity was in certain respects highly desirable, there was a widespread feeling that it carried too much weight at the expense of studies of local application. This feeling may or may not have been justified, but its existence caused considerable difficulty for the institute.

The second major deficiency of the so-called university model of organization, that there was no way of ensuring that the research and development efforts of the institution would be focused on specific objectives, was tackled, as already indicated, on the assumption that the necessary coordination could be provided by internal review boards. These bodies would appraise proposals for projects and would be able to recommend the allocation of funds in such a way as to ensure both a high quality of work and a concentration of effort according to a system of priorities. One problem was that it was difficult to expect impartial decisions from those who might before long expect to find themselves in the position of seeking approval and funds for their own proposals. It would be expecting a great deal of human nature to suppose that there would be no room in the set-up for influence-peddling or favouritism. Again, evidence of partiality might be lacking, but the impression that it existed was an obstacle to the successful functioning of the institute. Of course, if administrators had been given the responsibility for outlining the program, similar weaknesses, or perhaps even more serious ones, would exist.

What really gave the review process a chance to show effective results, inevitably to the accompaniment of cries of influence and favouritism, was a slackening in the original relatively abundant flow of government funds. As long as there was plenty of money and no serious administrative control over the initiation and conduct of projects, there was a good deal of opportunity for activities that should have had low priority by any criteria, as well as for downright waste. With growing financial stringency, the controlling bodies had at least some prospect of reducing the number of studies that tended to embarrass the institute and provide fuel for critics. Provided that there was sufficient continuity in co-ordinating structure and in the elected or appointed office-holders who assumed responsibility, it appeared possible to deal more effectively with those who gave the institute a bad name by abandoning projects before completion or in other ways failing to carry out commitments. Those who acquired a poor reputation in this way would cut themselves off from further supplies of funds. Whether informal arrangements for academic security could protect those who consistently failed to secure funds was a question that had not been settled by 1971, but it seemed clear that the taxpayer would ultimately have something to say in the matter if it were not settled by internal discipline.

The formation of the Institute Assembly was accompanied by a development that could not help but cause concern among those who were used to the university practice of having a professor's work in his field of special expertise evaluated by his peers. Beginning in the fall of 1971, the work of detailed appraisal of certain professors' efforts was assigned to committees consisting of a combination of staff members with full academic status, students, and other categories of staff, some with no training for the task. These committees undertook to criticize the proposals in detail, and requested changes to make them more acceptable. Obviously the assignment to relatively inexperienced students and untrained staff of this kind of responsibility went far beyond the question of representation of such individuals on policy-making bodies.

There were important governmental decisions in 1971 bearing on the role and mode of operations of OISE. The institute was removed from the jurisdiction of the minister of education and placed under that of the minister of colleges and universities. Like other institutions of higher education, it was henceforth to receive formula grants based on its student enrolment, an arrangement which made it possible to identify more precisely the cost of its graduate studies component. The government also announced that the research and development grants made to it on the former basis would be reduced by successive stages to 80, 60, and 40 per cent of the total of provincial funds available for such purposes. The remainder would be assigned by a review body established by the Department of Education, which would receive submissions from faculty members of OISE or of other university-level institutions and fund them on the basis of merit. The review body, which came to be called the Grants-in-Aid of Educational Research and Development Committee, had a minority of representatives of the Department of Education, along with others representing the organizations of teachers and trustees, the faculties of education, and the rest of the university community.

The new body was an inevitable consequence of the development of faculties of education, which would and should have growing resources of research talent deserving funding. It was difficult, however, not to think of it as a partial answer to criticisms that the institute had not been operating according to the usual pattern of fiscal accountability. There may have been some signifiance to the fact that the universities were at the same time arranging, after the matter had been made an issue by opposition members of the Legislature, to make public their financial records in more detail than heretofore and in a form that encouraged more inter-university comparisons.

As an experiment in democratic institutional government, OISE in its early stages offered some valuable lessons. When power, or at least the potentiality of exerting power, was first extracted from the administrative officials, there was considerable willingness to participate in committee activity, even though there was some grumbling about the amount of time required. As time went on, it became increasingly difficult to secure a good attendance at meetings, and some had to adjourn for lack of a quorum. It also became more difficult to persuade capable individuals to stand for election to committees. Repeated appeals had to be made for nominations, and elections were frequently settled by acclamation. There was a clear danger that matters would be dominated by the "politicians" who enjoyed the manœuvring needed to get and keep influence. Part of the evident disillusionment resulted from the realization that the power taken from the administrators had not all fallen into the hands of committees, but had been to some extent lost along the way.

It must be acknowledged that a system offering the maximum opportunity for individual initiative does produce certain advantages. Some ideas and insights are highly personal, and can best be formulated and publicized by their originator untrammeled by the kind of administrative formalities that tend to develop when groups of people must work together. A great deal of inspiration would be lost if every researcher were required to operate as part of a team. Moreover, an atmosphere of almost complete freedom tends to foster the kind of critical thinking that offers the educational system some hope of ultimate improvement, even though the immediate effects may be painful. Some of the adverse reaction to OISE stemmed from resentment on the part of those whose comfortable doman was subject to criticism.

While OISE was incapable in its early stages of executing any large number of commissions from outside agencies, it was possible for some individuals and groups to undertake such projects with their own personal integrity as security. Enough contributions of this kind were made to produce considerable good feeling toward the institute as a whole. To a distressing extent, however, the organization developed an image of remoteness and lack of interest in ordinary educational affairs. The critics refused to believe that a chaotic crowd of people "doing their own thing" would lead to ultimate benefits for education. Influential elements of the press took delight in pointing to the institute as a supreme example of waste and extravagance, even though the budget, which hovered around the $10 million mark after the first few years of operation, represented only a tiny percentage of the total provincial investment in education.

A rather promising step was taken in 1968 with a decision to establish what were called extension development centres or field centres. Three of these came into operation in 1969–70, two in 1970–1, and two in 1971–2. There was some consideration of the possibility that they might eventually share most or all of the functions assumed by the central headquarters in Toronto. In the early stages, however, they undertook to provide assistance with research and development projects in local school systems and agencies and to offer informational services about interesting and useful developments occurring elsewhere. It was thought particularly desirable that they establish a close working relationship with the regional offices of the Department of Education. According to reports, their offers of practical assistance were eagerly welcomed by local educational officials, and fruitful relationships were established. These varied very substantially from one part of the province to another, much depending on the training and outlook of the people involved. There was a good prospect that some of the unfavourable impressions of OISE would be counteracted and, what was perhaps more important, that an awareness of the potential of competently conducted research and development activities might begin to suffuse the educational establishment. The ultimate success of the centres would depend to a large extent on how well they were financed and supported. The growing reluctance of the provincial government to invest more in the OISE enterprise as a whole did not augur well for them.

INSTITUTE ACTIVITIES

The research and development programs and the field service activities of OISE covered a tremendous amount of ground from the beginning. It was never intended that they should be limited to any specifically defined area or areas of education. In the early stages a considerable amount of favourable comment was received from recipients of reports based on projects initiated by the Ontario Curriculum Institute, which merged with the new organization in 1966. During the first year or two, many studies represented a continuation of those inherited from the Department of Educational Research. At that stage a classification of studies could be fairly realistically based on the departmental structure, but as time went on departmental lines tended to become increasingly blurred.

An attempt is made in ONTARIO'S EDUCATIVE SOCIETY to indicate something of the scope and flavour of OISE activities over the years.* Perhaps it is sufficient here to indicate briefly some of the major groupings of studies funded for 1971–2. The first group, or Group A, had subdivisions called

*See ONTARIO'S EDUCATIVE SOCIETY, volume V, chapter 14.

"Innovative Learning Programs," "Productive Thinking and Inquiry," and "Aims and Means of Education." The first of these three sub-groups included studies of individualization of instruction through computer-aided instructional techniques, studies of adult learning and means of assisting adult learners, the conduct of an infant day care and education demonstration centre involving studies of infant development, and studies of reading problems in inner city areas. The second sub-group involved attempts to stimulate thinking among learners over the whole range of schooling, a so-called moral education project, attempts to develop programs for teacher training, and others. The third sub-group included studies on the establishment of policy goals and the implementation of planning policies, the allocation of resources for education, the economics of education, and the development of organizations, as well as the creation of an econometric model of education.

Group B had sub-divisions entitled "Canadian Studies and Bilingualism," "OISE Participation in School Program Development," and "Development of School Programs and Curricula." Most of the studies under the first headings were related to the teaching of Canadian history and social studies and the development of bilingualism in students. Some were conducted in the Modern Language Center of the Curriculum Department. Specific studies in Group B had to do with the theory of second language teaching, speech role and linguistic variations, the development of Canadian French teaching materials, experiments in bilingual education among English-speaking pupils, a French-language schools project, a Canadian Public Issues Project, a study of innovations and alternatives in education, a study of innovative schools and regions, the development and design of a program for teaching music, and the publication of a *Math Letter* for high school students.

Examples of Group C studies involved the exceptional child and the school system, perceptual-motor handicap, the development of psychological services for county school boards, the evaluation of practices and programs for emotionally disturbed children, and studies in measurement theory and methodology. Group D studies included a communications program, the operation of an educational laboratory, an educational evaluation program, the development of a test item bank for the physical sciences, and the development of the so-called perception bag. Group E studies involved international education. Group F studies included those dealing with counselling procedures, the training of counsellors, concepts, and strategies in adult education, post-secondary art education in Ontario, the application of computer technology to education, the implications for education of the socialization process and student activism, educational systems and the labour market, and various studies in statistics, test construction, and experimental design.

After a perusal of these plans and activities, even the severest critic could hardly fail to conclude that the institute was responsible for a potentially large contribution to education. With the addition of a multitude of field development projects, the total was even more impressive. An important feature of the 1971–2 research and development program was that it included a much greater proportion of what at least appeared to be large-scale studies than had previously been the case. The fact that such studies had much the best chance of being funded under the tightened system of control that had developed was the primary explanation for the change.

No organization for educational research and development, no matter how tightly organized or efficiently operated, could escape certain difficulties. One of the most serious of these is the general lack of understanding, not only among the public, but on the part of most educators as well, of what may reasonably be expected from the application of scientific methods to educational problems. Even if the researcher meticulously avoids unnecessary jargon and reduces special terminology to a minimum, he cannot make inherently complex matters simple. What he has taken years to learn cannot be explained to the average teacher in a weekend seminar. The non-researcher often expects too much. He thinks that a few studies should be able in short order to clear up the uncertainties surrounding the major problems in education. When the results of what appear to be concentrated and sustained efforts produce a verdict of "no significant difference," he becomes impatient. When he is given conclusions hedged about with restrictions and qualifications, he blames the researcher for excessive timidity. Research is said to be capable of leading only to more research.

Some of the most severe critics are those who realize, quite correctly, that research can usually do little to help a person make the vital value judgments on which the role and purposes of education must rest. It is not enough that research evidence may provide some subsidiary assistance by demonstrating what is feasible. Nor are such critics satisfied to have some illumination of the best means to an end. Their usual complaint is that research is confined to trivialities, and is incapable of dealing with anything that really matters.

The researcher is often accused of failure to communicate his findings because he is either unwilling or unable to do so. Recent studies of the innovative process have shown that the steps by which a novel idea becomes a matter of established practice are much more complex than most people have imagined. An organization like OISE accepted development as one of its major functions, but that phase included only the engineering stage by which an idea was translated into a device, a technique, or a practice that could be installed in the system. There was a large and difficult problem of implementation still to be considered. A genuinely innovative system must have a large group of people to carry out this task or risk wasting its investment in research and development. Where research and development are supported in an independent institution, as in Ontario, it is imperative that very close links be established with the Department of

Education and with local school boards, which must necessarily assume responsibility for the installation phase. These agencies must not only disseminate information about new ideas, but must also make it feasible and attractive for teachers and administrators to adopt them. The framers of the reorganization of the Department of Education in early 1972 showed a considerable understanding of these facts, and the prospects for progress were hopeful.

Far too much confidence is placed in publication as a means of producing innovation. It is assumed that if the researcher would merely take the trouble to report his findings in clear and simple language, and see that the results got into teachers' hands, all kinds of changes would follow. In fact few teachers can be expected to read in search of ideas for implementation. They ordinarily need to be able to observe a demonstration before they can be induced to depart radically from existing practice. Many educators feel that it is practically impossible to introduce the concept of the open classroom on a large scale with the assurance that it will produce anything but chaos unless teachers are thoroughly prepared for it during the period of initial training, when they can be given an opportunity to observe numerous examples in successful operation.

It is quite possible to overestimate the receptivity of teachers and administrators to innovate ideas. Generally speaking, of course, they will readily welcome any suggestion that promises to facilitate their work or to make it more effective with no drastic change in approach. A change that requires extensive retraining or a disruption of familiar patterns of activity is likely to be looked upon in quite a different light. The would-be innovator who proposes it may be considered impractical or hare-brained and be treated with hostility.

A final problem confronting those engaged in educational research and development, and one that looms largest in relation to some of the activities with the greatest practical import, is that certain investigations require that school routines be more or less seriously disrupted. Even if it can be shown that the welfare of the children will not suffer any permanent ill-effects, there may be an unacceptable amount of inconvenience. Those responsible for the studies can help matters, of course, by demonstrating a maximum amount of consideration of school personnel. In some cases they can produce a sense of involvement by a full disclosure of information about their purposes and findings. This approach is no panacea, however, since teachers and principals may have much more difficulty than researchers in seeing value in some of the more abstract studies. In certain cases, the less practitioners know about the nature of an investigation, the less difficulty there may be in securing their co-operation. Whatever the degree of success in carrying out single projects, resistance must be expected to accumulate as the number of demands on the system increases. Even if every possible precaution is taken, the point of saturation may eventually be reached. Once a local system develops a resistance to research and development activities conducted from outside, it may be very difficult to re-establish a co-operative relationship.

Although the cause of research and development faced serious difficulties in 1972, there were certain grounds for hope. One of these was that the annual meetings of the Ontario Educational Research Council produced an abundance of papers falling within a very broad definition of research, and large numbers of educational practitioners assembled to hear and discuss them. The numerous conferences, meetings, and seminars held by OISE commonly attracted many interested participants. This degree of receptivity offered a good deal of promise for the future, provided that the effects of internal confusion and bad public relations could be overcome.

EIGHT

Religion and language

The history of the organized educational system in Ontario was characterized during the period covered by contention over minority religious and language rights. The main religious and linguistic minorities involved were to some extent overlapping, since an overwhelming percentage of Franco-Ontarians were Roman Catholic. On the other hand, many English-speaking Roman Catholic Ontarians had no desire to promote French-language rights and were at times actively hostile toward them. The fact that the two linguistic groups of Roman Catholics maintained separate teachers' federations and trustees' organizations was indicative of their differences in outlook and their desire to maintain distinctive identities.

Both the religious and the linguistic issues aroused heated emotions, and the debate over them was characterized by different versions of the facts, one-sided arguments, and prejudice. Opposing positions were difficult or impossible to reconcile because each was based on a different set of assumptions and values. As far as the linguistic issue was concerned, many of the differences had faded by the end of the 1960s and the basis for a reasonably satisfactory arrangement seemed to have been reached. The religious issue, on the other hand, remained very much alive, and it was evidently impossible to meet the demands of one side without leaving a residue of bitterness on the other.

THE DEVELOPMENT OF THE ROMAN CATHOLIC SEPARATE SCHOOL SYSTEM
The first common schools were established without particular attention to the religious persuasion of the teacher or the pupils. In the nature of the early settlement of the province, it was not unusual to find that most or all of the local community consisted of members of one particular faith, and there was no basis for difficulty. Legislation passed in 1841, when Upper and Lower Canada were united, was designed to give Protestants and Roman Catholics the right to establish separate denominational schools. The arrangement was appropriate for small communities with one-room schools. If the teacher was a Protestant or a Roman Catholic, the members of the opposite denomination, on the application of ten or more resident freeholders or householders, had the right to establish a school and

hire a teacher of their own persuasion. Since each group might feel as strongly as the other about the possibility of undesirable religious indoctrination, it is not surprising that many of the early separate schools were Protestant. No distinction was made among Protestant denominations, and although some might be as deeply divided from one another as they were from the Roman Catholics, they could not establish a publicly supported dissenting school except under the conditions mentioned. That is, there could be no fragmentation of the common schools among different Protestant groups.

Comparisons were often made between the dual systems of Quebec and Ontario, with praise for toleration going to the former. The situations were not, however, comparable, since Quebec did not have a non-denominational school system, but rather one for Roman Catholics and another for Protestants and non-Christians. Yet the difference was not as great in practice as in theory, since Ontario Protestants were commonly unwilling to let the common school system develop as a purely secular one. The usual position was to assert that the schools ought to make provision for religious exercises that would involve only fundamentals acceptable to every denomination and be offensive to no one. Since it was almost impossible to identify such fundamentals, the common or public elementary schools became characterized by a vague sort of Protestantism that pleased or displeased different groups in varying degrees. This situation gave the Roman Catholics a continuing and legitimate cause for complaint.

Of course there was no feasible arrangement for religious instruction in a common school system that could have satisfied the leaders of Roman Catholic opinion. They did not want "godless" or purely secular schools any more than they wanted a Protestant view of religion mixed up with the curriculum. Provision for clergymen of various denominations to instruct their own adherents on a voluntary basis at the beginning or end of the school day was not satisfactory either. If religion was to be truly effective it must suffuse the entire program every hour of the school day. The strongest proponents of the position even suggested that the Roman Catholic teacher could communicate a subtle religious message in teaching arithmetic. Religion was an attitude to be conveyed and an example to be set rather than a subject to be taught.

There was never any serious quarrel with the right of Roman Catholics, or any other group, to hold this view. The dispute was centred on the extent to which they should be allowed to divert their own tax funds, or receive the benefit of other public levies, for the support of schools exemplifying their own views, with a consequent withdrawal of support from the public school system. Opposition was based on the threat of fragmenting and destroying the public system, an outcome that was thought to be in danger of being realized if other dissenting groups were given privileges comparable to those of the Roman Catholics.

When Egerton Ryerson assumed his position as assistant superintendent of education in 1844, he found that provision for separate schools had already been made. He accepted the situation, while hoping that the schools would eventually disappear as a result of the growth of Christian tolerance. The opposite happened as the doctrinal basis for the schools was strengthened, particularly as a result of the influence of Pope Pius IX. Ryerson's own work in structuring the educational system and in establishing central control over it contributed to the same effect, since there was an increasing apprehension among Roman Catholics that such control might be used as an instrument for Protestant indoctrination.

During the pre-Confederation period the position of the separate schools was strengthened considerably. Although the number of petitioners for the establishment of a separate school was raised from ten to twelve, the obligation of the town authorities to act on the petition became binding. As of 1853, supporters of a separate school were exempted from taxation for common school purposes only if they contributed an amount equal to what they would have paid to support the common school had the separate school not existed, but this restriction was removed in 1855. However, the Roman Catholic bishops were defeated in an attempt to have all their adherents automatically treated as separate school supporters. The actual procedure by which a taxpayer became a separate school supporter was subject to a good deal of controversy at intervals during the remainder of the nineteenth century, but the principle of voluntary choice was preserved.

The strongest evidence of official determination to prevent undue expansion of separate schools was a provision that in rural areas supporters must reside within three miles in a direct line from the site of the school house. The formation of union school sections was subject to this restriction. Not until 1963 was the centre of the radial zone changed from the school site to a point designated by the separate school board. After that, a separate school zone could be established if the required number of petitioners could be found, without the necessity of building a school. It was necessary to establish and dissolve such units in order to link up zones to form larger units of administration. There was no comparable problem in incorporated towns and cities, which after 1863 were treated as units for separate school purposes.

The British North America Act was extremely important for the separate schools in that, in giving the legislature of each province the exclusive right to make laws in relation to education, it prohibited any law that would prejudicially affect any right or privilege with respect to denominational schools which any class of persons had by law in the province at the time of the union.[1] The effect of this provision was to ensure that separate schools could not be abolished or their status in any way reduced. Subsequent dispute was not so much over whether they should lose any right or privilege, but whether they should be allowed to extend their operations with public support along with the rest of the formal school system. Opponents took the legalistic view that the provisions of the BNA Act defined both minimum and maximum privileges, and that no further concessions were to be made. Supporters of extension claimed that it was unreasonable to suppose that the framers of the act intended to freeze the development of separate schools in the face of the changing needs of society. The most controversial issue had to do with secondary schools. Although the grammar schools were in transition by 1867, there was no real system of publicly supported secondary schools representing a stage between elementary schools and university until after Confederation. When such a system was established, there was no provision for institutions maintained by special groups to receive public support.

During the period after Confederation, the separate schools did in fact make some substantial advances. The privilege of support was extended to those who lived outside the municipality in which the school was situated, but within three miles of the school, and to those who owned unoccupied land within the separate school zone, regardless of their place of residence. Provision was made for the establishment of Roman Catholic model schools which trained teachers for the Third Class Certificate. Although Ryerson had made sure that separate schools would not escape from provincial inspection, the practice of appointing Roman Catholic inspectors for schools of their denomination was begun in 1882.

One of the most significant developments was an arrangement made in 1899 by which a separate school might be formed in an area not organized into townships, even though there was no public school. Thus the separate school lost its exclusive status as an institution established by dissenters from the public system, and an essential step was taken to make the separate schools into a genuine system.

Formal approval was given in 1889 for elementary schools, both public and separate, to add fifth classes, which meant in more modern terminology grades 9 and 10, with public support. These were always regarded as elementary grades, even when they followed the same curriculum as grades 9 and 10 in high schools, and government grants were paid accordingly, that is, at a much lower rate. Legislation in 1908 made important distinctions between the fifth classes and continuation schools. For a time it seemed possible that separate schools might be permitted to add the remaining high school grades with public support, but this privilege was limited to continuation schools operated by continuation school boards, which were set up on a non-denominational basis similar to that of high school boards.

The Tiny case, which extended over a period of several years in the 1920s, marked a watershed in the claims of the supporters of Roman Catholic separate schools for a right under existing constitutional provisions to public support for secondary schools. The separate school board of Tiny Township submitted a petition of right claiming for itself and other such boards the right to conduct their own secondary schools with exemption from municipal taxation for the support of secondary schools other than their own and with government grants awarded under the same conditions as those existing at the time of Confederation. The British Privy Council finally settled the matter by ruling against the board. From that time on, although various spokesmen continued to talk about the denial of constitutional rights, the campaign for the achievement of the same objectives aimed primarily at the passage of new legislation, which was to be justified by equity and fairness.

The main issue during the 1930s was financial. At the time the separate schools were first established, the economy was simple, and financial support was largely obtained by rates levied on individual property. As time went on an increasing amount of wealth was held in the form of corporate shares. It was theoretically to be expected that a corporation would distribute its taxes to local public and separate school boards in direct proportion to the value of the shares held by the supporters of each board. In a large corporation, however, it is impossible to carry out this procedure, since shares are changing hands all the time. Mitchell Hepburn brought in legislation in 1936 to solve the problem, but it was so unsatisfactory and opposition was so strong that it was repealed the next year. At the end of the decade a major legal contest occurred when the Windsor Board of Education brought successful action against the Ford Motor Company, claiming the full amount of the company's school taxes, on the grounds that the proportion of separate school supporters among its shareholders could not be exactly determined, and that there was thus no legal basis for awarding any given amount to the Windsor Separate School Board. The passions aroused at the time had a good deal to do with the formation of the Public School Trustees' Association of Ontario, which devoted itself to resisting further concessions to the separate school system.

SEPARATE SCHOOL ISSUES
AFTER THE SECOND WORLD WAR

The majority of the Royal Commission on Education, reporting in 1950, took a distinctly unfriendly attitude toward the separate schools. The commission's scheme for reducing the elementary school program to six years and the secondary school program to four years involved cutting back the sphere of operations of the separate school boards. It is doubtful that such a change could have been made in accordance with the terms of the BNA Act, even though the commissioners seemed to think it could. The import of a fairly detailed set of recommendations was that the additional rights and privileges granted to the separate schools after Confederation should be cut back. A position was taken against the formation of central schools to accommodate the former individual separate schools. In rural areas at least there was to be little room for anything but one-room schools. As might have been expected, several members of the commission supported a minority report which protested against these and other recommendations. The result of the controversy was that the issue, an emotionally charged political one, overshadowed other aspects of the report and helped to prevent the adoption of many of its basic proposals.

The lack of taxable resources continued for some time to be a very serious handicap for the separate schools. They suffered increasingly from their inability to pay adequate salaries to their teachers as the members of religious orders, who customarily served for very low remuneration, declined as a proportion of the teaching force. The solution to the problem was eventually found in the operation of the provincial grant system. The introduction of the Ontario Foundation Tax Plan, which took effect in 1964, brought the separate school boards up to a level that was within reasonable reach of that of the public school boards, although some difference still remained. The action of the Robarts government did not have universal approval, but won support on the grounds that the tens of thousands of separate school pupils should not be deprived of educational advantages because of their parents' desire to exercise a constitutional right. As a result of the improved financial position of the system and the growing proportion of Roman Catholics in the population, separate school enrolment grew much more quickly than public school enrolment after the Second World War.

While the financial issue continued to be a matter of major concern until the Ontario Foundation Tax Plan came into operation, there was increasing interest among separate school supporters in the possibility of enlarging the scope of the system. A leading part was played in this movement by the English Catholic Education Association which in 1970 had as member organizations the Ontario Separate School Trustees' Association, the Association of Catholic High School Boards of Ontario, the Federation of Catholic Parent-Teacher Associations of Ontario, and the Ontario English Catholic Teachers' Association, and as associate members the Ontario Catholic Superintendents' and Inspectors' Association, the Ontario Diocesan Directors of Religious Education, the Ontario Catholic Students' Federation, and the Ontario Separate School Business Officials' Association.

The issue received a great deal of attention in 1962 when the Roman Catholic bishops of Ontario sent a brief to the prime minister of the province and to members of the Legislature appealing for a number of privileges: a share in curriculum planning, the development of separate colleges for the training of Roman Catholic school teachers, the extension of support for separate schools through the secondary school level, and a revision of the system of financial support for the separate schools. These were not expressed as demands to be met immediately but, particularly in the case of separate teacher training, as objectives that might be gradually attained over a period of time. Prime Minister Robarts responded favourably to the last item, as already indicated, in the Ontario Foundation Tax Plan, but he took a resolute stand against the others. He said he did not intend to reverse policies that had been followed by governments under all parties during the previous hundred years – policies which at that time had the support of the Liberal and New Democratic parties. His reason was that the cost of duplicating facilities in secondary schools, both academic and vocational, and in colleges and universities, would be unbearable. He told the Legislature: "From an educational point of view as well it could only lead to a lesser degree of excellence of instruction as a result of poor facilities, smaller concentration of students and, thus, less diversification of courses and the necessity of spreading our teachers over a wider and wider area."[2]

The essence of the position taken by the proponents of the addition of the remaining high school grades to the separate schools was that the system, as it existed with constitutional guarantees and by long tradition, was incomplete. They maintained that it was undesirable for students to have to shift to the secular high school system mid-way through their high school careers. While theories of continuous progress might suggest that a particular student should be working at the grade 8 level in one subject area but at the grade 11 level in another, such an arrangement seemed to be administratively difficult for a student who transferred. The report of the Hall-Dennis Committee, with its advocacy of unbroken development from kindergarten through grade 13, was cited in support of two complete systems. In actual fact, however, some of the committee members had no intention of providing that kind of ammunition. They felt that the flexible system they were advocating would make it easier for a child to transfer in at various points.

The proponents of the scheme were not interested in extending the privilege of public support for high schools to any other religious or secular group. They thought it was enough to complete the second publicly supported system which already existed on the strength of historical tradition. They felt that even those who believed that the original steps to establish separate schools were a mistake would see logic in this position. They placed great stress on the idea that the separate schools were public schools of a special type. It did not seem incompatible with this concept that Protestant teachers recruited to help staff the separate schools in some areas during a period of shortage could be fired as soon as Roman Catholic teachers were available for no better reason than "after all, we must look after our own first."

It was claimed that separate school boards would show no great desire to develop their own secondary schools in communities where it would be clearly impossible to maintain a second school on an adequate scale of operations. Past restraint was cited as support for this claim. There was also said to be no reluctance to share facilities and equipment with secular high schools. Opponents were suspicious of the assurances of restraint, pointing out that what separate school supporters had done when they lacked funds was not necessarily a good indication of what they might do when that handicap was overcome. This view received some support in

Toronto in the fall of 1971, when the rapid extension of separate schools in some areas left the public school system with fewer pupils than it had planned for, and thus with more facilities and staff than were required to meet minimum needs.

A development that added particular urgency to the cause was that the private Roman Catholic high schools, which had to operate entirely on fees and voluntary contributions, were finding it more and more difficult to survive in the face of rising education costs. They had been conspicuously unable to offer the variety of programs available in the public system after the Reorganized Program was introduced. It appeared by the early 1970s that, under existing methods of finance, most of them would soon have to close. Thus there would be no way for parents who placed a high value on a Catholic religious atmosphere to give their children the kind of education they wanted beyond grade 10. A large proportion of the private schools were apparently prepared to turn over their assets to an extended separate school system. Another development that encouraged haste was the demonstrated willingness of many of the French-speaking Roman Catholic private secondary schools to move into the public system once their linguistic rights were guaranteed. There might soon be none left to form part of a separate school system.

Some of the supporting arguments were expressed after a joint study project was carried out under the sponsorship of the Ecumenical Institute of Canada in co-operation with the Archbishops' Commission.[3] The plans for the study were drawn up in 1968 and a statement was issued in 1969. The point was made in this statement that the existence of a separate school system as a right guaranteed by the BNA Act was not a current issue. The main argument offered in favour of adding grades 11, 12, and 13 to the separate schools was that of the advantages of continuity already mentioned. There was said to be no dispute that the proposed action would increase the total amount of public money spent on education. This would not, however, be because the province's educational operations would become more expensive, but because parents would be relieved of the extra costs of sending their children to private high schools in addition to having to pay taxes to support the public system. Three "possible" answers were given to the objection that it would be difficult to allow public financing of a complete separate school system without stimulating requests for similar privileges for private schools. 1 / Roman Catholics alone were recognized by the Constitution as having the special rights in question; 2 / they proposed to bring with them the dowry of many of their buildings; and 3 / it was doubtful if non-Roman Catholic private schools would wish to surrender their sovereignty and become part of the public educational system. Fragmentation of education was to be avoided, if necessary by departmental regulation.

Opponents of the proposed development felt that the fragmentation issue was not to be dealt with so easily. They could not see why other groups could be resisted when, on the basis of fairness and equity, they had just as good a claim to public support for their own schools as had the Roman Catholics. The Catholics seemed to be arguing from the premise that to him who hath, more ought to be given, and that he who hath nothing is entitled to nothing. However, if equal opportunities were extended to all groups, fragmentation would be unavoidable, and it would be impossible to maintain any system on a high qualitative level.

A second opposition argument was that separate schools operated as a divisive influence in society. A student who attended one of them could not help but feel that he was different, and probably in some vital respect superior. Restricting his contacts to other members of a homogeneous group during a major part of his working hours might breed narrowness and prejudice. Further, there seemed little evidence to show that education in a separate school achieved its intended purpose of making the individual more truly religious than he would otherwise be.

A booklet entitled *Public Funds for Separate Schools?* prepared by the Inter-Church Committee on Protestant-Roman Catholic Relations, which included representatives of the Anglican Church of Canada, the Baptist Federation of Canada, the Churches of Christ (Disciples in Canada), the Presbyterian Church of Canada, the Salvation Army of Canada, and the United Church of Canada, suggested that all Christians should work together so that religious education could become an integral part of the school curriculum.[4] Others found it more reasonable to try to make the publicly supported system acceptable to all by excluding religion except perhaps as a voluntary subject of study.

The legislation establishing separate schools never imposed an obligation on anyone to support them. The fact that a large proportion of Roman Catholic parents always chose, even where a separate school was readily accessible, to send their children to the public school was often cited as evidence that they were apprehensive of the divisive effects of a segregated education. It is actually impossible to tell how many held this conviction and how many simply felt that a better quality of education was available in the public school. Not to be ignored were numbers of Roman Catholics who took an open stand against separate schools.

The separate school cause gained important new strength from platforms adopted by the Liberal and New Democratic parties in 1969. Both parties accepted the view that the welfare of pupils in the separate schools demanded an unbroken educational experience to the end of grade 13. The Liberals claimed to have been strongly influenced by the Hall-Dennis report and by a brief by the Ontario Separate School Trustees' Association entitled *Equal Opportunity for Continuous Education in the Separate Schools of Ontario*.[5] The New Democratic party sympathized with the desire of Roman Catholics to have the form of education they wanted, and to have adequate financial support to maintain it. Both parties stressed the necessity of keeping costs down by having publicly supported separate high schools share facilities with the public system. Both declined to recognize that other religious groups had any claim to privileges they thought reasonable to extend to Roman Catholics. They offered no support for private schools, Roman Catholic or otherwise. Roman Catholic high schools would be assisted only if they chose to come under the jurisdiction of the separate school boards.

The Conservative government continued to adhere to its traditional stand that the proposed change would be too expensive and that it would lead to deterioration in the quality of education. At a time of rapidly rising concern over the costs of education, the first point had considerable appeal. During the Conservative leadership campaign early in 1971, the candidates were pressed for a promise of concessions, but declined to depart from past policies, and tried to play down the issue as much as possible. During the election campaign in the fall of the same year, Davis again refused to yield. Robert Nixon declared that the Liberals would not let the issue become a divisive one, and candidates for his party and for the New Democrats suggested from time to time that there were much more important matters at stake.

The Conservative sweep in the election suggested one of two things: either that, despite some noisy demonstrations in favour of an extended separate school system that Davis encountered in the campaign, the issue was not of deep concern to any large number of people or that those voters who turned away from the Conservatives because of their stand were more than counterbalanced by newly-won supporters, the strength of whose sentiments were made clearer in the ballot box than they were in public debate. In any case, the election results seemed likely to confirm the status quo for several years at least.

THE BACKGROUND OF THE FRENCH-LANGUAGE ISSUE
The issue of language developed less obtrusively than that of religion. For a time during the nineteenth century there was no pronounced resistance to the use of a language other than English in schools in settlements of non-English-speaking people. In the 1850s the Council of Public Instruction made a knowledge of French or German an acceptable substitute for English as a qualification for teaching. The situation later became more difficult for those who wanted one or other of these languages used as a medium of instruction. There is no reason for concluding, however, that the authorities had consciously hostile designs on French culture, or intended to try to stamp out the use of French. Attempts at various stages to restrict the language were usually attributable to one or more of three reasons: 1 / parents of English-speaking pupils in some communities complained that there was no alternative to purely French instruction in the local school; 2 / there were fears that the exclusive use of French would deprive the children of an opportunity to make their way economically in a province where most communication was in English; and 3 / the

qualifications of teachers and the quality of instruction in some of the schools were demonstrably bad.

In 1885 the Minister of Education, G.W. Ross, ordered that English be taught in every school in the province. This seemingly reasonable requirement was followed at the end of the decade by a regulation that instruction and communication were to be in English unless the children were unable to understand it. At the same time, trustees in sections where French or German prevailed might require, with the approval of the inspector, that instruction be given in reading, grammar, and composition in either of these languages if the parents so requested. Inspectors were supposed to ensure that standards in the schools where this extra work was taught were as high as in those where it was not. Model schools might be established for the preparation of French and German teachers.

The beginning of the second decade of the twentieth century was a period of high tension between the English- and French-speaking populations of Ontario. The influx of French-Canadians from Quebec had been substantial, and their increasing numbers, along with their well-deserved reputation for fecundity, raised the spectre of eventual French linguistic and cultural dominance in the minds of some alarmists among the descendants of the original settlers. There was also considerable antagonism between French and Irish Catholics who were struggling for control of their church in certain parts of Ontario. The Orange order had considerable political power, which it used to combat the extension of French-Canadian influence. Prejudice was expressed in speech and print in a manner that would have been considered outrageous in later years. What subsequently happened in the educational system was a result of a mingling of influences, some but not all of which were worthy of condemnation.

Taking account of protests by English-speaking citizens in some parts of eastern Ontario that French instruction prevailed in local schools and because standards in many of these schools were known to be very low, F.W. Merchant studied the situation and made a series of recommendations which formed the basis for Regulation 17, issued in 1912. According to this regulation, the use of French for instruction and communication was restricted to form 1, although it might be carried beyond that level with the approval of the chief inspector if the pupils did not understand English. French could also be taught as a subject of study beyond form 1 in schools where it had previously been offered, but for no more than one hour a day unless the chief inspector agreed. The issuance of Regulation 17 marked a high point in bitterness among Franco-Ontarians and a low point in sympathy and understanding on the part of the education authorities.

A revised and somewhat more moderate form of the regulation was issued in 1913, providing for more adequate inspection of the bilingual schools. Franco-Ontarians were not mollified, however, and the Ottawa Separate School Board took legal action to have the measure retracted.

While a decision was awaited, the Ottawa separate schools were closed for several months in 1914. The Supreme Court of Ontario eventually ruled that Regulation 17 was legal; the British North America Act protected rights based on religion but not those based on language. In fact it was not until the 1960s that the use of French in Ontario schools was guaranteed by legislation.

During the period that followed the Ottawa case, the regulation was not rigidly enforced. However, performance and retention rates in the bilingual schools remained at an unsatisfactory level. A committee chaired by Merchant made a further study and reported in 1927 that almost half the pupils were concentrated in form 1 and only one in ten reached grade 8. Only 13.5 per cent of the teachers held First Class or Second Class Certificates while all the others had lesser qualifications or none at all. A new policy adopted that year involved the abandonment of the attempt to limit French as the language of instruction to the first form, or to dictate when it could be studied as a subject. The University of Ottawa Normal School was established as a means of improving teachers' qualifications and the model schools were gradually phased out. An effort was made to improve instruction by providing for a committee consisting of the Chief Inspector, the Director of French Instruction, and the Director of English Instruction.

The new policy produced encouraging results. By 1935 the percentage of teachers with First and Second Class Certificates rose to 60, and pupil retention rates increased substantially. Those completing the high school entrance program in form 4 were not, however, faring very well on the entrance examination, as might have been expected in view of their relatively limited use of English. What was obviously needed, given the assumption that French culture and the use of the French language in Ontario should be encouraged, was a continuous program carrying through both levels rather than a sharp break at the end of the elementary school.

DEVELOPMENTS IN THE IMMEDIATE POST-WAR PERIOD

The report of the Royal Commission on Education conferred a cautious blessing on the existing situation by recommending that, under specified conditions and with the approval of the minister of education, a local education authority might provide for French as a subject of study and a language of instruction in public or separate schools under its jurisdiction. French was to be used in this way in addition to English, in which the pupils were to attain reasonable proficiency at each level. The use of French was not to be allowed to excuse an inferior standard of achievement. In view of the commission's proposal to cut back the elementary school to the first six grades, the implication for French was that its use would also be curtailed. There was no suggestion that it be used for instructional purposes in secondary school. While the commissioners approved of special courses in French for those who used it as a first language and were proficient in it, they did not favour a special curriculum for French-speaking students. The majority recommended the abolition of the University of Ottawa Normal School on the grounds that it was undesirable to segregate students on the basis of language, and proposed that other normal schools maintain suitable programs for French-speaking trainees. The minority opposed this recommendation, which was not implemented.

Until the 1960s those graduates of the bilingual schools who wished to continue their education in the publicly supported system were dumped into the secondary schools to get along as best they could despite their handicap. Since special programs in French, which came to be identified as "Français," were not always available, many of such students had to participate in classes of beginners and waste their time going through the fundamentals of the language. Those who wanted an education in their own language were forced either to attend private schools or leave the province.

A significant advance was made in 1962 when schools were permitted, with the approval of the minister, to have Latin taught through the medium of French. This privilege was extended to history and geography in 1965. A special course in English, labeled "Anglais," was developed to meet the needs of secondary school students who had come from bilingual schools. During these years efforts were concentrated on the production of suitable textbooks for the new courses.

PROGRESS MADE IN THE LATE 1960s
The great achievements of the latter part of the 1960s were 1 / the provision of a complete secondary school program in the French language, either in special schools constructed or set aside for the purpose or in special classes where there were too few students to justify a complete school, and 2 / the enactment for the first time of legislation giving bilingual and French schools at both the elementary and secondary levels a legal basis for existence. These developments reflected a growing trend toward separatism in Quebec, and a desire on the part of the government of Ontario to help make French Canadians feel more at home in that province. Developments in Ontario paralleled rising expressions of concern on the part of the federal government. They came at the same time as, or before, certain recommendations were made by the federal Royal Commission on Bilingualism and Biculturalism. They are best considered as a response to the same conditions that inspired the work of that body rather than as a direct result of its recommendations. The Ontario measures were essentially in harmony with the commission's proposals, although the guarantees provided were not as watertight as those advocated by the commission.

The commission, in the first volume of its report, urged that a formal procedure be established in all provinces whereby either a French- or an English-speaking minority could ensure reasonable provision of schooling in its own language.[6] School boards must not be in a position to reject the minority's request. The nature and extent of the provisions would depend on the number of potential pupils. In some cases it might be possible to have minority-language schools at both the elementary and secondary levels, and in others at only one. Where the maintenance of schools was not feasible, special classes might be set up. Boarding schools and television instruction might help to overcome the problem of small and scattered numbers.

In 1967, a few months after the appearance of the commission's report, Prime Minister Robarts announced the new Ontario policy. French-language secondary schools would be provided within the publicly supported school system. This policy ruled out the possibility of having a special system of French-language schools. The program in the new schools would include English in the hope that students would be able to hold their own in the Ontario labour market. Later in the year the minister of education appointed a committee, headed by R. Bériault, to help round out various aspects of the program. Davis was particularly concerned about the welfare of French-speaking students who were dispersed among English-language schools. The committee drew up legislation defining procedures for establishing bilingual and French-language schools at both levels.

Bill 140, an amendment to *The Schools Administration Act* passed in 1968, made the establishment of French-language classes mandatory on the request of ten or more French-speaking ratepayers where there were at least thirty French-speaking pupils in the primary, junior, or intermediate division. Where the number was adequate, a French-language school must be maintained. Bill 141 amended the same act to define the conditions under which French-language secondary schools and courses must be provided. Again depending on the number of students, there were three possible courses of action: the teaching of certain subjects in French, the creation of a French-language department within a secondary school, and the establishment of a French-language composite school. The third was considered to be the most satisfactory arrangement, especially where it was possible to offer a full range of options. The legislation gave to English-speaking minorities in predominantly French-speaking areas much the same guarantees of instruction in their own language. On the request of a parent or guardian, an English-speaking student might be admitted to a French-language class or school as long as the principal felt that his presence would not be detrimental to the work of the rest of the class.

The legislation establishing divisional boards of education provided for the formation of a French-language committee by a board of education on receipt of a written request by at least ten French-speaking taxpayers that school instruction be provided in French. Such a committee was to consist of seven members, three appointed by the board and four elected by the French-speaking taxpayers of the area. Its main function was to recommend measures to meet the educational and cultural needs of French-speaking students.

In 1968 the new policy led to the transfer of responsibility for a number of private French-language secondary schools to the jurisdiction of the local high school board or board of education. There were seven of these in Ottawa alone. By 1968–9 the number of such schools in the province under private control had been reduced from approximately twenty to four. As previously noted, this development was a blow to those who were campaigning vigorously for the extension of the separate school system to the end of grade 13. There were some who foresaw the wholesale transfer of French-speaking pupils at both levels to the public school system. Attention was called to certain historic conflicts between the two linguistic groups within the Roman Catholic separate school system. Another factor was that even those Franco-Ontarians who had a firm belief in the values of a Roman Catholic oriented education had less apprehension about the public system than their English-speaking co-religionists, since language and religion would reinforce one another in schools and classes that were both French and Catholic. English-speaking Catholics, with less to distinguish them from most Protestants, had to struggle harder to maintain what differences there were.

The legislation was passed with the general approbation of the public and the media. However there was a certain amount of opposition to the establishment of French-language schools, as opposed to special classes, on the grounds that the students, who were going to have to get along with one another as adults in a single society, ought to have opportunities to mingle in recreational and other extra-curricular activities. The position was somewhat similar to that taken by opponents of schools segregated on the basis of religion. On the other hand, it was pointed out that the English culture tended to be dominant, reflecting the situation in the province generally, unless a substantial majority of the students were French-speaking. Thus segregation seemed to some people to be a necessity if French culture were to survive as a living reality. The idea of having two school organizations under one roof was one that had little appeal for administrators.

The report of the Comité franco-ontarien d'enquête culturelle, released in January 1969, indicated varying degrees of weakness in the cultural life of Franco-Ontarian communities in different parts of the province, and recommended means of improving the situation.[7] A good deal of stress was placed on education as an ameliorative force. Within its terms of reference, the committee's proposals were undoubtedly imaginative and sound. Yet a basic dilemma was not resolved. If Franco-Ontarian culture were to be brought up to and maintained in a position of such strength that a person's cultural needs could be met within it and he could make a creative contribution to it, could he at the same time deal effectively with the predominant English-language culture? To do so would place a very great strain on him. If he could not reach a reasonable level of competence in English, his employment prospects might be seriously limited and his mobility severely curtailed. He might well find that migration to Quebec was the best course of action open to him.

By 1971 there was considerable dissatisfaction developing in certain parts of the province over the implementation of the legislation of 1968. The problem centred around the reluctance of certain school boards to establish French-language secondary schools, as opposed to special classes or programs for Franco-Ontarian students. The legislation appeared to the critics to leave too much to local discretion. Further, such organizations as the Association canadienne-française de l'Ontario were calling for an adaptation of the structure of the Department of Education to ensure that more attention was given to their language group. There was a feeling that French-language education ought to be the particular concern of an associate deputy minister, with other appropriate officials at various levels answering to him.

FRENCH INSTRUCTION FOR ENGLISH-LANGUAGE STUDENTS

A complementary facet of the attempt to accommodate Franco-Ontarians by providing opportunities for education in their own language was the extension of French as a subject of study among the rest of the school population. There is no question that this movement was fundamentally a gesture of good will toward French Canada. There were two major aspects to the program in the school system: renewed efforts were made to stress the oral aspects of the language in the secondary school course and instruction was extended down into the elementary school grades.

The secondary school course was formerly criticized for being too bookish and pedantic. There was said to be too much stress on memorizing vocabulary lists, on teaching fine points of grammar, and on artificial translation exercises. Students actually regarded French in practically the same category as one of the dead languages. The Department of Education did not encourage this kind of treatment, but in fact actively promoted the training of the ear and the development of oral skills. In the course of study for 1936, for example, teachers introducing the subject in grade 9 were urged to dispense with the textbook for the first six weeks while the students concentrated on learning the sounds of the language. French was to be used to the fullest possible extent as the medium of instruction. Naturally obedience to this last exhortation depended on the degree of oral competence attained by the teacher. It was uncommon to find a native speaker of English educated in the Ontario system who had anything approaching an authentic French accent.

The Department of Education in fact spoke to the school system with two contradictory voices. The stronger of these said that students who were aware of their own best interests would keep in mind that their ultimate hurdle was the departmental grade 13 examination, which would test their ability to read and write French. When a so-called oral feature was introduced, it called for a written response to a voice on a record, and thus gave no opportunity for active oral expression. Further, it counted for only a small proportion of the marks awarded on the whole examination. Students were seldom willing to accept the theory that time and effort spent on the oral aspects of the language would reinforce their competence in the skills that really counted for examination purposes. As the critical time approached, teachers demonstrated much the same attitude.

Statements of objectives for the teaching of French typically stressed cultural values. The student was supposed to acquire an understanding of the outlook, attitudes, and feelings of French-speaking people, to see the world as they saw it, to appreciate their sense of humour, and to share their perception of reality. Logic would have dictated that French Canada be the main centre of interest if this set of objectives were considered important. To judge by most of the textbooks in use in the schools, however, the study of French seemed to be intended mainly to illuminate life in France. Not a few students got the impression that all the French spoken in Quebec was an inferior brand and not worthy of attention.

While public concern for the continued existence of Canada and a growing conviction that the country could survive only as a bilingual entity provided the essential support for the addition of French to the elementary school curriculum, educators were also taking increasing cognizance of the fact that oral competence became difficult to achieve if study was begun too late. As a result of his observation of the physiology and functioning of the human brain, Wilder Penfield suggested that a child be introduced to the language not later than age eight to eleven.

A few educational leaders opposed the addition of French to the elementary school curriculum on the grounds that the time taken for it would reduce the effectiveness of the rest of the program. Reference was made to the lack of evidence that an earlier beginning actually resulted in a higher level of achievement by the end of secondary school. Certain administrators were not keen on facing the problem of recruiting enough well qualified teachers, particularly where there were few native speakers of French in the local community. However for the most part the extension of French-language instruction in the elementary schools was accepted with reasonable enthusiasm, and most of these objections were overcome.

Instruction in French was begun in schools under the control of the Ottawa Public School Board in 1930, and by 1940 was given in grades 5 to 8. In most of the province, however, school boards did not begin to follow suit until the early 1960s. The Department of Education appointed a director of French instruction in 1964 to co-ordinate the program. By 1965 nearly 167,000 elementary school pupils were studying the language in schools operated by 231 public and separate school boards. The usual procedure was to begin with grade 8 or grades 7 and 8 and work down through the grades in later years. Each extension called for curricular adjustments at the higher levels to accommodate pupils with better prior preparation. Some school systems used teachers with special qualifications on an itinerant basis while others relied on regular classroom teachers. The Department of Education introduced immersion courses into its summer school program.

The department, rather than pressing boards to introduce the subject, approved the program only when evidence was presented that enough teachers were available with a high level of oral competence. Only under special circumstances might a course be offered below the grade 7 level if fewer than four classes a week were provided. Restrictions were relaxed after the beginning of the 1968–9 school year. At that time the system had a long way to go to meet the recommendation of the Royal Commission on Bilingualism and Biculturalism that all English-speaking pupils should begin French lessons in grade 1. Some of those who approved the program in general thought that grade 2 was early enough, and that grade 1 pupils faced sufficient challenge in acquiring the other skills that were called for under existing conditions.

While the necessary gesture was being made to French Canada, the school program did not appear to be succeeding in making Ontario English-speaking pupils bilingual, or even in giving them a solid basis for becoming bilingual. In most areas the practical motive for achieving this objective was absent. It was impossible to use the argument, however persuasive it might be in Scandinavia or the Netherlands, that a good working knowledge of a second language, or even a third or fourth, was necessary for one's future economic welfare. This being the case, the only hope for success would lie in a much greater effort in the schools than had been seriously proposed. Necessary steps would involve the exclusive employment of teachers who were either native speakers of French or approached them in pronunciation and fluency, the expenditure of enough class time to ensure that each child got regular, frequent, and intensive practice, and the occasional use of French as a medium of instruction for other subjects. Every effort would also have to be made to place English-speaking children in a French environment for a significant amount of time, perhaps during vacation periods, either inside or outside the province. If the public was unwilling to support a program of these dimensions, educators had an obligation to point out that the half loaf it was getting might be little better than nothing. Study of a second language does not begin to pay dividends until one reaches a fairly high level of competence.

OTHER RELIGIOUS AND LINGUISTIC MINORITIES
Ontario society was always tolerant, in a laissez-faire sort of way, of smaller and less powerful religious and linguistic minorities than those already dealt with. These minorities were quite at liberty to provide special schools for their children, as long as such schools met certain provincial standards, and to offer out-of-school classes for any interested age group. They were, however, obliged to raise all the required funds without public assistance, while at the same time retaining the obligation to pay taxes to support the public schools. The theoretical government position that all taxpayers had to support a single public system, which they might use or not as they pleased, but had to pay the full cost of any alternative they chose to support, was made into somewhat of a mockery by the publicly supported Roman Catholic separate school system.

One major group that insisted on the maintenance of its own educational facilities was the Ontario Alliance of Christian Schools. This fundamentalist group of Protestants maintained that the public school system had abandoned God and defied divine revelation by encouraging children to think that they could discover truth through the exercise of their own individual powers. Like the Roman Catholics, members of this group believed that true education could take place only in an environment suffused by acceptable religious beliefs. In a brief to Prime Minister Robarts in 1968, the Alliance based an appeal for public support on two main arguments: that parents should have the freedom to choose the kind of schools they wanted without suffering financially and that it was unhealthy for the state to have a monopoly on education.[8] These appeals did not, as has already been pointed out, result in any change in government policy.

The Jews constituted another example of an important cultural group attempting to maintain its identity in part by education. In 1968 there were reported to be over three thousand children attending Jewish day schools, which were privately maintained.[9] Many others who attended public schools received instruction in special classes held outside of regular school hours, an arrangement that was regarded as a rather ineffective method of ensuring the survival of the desired traditions. The day schools met all the demands of the provincial curriculum, which they supplemented by Jewish learning. The Jewish community made repeated appeals for modest financial support from the provincial government, but got essentially the same answer as did the Ontario Alliance of Christian Schools.

There were a great many groups and communities of immigrants, mostly in the larger cities, who made some attempt to keep alive the languages and cultures of their countries of origin through educational activities. Most of the classes set up for this purpose were sponsored by "ethnic" associations of one kind or another. For most of the groups involved, it did not appear likely that they would maintain a very strong offshoot of the homeland culture for more than a generation or two, since the children tended to assimilate rather rapidly into the English-speaking community. The provincial government made a move in 1971 to assist languages other than English and French to survive when the minister of education, Robert Welch, announced that the range of foreign languages that could be studied in school would be extended to meet the wishes of parents and students.

NINE

The burden of support

No one has any clear idea of the full cost of education, as the term is defined in this volume and in ONTARIO'S EDUCATIVE SOCIETY. The best that can be done is to ignore the informal and indirect educational processes and try to secure estimates applying to the formal system. Even in dealing with this area, it is customary to take into account only those expenditures required to provide and operate facilities and to offer instruction, and to exclude private costs such as those of maintaining students while they attend educational institutions and the amount of earnings foregone if they are of employable age.

It is not beyond dispute that the value of services withheld by students who might otherwise be productively employed ought to be considered a real educational cost. This assumption is not justifiable if education increases productivity enough to compensate for the reduced number of working years at the end of the process. There is certainly no dispute that many highly educated individuals have a greater lifetime income than those who lack the same preparation. Income can, of course, be equated to productivity only in a very general fashion.

A SUMMARY OF SOME ASPECTS OF POST-WAR COSTS
Whatever the limitations of the approach, there is a good deal to be gained by considering some of the gross figures emerging from the cost estimates relating to the provision of instruction and the maintenance of facilities. It is not the intention here to review these in detail and thus repeat material presented in ONTARIO'S EDUCATIVE SOCIETY, particularly in volume I, chapter 7. In the identification of general trends, rough approximations are used rather than the exact figures.

During the first year after the Second World War there were approximately 665,000 children in the publicly supported school system at the elementary and secondary levels. As a starting point, it will be useful to examine the cost of maintaining this establishment, not only in absolute terms, but also in terms of each pupil and each member of the population. The extent of the burden becomes meaningful, of course, only when considered in the light of the economic resources available at the time.

During 1945 school boards spent approximately $62.1 million, of which they received about $26.6 million, or 42.9 per cent, in the form of grants from the provincial government and obtained the remaining $35.5 million from local sources. While only $34.5 million, or about 97 per cent of local revenues came from taxation, the entire amount may be counted as a burden on the Ontario citizen. According to a common approach, the average expenditure per pupil, ignoring distinctions between the elementary and secondary school levels, is obtained by dividing the total $62.1 million figure by 665,000, which produces something over $93 as the average cost per pupil. In a search for the real cost, it is desirable to add expenditures by the Department of Education other than those for school grants. These included the cost of maintaining the department, running the examination system, operating teacher training institutions, and making small grants to universities, along with other miscellaneous items. Since the total provincial budget for education for the fiscal year beginning on April 1, 1945 was $34.2 million, the excess of this amount over $26.6 million, or $7.6 million, may be added to the $62.1 million already referred to, raising the total to $69.7 million. With the population of Ontario estimated at an even 4 million, it cost the average individual less than $17.50 to maintain the formal educational system. Of this amount, about $8.60 represented the amount raised by local taxation.

The cost of education may be viewed in relation to that of other financial transactions of local and provincial governments at the time. The part of municipal expenditure raised by all forms of municipal taxation,* including school taxes, was a little more than $108 million, or an average of about $27 per person. The total of net ordinary and capital provincial expenditure was $124.8 million, or slightly over $31 per person. The amount raised for specifically educational purposes constituted about 30 per cent of the total of provincial and municipal levies. Education took approximately 27.4 per cent of the provincial expenditure budget. It would be impossible from existing statistics to determine the relationship between expenditure for education and that for all public expenditure for Ontarians specifically because, although the federal government contributed little to the operation of the formal educational system, it provided other social and economic benefits which could not be isolated by province.

In 1945 the provincial government contributed only a very small proportion of the operating and capital costs of provincial universities, its grants amounting to $65,639 for capital purposes and $3,610,281 for operating purposes. A considerable proportion of these funds went to the colleges at Guelph which were under the control of the Department of Agriculture.[1] Federal contributions came largely under the program handled by the Department of Veterans Affairs and, although undoubtedly a burden on the taxpayer, had best not be counted in the search for an esti-

---

* Revenue from local taxation is used in this comparison rather than expenditure in order to avoid the necessity of accounting for provincial grants. The total of municipal revenue raised by taxation plus net ordinary and capital provincial expenditure is approximately the amount spent at the two levels combined.

mate of the extent of the normal cost of formal education at that time. Other federal assistance programs contributed a small proportion of educational and training expenditure. The remaining funds needed to support the educational enterprise came from private sources.

The gross provincial product of Ontario for 1945 was estimated at $4.8 billion. If the $69.7 million figure is used for the total amount spent at the municipal and provincial levels for education, it may be said that education took less than 1.5 per cent of the gross provincial product. For the same year, personal income reached a total of $3.7 billion of which the cost of education accounted for 1.9 per cent. The burden of paying for formal education at this particular time thus does not appear to have been excessive.

Figures used in these calculations do not cover educational programs conducted by departments of the provincial government other than education or direct educational services provided by the federal government. As indicated in volume II, chapters 13 and 15 of ONTARIO'S EDUCATIVE SOCIETY, and in chapter 5 of this volume, these activities have come to be very comprehensive and pervasive. Apart from the actual conduct of schools, their costs are almost impossible to estimate, since a great deal hinges on the definition of education one recognizes. Because they are not considered in the figures presented here, the estimated cost of the educational enterprise must be recognized as under the real figure by a substantial amount.

The year 1960 provides a convenient point of comparison with 1945, not only because it marked the completion of a decade, but also because it came just before a period in which education was deliberately identified as the highest priority of the provincial government. During that year, total school board expenditure reached almost $430 million, of which slightly under $161 million, or about 37.6 per cent, came from the provincial government, nearly $254 million came from local taxation, and the rest from other sources. During the 1960–1 school year there were roughly 1,389,000 pupils attending publicly supported elementary and secondary schools. Average school board expenditure per pupil, without distinction according to level, amounted to almost $310, or nearly three and one-half times as much as the cost in current dollars in 1945. Provincial government expenditure on education at all levels, including university education, and on departmental administration, was $209.1 million, an excess over that spent on school grants of about $48 million. For a population now grown to 6,111,000, the average cost per person, obtained by dividing the sum of $430 million and $48 million, or $478 million, by that number was slightly over $78, or nearly four and one-half times that in 1945. Included in these figures were $16.1 million and $12.7 for operating and capital grants to provincially assisted universities. That is, of the $78 raised provincially for all types of formal education, the cost per person for university education was about $4.70. This amount did not, of course, take any account of fees, or of corporate giving, which represented funds that had ultimately to come from the ordinary citizen.

In 1960 the $254 million raised by school boards through local taxation amounted to 44.4 per cent of the total of about $574 million for all municipal purposes. Thus in terms of local taxation, the cost to the average person was $41.50 for education and $93.90 for all municipal services. Since 1945 the local levy for education had been multiplied by almost five while that for all municipal services had been multiplied by only about three and one-half. To present a sharper contrast, the levy for all municipal services *except* education was only about three times as much as in 1945.

Total provincial government expenditure for the fiscal year ending on March 31, 1961, was $828,230,000, or about $135.50 per person, that is, well over four times the per capita amount in 1945. Expenditure on education was about 25.2 per cent of the provincial budget.

In 1960 the federal government's contributions to university education were at a rate of $1.50 per capita. The necessary funds had to come from the taxpayers, and may be counted as an additional burden on them. Along with some other small amounts, federal grants for higher education reached $13,555,000 by the end of the fiscal year 1960–1. As a matter of fact, as a rough estimate, Ontario contributed something like $4 in federal taxes for every $3 it received in benefits from the same source. Looked upon as a method of financing provincial education, this procedure was obviously not very efficient. As a contribution to equalizing opportunities across Canada, the matter must be looked upon in quite a different light. If only the amount actually spent in Ontario, a sum which is much easier to ascertain than the amount raised in Ontario by the federal government for educational purposes, is counted as cost, federal and provincial contributions to all forms of education totalled about $492 million, or about $80.20 per capita.

There were also federal contributions to shared cost programs for training various categories of people in the labour force. The Ontario government received approximately $3,372,000 for this purpose for 1960. This amount has been accounted for in Department of Education expenditure figures.

The gross provincial product for Ontario was about $15.2 billion in 1960. Total municipal and provincial expenditures for education amounted to approximately 3.1 per cent of this amount. The total amount of personal income received by Ontario citizens in 1960 was about $11,024 million, or an average of $1,804 per person. Contributions to educational expenditure at all three levels of government were approximately 4.4 per cent of the former amount. As in 1945, these calculations do not cover educational activities, formal or informal, undertaken by provincial government departments other than Education or those conducted by various branches of the federal government.

A comparison between 1960 and 1970 shows costs increasing at an accelerating rate. School board expenditure for the latter year was approximately $1,702,420,000, of which a little more than $848,426,000 or 49.8 per cent, came from the provincial government, $799,203,000 came from local taxation, and $54,791,000 came from other sources. At this time, these other sources included $12,564,000 from the federal government. The number of pupils attending publicly supported elementary and secondary schools was about 2,022,000. Thus average school board expenditure per pupil was approximately $842, that is, well over two and one-half times as much as in 1960 and over nine times as much as in 1945. Some of the increase could be explained in terms of the larger proportion of students in the secondary schools where the costs were higher. In 1945–6 these constituted 18 per cent of the total, in 1960–1, 19 per cent, and in 1970–1, 27.5 per cent. The average expenditure per elementary school pupil in 1970 was approximately $703 and the average per secondary school student, approximately $1,251.

Total expenditure through the Department of Education in 1970–1, according to interim reports, was almost $1,123 million, exceeding that spent on school grants by about $289 million. This excess covered the capital and maintenance costs of colleges of applied arts and technology, amounting to about $91 million, which were much greater than those of post-secondary institutions for technological and trades training in 1960. Other expenditure items included teacher education, both in the teachers' colleges and in the universities, and the Ontario Institute for Studies in Education. If the excess over grants to school boards is added to the amount spent by schools boards, the total comes to $1,991 million. On the basis of an estimate of 7,637,000 for the provincial population, the per capita cost amounts to about $261.

In 1970–1 provincial grants to universities were made through the Department of University Affairs. The amount spent by that department for all purposes except capital grants was approximately $434 million, according to interim figures. This total covered operating grants to universities and other institutions (including capital repayment), as well as student grants and departmental operating expenditure. If this sum is added to that spent by the Department of Education and the local school systems, the grand total reaches $2,425 million, or $318 per capita. The per capita amount was about eighteen times that in 1945 and over four times that in 1960. Expenditures on education amounted to about 41 per cent of the provincial expenditure budget.

Under the terms of the *Adult Occupational Training Act*, which was in force in 1970, the federal government purchased from the provinces the training required in its manpower development programs and made direct subsistence payments to those taking the courses. Amounts in the first of these two categories show up as expenditures by the Department of Education and the local school boards, and thus have already been accounted for. Direct federal payments to trainees totaled approximately $45.0 million, or about $5.87 per capita of the Ontario population. These figures bring the total cost of education up to about $2,470 million, and the per capita cost to $323.

In 1970 all municipal governments including school boards raised a total of about $1,605 million by local taxation. To obtain the actual burden on the local taxpayer, however, we must reduce this sum by the residential property tax reduction of roughly $147 million, leaving a total of $1,458 million. The $810 million raised by school boards was a little more than 56 per cent of the latter sum. The amount levied locally for school purposes was thus $106 per capita and that for all municipal purposes, $191. Thus the local per capita levy for education was about twelve times as much as in 1945 and over two and one-half times as much as in 1960. The comparable per capita levy for all municipal services other than education was a little more than four and one-half times as high as in 1945 and somewhat more than one and one-half times as high as in 1960.

The gross provincial product in 1970 was approximately $35.0 billion. Municipal and provincial expenditures for education were about 6.9 per cent of this amount. Federal subsistence allowances to manpower trainees bring this percentage up to approximately 7.1 per cent. Total personal income for the province was about $27.1 billion, or $3,550 per capita. Expenditure for formal education and training, according to the definition used here, was 9.1 per cent of this amount.

Perhaps a better way of comparing the financial burden of education at various times during the post-war period is to estimate costs in terms of constant rather than current dollars. Thus the cost of education in 1960 and 1970 respectively, including federal, provincial, and school board expenditures, and eliminating transfers between levels, would be about $322 million and $1,282 million in terms of 1945 dollars. The per capita cost in 1945 dollars would be $52 in 1960 and $168 in 1970. This type of comparison makes the increase seem considerably more modest. In constant dollars, the total cost was about eighteen and one-half times as great in 1970 as in 1945, and about four times as great as in 1960. By similar calculations, the per capita cost was about nine and one-half times as great in 1970 as in 1945, and about three times as great as in 1960.

THE NATURE OF CRITICISM OF THE
COST OF EDUCATION

Much of the controversy about educational costs during the post-war period centred around the distribution of the financial burden. Many accepted claims for the benefits of education and were prepared to see the necessary funds raised provided that the process was equitable. Criticism centred on the alleged unfairness of the levy on real estate and there was continuous clamour to have it reduced or eliminated. It nevertheless persisted as the most important single source of revenue for education. In theory one of its advantages was that it was highly visible, and those who paid it had a basis for protest if it got out of hand. It was also comparatively uncomplicated to administer, since varying amounts of money could be raised simply by adjusting the rate. Because it was levied on relatively immovable and tangible assets, it was very difficult to escape. Among its disadvantages were that there was seldom a corresponding tax levied on other types of assets, and it thus tended to be discriminatory. It was decidedly regressive in that the value of real property owned by householders tended to be a declining proportion of their total assets as the latter rose. There were particular difficulties in levying it fairly on farms in communities where these were mixed with other types of property. Unlike residential property, a farm usually provided both a dwelling for the owner and a means of earning a living. A major source of unhappiness among many of those who paid high real estate taxes was that, because they had no children to educate and no need of formal education themselves, they felt that they were deriving no benefit from their contributions. An argument which they found difficult to understand was that the value of the land ultimately depended on the state of the economy, and the general welfare of society in terms of its enlightenment, culture, standard of living, and social services, depended on the general educational level of the citizens. Somewhat easier to accept was the fact that land was relatively valuable in a community that could offer good schools and other amenities.

Until shortly after the turn of the century, municipal governments in Ontario attempted to levy a more broadly based property tax. Because of the extreme variations and inequities with which the procedure was carried out, there must have been few who were unhappy to see it abandoned. Some communities collected so little that they gained a reputation as tax havens where the wealthy tended to congregate. It commonly happened that any attempt at fair assessment was so forbidding that the process was reduced to the collection of fixed amounts on certain standard items.

Assessment for the purposes of levying real estate taxes was long a haphazard process which left many problems to be settled even in the 1970s. There were traditionally two major sources of difficulty: variations from one local area to another and variations in the assessment of different types of property within the same municipality. During the fifties and sixties the Department of Municipal Affairs undertook to improve matters by such measures as preparing assessment manuals and providing in-service courses for municipal assessors. A step forward was taken in 1957 when equalizing factors became available to enable the provincial government to compensate for local variations in the general level of assessment. These factors were obtained by using a sampling technique for properties of different kinds in each area and relating the results to a provincial standard. Before this time school grants could be based only very imperfectly on ability to raise funds, varying according to such factors as size and type of school and size and type of municipal unit. A new grant scheme in 1958 placed greater emphasis on local assessment per classroom and per student. The use of provincial equalizing factors of course did nothing to ensure that different types of property within a municipality would be dealt with according to a uniform pattern. It was a well-known fact that some municipalities assessed apartment buildings more heavily than others in relation to single family dwellings, and that industrial property fared quite differently in different communities. Another problem that caused increasing difficulty was that property in general continued to be assessed at 1940 values. The source of inequity was that actual values had increased at widely varying rates in different parts of the province and particularly between rural and urban areas.

Many of the widespread reforms advocated by the Provincial Committee on Taxation (the Smith Committee) in its report released in 1967 hinged on an assessment of all real property at its actual market value and on keeping this valuation up to date.[2] In his budget address in 1969, Provincial Treasurer Charles MacNaughton forecast fundamental changes in the taxation pattern which would await the completion of this process. As a major step toward improved efficiency, the provincial government assumed direct responsibility for assessment in January 1970. Reassessment was a painful procedure which had substantial adverse repercussions for the government. Although it did not necessarily involve any general increase in the real estate tax, since the rate could go down as the assessed value of real property was adjusted upward, there was a substantial change in the balance between one owner and another. Where the previous assessment and actual value diverged least, the owners were inclined to consider the advantage they gained by reassessment as their due. Where the two values diverged most, and reassessment meant a sharp tax increase, there were bitter complaints. Whatever the difficulty, it was becoming obvious that stringent action had to be taken if the real estate tax was to continue to be considered a practicable method of raising revenue.

A nettle which the Smith Committee found much easier to grasp than did the provincial government was that of exemptions from the real estate tax. The major categories of property that had traditionally enjoyed such exemptions were federal government property, including federal crown corporations; provincial government property, including provincial crown corporations; municipal government property; educational institutions, including universities and publicly supported and private schools; hospitals; religious institutions; and charitable institutions. Generally speaking, the Smith Committee recommended the elimination of these exemptions, or at least their drastic reduction. The federal and provincial governments had already established precedents by paying grants in lieu of taxes on certain properties, a practice that might be extended to ensure that the full equivalent to municipal taxation was paid, and that municipal taxes were recognized as including those levied by school boards. It might appear to be a matter of mere bookkeeping for a municipality to pay real estate taxes on its own properties. The Smith Committee, however, saw some advantage in at least assessing these properties so that it would be easier to estimate the cost of maintaining and operating them in relation to similar facilities in the private sector.

The principle with respect to publicly supported educational institutions and hospitals was that the government could allow municipal agencies to tax them and could compensate them by provincial grants. The politically awkward factor in making this change was that a relatively invisible cost would be made highly visible. Adverse repercussions could be anticipated with respect to universities and hospitals in particular because the costs of both were rising rapidly in any case. Nevertheless, the provincial government introduced the policy in the budget for 1970–1 of compensating municipal governments for funds lost because of exemptions on university property. The first steps were very modest, and it was expected that this policy would be completely implemented only over a period of time.

According to the Smith Committee, privately maintained educational and charitable institutions should surrender the tax exemption on their real property in favour of an annual grant from the Legislature. In order to demonstrate their entitlement to such a grant, they would have to detail their contribution to the welfare of the community. It is easy to understand why they showed a strong preference for the continuation of the exemption. Facing what could be an irascible or penny-pinching government every year could be a very trying task. The Smith Committee found it most difficult of all to deal with the problem of religious agencies. Although these might in theory be treated in the same way as private educational and charitable institutions, it would probably be more difficult for them to demonstrate their contribution to the general welfare. It was also against Ontario tradition to make grants of public funds to religious agencies. The Smith Committee proposed a kind of compromise with the textbook approach by suggesting that these agencies pay only part of the amount for which they would be liable according to regular rates, beginning with 5 per cent and going up to 35 per cent. The Robarts government, however, preferred not to stir up the turmoil that might have followed an attempt to implement this recommendation, and assured the churches that they would not be taxed. No active steps seemed to be contemplated to remove the exemptions from private schools or charitable organizations either.

Some of the most serious difficulties would be overcome if full real estate taxes, or their equivalent, were paid on property held by the two senior levels of government and by universities. There would be great relief in Kingston, for example, where in 1969 approximately 35 per cent of the real property in the city was beyond the reach of the tax collector. The situation created sharply ambiguous feelings among the tax-paying citizens toward Queen's University. On the one hand, they were proud of the great and growing institution in their midst, which was the source of a good deal of prestige and made a substantial contribution to the prosperity of the community. On the other hand, its expansion involved the gobbling up of revenue-producing properties and the shifting of an additional burden to those that remained in private hands. In other university cities, where there were many public buildings and institutions of other types in relation to the population, the problem was comparable, although less serious.

The Conservative party, under the leadership of George Drew, won the election of 1943 at least partly as the result of a promise that, although ambiguously worded, was widely taken to mean that a Conservative government would institute a policy of paying half the cost of education in the form of provincial grants. For the next twenty years, opposition critics berated the government for failing to live up to this version of the commitment. As long as he was in a position to do so, Leslie Frost, who became Prime Minister in 1949, denied the validity of their case. Although he had played no part in formulating the policy implied by the promise, he was responsible, as Provincial Treasurer in the Drew government, for carrying it out. He did so, according to his interpretation, by making grants equal to half the *approved* costs, rather than the total costs, and only for the single year to which he said the promise applied.

Although provincial grants rose rapidly, they constituted far less than half the total cost of education during most of the post-war period. In 1955 they amounted to only 37.5 per cent of school board expenditure, and did not begin to rise proportionately until after 1960. The continuous opposition pressure for a relative increase reflected complaints that the level of municipal taxation was reaching a maximum. This premise was obviously false, since municipal taxes could and did go up. Expressions of irritation, however, did not diminish.

Both the Liberal party and the CCF, which became the New Democratic party in 1961, consistently advocated that the provincial government pay the lion's share of education costs. For a time in the early 1960s, when John Wintermeyer headed the party, the Liberals advocated that the entire financial burden be borne by this level of government. Later in the decade, both Liberals and NDP supporters generally felt that 80 per cent might be a reasonable figure. In 1969 the government instituted the policy of working toward the 60 per cent level, an objective which was to be reached in 1972–3. The Conservative election victory in 1971 seemed to ensure that this plan would be carried to completion on the scheduled date.

As of 1962–3, the suggestion that a larger share of the cost of education be paid from provincial revenues meant that it would have to come from the income tax collection agreement with the federal government, the retail sales tax, the corporation tax, the gasoline tax, the succession duty, the motor vehicle fuel tax, the Liquor Control Board of Ontario, and miscellaneous other sources. During that year, comparable amounts were collected from the first four of these sources, which were by far the best revenue producers. The corporation tax was somewhat in the lead, yielding nearly $186 million, or almost 19 per cent of the total of $994 million in net general revenue. The opposition parties, particularly the NDP, felt that more revenue could be obtained from this source without damaging the economy. The income tax also appealed as a progressive tax falling most heavily on those with the greatest ability to pay. The retail sales tax was kept from being highly regressive by the exemption of a list of necessities, but was nevertheless not greatly favoured by either opposition party.

By 1971–2 the income tax had become the most lucrative, yielding, according to budget estimates, about $1,050 million, or more than one-fourth of the estimated total net general revenue. The retail sales tax was expected to yield $745 million and the corporation tax $290 million. The succession duty and the province's share of the federal estate tax, first paid in 1964–5, had ceased to improve as revenue producers. The gasoline tax, which was expected to yield more than twice as much as in 1962–3, constituted a declining proportion of the total. A capital gains tax was included in the federal government's reforms legislated at the end of 1971, but had not yet had any impact on provincial revenues.

Undoubtedly a pattern of taxation could be developed that would be much more equitable, especially for low-income people attempting to retain ownership of a home, than would continued heavy reliance on a real estate tax. Of great importance also would be the psychological factor of shifting to less visible forms of taxation. Deduction of income tax at the source had made this exaction less painful than it would be if collected in a lump sum. Further, the federal government, because of joint collection, tended to be blamed even for that part of it that was returned to the provincial government. Corporations might have influence, but had little direct command over votes. Although they might shift a large part of their taxes to the consumer, the process was very involved and not at all obvious to the latter. The retail sales tax was extracted little by little, and few consumers ever estimated what it cost them over an extended period. As an irritant to the taxpayer, the real estate tax stood practically alone. There would nevertheless be some difficulties for any government attempting to reduce it drastically and compensate by other levies.

During the election campaign of 1971, both the Liberal and New Democratic parties promised that, if they won the election, they would pay 80 per cent of the costs of education with revenues raised through taxes other than those levied on real estate. Whatever the popular feeling about this particular issue, neither party secured the opportunity to implement its scheme.

Arguments against the assumption of too much financial responsibility by the provincial government have centred around the claim that there was a danger of destroying local interest, initiative, and control. It was pointed out that one level of government simply did not raise money and turn it over, with no strings attached, to be spent at another level. If school boards had to continue to raise a substantial part of the revenue, they would presumably face the wrath of the taxpayers if they were too extravagant. While it was true that some of the poorest boards long received up to 95 per cent of their funds from grants, it was claimed that boards where most of the revenue was raised locally provided the yardsticks for expenditure that applied to all. If the provincial government were to supply anything approaching 95 per cent of the revenue for all boards, or even a much lower percentage, it would have to place them under rigid controls to prevent extravagance.

As grants were increased sharply in 1969 and 1970, some of the pessimistic forecasts showed signs of being substantiated. There was too little pressure on the new divisional school boards to keep local levies from rising, let alone holding them constant or reducing them. Thus there was a danger that they would defeat the government's attempt to raise its contribution to 60 per cent of the cost. The inevitable result was that the minister of education announced measures in the fall of 1970 to curtail the freedom of school boards to increase local levies. They were limited to an average expenditure of $545 per elementary school pupil and $1,060 per secondary school student. In view of the widespread concern at that time over the increasing costs of education, this measure met with vociferous approval, along with protests from some school boards and many teachers. Boards in some of the large urban areas such as Metropolitan Toronto felt that the limits were being applied too rigidly, with insufficient allowance for the special needs and unusual costs which confronted them. Teachers felt that, in view of strong inflationary trends, they might be expected to make financial sacrifices out of proportion to those exacted from other elements of society. There was little evidence of public anxiety over the consequences of centralizing financial control when other aspects of education were supposed to benefit from decentralization.

THE FINANCIAL OUTLOOK FOR THE FUTURE

The 1970s promised to confront the province with a major crisis in educational finance. The cost implications of programs and policies adopted in the 1960s were still to be completely felt. The most serious problem would be at the post-secondary level. A continuously rising unit cost would have to be multiplied by enrolments which would continue to grow despite disillusionment over the declining economic values of education. According to projections, the population in the eighteen-to-twenty-four-year age group would rise from 934,800 in 1971 to 1,191,600 in 1981, that is, by about 28 per cent.[3] There was certain to be an intensification of the impression that occupational security and satisfaction depended on some measure of post-secondary education, which would ensure a continuing increase in the proportion of young people enrolling in the appropriate institutions. To judge by developments in the state of California, such a trend could continue until education at this level came to be a normal expectation of a substantial majority of youth.

According to an estimate by the Economic Planning Branch of the Department of Treasury and Economics in 1971, the average cost per student in Ontario universities would rise from $3,677 in 1970–1 to $4,277 in 1975–6, that is, by about 16 per cent. The Department of University Affairs earlier projected total university expenditure by the provincial government to $740 million for 1974–5 on the assumption of a continuation of policies being pursued in 1970. This figure included operating grants (which covered capital repayment), the expenses of the department, and grants (although not loans) to students. The estimates were based on a projected enrolment of 169,000, which included a full-time enrolment allowance of 24,000 for part-time students. Church-related institutions, which received half the grant of those given full provincial assistance, would presumably have about 12,000 additional students.

Before certain administrative changes were made in 1971 and 1972, educational programs administered by the Department of Education were officially grouped for convenience in six categories: 1 / departmental administration, 2 / formal education from kindergarten to grade 13, 3 / assistance to school boards, 4 / special educational services for the handicapped, 5 / continuing education, and 6 / community services.[4] The first of these categories included a number of programs and institutions such as the Elliot Lake Centre for Continuing Education, the Moosonee Education Centre, the Ontario Institute for Studies in Education, the Province of Ontario Council for the Arts, and the Teachers' Superannuation Fund. The second included certain amounts to assist in the transfer of the elementary teacher training programs from the teachers' colleges to the universities. These amounts were only a small percentage of the cost of teacher education. In the same category were expenditures for educational television. The third consisted mainly of general legislative grants to school boards. The fourth, although involving rather small amounts of funds in comparison with the others, included some important activities in the special education field such as the maintenance of the provincial schools for the deaf and blind and education of retarded children in institutions. The fifth included transfer payments to the colleges of applied arts and technology, Ryerson Polytechnical Institute, and the Ontario Manpower Retraining Program. The sixth involved non-profit camps, recreational programs, and other community services.

The cost of all these programs for the fiscal year 1970–1 was approximately $1,125,204,865. On the basis of previous experience, if normal growth factors were taken into account, a continuation of the same programs would involve a cost increase of at least 65 per cent by 1974–5. This would mean a total expenditure for that year of more than $1,850,000,-000. The extent of the increase would reflect the completion of the policy according to which provincial grants would account for 60 per cent of school board expenditure. If any additional programs were undertaken, and none of the existing ones was cut, the costs would be still higher. On the basis of a continuation of existing trends, sources of revenue being drawn upon in 1970–1 would fall short of meeting projected costs by nearly $200,000,000.

The government was committed to raising legislative grants to the point where they amounted to 60 per cent of school board expenditure by 1972–3. Thus, although the total sum spent by school boards might be expected to rise from $1,640,000,000 in 1970–1 to a sum approaching $2,300,000,000, or by about two-thirds, the boards would need to increase the amount raised locally, which was estimated at $815,000,000 in 1970–1, by only a little more than 10 per cent.

INCREASING COMPLAINTS ABOUT EDUCATIONAL COSTS

In 1970 there was a new note in the perpetual complaints about the high and still rising costs of education. The concern was particularly acute because of the stagnant condition of the economy. In farming areas where the effects of the school board reorganization of 1969 and the related pursuit of equality of educational opportunity had resulted in particularly large tax increases and where the cost/price squeeze threatened to put numbers of farmers out of business, some protested by engaging in "tax strikes." This tactic meant withholding school taxes for periods of up to three years. There was, of course, a small penalty for each month by which the taxes were in arrears, but the property could not be offered for sale by the government until the end of the three-year period. If considerable numbers of farmers engaged in the campaign, it is hard to imagine any government facing the political consequences of carrying out large-scale tax sales. A united campaign thus threatened serious embarrassment for the government. In recognition of the strength of the farmers' case, the government announced a Farm Tax Reduction Program for 1970, by which those whose property was assessed as a farm in that year received a grant amounting to 25 per cent of their net municipal taxes provided that the property consisted of at least eleven acres or, if smaller, yielded at least $2,000 in gross income. Net municipal taxes consisted of the total of municipal and school taxes minus the basic shelter tax reduction. Some farmers' groups announced that they would not be mollified by such measures, and that they would continue in their determination to withhold their tax payments until what they regarded as a fairer tax scheme had been devised. Since machinery for deducting the grants from tax payments had not been set up, and the grants were paid directly, farmers could be in the position of receiving relief on unpaid taxes.

While those who advocated a tax strike were protesting against a particular form of taxation, there was evidence of increasing scepticism about the value of the educational enterprise itself. Economists had been busy for some years devising techniques for estimating the specific contribution of education to economic productivity. Most of their studies had provided strong support for the value of education as investment. In its Second Annual Review, released in 1965, the Economic Council of Canada had estimated the returns from this investment at between 15 and 20 per cent for the individual.[5]

There had, of course, always been sceptics who, while not denying the statistical evidence that education was usually financially profitable for the individual who obtained it, maintained that a large part of the supposed benefits to society were illusory. Actual losses might even be sustained when employers insisted on higher and more expensively obtained paper qualifications for jobs that did not actually require increased skill. Whatever the validity of this case, it appeared to be gaining strength by 1970. Particular suspicion was thrown on the capacity of general arts and science programs in universities to make an economic contribution. If this impression gained more general acceptance, and certain kinds of higher education were regarded as largely or exclusively of benefit to the recipient, there would be increasing pressure to shift the financial burden back on him and his parents, as witness the Draft Report of the Commission on Post-Secondary Education in Ontario. When education is regarded as consumption, it seems natural to expect the consumer to pay.

PROSPECTS FOR REDUCING THE RATE OF
RISING EDUCATIONAL COSTS

There was sure to be an intensive search during the 1970s for ways to cut costs. The Committee on University Affairs gave a good deal of attention to the problem, and devoted considerable space to it in its annual reports. One obvious approach was to squeeze out the remaining inclination of universities to compete with one another by offering courses and programs that had little chance of attracting enough students for the most efficient operation. A major step was taken in this direction in 1967 when provincial operating grants for graduate programs were restricted to those programs which had been approved under the appraisals procedures designed and carried out by the Ontario Council on Graduate Studies. There was nevertheless still thought to be considerable room for further savings. Something might be accomplished by a skilful manipulation of the per-student operating grant formula, and a major contribution might be made by the co-operative efforts of university representatives working through the Council of Ontario Universities. If there remained too much suspicion of waste, the universities faced the prospect of a reduction in the autonomy they had maintained while the provincial government took over most of the responsibility for their financial support. There was a serious danger that the trend toward internal democracy, involving the dispersal of authority through a network of committees, would reduce their responsiveness to the interests of the province as a whole, and thus make inevitable the imposition of stronger controls from outside. The interim recommendations of the Commission on Post-Secondary Education, which were being debated hotly in the spring of 1972, made the threat of a further loss of autonomy seem very real.

In 1971–2, graduate programs were the object of increasingly intensive scrutiny. During the sixties the official policy toward these programs was an expansive one. Ambitious administrators in the smaller and newer institutions were heeded when they declared that they could not hope to achieve high standards in their undergraduate programs if they could not attract faculty members who would have an opportunity to teach some graduate work and engage in the research that was associated with it. At a time of extreme scarcity of qualified faculty, when it was obviously necessary to attract competent people from abroad, there was a good deal of validity in this claim. Further support for the policy of expansion was provided by the need to prepare teaching faculty as quickly as possible to overcome the scarcity. Throughout the period, nevertheless, there were thoughtful university people who had misgivings about the ultimate effects of the policy. They could not believe that fourteen provincially assisted universities and a couple of others could offer strong graduate programs, even if each one concentrated on a limited number of areas, and they feared that the dispersal of resources resulting from the attempt to support the ambitions of all universities would prevent any one of them from maintaining a position of excellence. Their case was strengthened by evidence that some universities seemed to find it profitable to encourage the enrolment of an inordinately high proportion of foreign students in order to obtain the maximum of operating grants under the formula. The surplus of PhD graduates which began to appear in a number of fields in 1970 suggested that some graduate programs had been expanded a bit too far, particularly in the light of a comment attributed to the principal of Erindale College, J. Tuzo Wilson, that a large proportion of them were not good enough to be hired as university instructors.

A possibility that is always open to consideration is that university faculty might work somewhat harder, or more efficiently, or both. In delivering the Gerstein Lectures at York University in 1966, the minister of education, William G. Davis, pointed out that the ratio of students to instructors in Ontario universities was considerably more favourable than it was in some American institutions that managed to maintain a reputation for first class work. Despite his suggestion that the load might be increased without ill effects, the ratio for all Ontario universities combined fell from 14.1 to 1 in 1965–6 to 13.3 to 1 in 1966–7, and to 12.6 to 1 in 1967–8. A change of direction began to show itself in 1968–9, with a small increase to 13.0, followed by a figure of 12.9 in 1969–70 and one of 13.0 in 1970–1. Those who did not take kindly to the idea that the ratio should rise by a substantial amount commonly pointed to the over-sized classes, sometimes consisting of several hundred students, that were common in the larger universities. These were, of course, balanced by faculty members who had few teaching hours, very small classes, or both. The main defence of what appeared to be light teaching loads was that the faculty were expected to put a great deal of effort into increasing the fund of knowledge, which was a major aspect of the university's business, and that only in research and study could they retain and improve their teaching competence. If funds could not continue to be provided on the scale demanded, however, they faced the prospect of having to manage under less favourable conditions.

Some people retained a hope that instructional media might help to reduce costs. If the basis for comparison was an uninspiring professor standing in front of a large class to review a set of notes that might or might not reflect the most up-to-date knowledge in the field, substantial advantages could be cited for television. Since the same video tape could be used repeatedly, it was practical to take special measures to ensure its quality. A particularly good lecturer might be selected, extra effort might be devoted to the preparation of the lecture, and the quality of the final product might be improved by redoing certain sections or by judicious cutting. In the actual presentation, the use of strategically placed sets might produce a much greater sense of intimacy than could be expected of a live lecturer in a large hall. It was also possible to reduce or eliminate hearing problems.

Those who were unenthusiastic about attempts to save substantial sums in this way pointed out that, although the television approach might be an improvement over the mediocre live lecture, neither one ought to be held up as the essence of university education. The inefficiency of the lecture as a means of conveying information was repeatedly pointed out. Its defenders were forced to fall back on claims that it enabled the student to observe a mature and well disciplined mind work over complex material, and that it gave the professor an opportunity to introduce findings or insights that were so new that they had not yet found their way into written records. Unfortunately, the greatest potentialities for saving lay in producing the kind of televised lecture that could be taped and used repeatedly, that is, the kind that was least likely to show the professor's ability to deal spontaneously with novel situations or enable him to introduce the latest findings. The medium was most in harmony with the university's purposes if it was used to convey a live lecture of high quality, possibly to students in several different locations, or where it was used to provide close-up illustrations of what was being explained. Unfortunately, administrative arrangements and the cost of equipment and facilities were likely to nullify any savings in manpower in this type of use.

What concerned the sceptics even more was that television could not provide any substitute at all for direct personal contact between instructor and student, whether in a seminar group or in individual consultation. It could not give him the opportunity of engaging in active, strenuous intellectual contest. The quality of education, particularly in the larger universities, was widely faulted because too few of these opportunities had been provided. It seemed regrettable to abandon hope that dehumanizing trends could be halted and to plunge further into the use of the instruments of mass entertainment, embracing the process of mass education when the universities had so persistently clung to the ideal of education as an individual phenomenon.

Attempts to incorporate television viewing as a regular and substantial feature of instruction in Ontario universities had almost completely failed by the early 1970s. Particular disillusionment was reported from Scarborough College, which had initiated bold new programs a few years earlier. Costs turned out to be unexpectedly high, administrative adaptations excessively difficult, the problems of producing effective programs surprisingly great, and the benefits elusive. Heavy reliance on television conflicted with the style and work habits of the faculty, many of whom had no incentive to adapt to the peculiar demands of the medium.

Yet the financial problem facing the province in the early 1970s was such that further efforts, perhaps under such auspices as those of the open University of Ontario proposed by the Commission on Post-Secondary Education, might have to be made to take advantage of television instruction. Under conditions as they were developing, great masses of students could probably not be given the personal attention of highly qualified scholars. For them, televised presentations might well be more effective than submitting to the ministrations of partially-educated and inexperienced graduate students.

Extension courses had long provided a way of accommodating numbers of students for whom full-time attendance was inconvenient or impossible. These courses were usually managed in such a way that the cost per student credit was relatively light. One reason was of course that overhead costs had been small because existing buildings and facilities, which would otherwise have been idle, could be utilized. Many professors could be persuaded to lecture in night classes for remuneration at a lower rate than they were paid for their regular activities. If the program was not managed with considerable care, of course, standards might fall substantially below those of regular programs, but such an outcome was by no means unavoidable. It was conceivable that unmanageable costs for full-time programs might be reduced if restrictions on admission to the latter were accompanied by an increase in opportunities for part-time study. There would be a very serious problem, however, arising from the fact that it would be difficult to exclude students from full-time programs except on the basis of merit. Yet if the less promising students were diverted to part-time work, standards would be impossible to maintain, the program would be discredited, and new pressure would develop for opportunities for full-time study.

In early 1971 there were suggestions, based, as it turned out, on an excessively pessimistic viewpoint, that there would not be enough full-time places in 1971–2 for all those qualifying for admission in terms of the previous year's requirements, and that three thousand or more applicants might be turned away. Theoretically, the same solution might be extended in subsequent years in order to keep enrolment constant or to permit it to grow only very gradually. This kind of negative approach would be both the least satisfactory and the least feasible. It would deny the implications of the bold educational initiatives of the people and government of Ontario during the 1960s. Whatever the doubts about the extent of the contribution of education to economic productivity, parents were still determined that their children should go as far as their talents would take them, or even further, if possible. To place additional restrictions on educational opportunity, and thus confine it to a smaller proportion of the population, would arouse particular resentment at a time when the financial burden was being distributed over the entire population. Ontario did not have the alternative of turning back the clock.

The determined cost-cutter would be sure to turn his attention to university professors' salaries. Particularly, if he thought professors had a rather easy time, with a light work load and freedom from many of the restraints that those in other occupational groups had to endure, he might suggest that existing salary levels be frozen, or at least allowed to rise rather slowly. That is, university faculty might be singled out among occupational groups as the ones who must, for the public good, submit to special financial sacrifices.

According to information compiled by the Ontario Council of University Faculty Associations, university salaries demonstrated a tendency to rise more slowly than either provincial productivity or wages and salaries in general between 1937–8 and the end of the sixties. Between 1960–1 and 1963–4, for example, the average annual increase for all ranks was in the neighbourhood of 3.5 per cent as compared with 5.0 per cent for all professionals and 4.0 per cent for wages and salaries. There was some improvement after that time, although it occurred against a background of accelerating increases for all occupational groups. Salaries for all ranks in all Ontario universities rose by 9.4 per cent between 1966–7 and 1967–8, and by 8.5 per cent the following year. In 1969–70 mean salaries for all ranks ranged from $12,100 to $15,900.

There is no objective way to determine whether any specific occupational group receives fair or just remuneration. It is not necessarily justifiable to take a year such as 1937–8, when a period of deflation had left salary-earners in relatively secure occupations in an unusually favourable financial position, and to treat any decline in that position as social injustice. University faculty members in 1937–8 had a very different role from that of their counterparts in 1970. They were a much scarcer commodity, and could conceivably have been overpaid in terms of their social value without putting undue strain on the economy. With 6,685 full-time teaching staff in the provincially assisted universities in 1968–9, or more than twice as many as there had been just four years earlier, the situation was quite different.

The most important influence on salaries in universities, as in all occupational fields, is supply and demand. During most of the 1960s rapid expansion and inadequate facilities for graduate study produced a desperate shortage of qualified instructors, and heavy reliance had to be placed on foreign recruits. Since other countries, including the United States, had no surplus of highly competent people, it seemed safe to assume that Ontario universities had either to offer good salaries or see the quality of their programs deteriorate. The implication of being in an international market was that a small salary lag could produce very serious adverse results. Matters promised to be quite different in the 1970s. While outstanding scholars would no doubt continue to be scarce, and able to command a high price, the supply of second-rank instructors, who would have to form the mainstay of most universities, was easing considerably. Universities might well be able to keep salaries from rising very quickly, without giving the appearance of reducing academic standards.

To present such possibilities is by no means to support them. In higher education, as in every other sphere of life, the buyer gets what he pays for. If the taxpayers of Ontario should decide that they wanted to save some of the costs of higher education by freezing or reducing professors' salaries, they might easily deliver such a blow to the quality of higher education that the value of their tremendous educational investment would decline disastrously. Entirely aside from the question of whether or not professors suffered any actual hardship, a successful attack on their level of remuneration would effectively reduce the prestige they enjoyed in Ontario society. One can see another example of the familiar vicious circle developing: the more quality declines, the less the population is willing to pay for what it gets.

So much for the universities, which in some ways constituted the most vulnerable target, since it was hard to demonstrate the value of some aspects of their contributions, and they had too few faculty members to carry much clout at the polls. The colleges of applied arts and technology also seemed to offer the possibility of some savings, or at least the postponement of expenditure, largely in terms of capital development. They began operations, mostly in 1967, in buildings constructed for the institutes of technology and the Ontario vocational centres and in converted structures rented or taken over from other agencies. It was always possible, although in many respects undesirable, to continue with makeshift and temporary arrangements for longer periods than originally planned. The approach to erecting new campus buildings adopted by the provincial government from the beginning was conducive to this kind of stretch-out. There were to be no grandiose structures with surplus space to allow for several years of expansion, but instead a series of flexible plans allowing for the addition of modular units when needed. A period of severe austerity might thus mean, not a choice between a new building and nothing, but a diminished number of new units and perhaps continued operation from more sites than were desirable for maximum efficiency.

Apart from a decision to change the policy of attempting to provide for all comers, there were few places where additional savings could be made. Salaries were already largely determined by competition with those in industry and other educational institutions. Complaints that a qualified person could do better financially in a secondary school system and examples of substantial sacrifices made by some who chose college teaching in preference to other occupations suggested that any hope of saving on salaries would be unrealistic. There was no better prospect of reducing expenditure on equipment and supplies. The colleges were already starved for the kind and range of library materials that could make education an exploratory and in part a self-guided experience. A reduction in machinery and equipment for technological, technical, and commercial courses could deal a fatal blow at the attempt to keep them relevant to the needs of the economy.

The Ontario Institute for Studies in Education was often cited as an example of unnecessary extravagance. While there might be a case for the accusation that its funds were not all spent judiciously, no institution is exempt from such a charge. In fact the sum of $10 or $11 million, covering the major program of graduate work in education, as well as a large proportion of the research and development activities conducted in the province, represented a tiny proportion of the total expenditure on education. It would be unfortunate if impressions of ineffectiveness at the institute were to lead to a retreat from this type of investment.

The massive size of the elementary and secondary school system would make it a main target for the pruner's knife. Despite the growing tendency to look on both levels as part of a single system, it was still possible to appraise them separately in terms of costs. The secondary school level would get the most attention because it was still expanding, largely as a result of growing enrolments which responded to declining birth rates some years later than did those in the elementary schools. Although it was expected that the percentage of the fifteen-to-nineteen-year age group in attendance at school would continue to rise slowly until it reached about 82 per cent in 1975, the increase in numbers attributable to this factor would not be very great.

Instructional salaries, which rose from 52.3 per cent to 58.7 per cent of school board expenditure between 1950 and 1970, were by far the largest single expenditure item for secondary schools. In the larger school systems, annual salaries in 1971–2 ranged from a minimum of about $7,200 for a teacher with a three-year degree and no prior experience to over $16,000 for one with an academic honours degree or equivalent, an appropriate specialist's certificate, and about fourteen years' experience. There were also extra payments for administrative and supervisory responsibilities and for teaching night-school classes. In relation to wages and salaries in other occupations, Ontario secondary school teachers were the best paid in the world. Whether or not they were worth every cent of their salaries might count for little in the interplay of economic and social forces that would determine their status in the future.

The relatively favourable position of 1970 was mainly the result of the seller's market that existed throughout the fifties and sixties. While the population was increasing at an extraordinary tempo because of the high post-war birth rate and the major influx of immigrants, the line was held, as noted earlier, in terms of a university degree as a minimum basic requirement for academic teaching. Under the guidance of such expert tacticians as S.G.B. Robinson and I.M. Robb, the Ontario Secondary School Teachers' Federation made the most of the teachers' essentially favourable position to extract regular and substantial salary increases from school boards. At the end of the 1960s, there were strong pressures within the federation to continue the campaign for an improvement in the teachers' position in relation to that of other groups. These forces experienced a rebuff in Metropolitan Toronto in early 1970 when the threat of mass resignations was dropped and the teachers went back to work the following term without having gained their salary objectives.

The sense of urgency about the 1969–70 campaign reflected a realization among federation leaders that their bargaining position was turning unfavourable. Supply and demand were just about in balance, and the possibility of a surplus of qualified teachers loomed in the future. The colleges of education had far more candidates than they could handle in the fall of 1970, and found themselves for the first time in many years in a position to make a genuine selection. Tight federation discipline would be increasingly difficult to maintain if school boards could turn to a pool of unemployed but well qualified candidates eager to get into the profession.

The very number of teachers required to maintain the schools was becoming a major obstacle to further salary advances. When the Metropolitan Toronto teachers asked both for higher pay and for a further reduction in the student/teacher ratio, it took a relatively simple calculation to show that the total sum involved looked forbidding. The result was that the case had little support among the general public. For the 1970s there was every prospect that the attempt to control educational costs would confront the teachers with an inescapable choice between two essentially conflicting demands. If they wanted to be a highly paid professional group, they might have to accept a reversal of the trend toward a lower student/teacher ratio. For the province, as in the case of the universities, there was a danger that an excessively penurious outlook might reduce the quality of education, to the detriment of the whole of society.

A mere return to past practice would result in a poorer quality of education. Experience has made it abundantly clear that solid working days broken by two or three spare periods a week leave a teacher with little time or energy to keep up with new developments in content and methods and all too often drain him of the patience needed to maintain a sympathetic, understanding relationship with students. There are, however, alternatives. One which Ontario teachers had not accepted with excessive enthusiasm was the possibility of using many more teacher aides, who might be employed at much lower salaries than teachers. The colleges of applied arts and technology had shown themselves willing and eager to provide appropriate training. If the teaching task were scrutinized carefully, and the tasks requiring a lesser level of preparation carefully identified, the teacher's special competence might be spread over a larger group of students. It was quite possible that the result would not be quite as favourable as having highly qualified teachers handle the entire process, but the situation in the 1970s threatened to place that ideal arrangement out of reach.

Teachers often observed that the declining student/teacher ratio was not particularly reflected in smaller individual classes, at least in the major subjects. The reduction could be traced largely to an increase in administrative and supervisory staff, to the offering of a wider range of optional courses, some of which did not attract large enough enrolments to be efficiently operated, and to the provision of special programs for the mentally, physically, and emotionally handicapped, which required relatively large investments of highly qualified teacher power. All three of these areas offered the possibility of savings. With respect to the first, it would probably be cheaper to ensure that teachers were given the maximum incentive and opportunity to improve their own preparation than to hire large numbers of consultants to help compensate for their deficiencies. These were not, of course, mutually exclusive alternatives, since consultants often had in-service training as one of their most important responsibilities. Nevertheless, there was a strong feeling in many quarters that the educational system might be operated at less expense and with greater effectiveness if the bureaucratic superstructure, all designed with the commendable aim of assisting the teacher, were somewhat reduced. It would be more ominous and in the long run probably much more regrettable if expenditure were cut substantially by a reduction in subject options, which promised to help young people adapt to an increasingly complex society.

As far as special programs for the handicapped were concerned, the most progressive systems in the province, mainly in the larger cities, had over a period of years worked out effective means of handling children in these categories. Where trained teachers and consultants were available, such children had been placed in special schools or classes and given appropriate individual therapy. But the advanced preparation required for the teachers was expensive, and the number of pupils that a single teacher could handle successfully tended to be extremely small.

There might actually be a threat to some existing classes. Education officials in Metropolitan Toronto feared so as they protested against the provincial per pupil ceilings on expenditure that were first announced in the fall of 1970. The most serious prospect was that the drive to extend similar facilities into other parts of the province would be seriously hindered. One of the main objectives of the school board reform of January 1, 1969 was to create divisional boards that could operate on the scale needed to provide adequately for the handicapped. The boards were for the first time given complete responsibility for the mentally retarded, as well as for those with other special needs. An element of coercion was removed in the provincial grant scheme when stimulation grants for classes for the handicapped were abolished on the assumption that the boards would assign these classes a high priority if they were given the money without strings. But parents of handicapped children were always a minority of the population, and might not succeed in applying the necessary pressure to have facilities expanded. The damage would lie in opportunities missed – in hopes not fulfilled.

It is not difficult to trace the consequences of neglecting the handicapped. Even if humanitarian considerations, which ought to be paramount, are ignored, and economic factors alone are taken into account, the case against reducing effort is a powerful one. Those who are taught to make the best of their abilities may be reasonably contented contributors to their own welfare and to that of society. Those who are not often remain the responsibility of welfare agencies throughout their lives at a cost vastly greater than that of the best education available at the appropriate stage. Yet it may be politically easier to spend more on welfare and less on education even though such a decision involves neglecting the sole means of relieving the situation in the long run.

The remaining major area where it seemed that costs could be cut was that of buildings and facilities. Critics of the high level of expenditure on these items during the post-war period referred to "palaces" of learning. Time and again, debates in the provincial Legislature centred around the possibility of reducing architects' fees and other expenses by devising a few standard plans from which all school boards would be compelled to make a selection. This approach did not, however, have much appeal. It was pointed out that differing conditions of site, size, range and type of offerings, climatic conditions, and other factors would make it necessary to provide far more than a few standard plans. If an agency such as the Department of Education undertook to provide for all types of needs, there might be excessive bureaucratic inefficiency. If prompt account were not taken of the latest developments in heating, lighting, air conditioning, the arrangement and use of space, and other features, the ultimate financial losses might be much greater than any apparent gains. A much more promising approach was developed through the Study of Educational Facilities conducted under the aegis of the Metropolitan Toronto School Board. The essence of this concept was that standardized specifications were defined for the various components of buildings and produced in large numbers by whatever firms could turn them out most efficiently. An infinite variety of buildings might be constructed using combinations of these same standard components. Initial steps to implement the scheme produced promising results. The hope of savings from this approach depended, of course, on the existence of a large market.

In the 1950s there was apparently a clear idea in the minds of the minister of education and his officials about what was most important in education, and what could be placed on a lower level of priority in times of financial difficulty. Provincial grants were paid for the construction of classrooms, but not for gymnasiums, auditoriums, teachers' rooms, or other such facilities. School boards might provide these, but had to do so solely at the expense of the local taxpayers. W.J. Dunlop left himself open to sharp criticism for using the term "frill" for such amenities. Since the department did not, until the end of the fifties, provide grants for school sites, opposition critics were able to point out that the land a school stood on was apparently considered to be a frill. During the sixties, the government's policy was eased. It even became possible to receive provincial support for a swimming pool provided that the school managed with a pool and one gymnasium where the enrolment would have justified the construction of two gymnasiums. Some educators were beginning to feel that if the need to reduce costs became sufficiently urgent, it might be better to build an auditorium, a gymnasium, a swimming pool, and a library and forget about the classrooms.

A much more constructive alternative to cutting back athletic, recreational, and cultural conveniences was to share them more fully with the community at large. Some of the major school systems such as those in Ottawa, North York, and Scarborough were demonstrating how the costs of construction could be shared with municipal councils, and the use of facilities could be made available to all citizens. School children had priority during the day and adults during the evenings and weekends. In this way, what might otherwise have been regarded as educational expenditure could be looked upon as investment in community improvement.

In an address delivered in the Legislature in March 1970, Tim Reid, the Liberal education critic, reviewed some of the large expenditures on construction and vocational equipment for the secondary schools and colleges of applied arts and technology, and deplored the duplication involved. "A carefully planned and well administered sharing of such expensive facilities and equipment," he said, "would not only reduce immediate and long-run construction costs, but would also reduce the total annual operating costs of vocational training in the colleges of applied arts and technology and in the secondary schools ..."[6] It was true that the supervisory powers of the Department of Education were exercised over the secondary schools and the colleges as if they were largely separate empires, and such a situation suggested the possibility of duplication. Before real savings could be expected from sharing arrangements, however, certain conditions had to exist: the equipment at one level had to be suitable for use at another; the equipment to be shared had to be under-utilized by the institution for which it was primarily provided; scheduling of use by the students of another institution had to be possible without excessive disruption of the program at the institution providing the service. Another factor to be considered was that the development of co-ordinating machinery required for complete sharing might lead to excessive centralization of authority over the institutions concerned. Despite these considerations, Reid was on solid ground in advocating a study of the situation.

There has been much invalid criticism of certain items of construction cost. Carpeting on floors may actually be the least expensive covering to install and maintain, to say nothing of its acoustical properties which may be an essential aspect of certain instructional techniques. Air conditioning alone may make it possible to use rooms without an exterior wall – rooms that may be constructed at considerably reduced expense in certain building plans. The same device may make a vital contribution to efficiency in summer courses, which have become an increasingly common feature in school programs.

The decline in the rate of increase in secondary school enrolment was expected to reduce the demand for further construction during the 1970s. Even if a point of numerical stability was reached, however, the continuation of population shifts would call for many additional new buildings. Where new suburban developments occurred, it would be practically impossible to avoid substantial investment for this purpose. A certain amount of expenditure could be postponed by continuing to use some of the old and often obsolete buildings in the central areas of cities and in long-established towns.

In the elementary schools, instructional salaries accounted for 60.0 per cent of total expenditure in 1950, 57.8 per cent in 1960, 54.0 per cent in 1965, and 56.7 per cent in 1970. Most of the rest of school board expenditure was for plant operation and maintenance, including administration and instructional supplies. Transportation costs and debt charges rose rather sharply during the period.

The prospect of reducing the rate of increase in teachers' salaries seemed less likely than in secondary schools. Although there were the same indications of an adequate supply, or even a surplus, of candidates for teaching at this level, what made the situation different was the clearly established policy of requiring progressively higher qualifications. There was no chance of a reversal of this policy on the grounds of cost short of a considerably more forbidding financial nightmare than any yet faced. Practically every vocal group had clamoured for the change for years, and the government had been consistently criticized for failing to move quickly enough. The increase in costs would be the result of two main influences: new teachers would enter the system at higher points on the salary schedule and the increased investment in pre-service preparation would presumably improve retention so that the balance would shift toward higher allowances for experience. Countering these influences would be the relative numerical stability in elementary school enrolment as compared with that at higher levels.

The main pressures for the construction of new elementary schools would come from population shifts and the desire to put into practice some of the instructional techniques revolving around the concept of the open classroom. School boards in urban areas were frequently criticized for using portable classrooms, even when it could be shown that these would tide a particular area over a temporary bulge in school enrolment as demographic development followed standard patterns. The portable came to be regarded as an example of educational deprivation. Thus it was hard to resist pressure to accommodate children in permanent structures. On the other hand, it was comparatively easy to retain older buildings with whatever implications they had for instructional methods. Some school boards would chafe over their inability to attract the best teachers when they could offer only obsolete facilities, but their case could not be expected to attract much sympathy under conditions existing during the early 1970s.

There was one influence that might result in unused classrooms even before a widespread acceptance of the philosophy of zero population growth. Large numbers of Roman Catholic children continued to attend the public schools in 1970, despite the enticements of the separate schools. Many did so because their parents were not persuaded of the desirability of segregation on religious grounds. Other parents had traditionally felt that the public schools offered a higher standard of education. When separate schools were forced to operate on much tighter budgets, and could not afford teachers' salaries or facilities comparable to those in the public schools, there may have been some basis for this belief. At least it is understandable that it should have been held, whether soundly based or not. However, the situation changed considerably during the 1960s. School board expenditure for 1968, divided by enrolment for 1968–9, produced an average of $477 per pupil in the Roman Catholic separate schools and $538 in the public schools. The narrowing of the difference in resources between the two systems had been achieved through the grant system. In 1968, provincial grants amounted to 40.7 per cent of public school board revenues and to 74.7 per cent of separate school board revenues. By 1968–9 the median salary for female separate school teachers was less than $400 lower than that for their counterparts in the public schools. It was suggested that separate schools were attracting enough pupils away from the public schools to cause some waste of facilities. On the other hand, a number of Roman Catholics feared that the trend toward integration of the elementary and secondary school levels might persuade some parents to enrol their children in the public schools from the beginning to avoid the awkwardness of a transfer at the end of grade 8 or grade 10, that is, unless the publicly supported separate school system was extended to the end of secondary school.

It was doubtful that worthwhile amounts of funds could be saved by restricting equipment and supplies in the elementary schools. The possibility of exploiting educational television, to which the province was deeply committed, depended on a large expenditure for receiving sets, video tape projectors, and other items. Because of the rapid advances in technology, substantial sums would have to be provided for replacements. Also, as learning was increasingly defined in terms of self-directed exploration and discovery, the need for more traditional materials such as library books, to say nothing of other items required in an up-to-date resources centre, continued to increase.

There was no objective way of determining what level of expenditure or what proportion of its financial resources Ontario society might be expected to devote to education. The past held no answers because the nature of current society, the character of economic and social issues, the accumulation of knowledge and the problems involved in its application, and the implications of the revolution in communications all combined to nullify the value of past experience. Although there might be value in studying the efforts of other provinces and countries, none of these could proclaim triumphantly that it had found the answers.

Ontario society could certainly afford to spend a much larger proportion of its income than even the maximum estimates based on a projection of the costs of the programs of the 1960s called for. While it might be realistic to say that the province had got involved in more than it *would* pay for, no one could honestly say that its commitments were more than it *could* pay for. During the post-war years, most of the population had got into the habit of expecting a steady rise in the standard of living. Increasing costs of education were assessed as a growing proportion of the extra increment in real income rather than as a threat to existing standards. The people as a whole were never confronted with the difficult decision whether or not to purchase more education at the sacrifice of some convenience or comfort already enjoyed. The issue was whether more education would limit the prospect of more entertainment, better clothing, a more luxurious automobile, better living quarters, or more liquor. The fact that some of the less fortunate groups such as pensioners and the unemployed did actually have to sacrifice at times for education does not change the overall situation.

The crisis over educational costs in the early 1970s reflected a lack of public confidence in the more enthusiastic claims for the economic and cultural values of education. It is always difficult to accept the contention that if one's neighbour is given special educational privileges, the result will be not only highly visible gains for him but ultimate, indirect, and diffuse benefits for oneself as well. When one begins to fear that the latter benefits are exaggerated or illusory, one's attitude toward the whole proposition becomes distinctly unfavourable. Despite the growing skepticism about the economic benefits of education, it is probable that the most serious doubts had to do with other aspects. Education had long purported to make its recipients better citizens, keener thinkers, more rational decision makers, and many other things that sounded very desirable and worth working for, but there seemed to be increasing grounds for uncertainty that the desired results were being achieved.

Educators contributed to the situation by losing the former air of certainty with which they proclaimed the values of education. No one saw as unequivocally in any subject of study the virtues that were once attributed to the supposed great mind-trainer, Latin. Education might be in a fundamentally healthier state when the multitude of unproved assumptions underlying practice were held up to scrutiny, but the new emphasis on research probably raised doubts that were reflected in public hesitation to provide financial support. Although it might seem commendable to conduct research for the improvement of education, a process that required so much improvement could obviously not be accepted on faith.

It is quite possible that misinterpretations of the implications of the knowledge explosion helped to create scepticism about the need to continue with a limitless expansion of the educational enterprise. Hordes of superficial thinkers repeated with an air of awe the statement that knowledge had increased at an accelerating rate until it reached the point about 1960 when it doubled every ten years. Apart from the disturbing tendency to equate knowledge with information, there may have been a reasonable basis for such a statement. But the average citizen could sense, if he did not articulate his suspicion, that there was something completely absurd in the deduction that so often followed: that the student must try to keep up with the development by using his memory more efficiently and stuffing his mind with greater and greater quantities of data. Although the capacities of the mind are impressive, and far from fully tapped, it takes only common sense to realize that any attempt to keep up with accumulating information would be futile, and that an educational system that undertook such a quest would not justify ever-growing infusions of funds.

In spite of all the uncertainties about the values of education, there were plenty of sound grounds for defending it as the most worthy preoccupation of a society that had found the means of meeting its basic material needs. Educators and leaders in other spheres of life had the responsibility of clarifying those grounds and of standing firmly on them. If they could assert with conviction, and could convince the public, that the truly educative society was the happy, the productive, and the fulfilling society, money problems would rapidly diminish.

A certain position taken by Walter Pitman, who acted as education critic for the New Democratic party until the leadership convention in the fall of 1970, was linked with efforts to reduce educational costs. He propounded the view, heard with increasing frequency during the previous two or three years, that a good deal of trouble in the secondary schools was caused by a rigid enforcement of compulsory education legislation that forced a number of young people to remain in school after they had become totally resistant to everything the school had to offer. At this and later stages, Pitman felt that opportunities for withdrawal should be accompanied by easier opportunities for re-entry at later stages when a little experience in the employment field had demonstrated the value of education. There would also have to be more numerous and adequate provisions for on-the-job training and night school.

To many educators, these opinions seemed to make good sense. While the educational system had to bear a considerable part, although by no means all, of the responsibility if young people became completely "turned off," there was no question that such individuals lowered the quality of education for all when they were forced to remain in school, and that compulsory attendance made them more antisocial than they would otherwise be. Yet it would be unrealistic to suppose that, if compulsory attendance were ended at fourteen instead of sixteen, large numbers of troublemakers would leave the schools and enable boards to reduce expenditure by substantial amounts. Regulations would have to be framed so that teachers could not oust students simply because they were unusually difficult to teach or because they passed through a temporary stage of uncooperativeness. Further, according to Pitman's scheme, an unknown part of what was saved by the early departure of those who reached an impasse would have to be spent to provide facilities for some of them to return after they had acquired a fresh incentive to learn.

Much of the trouble that Pitman identified was not the result of compulsory education in the narrow sense, but rather of society's insistence on the certificate or diploma that indicated the successful completion of a formal course. Young people who were convinced of the necessity of the end but saw little relevance in the means were a source of a more pervasive problem than those who saw no need for either. While something could be done to appease them by improving the quality of educational offerings, a fundamental solution for their difficulties lay in a changed social attitude that involved less reliance on formal documents and more on individualized appraisal. Once they could see that a particular line of study had a direct bearing on what they wanted to do later, rather than simply providing the means to surmount a barrier, their motivation might be expected to improve.

FORMATION OF COMMITTEE
TO INVESTIGATE EDUCATIONAL COSTS IN 1971

On taking over the portfolio of Education in the new Davis cabinet, Welch acted promptly to investigate the whole question of costs by appointing a Committee to Study the Costs of Education in the Elementary and Secondary Schools of Ontario. The study, under the direction of the former deputy minister, J.R. McCarthy, had six very comprehensive objectives:

1. To study the use of the financial resources being provided for elementary and secondary education in Ontario in the attainment of the educational goals;

2. To examine the present grant plan to determine if the various differentiating factors such as course, level – that is elementary and secondary – and type – ordinary and extraordinary – generate funds in proper balance consistent with the needs for the attainment of desirable educational objectives;

3. To examine the implications of ceilings on expenditures by local school boards, including the effect on the decision-making and autonomy of local school boards;

4. To examine the various aspects of school programmes with particular reference to innovations and new concepts, as, for example, the open plan organization, technical and commercial programmes, and use of educational technology, with a view to designing and recommending research studies to determine the effectiveness of these concepts in relation to the aims and objectives of education, these studies to be conducted by contract arrangements with research agencies;

5. To communicate and consult with groups and organizations representative of parents, teachers, trustees, students, and other interested parties;

6. After due study and consideration, to make recommendations and to submit a report or reports to the government with respect to the matters inquired into under the terms set out.

The auspices under which the study was to be conducted seemed well designed to counter any suggestion that the project was intended as a mere whitewash.[7]

TEN

Future prospects
for formal education

In some quarters disillusionment with schooling has reached the point where the school has been seen as a destructive institution. One of the more extreme positions on this issue has been taken by Ivan Illich in publications such as *De-Schooling Society*.[1] His case against the school includes a number of specific charges: that it discredits self-teaching; that, in fitting the individual into a niche defined by others, it prevents him from developing his own individuality; that it initiates man into a world where everything can be measured and, although personal growth is not in any real sense measurable, he comes to think of everything immeasurable as second class; and that it perpetuates and even accentuates social inequality rather than reducing it according to the common supposition.[2]

In his *Celebration of Awareness*, Illich characterizes the non-educational function of the school in severely condemnatory terms.

As much as anything else, schooling implies custodial care for persons who are declared undesirable elsewhere by the simple fact that a school has been built to serve them. The school is supposed to take the excess population from the street, the family, or the labor force. Teachers are given the power to invent new criteria according to which new segments of the population may be committed to a school. This restraint on healthy, productive, and potentially independent human beings is performed by schools with an economy which only labor camps could rival.[3]

It is not necessary to accept some of the most emphatic denunciations of the school in order to agree that the future may well see a drastic reduction in the importance of institutions of formal education in favour of educational experiences that are more directly related to community life. In support of this idea, attention is drawn to the multitudes of purposeful activities that characterize modern urban society. Through a carefully designed selection of contacts, in some cases prolonged into a brief period of service like that of secondary school students in the Occupations course under existing conditions, children and young people might observe how countless articles and substances are produced, distributed, exchanged, and used, how buildings, roads, bridges, sewers, and subways are constructed, how transportation and communication systems are operated, how order is maintained through the maintenance of police services and of the judicial system, how government is conducted at different levels and through different agencies. They might see at first hand how the surplus wealth of the community above that required for subsistence is devoted to recreational and cultural pursuits. They would be exposed to the best available manifestations of creative artistic expression. Much of their time would be spent in libraries or using library resources at home so that their minds could be transported beyond the immediate horizons in terms of both space and time. The best of television programs would be available to provide them with useful information and to fire their imagination.

Paul Goodman refers to educational activities that might be performed better by agencies other than the school: "Modern languages are best learned by travel ... Most of the money now spent for high schools and colleges should be devoted to the support of apprenticeships; travel; subsidized browsing in libraries and self-directed study and research; volunteer programmes at home and abroad; student political activities; rural reconstruction; work camps for projects in conservation and urban renewal."[4]

The proposed approach would differ in two fundamental ways from the kind of access children have to direct experiences organized by the schools under existing conditions. First, there would be a planned program for each child, which would enable him to obtain a systematic and comprehensive view of his environment through both direct and vicarious experience and to pursue a particular line of development in accordance with his talents and interests. Such a program would have to be devised under the guidance of an expert and sympathetic adult, who would be a successor to the traditional teacher. As the child grew in knowledge and competence, he would increasingly take responsibility for his own educational career. Second, adults engaged in all kinds of occupations – manufacturing, commerce, communications, personal service, construction, entertainment, artistic creation, and public service – would recognize and accept an educational role. They would expect to spend some of their time explaining to young learners, at times individually and often in groups, what they were doing, what feelings they had about their work, what significance they saw in it, if any, and whether or not they felt their example was one to be followed. There would be a new concept of work as a combination of doing and teaching.

The benefits from this procedure would not be by any means confined to the learner. While many people are not attracted to a career in teaching in the usual sense of the term, it is normal to enjoy communicating about matters within one's own range of experience. A regular opportunity, or even a kind of social obligation, to do so would lend a new sense of dignity and importance to various occupations. In many cases employees would feel less like the cogs in a machine to which advanced technology seems to have reduced them. Many a dull task might be enlivened if it were seen in part as a means of educating the young. Even the expert practitioner in a highly specialized field might benefit from occasional diversions from the straightforward exercise of the skills for which he was primarily trained. As automation reduced the need for many kinds of human effort, a general diffusion of the responsibility for education could help to take up the slack.

Those who participated in the process, or at least their employers, would have to have financial as well as social incentives for assuming the required role. Enterprises that were run for profit would have to be compensated for diverting some of their efforts from their primary objective. Thus there would be a need for the funds saved from the curtailed operation of schools, as Goodman suggests.

There would, of course, be some forms of learning that could not take place effectively in community institutions and agencies operated primarily for a non-educational purpose. The modified successor to the school would have to offer opportunities to learn skills such as reading, arithmetic, principles of good writing, and foreign languages. Children would go there when their over-all program indicated a need for the skill, and would stay only until they reached a level of competence that suited their purpose. Since the humanizing aspects of education would be adequately looked after through association with the teacher who was responsible for helping to plan their program, through contacts with the numerous incidental teachers whom they encountered in their varied experiences, and through play and other forms of recreation, skill training could make maximum use of programmed learning devices, films, television programs, and textbooks.

At the highest levels of skill training in fields such as engineering, the law, or medicine, training facilities would have to bear a considerable resemblance to existing professional schools. There would, however, be no attempt to offer instruction in anything but the skills needed for successful practice. The production of doctors, lawyers, and engineers with cultured minds and social consciences would require the non-institutional component of learning that was gained from informal experience. For skill training, maximum use would be made of successful practitioners as part-time instructors, as is often now the case. The liberal arts faculties of universities would operate in accordance with an ideal that has often been expounded but imperfectly followed. They would be essentially places where qualified people extended the intellectual and cultural resources of society, and justified their positions there solely on the basis of their proven ability to make such a contribution. Like the policeman, the bus driver, and the judge, their teaching contribution would arise from their expertise in their basic task, and would be offered only to those attracted by a genuine interest and sense of need. They would no longer be faced with masses of students primarily interested in securing the credit that resulted from the successful passing of an examination or the submission of acceptable term work.

Another successor to the present-day school would be the place where the learner would meet his guiding teacher from time to time to engage in individual consultation and to give an account of his progress. These meetings would supplement associations which the two would have on numerous occasions in the "field," when the teacher might guide groups of various sizes depending on the objective. There would also have to be a variety of places where children could meet for social activities, games, sports, clubs, model parliaments, and the like. These would be best regarded as community facilities catering to all age groups at appropriate times of the day. Thus it would be possible to avoid the impression of the school as a place where children are walled off from the outside world in an artificial little society of their own.

The question arises as to how candidates for various occupational roles would be evaluated if formal educational institutions ceased to perform the function. The answer is essentially that evaluation for certification is a need resulting from the alienation of the school from society. If young people's interests enabled them to seek education directly through experience, there would be no distinct hiatus between education and work; one would blend into the other. In acquiring information about a particular occupation, the individual would leave evidence of his interest and capacity that would probably be better indicators of success than any certificate or diploma he could earn in a school. His recommendation would come from his record as a student on the job. For many young people the scheme would in effect be a variant of the work-study concept.

What of the young people who would refuse to learn without the regimentation and discipline of the school? This question contradicts the assumptions on which the whole approach is based. One of these, already expounded in chapter 6, is that there is little value in those things that pass for learning as a result of compulsion. What penetrates the barriers of indifference, or is acquired as a response to extraneous motives, is soon sloughed off and forgotten. Real learning can result only from interest and need. It is assumed that the child has a natural desire to learn and to participate in the life of the community. Provided that he is not spoiled by threats to his security and the suppression of his natural curiosity, he will learn those things that seem relevant to his existence – an existence that encompasses the imagination and the intellect as well as the mundane experiences of ordinary life. Given the kind of family and neighbourhood environment from which many children emerge, however, it would be naive to suppose that they would all respond immediately and productively to the kind of freedom and individual responsibility that the school-in-society would offer. For some there would have to be institutional restraints, somewhat like those provided in the most enlightened correctional institutions. However, release would constantly beckon, not at some arbitrarily determined age level such as that marking the end of compulsory schooling, but as soon as the child was able to meet the challenge of freedom to pursue a constructive learning program.

Another group that would present special difficulties would be children in remote areas of the province and in rural communities where the range of human institutions and cultural contributions is limited. There is no easy solution for such children, whether education is provided within institutional walls or otherwise. Obviously much more of the process would have to be indirect and vicarious than in urban areas, although a prosperous society might find it advantageous to expend extra sums of money to enable the students to visit other parts of the province. The procedure would be increasingly feasible in financial terms because the proportion of the population outside urban areas is expected to continue to decline.

The value of education through direct experience has, of course, long been recognized in the field trip. At best, this device is carefully planned, systematic, and integrated with a broader learning program, and each child recognizes in it an individual objective. Instruction is shared by the teacher and those who are involved in the enterprise being observed, whether it is a museum with trained guides or a water purification plant where a manager takes the trouble to explain what is going on. However, when the field trip is a relatively rare event, it tends to be regarded as a special treat or a diversion from the serious business of schooling rather than the very essence of education.

Considerably closer to the school-in-society concept is the Summer of Experience, Exploration and Discovery (SEED) project introduced in the city of Toronto in 1968. A considerable number of pupils were given the opportunity to participate in a variety of challenging experiences which brought them into contact with experts in many fields. Some of them showed a keen interest in and an ability to profit from instruction in subjects normally considered beyond their age group. A major value of the program was the opportunity for direct contact with certain aspects of society that they would have learned about only vicariously in school.

In 1970 the SEED program was extended into the regular school year. The inspiration for this initiative was the "school without walls" concept developed in the Parkway program in Philadelphia by John Bremer. A controversy centred around Bremer when he emerged as the favoured candidate for the position of director of education in the Toronto system. The Board of Education was, however, prevented from hiring him when the minister of education took exception to his lack of qualifications in terms of Ontario requirements.

Bremer felt that the factory had been the model for the school in the previous century, and that the school had never recovered. In demanding factory-like efficiency, it destroyed the continuity of life. The curriculum reflected distinctions between learning and doing, between child and adult, between the academic and the "real" world.[5] The solution had to be more drastic than taking the students on an occasional field trip. They had to gain experiences in stores, offices, factories, and public institutions for sufficient time to learn what life was really like. The whole process was to be democratically organized to encourage students to take responsibility.

The students had to meet the state requirements for a high school diploma: four years of English and physical education and two years of mathematics and of American history and government. Attendance at scheduled activities was compulsory. The ultimate success of the program depended on how well its graduates did in college, in the job market, and in life in general. Apart from restrictions reflecting these realities, there was a great deal of freedom and spontaneity. The program offered a wide variety of electives that might be studied in realistic suroundings. The two tutors who accompanied each group of fifteen students were more like companions and guides than like the conventional teacher, although they were responsible for ensuring that each member of the group acquired the necessary basic skills. Freedom was reflected in the absence of restrictions on dress or on activities that were frowned on in some city schools, such as publishing a newspaper.

Many of the teachers who applied for positions in the program were eager to escape the same routine and regulations that oppressed so many students in regular schools. They welcomed the opportunity to treat each student as an individual and to help him devise a meaningful program. Not all the parents, however, were as enthusiastic as their offspring. They had difficulty getting over the idea that learning had to involve a room, a teacher, and a book. There was thus considerable pressure to demonstrate that the program could actually produce results.

The Parkway program was obviously quite conservative in comparison with the concept being expounded here in that the students were always subject to the implied threat that they might be put back in the ordinary program if they did not measure up. Thus there was little indication of what would happen if an attempt were made to handle most young people in the same way. Further, the impact of a few students pursuing educational experiences wherever they could find them gave no real indication of the impact on the community if education underwent a wholesale integration with other aspects of community life.

Schemes such as the Parkway and SEED programs are constantly menaced by the continued existence of the framework within which regular schools operate. There are standard requirements for graduation diplomas and admission to higher institutions which employers and education officials insist upon. Those who manage or participate as students in the innovative program are not really free to pursue new objectives, but are instead constantly on trial to show that they can beat regular classes at their own game. Thus the programs are prevented from demonstrating the full extent of their promise.

The success of the scheme under consideration here would depend on highly developed techniques of administration, not as they apply to the organization and management of school classrooms, but as they enable the individual to achieve his own objectives in complex and varied surroundings. The science of educational and psychological measurement would have to be developed to a high level and established principles expertly applied to ensure that each child's capacities, interests, and needs were identified with a reasonable degree of accuracy, and that his progress was continually assessed. The task of administration would then be to ensure that, at any given time and for the optimum period of time, each learner would be in what was for him the most fruitful learning environment. The tools, particularly the modern computer, are available for such a task, which would have been impossibly difficult a generation ago. The fact that they have not been fully applied to education merely indicates that technology has given this field a low priority.

If most children were to be educated in the suggested fashion, there would clearly have to be some major transformation in social practices and attitudes. Those working in various occupations and professions would have to acquire an entirely new outlook if they were called upon to serve as part-time teachers. Whether the political system was organized along capitalist or socialist lines, there would have to be safeguards to ensure that efficient production and distribution of goods and services was not excessively disrupted. Effective financing of the process would be a major challenge to administrative ingenuity.

Many adults, thinking of the special problems arising from youthful idleness during the traditional summer vacation, will be horrified at the thought of hordes of children dispersed through community institutions and agencies throughout the year. They feel, perhaps subconsciously, that the school walls serve as a protection as they go about the business of the adult world. In actual fact, the removal of the isolating influence of the school might eliminate the chief cause of alienation and misunderstanding. Young people brought up in closer contact with community life should feel less baffled by it and less inclined to drop out. Alternatively, if in a surge of youthful idealism they felt impelled to work for improvement and reform, they would be less inclined to approach the task with over-simplified, unrealistic solutions. There would be a better chance that people of all ages would face the bewildering pace of change with common understanding and on a united front.

The youthful sub-cultures that arise from the isolated environment of the school are in varying degrees unhealthy. They contain a strong element of resentment and blind resistance to adult authority and values, whether bad or good. They are characterized by views of adults as custodians, agents of repression, and hypocrites. The natural drive for independence is exaggerated to the point where self-destructive activities are embraced as acts of defiance. Every perceptive teacher knows that it is common for adolescents to resort to smoking, drinking, and drug-taking, not in spite of the school's propensity to inveigh against them, but because of it.

The close integration of education and life is thought to be the basic reason why primitive societies do not have this kind of sub-culture. Children acquire, in harmony with adults, the ability to function effectively as members of society. Each learning experience is clearly related to a vital aspect of life such as obtaining food and shelter, recreation, and worship. An advanced civilization may come to realize the advantage, even the necessity, of returning to a principle that unfortunately got lost along the path of progress. When it does, it will have gone far toward a solution to the problem of perpetual overt unrest on university campuses and that of more passive resistance at earlier levels of the educational system.

While the scheme would seem certain to dampen some of the more flamboyant and destructive protests of youth against various social, political, and economic aspects of the established order, it would by no means extinguish the idealistic ardour that characterizes that period of life. On the contrary, it would enable young people to learn specifically and at first hand where the real problems and difficulties lay. They might observe directly whether certain forms of work were more routine and deadly than they need be, whether labour unrest was caused primarily by inadequate remuneration or was a reaction against unnecessary regimentation and unpleasant working conditions. They would have a chance to judge for themselves whether the police had an unduly repressive attitude or reflected the views of most citizens toward law enforcement. They might form their own conclusions about the extent to which local politicians did their homework before making decisions affecting the prosperity and welfare of their fellow citizens. They might be a much greater threat to the complacent and to those with an easy conscience if they had the force generated by a combination of idealism and knowledge.

The concept of education as an inherent function of many social agencies is in harmony with progressive theories of education, although it would remove the barriers between the school and society rather than trying to make of the school a small replica of society. It assumes that an interest in every manifestation of the human spirit, including aesthetic and intellectual activities, is in harmony with direct involvement in the affairs of men. It assumes that a constructively critical attitude may develop from familiarity with such concerns rather than being stultified by them. If properly organized, of course, it would not require that everyone be immersed in a continuous swirl of activity, but would allow for the individual who found his most attractive learning environment in the library or the cloister. It differs fundamentally, however, from a certain traditionalist viewpoint, expounded very effectively by Northrop Frye, to the effect that the individual can appraise society objectively, and reach his highest intellectual development, only by withdrawal.[6]

A community-integrated education is not a utopian idea – a mere exercise of the imagination. Neither is it an immediate prospect that some political party could espouse as a panacea and proceed to berate the opposition for being too stodgy to support it. It is rather an objective toward which the Ontario system, surely one of the best in existence according to traditional standards, could be steered gradually as the necessary procedures are developed and the necessary public attitudes created. The isolation of particular schools could be broken down a small step at a time for selected groups in the hope that the advantages would be obvious enough to create pressure for more radical departures from tradition. Teachers would have to be prepared very carefully to avoid the adverse reaction that chaos would surely produce. The whole process would have to be facilitated by a carefully expressed rationale and by skilful and enthusiastic promotion. The utmost precautions would have to be taken to ensure that people did not equate the approach with the kind of permissiveness that encourages children to do whatever their whims dictate and in the process grow up self-centred, ignorant, and lazy.

It would be impossible to estimate beforehand how much the scheme would cost. Much would depend on the depth and variety of experience the children were given. Just like regular schooling, the program could be tailored somewhat to the public's ability and willingness to pay. However, to reiterate a view already expressed, Canadians have shown themselves unequivocally prepared to finance education at a high level provided that they have confidence in the value of the product. If their offspring were systematically integrated into the ordinary affairs of life, visibly learning and gradually working their way into productive roles, there would be every reason for gratification, and little temptation to pinch pennies.

Notes

CHAPTER 1

1 Dominion Bureau of Statistics, *Eighth Census of Canada, 1941*, Vol. II: *Population by Local Subdivisions* (Ottawa: King's Printer, 1944).

2 *Ring of Iron: A Study of Engineering Education in Ontario*. A report to the Committee of Presidents of Universities of Ontario, Toronto, December 1970.

3 Commission on Post-Secondary Education in Ontario, "Post-Secondary Education in Ontario: A Statement of Issues," 1970, p. 6.

4 Sylvia Ostry, *The Occupational Composition of the Canadian Labour Force*. One of a series of labour force studies in the 1961 Census Monograph Programme (Ottawa: Dominion Bureau of Statistics, 1967).

5 Ontario Council on Graduate Studies, "Supplement #1 to Survey of Employment of Ontario Ph.D. Graduates – 1964–69," January 1971.

CHAPTER 2

1 Dominion Bureau of Statistics, Education Division, Student Information Section, *Survey of Vocational Education and Training, 1968–69*, Ottawa: Information Canada, May 1971, pp. 107, 110.

2 Ontario, Legislative Assembly, *Debates*, 25th leg., 1st sess., 1 February 1956, p. 23.

3 *Ibid.*, 26th leg., 1st sess., 28 March 1960, p. 1812.

4 University of Toronto, *President's Report for the Year Ended June 1959*, p. 1.

CHAPTER 3

1 Ontario, Department of Education, *Report of the Minister, 1963*.

2 Ontario, Department of Education, *Programme of Studies for Grades I to VI of the Public and Separate Schools, 1937*.

3 Hilda Neatby, *So Little for the Mind* (Toronto: Clarke, Irwin, 1953).

4 Ontario, Legislative Assembly, *Debates*, 28th leg., 3rd sess., 8 April 1970, p. 1270.

5 Ontario, Provincial Committee on Aims and Objectives of Education in the Schools of Ontario, *Living and Learning* (Toronto: Newton Publishing, 1968), p. 157.

6 Robin S. Harris, *Quiet Evolu-*

tion: A Study of the Educational System of Ontario (Toronto: University of Toronto Press, 1967), p. 133.

7 "Merge education bodies – OSSTF," *Telegram*, 13 May 1971.

8 Ontario, Legislative Assembly, *Debates*, 29th leg., 2nd sess., 14 March 1972, p. 364.

9 Ontario, Legislative Assembly, *Debates*, 27th leg., 5th sess., 17 May 1967, p. 3541.

10 John P. Robarts, address given at the dedication of an addition to Southwood Secondary School, Galt, Ontario, 14 November 1967.

11 Ontario, Legislative Assembly, *Debates*, 28th leg., 2nd sess., 24 April 1969, p. 3505.

12 Revised Statutes of Ontario, 1960, "The Schools Administration Act," chap. 361, sec. 36.

13 Revised Statutes of Ontario, 1964, "An Act to Amend the Schools Administration Act," chap. 105, sec. 8.

14 Revised Statutes of Ontario, 1968, "An Act to Amend the Schools Administration Act," chap. 121, sec. 10.

15 Ontario, Legislative Assembly, *Debates*, 27th leg., 5th sess., 9 March 1967, p. 1212.

16 W.J. McCordic, "An Experiment in Metropolitan Government," *Canadian Education*, XIV, March 1959, pp. 3–15.

17 W.J. McCordic, "The New Challenge for Metro," address delivered at a meeting of the Ontario College of Education Chapter of Phi Delta Kappa, Toronto, 28 January 1966.

CHAPTER 4

1 *The Department of Education Act, The Schools Administration Act, The Secondary Schools and Boards of Education Act, The Public Schools Act*, and *The Separate Schools Act*.

2 Ontario, *Report of Royal Commission on University Finances*, vol. I (Toronto: King's Printer, 1921), p. 29.

3 University of Toronto, *President's Report for the Year Ended June, 1960*, pp. 9–10.

4 Presidents of the Universities of Ontario, Report to the Advisory Committee on University Affairs, *Post-Secondary Education in Ontario, 1962–1970*, May 1962, Revised January 1963 (Toronto, 1963), p. 28.

5 *Financing Higher Education in Canada*. Report of a Commission to the Association of Universities and Colleges of Canada, successor to the National Conference of Canadian Universities and Colleges, and its Executive Agency, the Canadian Universities Foundation, Vincent W. Bladen, chairman (Toronto: University of Toronto Press, 1965).

6 Ontario, Legislative Assembly, *Debates*, 27th leg., 2nd sess., 22 April 1964, p. 2333.

7 *Report of the Commission to Study the Development of Graduate Programmes in Ontario Universities to the Committee on University Affairs and the Committee of Presidents of Provincially-Assisted Universities, J.W.T. Spinks*, chairman (Toronto, November 1966).

8 *Ibid.*, p. 77.
9 "Report on the Joint OCUFA/ CPUO Meeting," *OCUFA News-letter*, IV, 2, November 1970, p. 1.
10 Ontario, Legislative Assembly, *Debates*, 27th leg., 5th sess., 5 June 1967, p. 4299.
11 *Ibid.*, 28th leg., 4th sess., 3 May 1971, p. 1112.
12 Committee of Presidents of Universities of Ontario, *Monthly Review*, II, 5, March 1971.
13 Ontario, Legislative Assembly, *Debates*, 28th leg., 4th sess., 25 May 1971, p. 1955.
14 Commission on Post-Secondary Education in Ontario, *Draft Report*, Douglas Wright, chairman (Toronto: Queen's Printer, 1971).

CHAPTER 5
1 "Brief on Libraries in Ontario presented to the Royal Commission on Education by the Ontario Library Association, 1945," in W. Stewart Wallace, *Report on Provincial Library Service in Ontario*, appendix B (Toronto: Ontario Department of Education, 1957), p. 38.
2 Francis R. St John Library Consultants Inc., *Survey of Libraries in the Province of Ontario, 1965* (Toronto: Ontario Library Association through the co-operation of the Ontario Department of Education, 1965), p. 20.
3 For example, see Ontario, Legislative Assembly, *Debates*, 28th leg., 3rd sess., 10 June 1970, pp. 3861–6.

CHAPTER 6
1 Honora M. Cochrane, ed., *Centennial Story: The Board of Education for the City of Toronto 1850–1950* (Toronto: Thomas Nelson & Sons, 1950), pp. 42–3.
2 *Ibid.*, pp. 211–12.
3 John Seath, *Education for Industrial Purposes* (Toronto: King's Printer, 1911), pp. 282–3.
4 J.M. McCutcheon, *Public Education in Ontario* (Toronto: T.H. Best, 1941), p. 187.
5 Ontario, Department of Education, *Programme of Studies for Grades I to VI of the Public and Separate Schools*, 1937, p. 5.
6 *Report of the Royal Commission on Education in Ontario, 1950*, J.A. Hope, chairman (Toronto: King's Printer, 1950), pp. 25–6.
7 Hilda Neatby, *So Little for the Mind* (Toronto: Clarke, Irwin, 1953).
8 J. Bascom St John, "Why the Children Forget History," *Globe and Mail*, Toronto, 14 February 1964.
9 Northrop Frye, ed., *Design for Learning*, Reports submitted to the Joint Committee of the Toronto Board of Education and the University of Toronto (Toronto: University of Toronto Press, 1962).
10 Ontario, Department of Education, Submission Regarding Allocation and Use of the UHF Broadcasting Band, 25 October 1966, p. 1. (Mimeographed.)
11 *Report of the Grade 13 Study Committee, 1964*, F.A. Hamil-

ton, chairman (Toronto: Ontario Department of Education, 26 June 1964), terms of reference.

12 Presidential Advisory Committee on Undergraduate Instruction in the Faculty of Arts and Science, University of Toronto, *Undergraduate Instruction in Arts and Science* (Toronto, 1967).

CHAPTER 7

1 *Report of the Royal Commission on Education in Ontario, 1950*, J.A. Hope, chairman (Toronto: King's Printer, 1950), p. 161.

2 Commission sponsored by the Canadian Association of University Teachers and the Association of Universities and Colleges of Canada, Report of the Commission, *University Government in Canada*, Sir James Duff and Robert O. Berdahl, commissioners (Toronto: University of Toronto Press, 1966).

CHAPTER 8

1 *A Consolidation of the British North America Acts 1867 to 1965*, consolidated as of 1 January 1967 (Ottawa: Queen's Printer, 1967), pp. 28–9.

2 Ontario, Legislative Assembly, *Debates*, 26th leg., 4th sess., 21 February 1963, p. 923.

3 Memorandum re the record of the Ecumenical Study Commission on Religion in Education to support the basic stance of the

Brief entitled "Equality in Education," presented to the Prime Minister and the Minister of Education by the Ontario Separate School Trustees' Association, 26 May 1969.

4 Inter-Church Committee on Protestant–Roman Catholic Relations, "Public Funds for Separate High Schools? Reasons for Maintaining the Integrity of the Ontario Public School System." [n.d.]

5 Ontario Separate School Trustees' Association, Brief entitled "Equal Opportunity for Continuous Education in the Separate Schools of Ontario," May 1969.

6 *Report of the Royal Commission on Bilingualism and Biculturalism*, I: *General Introduction* and *The Official Languages* (Ottawa: Queen's Printer, 1967), 122–3.

7 La Vie culturelle des franco-ontariens: Rapport du comité franco-ontarien d'enquête culturelle (Ottawa, Janvier 1969).

8 The Ontario Alliance of Christian Schools, "A Brief Submitted to the Cabinet of the Province of Ontario," July 1968.

9 The Parents Committee of Jewish Day Schools of the Province of Ontario, Submission of the Committee to the Prime Minister of Ontario and the Minister of Education for the Province of Ontario, January 1968.

CHAPTER 9

1 Edward E. Stewart, "The Role of the Provincial Government

in the Development of the Universities of Ontario, 1791–1964" (Ed. D. dissertation, University of Toronto, 1970), pp. 559–60.

2 Ontario, Committee on Taxation, *Report of the Ontario Committee on Taxation*, 3 volumes, L.J. Smith, chairman (Toronto: Queen's Printer, 1967).

3 Ontario, Department of Treasury and Economics, Economic Planning Board.

4 Ontario, *Expenditure Estimates, 1970–71* (Toronto: Queen's Printer, 1969–70).

5 Economic Council of Canada, *Second Annual Review: Towards Sustained and Balanced Economic Growth* (Ottawa: Queen's Printer, 1965), p. 90, citing J.R. Podoluk, *Earnings and Education*, Dominion Bureau of Statistics, 1965.

6 Ontario, Legislative Assembly, *Debates*, 28 leg., 3rd sess., 10 March 1970, p. 439.

7 *Ibid.*, 4th sess., 29 June 1971, p. 3347.

CHAPTER 10

1 Ivan Illich, *Deschooling Society* (New York: Harper & Row, 1970, 1971).

2 Ivan Illich, "The Roots of Human Liberation," *Times Educational Supplement*, 16 July 1971.

3 Ivan Illich, *Celebration of Awareness: A Call for Institutional Revolution* (New York: Doubleday, 1970), pp. 110–11.

4 Paul Goodman, "Pitiful Waste of Youthful Years," *Times Educational Supplement*, 16 July 1971.

5 Stratton Holland, "This Philadelphia School Uses the Whole City as Its Classroom," *Toronto Daily Star*, 15 March 1969.

6 Freeman K. Stewart, ed., *The Aims of Education*, Conference Study No. 1 (Ottawa: Canadian Conference on Education, 1961).

General index

Act to Improve the Common and Grammar Schools of the Province of Ontario, 179

Adult education, associations for, 168–9

Adult Occupational Training Act, 17, 276

Advisory Committee on University Affairs, 121, 122, 124–5

Advisory committees established by boards of education, 105

Advisory Council of Directors, Metropolitan Toronto School Board, 114

Advisory Council on Education, 71

Advisory vocational committees, 99

Age distribution of Ontario population, 34

Air Services Training School, 157

Albion Hills Conservation School, 149

Algoma College, 60

Allanburg Women's Institute, 59

Althouse College of Education, 47, 48

Applied Arts and Technology Branch, Department of Education, 24, 79, 88, 92, 151

Apprenticeship Act, The, 151

Archives, provincial, 151, 152

Archbishops' Commission, 259

Art Gallery of Ontario, 148

Arts and Science Branch under Reorganized Program, 41, 204

Assessment, 278–9

Associated High School Boards of the Province of Ontario, 166

Association canadienne-française de l'Ontario, 267

Association des commissions des écoles bilingues d'Ontario, 100, 166

Association of Directors of Education of Ontario, 166

Association des enseignants franco-ontariens, 164

Association of Secondary School Superintendents, 166

Associations concerned with education, 162–70

Assumption College, 50, 53–4

Assumption University of Windsor, 55

Atkinson, Charitable Foundation, 192, 193, 235

Atkinson, College, York University, 18

Atkinson Study of Utilization of Student Resources, 27, 191–2, 209, 235

Baldwin Act, 1849, 65

Basilian Order, 54

Bill 140, 1968, 265

Bill 141, 1968, 265

Birth rate in Ontario, 33

Board of Broadcast Governors, 202

Boards of education, origin of, 70

Boy Scouts of Canada, 168

Boys' Clubs of Canada, 168

British North America Act, 254, 255, 263
Brock University, 59
Brock University Act, The, 59
Brock University Founders' Committee, 59
Business and Commerce Branch under Reorganized Program, 204

Canada Council for the Encouragement of the Arts, Humanities and Social Sciences, 159
Canadian Association for Adult Education, 169
Canadian Association for the Social Studies, 167
Canadian Association of University Teachers, 164–5, 227
Canadian Broadcasting Corporation, 196, 199, 202, 203; School Broadcasts Department of, 196
Canadian Council for Educational Research, 234
Canadian Council for Research in Education, 168
Canadian Council of Teachers of English, 167
Canadian Education Association, 161, 162, 163, 234; Standing Committee of Ministers of Education of, 161
Canadian Girls in Training, 168
Canadian Government Travel Bureau, 158
Canadian Institute of Chartered Accountants, 8
Canadian International Development Agency, 157
Canadian Library Association, 144–5
Canadian National Commission for UNESCO, 160; Associated Schools Project of, 161
Canadian Penitentiary Service, 157
Canadian Teachers' Federation, 156, 164, 234

Canterbury College, 57
Carleton University, 7, 52, 228–9
Carnegie Corporation of New York, 233, 235
Carnegie Study of Identification and Utilization of Talent in High School and College, 235
Celebration of Awareness, 303
Centennial College of Applied Arts and Technology, 23
Churches, educational role of, 169
Civil Service Association of Ontario, 165
Claremont Conservation Field Centre, 149–50
College Entrance Examination Board, 191
Colleges of agricultural technology, 4, 149
Colleges of applied arts and technology, 22–5, 26, 291–2; enrolment in, 48–9; faculty representation in, 165; founding of, 48–9
Comité franco-ontarien d'enquête culturelle, 266
Commercial courses, early development of, 183
Commission on Post-Secondary Education in Ontario, 10, 23, 26, 138–41, 286, 287, 289
Committee of Board Chairmen, Metropolitan Toronto School Board, 114
Committee on Government Productivity, 93
Committee of Ontario Deans of Engineering, 7
Committee of Presidents of Universities of Ontario, 46, 52, 59, 123, 125, 129, 130, 131, 132, 133, 134, 135, 136, 137, 167; Committee on the Co-ordination of Academic Library Services of, 130; Joint Ad-Hoc Subcommittee on Regional Computing Centres of, 131;

Presidents' Research Committee of, 132; Subcommittee on Computer Services of, 131; Sub-committee on Librarianship of, 130

Committee to Study the Costs of Education in the Elementary and Secondary Schools of Ontario, 301–2

Committee on University Affairs, 125, 126, 131–2, 133, 134, 135, 136, 165, 286

Common School Act, 1816, 64

Community Programs Branch, Department of Education, 150

Computer assisted instruction, 198–9

Conservative party, policy re extension of separate schools of, 261

Consolidated school sections, 66

Consultative committees in counties and territorial districts, 95

Continuation schools, 69; origin of, 255

Costs of education, 272–302; projections of, 284–5; proposals for reducing, 286–302

Council of Ministers of Education of Canada, 161–2, 203, 206

Council of Ontario Universities, 136, 167, 286

Council of Public Instruction, 65

Council of Regents, Colleges of Applied Arts and Technology, 86

County boards of public instruction, 65

Crusader Cycle Club, 152

Cumming report, 107

Curriculum: changes in elementary schools in the 1960s in, 217–19; changes in secondary schools in late 1960s in, 210–12; characteristics of in early twentieth century, 181–4; in nineteenth-century Ontario schools, 176–80; reforms of 1930s in, 184–7

Curriculum Branch (Section), Department of Education, 84–5, 195, 218

Curriculum Bulletin No. 5, 218

Department of Agriculture and Food, 149

Department of Civil Service (Ontario), 155

Department of Correctional Services, 149, 150

Department of Education: activities of in educational television, 200–3; Applied Arts and Technology Branch of, 24, 79, 86, 88, 92, 151; Blind and Deaf Division (Section) of, 87; Business Management Program of, 87; Community Programs Branch of, 74, 87, 150, 158; Correspondence Courses Division (Section) of, 97; Curriculum Branch (Section) of, 84–5, 195, 218; Departmental Business Administration Branch of, 88; Division of School Planning and Building Research of, 88; Education Data Centre of, 88; establishment of, 65; ETV section of Curriculum Division of, 201, 202; Grants Division of, 88; growth of powers of, 67; Information Branch of, 89; Instruction Division of, 83–4; involvement in research of, 235–6; News and Information Services of, 89; Personnel Branch of, 79; Physical and Health Education Branch of, 74; Policy and Development Council of, 72, 79; Professional Development Branch of, 76; Program Branch of, 80, 83–4, 210; Provincial Library Service of, 88, 142, 143; Provincial Schools and Further Education Division of, 86; regional offices of, 83; Registrar's Section of, 84; relationship to Ontario Curriculum Institute of, 238; reorganization of, 76–92; School Business Administration Branch of, 82, 88; School Plant Approvals Unit of, 89; Schools for Retarded Children Division (Section) of, 87; Special Schools and Services Branch of, 87; Superintendency of Curriculum in, 76; Superintendency of Special Services in, 76; Supervision Division (Section) of, 80; Teacher Education Branch of, 76, 86; Technological and Trades Training Branch of, 79; Youth Branch of, 79; Youth and Recreation Branch of, 79, 87–8

Department of Educational Research, Ontario College of Education, 190, 191, 233, 235–6

Department of Energy and Resources Management (Ontario), 149, 152

Department of Fisheries and Forestry (Canada), 158

Department of Health (Ontario), 153

Department of Highways, 154

Department of Indian Affairs and Northern Development, 155

Department of Justice (Ontario), 149

Department of Lands and Forests (Ontario), 149, 151, 152, 154

Department of Mines (Ontario), 150, 152, 154

Department of Municipal Affairs, reform of assessment practices by, 278

Department of National Defence, 156

Department of National Health and Welfare, 157

Department of the Provincial Secretary and Citizenship, 150, 151

Department of Public Records and Archives, 151

Department of Social and Family Services, 153; Advisory Council for Public Welfare Training of, 154

Department of Tourism and Information, 151

Department of Transport (Canada), 157; Meteorological Service of, 158

Department of Transport (Ontario), 152

Department of Treasury and Economics, Economic Planning Branch of, 283–4

Department of University Affairs, 124–5, 134, 136, 289

Department of Veterans Affairs, 16

Departmental Business Administration Branch, Department of Education, 88

Departmental grade 12 testing program, 192

Departmental lower school examinations, 73

Departmental middle school examinations, 73

Deputy ministership of education, 80

De-Schooling Society, 303

Design for Learning, 193

Development in education, 232

District boards of education, 64, 65

District high schools, 70–1

Division of School Planning and Building Research, Department of Education, 88

Dominion Bureau of Statistics, 161

Duff-Berdahl report, 226, 242

Economic Council of Canada, Second Annual Review of, 286

Ecumenical Institute of Canada, 259

Education Data Centre, Department of Education, 88

Education for Industrial Purposes, 183

Educational Television Branch, Department of Education, 85, 202, 203

Elementary school buildings, 37–9

Elementary school system, establishment of, 64–8

English Catholic Education Association, 257

Enrolment: in Ontario elementary schools, 35–7; in Ontario private schools, 72; in Ontario schools, 32–7, 39–41; in Ontario secondary schools, 40–1

Equal Opportunity for Continuous Education in the Separate Schools of Ontario, 260

Erindale College, 60

Essentialist philosophy in education, 174–6

Essex College, 55

Examinations, 190–2; departmental grade 13, 191, 206–9, 235; early development of, 181; high school entrance, 190

Extended Graduate Program, 122

Facilities, school, 295–6

Farm Tax Reduction Program, 285

Federal government involvement in education, 155–61

Federal-Provincial Technical and Vocational Training Agreement, 20, 41–2, 47; Program 5 of, 17

Federation of Catholic Parent-Teacher Associations of Ontario, 105, 168

Federation of Women's Teachers' Associations of Ontario, 72, 163–4

Fifth classes, 255

Financing Higher Education in Canada, 123

Five-year program in secondary schools, 204

Ford Foundation, 237, 238

Ford Motor Company, 256

Forest Hill Board of Education, 106–7

Forest Ranger School, Dorset, 149

Four-year program in secondary schools, 204–6

Francis R. St. John Library Consultants Inc., 88, 144

Free Libraries Act, 1882, 142

French, use of in Ontario schools, 261–70

French-language advisory committees, 99, 265–6

French language schools, committee on, 94

General and Advanced Committee (for grade 13 reform), 207–8

General Board of Education, 64

General course in secondary schools, 182

George Brown College of Applied Arts and Technology, 48

German, use of in Ontario schools, 261, 262

Gerstein lectures, 1966, 126

Girl Guides of Canada, 168

Grade 13 Study Committee, 207, 208, 209

Grading in schools, emergence of, 180–1

Graduate Students' Union, University of Toronto, 29

Grants Division, Department of Education, 88

Grants to school boards, 278

Guelph Agricultural College, 4

Hadow reports, 73, 184

Hamilton Institute of Textiles, 6

Hamilton Teachers' College, 43, 44

Handicapped, classes for, 294–5

High school entrance examination, 69

Holy Redeemer College, 57
Home and School councils, 105
Huntington University, 58

Immigration statistics for Ontario, 33, 34
Imperial Oil, 234
Implementation Committee (for grade 13 reform), 208
Indians, education of, 156
Individualized instruction, 219
Industrial Education Act, 1911, 183
Information Branch, Department of Education, 89
Institute of Chartered Accountants of Ontario, 8
Institute of Child Study, University of Toronto, 234
Instruction Division, Department of Education, 83–4
Inter-Church Committee on Protestant-Roman Catholic Relations, 260
Interim school organization committees, 100
International Reading Association, 167
Iona College, 57

Jesuit Order, 58
Jewish schools, 270
Joint Committee of the Toronto Board of Education and the University of Toronto, 193, 194, 195, 218
Junior Forest Ranger program, 152

Kindergartens, emergence of, 181

Lakehead College of Arts, Science and Technology, 58
Lakehead Teachers' College 44, 86
Lakehead Technical Institute, 6, 58
Lakehead University, 47, 58
Lakeshore District Board of Education, 107
Lakeshore Teachers' College, 44
Laurentian University, 50, 58, 60
Laurentian University Act, The, 1960, 58
Law Society of Upper Canada, 9
Liberal party, policy on school grants of, 281, 282; support for extension of separate schools by, 260
Libraries, association, 142, 143
Library Association and Mechanics Institute Act, 1851, 142
Library boards, public, 143
Library co-operatives: county, 143, 144; regional, 144
Library systems, regional, 143–4
Living and Learning, 30, 31
London Teachers' College, 43

McArthur College of Education, 47
Macdonald Institute, 149
McLaughlin Planetarium, 147
McMaster University, 49
MacLeod Committee. See Minister's Committee on the Training of Elementary School Teachers
Macpherson report, 224
Man in Society course, 205
Matriculation examinations, 69
Mechanics' institutes, 142
Media, educational, 196–204
Medical Research Council, 159
Medical profession, increased training needs of, 8
Metropolitan Educational Television Association (META), 200, 202
Metropolitan School Board, 108, 109, 110, 111, 112
Metropolitan Toronto Act, The, 108
Metropolitan Toronto and Region Conservation Authority, 149
Metropolitan Toronto School Board, 113, 114, 115, 116; Advisory Committee of Directors of Educa-

tion of, 114; Committee of Board Chairmen of, 114

Metropolitan Toronto school system, development of, 106–16

Minister's Committee on the Training of Elementary School Teachers (MacLeod Committee), 12, 43, 44, 86, 222

Ministers' Information Systems Committee, 161, 236

Model schools, Roman Catholic, 255

National Advisory Council on School Broadcasting, 196, 199

National Conference of Canadian Universities, 50, 120

National Film Board, 158, 160

National Library of Canada, 160

National Museums of Canada, 160

National Research Council, 159

New Democratic party: policy on school grants of, 281, 282; support for extension of separate schools by, 260

News and Information Services, Department of Education, 89

Nipissing College, 60

North Bay College, 60

North Bay Teachers' College, 43

Northeastern University Executive Council, 60

Northern Corps of Teachers, 99

Northern Ontario Public and Separate School Trustees' Association, 166

Nursing education, 8–9

Occupational program in Reorganized Program, 41, 204

Ontario Admission to College and University (OACU) program, 209

Ontario Agricultural College, 119, 149

Ontario Alliance of Christian Schools, 270

Ontario Association for Continuing Education, 169

Ontario Association of Education Officials, 166

Ontario Association of School Superintendents and Directors, 166

Ontario College of Education, 46–7, 233, 235, 236, 238–9; Department of Educational Research of, 235–6; Vocational Department of, 47

Ontario Committee on Taxation (Smith Committee), 96

Ontario Conference on Education, 71

Ontario Conference on Local Government, 150

Ontario Council on Graduate Studies, 30, 129, 286

Ontario Council (Confederation) of University Faculty Associations, 122, 129, 136, 165, 227, 290

Ontario Council of University Librarians, 130

Ontario Curriculum Institute, 193–6, 218, 236, 247

Ontario Educational Association, 67, 71, 163, 167; Ontario Principals' Section of, 166; Research Section of, 234–5

Ontario Educational Communications Authority, 85, 131, 203

Ontario Educational Research Council, 167–8, 235, 251

Ontario English Catholic Teachers' Association, 164

Ontario Federation of Community College Faculty Associations, 165

Ontario Federation of Home and School Associations, 168

Ontario Fire College, Gravenhurst, 149

Ontario Foundation Tax Plan, 77–8, 257

Ontario Graduate Fellowship Pro-

gram, 122
Ontario Institute for Studies in Education, 83, 90, 91, 209, 223, 236–51, 292; Academic Council of, 240, 241, 243, 245; Administrative Council of, 242; contributions of, 247–51; field centres of, 247; Institute Assembly of, 244
Ontario Library Association, 143, 144
Ontario Mathematics Commission, 192, 193
Ontario Municipal Board, 107, 113
Ontario New Universities Library Project, 122
Ontario Police College, Aylmer, 149
Ontario Public School Men Teachers' Federation, 72, 164
Ontario Public School Trustees' Association, 166
Ontario School for the Blind, 42, 74, 87
Ontario Schools for the Deaf, 42, 74, 87
Ontario School Trustees' Council, 103, 166
Ontario School Trustees' and Municipal Councillor's Association. See Ontario School Trustees' and Ratepayers' Association
Ontario School Trustees' and Ratepayers' Association, 166
Ontario Science Centre, 151
Ontario Secondary School Headmasters' Association, 166
Ontario Secondary School Headmasters' Council, 166
Ontario Secondary School Teachers' Federation, 72, 92–3, 115, 164, 166, 293
Ontario Separate School Trustees' Association, 100, 166, 260
Ontario Teachers' Association, 67
Ontario Teachers' Federation, 73,

101, 103, 163, 164, 209, 222, 223, 235, 237; Committee on Mathematics and Science of, 192
Ontario Teachers' Union, 67
Ontario Universities Capital Aid Corporation, 134
Ontario Universities' Council on Admissions, 130
Ontario Universities' Television Council, 131
Ontario Urban and Rural School Trustees' Association, 166
Ontario Veterinary College, 149
Ontario Vocational Centre, London, 48
Ontario Vocational Centre, Ottawa, 48
Ontario Vocational Centre, Sault Ste Marie, 48
Ontario Vocational College, Hamilton, 46
Osgoode Hall, 9
Ottawa Public School Board, introduction of French in elementary schools by, 269
Ottawa Separate School Board, protest against restrictions on use of French in schools by, 262–3
Ottawa Teachers' College, 43

Parkway program, 307–8
Peterborough Teachers' College, 43
Policy and Development Council, Department of Education, 72, 79
Porter Plan, 188–9
Private schools, enrolment in, 42
Professional associations, educational role of, 168
Program Branch, Department of Education, 80, 83–4, 210
Program 5, 17
Programmed learning, 197–8
Progressive philosophy in education, 174–6, 184–7, 189

Province of Ontario Council for the Arts, 145–6
Provincial Committee on Aims and Objectives of Education in the Schools of Ontario (Hall-Dennis Committee), 11, 26, 30, 90–2, 145, 210, 218–23, 258, 260
Provincial Committee on Taxation (Smith Committee), 279, 280
Provincial government departments, educational activities of, 148–55
Provincial Institute of Automotive and Allied Trades, 48
Provincial Institute of Mining, 6, 48
Provincial Institute of Trades, 6, 48
Provincial Institute of Trades and Occupations, 48
Provincial Library Council, 144
Provincial Library Service, Department of Education, 88, 142, 143
Provincial Schools and Further Education Division, Department of Education, 86
Public Funds for Separate Schools?, 260
Public Libraries Act, The, 1966, 144
Public library system, 142–5
Public School Trustees' Association of Ontario, 166, 256
Public Service Commission of Canada, 158
Pupil-teacher ratios in Ontario schools, elementary, 39

Queen's University, 49, 50, 118–19; McArthur College of Education, 47
Quiet Evolution, 92

Radio, as used in education, 196–7
Regional offices, Department of Education, 83
Registered nursing assistants, 8–9
Registrar's Section, Department of Education, 84
Regulation 17, 262, 263
Rehab School, Toronto, 7
Religious education, 185
Reorganized Program (Robarts Plan), 4, 5, 17, 21, 22, 25, 41, 47, 77, 177, 204, 206, 210, 259; Arts and Science Branch under, 21, 41; Business and Commerce Branch under, 21, 204; Occupational Program under, 22, 41; Science, Technology, and Trades Branch under, 21
Report of the Commission to Study the Development of Graduate Programmes in Ontario Universities (Spinks report), 127
Research in education, 231–51
Retarded Children's Education Authorities, 87
Ring of Iron, 7
Robarts Plan. *See* Reorganized Program
Rockefeller Foundation, 234
Roman Catholic Bishops of Ontario, brief to provincial government of, 257
Roman Catholic separate schools, 252–61
Royal Canadian Academy of the Arts, 163
Royal Canadian Institute, 163
Royal Commission on Bilingualism and Biculturalism, 264–5, 269
Royal Commission on Education, 1945–50, 19, 72, 74, 75, 187–8, 194, 220, 234, 256–7, 263–4
Royal Military College, Kingston, 156
Royal Ontario Museum, 146–8; Division (Department) of Education of, 147; Saturday Morning Club of, 147
Royal Society of Canada, 163

Ryerson Institute of Technology. *See* Ryerson Polytechnical Institute

Ryerson Polytechnical Institute (Ryerson Institute of Technology), 6, 22, 23, 48, 153, 155

Sacred Heart College, 50, 58
St Catharines Teachers' College, 44
St George's School for Child Study, 233–4
St Jerome's College, 50, 57
St John report, 144
Scarborough College, 60
School Act of 1841, 65
School Act of 1850, 65
School administrators, associations of, 165–6
School board amalgamation, 1969, implications of for teachers, 101
School Business Administration Branch, Department of Education, 82, 88
School grants, 99
School of Mining and Agriculture, Kingston, 119
School Plant Approvals Unit, Department of Education, 89
School of Practical Science, 119
Schools for the handicapped: Ontario School for the Blind, Brantford, 42, 74, 87; Ontario Schools for the Deaf, Belleville, Milton, 42, 74, 87
Science, Technology, and Trades Branch, Reorganized Program, 204
Secondary school building, 41–2
Secondary school system, establishment of, 68–71
SEED program, Toronto, 307, 308
Select Committee of the Legislature on The Municipal and Related Acts (the Beckett Committee), 96, 97

Select Committee on Youth, 93
Separate school unit reorganization, 1969, 100–1
Service for Admission to College and University program, 209
Service clubs, educational role of, 169
So Little for the Mind, 75, 189
Society of Industrial and Cost Accountants, 155
Special Schools and Services Branch, Department of Education, 87
Special Vocational program, 41
Spinks report. *See Report of the Commission to Study the Development of Graduate Programmes in Ontario Universities*
Standing Committee on Broadcasting, Films and Assistance to the Arts, 203
Standing Committee of Ministers of Education, CEA, 161
Stratford Teachers' College, 43
Study of Educational Facilities, 295
Sudbury Teachers' College, 44

Taxation for school purposes, real estate tax, 278–83
Teacher Education Branch, Department of Education, 76, 86
Teacher preparation, 11–16, 86; High School Assistant's course, Type A, 46; High School Assistant's course, Type B, 46; Industrial Arts and Crafts program, 46; Intermediate Home Economics course, 46; Ordinary Vocational program, 46; special summer courses, 47; for vocational teachers, 48
Teachers' colleges, enrolment in, 43–4
Teachers' federations, 163–4
Teachers' salaries: elementary, 297–8; secondary, 293–4
Teaching certificates: Deferred In-

terim First Class, 12; Interim First Class, 12

Teaching Profession Act, The, 1944, 73, 164, 166

Technical Education Act, 1919, 184

Technical and Vocational Training Assistance Act, 1960, 17, 20

Technological and trades training, enrolment in institutions for, 48

Technological and Trades Training Branch, Department of Education, 79

Television, educational uses of, 199–204

Tests, 190–2; departmental grade 12 testing program, 235; departmental grade 13 examinations, 192

Textbooks, 186; emergence of uniform, 181

Thornlea High School, Thornhill, 211

Thornloe University, 58

Tiny case, 255–6

Toronto Board of Education, 106, 107, 147

Toronto and Suburban Planning Board, 107

Toronto Teachers' College, 43

Toronto and York Planning Board, 107

Traditionalist philosophy in education, 174–6, 187

Transfer review boards, proposals for, 102

Trent University, 59

Universities Capital Aid Corporation, 124

Universities: faculty representation in, 164–5; federal subsidies to, 120; formula financing of, 133–5; post-war growth of, 49–60; relations of with provincial government, 117–41

University Committee, 121

University government, 225–9; faculty participation in, 227; student participation in, 228–9

University Government in Canada, 226

University of Guelph, 4, 149

University Matriculation Board, 206

University of Ontario, 139; proposals for, 127–8

University of Ottawa, 47, 49, 50, 52

University of Ottawa Normal School, 263

University of Ottawa Teachers' College, 44, 86

University of Sudbury, 50

University of Sudbury Act, The, 1957, 58

University of Toronto, 49–50, 53, 60, 119–20, 137, 224, 225, 226, 228, 229, 240; Extension Division of, 148; Faculty of Law of, 9

University of Waterloo, 50, 57–8, 221

University of Western Ontario, 49, 50, 54, 120, 229; Althouse College of Education of, 47, 48

University of Windsor, 50

Upper Canada Village, 152

Vocational advisory committees, 69

Vocational education, early development of, 183–4

Vocational schools, control of, 69–70

Waterloo College, 50, 57; Associate Faculties of, 57

Waterloo Lutheran University, 50, 57

Weston Board of Education, 107

White, John, 229

Windsor Board of Education, involvement of in separate school issue, 256

Windsor Teachers' College, 43, 86

Women's Institutes, 169

World Politics course in secondary
schools, 205
York University, 52–3, 60
Young Men's Christian Association
(YMCA), 168
Young Women's Christian Associ-
ation (YWCA), 168

Youth Branch, Department of Education, 79
Youth organizations, educational
role of, 168
Youth and Recreation Branch, Department of Education, 79, 87–8

Index of persons

Althouse, J.G., 74, 77, 121
Arthur, M. Elizabeth, 133

Bériault, R., 265
Bishop, A.W., 84
Bissell, C.T., 122
Bladen, Vincent, 123
Blatz, William, 233–4
Bremer, John, 307, 308
Brown, C.A., 84, 206
Bruner, Arnold, 89
Bruner, Jerome, 194

Cameron, Maxwell, 233
Campbell, T.I., 77, 78, 79, 90
Cannon, C.F., 121
Crossley, J.K., 195
Cumming, Lorne R., 107

Davis, W.G., 72, 92, 93, 137, 236,
   294–5; administrative style of, 80;
   contribution to educational research and development by, 238–
   40; delivery of Gerstein Lectures,
   1966, by, 287; establishment of
   French-language schools by, 265;
   establishment of Ontario Educational Communications Authority
   by, 85; establishment of Policy and
   Development Council by, 79–80;
   explanation of curriculum changes
   in secondary schools in late 1960s
   by, 211–12; involvement of in
   educational television, 200, 203;
   policy re extension of separate
   schools of, 261; program for educational reform instituted by, 232;
   reconstitution of Committee on
   University Affairs by, 124–5; reorganization of Department of
   Education by, 76–92; restraints on
   school board expenditure by, 283;
   role of in curriculum reform, 196
   role of in establishing Council of
   Ministers of Education, 161–2;
   school board amalgamation by,
   95–106; on university-government
   relationships, 126–7
Dennis, Lloyd, 222
Dewey, John, 175, 184
Drew, George, 73, 74, 281
Duffin, G.L., 68, 84
Dunlop, W.J., 19, 50, 51, 59, 68,
   75, 76, 189, 296

Egerter, Mrs Grover, 59
Elborn, H.E., 84

Ferguson, G.H., 66
Froebel, Friedrich, 181
Frost, L.M., 51, 59, 121, 281
Frye, Northrop, 193, 310

Goldenberg, H. Carl, 111, 112
Goodman, Paul, 304, 305
Grant, G.M., 119
Greer, V.K., 67
Griffith, B.A., 51

Hagey, J.G., 57

Hall, G.E., 206
Harris, R.S., 92, 193, 235
Hepburn, Mitchell, 74, 256
Herbart, J.F., 182
Hope, J.A., 74

Ide, T.R., 85, 202
Illich, Ivan, 303

Jackson, R.W.B., 233, 234, 236, 241
Johnston, L.M., 24, 79, 84, 92

Keddy, J.A., 88
Kerr, G.A., 138
Ketchum, P.A.C., 191
Kinlin, J.F., 84, 94, 195
Koerber, W.F., 79

Long, John A., 107, 233, 234

Macaulay, Robert, 78
McCarthy, J.R., 80, 82, 83, 92, 121,
   190, 194, 302
McCordic, W.J., 107, 108, 114
Macdonald, J.B., 126, 136
McKague, A.H., 84
MacNaughton, Charles, 104, 279
Merchant, F.W., 71, 160, 262, 263
Minkler, F.W., 5, 236
Morgan, J.R.H., 237–8
Mustard, Thornton, 73, 184

Neatby, Hilda, 75, 189
Needles, Ira, 57
Nixon, Robert, 95, 103, 261

Orlowski, S.T., 89

Parnall, M.B., 84, 195
Patterson, Z.R., 88
Pelletier, Gérard, 203
Penfield, Wilder, 268
Phillips, C.E., 184
Phimister, Z. S., 80, 82
Pitman, Walter, 170, 300–1

Piux ix, 254
Porter, Dana, 75, 121, 188

Reid, Timothy, 85, 138, 296
Rendall, S.D., 21
Rickover, Admiral H., 212
Rivers, F.S., 82
Robarts, J.P., 26, 59, 76, 77, 78, 96,
   97, 121, 124, 125, 130, 161, 217,
   218, 257, 258, 265, 270, 280
Robb, I.M., 293
Robinson, G. de B., 51
Robinson, S.G.B., 293
Roedde, W.A., 88
Ross, G.W., 262
Rousseau, J.-J., 175
Ryerson, Egerton, 64, 66, 178, 181,
   253–4, 255

St John, Bascom, 76, 79, 122, 193
Sandiford, Peter, 233
Seath, John, 71, 183
Sharp, Roy, 193, 237
Sheffield, E.F., 50, 126
Sisco, N.A., 24, 79
Smith, Sidney, 191
Spinks, J.W.T., 127–8, 129, 130
Stephen, J.S., 77, 94
Stewart, E.E., 92, 94
Stewart, W.R., 84
Strachan, John, 64

Waldrum, G.H., 84, 94
Walker, H.H., 92
Wallace, R.C., 121
Wallace, W. Stewart, 143, 144
Watson, S.A., 73, 184, 190
Welch, Robert, 82, 92, 93, 271, 301
Wells, T.L., 93, 138
Westcott, C.H., 78
White, John, 92, 136, 137
Williams, C.H., 78, 89
Wilson, J. Tuzo, 287
Wintermeyer, John, 281
Woodruff, G.L., 86
Wright, D.T., 126, 141